Holy Bible

Aionian Edition

Aionian Bible

New Testament

Given to our family, friends, and fellowman for Christ's victory of grace!

Holy Bible Aionian Edition ®
Aionian Bible
New Testament

Creative Commons Attribution-No Derivatives 4.0, 2018-2021
Text source: AionianBible.org
Source copyright: Creative Commons Attribution-No Derivatives 4.0
Nainoia Inc Aionian Verse retranslation of New Heart English Bible via Marshall, 2018-2021
ISBN: 978-1-67811-689-7

Formatted by Speedata Publisher version 4.3.18 on 4/30/2021
100% Free to Copy and Print
AionianBible.org

Published by Nainoia Inc
http://Nainoia-Inc.signedon.net

We pray for a modern public domain translation in every language
Report content and format concerns to Nainoia Inc
Volunteer help is welcome and appreciated!

Celebrate Jesus Christ's victory of grace!

Preface
AionianBible.org/Preface

The *Holy Bible Aionian Edition* ® is the world's first Bible *un-translation*! What is an *un-translation*? Bibles are translated into each of our languages from the original Hebrew, Aramaic, and Greek. Occasionally, the best word translation cannot be found and these words are transliterated letter by letter. Four well known transliterations are *Christ*, *baptism*, *angel*, and *apostle*. The meaning is then preserved more accurately through context and a lexicon. The Aionian Bible un-translates and instead transliterates ten additional Aionian Glossary words to help us better understand God's love for individuals and all mankind, and the nature of afterlife destinies.

The Aionian Bible *un-translation* helps us to see these ten underlying words in context. Actually, the original translation is unaltered and a note is added to 63 Old Testament and 200 New Testament verses. Also the Aionian Bible is not one Bible, but an entire library of public domain and Creative Common Bible texts. In each of the Bible republications the original text is wholly unaltered, except for this particular translation which is specifically named the *Aionian Bible* translation. The *Aionian Bible* translation is a new translation identical to the public domain *New Heart English Bible* except for the retranslation of the verses containing Aionian Glossary words, the usage of 'non-Jew' is replaced with 'Gentile' and a few additional verses are revised to correspond with the underlying Hebrew and Greek. This new translation includes the same inline notes as every Bible in the Aionian Bible library, but also retranslates the Aionian Glossary words to more accurately reflect the underlying Hebrew and Greek words. Every verse retranslation in the *Aionian Bible* translation is based on meticulous reference to the underlying language sources. Also note that the *New Heart English Bible* considers Old Testament manuscripts beyond the *Masoretic Text* in its textual criticism as fully explained in *Scribal Skips* by Wayne Mitchell. The *New Heart English Bible* was chosen as a base text simply because it is the most readable public domain English translation.

The first three Greek words reconsidered are *aion*, *aionios*, and *aïdios*, typically translated as *eternal* and also *world* or *eon*. In fact, the Aionian Bible is named after an alternative spelling of *aionios*. Consider that researchers question if *aion* and *aionios* actually mean *eternal*. Translating *aion* as *eternal* in Matthew 28:20 makes no sense, as all agree. The Greek word for *eternal* is *aïdios*, used in Romans 1:20 about God and in Jude 6 about demon imprisonment. Therefore, *aïdios* remains translated as *everlasting* in the *Aionian Bible* translation. Yet what about *aionios* in John 3:16? Certainly we do not question whether salvation is eternal! However, *aionios* means something much more wonderful than infinite time! Ancient Greeks used *aion* to mean *eon* or *age*. The similar spelling of *aion* and *eon* is easily seen. They also used the adjective *aionios* to mean *entirety*, such as *complete* or even *consummate*, but never infinite time. Thus *aionios* is retranslated *consummate* 65 times, *of the ages* two times, and *wholly* one time in the *Aionian Bible* translation. *Aion* is retranslated as *age* 95 times and *lifetime* two times. Note that familiar Hebrews verses now say more accurately, but less poetically, '*Jesus is a priest for the age.*'

The wonderful rediscovery is that the *aionios* life promised in John 3:16 is not simply a ticket to eternal life in the future, but the invitation through faith to the *consummate* life beginning now! *Aionios* is the perfect description of God's Word which has *everything* we need for life and godliness.

The next seven words are *Sheol*, *Hades*, *Geenna*, *Tartaroo*, *Abyssos*, and *Limne Pyr*. These words are often translated as *Hell*, the place of eternal punishment. However, *Hell* is ill-defined when compared with the Hebrew and Greek. For example, *Sheol* is the abode of deceased believers and unbelievers and should never be translated as *Hell*. *Hades* is a temporary place of punishment, Revelation 20:13-14. *Geenna* is the Valley of Hinnom, Jerusalem's refuse dump, a temporal judgment for sin. *Tartaroo* is a prison for demons, mentioned once in 2 Peter 2:4. *Abyssos* is a temporary prison for the Beast and Satan. Translators are also inconsistent because *Hell* is used by the King James Version 54 times, the New International Version 14 times, and the *World English Bible* zero times. Finally, *Limne Pyr* is the Lake of Fire, yet Matthew 25:41 explains that these fires are prepared for the Devil and his angels. So there is reason to review our conclusions about the afterlife destinies of mankind and fallen angels.

The Aionian Bible project invites you to reconsider traditional Christian understanding. It may seem utterly ridiculous to suggest that the most well-known verse in the history of Christianity, John 3:16, was improperly translated. And it may seem preposterous to propose that a destiny of Heaven or Hell is not the complete picture. Yet is it ridiculous? Is it preposterous? Have we or our forefathers ever carried ignorance and errors along for decades and even centuries in the past? We have. Even so, the purpose of the Aionian Bible project is not to abandon tradition or Christian heritage. We have much to learn from the belief and practice of godly men and women throughout all ages. Instead the purpose of this project is to invite us to compare our current conclusions with Scripture. We should never be afraid to review our understanding. Do consider Dr. Heleen Keizer's article *'ETERNITY REVISITED' A Study of the Greek Word aion* and other resources at AionianBible.org/Aionios-and-Aidios. This article is a useful introduction to the first century usage and meaning of *aion* and *aionios*. Further resources can be found countless places online and in print. Then study the Scripture and ask the Lord for understanding. Hopefully you find this invitation to reconsider fair, thought-provoking, and above all, honoring to God's Word.

Again, the original text for each translation in the Aionian Bible library is unaltered, except for this particular Bible named the *Aionian Bible*, which is itself a new translation based on the *New Heart English Bible* as explained above. To help parallel study and Strong's Concordance use, apocryphal text is removed and most variant verse numbering is mapped to the English standard. We thank our sources at eBible.org, Crosswire.org, unbound.Biola.edu, Bible4u.net, and NHEB.net. The Aionian Bible is copyrighted with creativecommons.org/licenses/by-nd/4.0, allowing 100% freedom to copy and print, if respecting source copyrights. Check the Reader's Guide and read online at AionianBible.org and with the Android App.

Why purple? King Jesus' Word is royal… and purple is the color of royalty!

Table of Contents

NEW TESTAMENT

Matthew	1
Mark	20
Luke	32
John	52
Acts	68
Romans	88
1 Corinthians	96
2 Corinthians	104
Galatians	110
Ephesians	113
Philippians	116
Colossians	118
1 Thessalonians	120
2 Thessalonians	122
1 Timothy	123
2 Timothy	126
Titus	128
Philemon	129
Hebrews	130
James	136
1 Peter	138
2 Peter	141
1 John	143
2 John	145
3 John	146
Jude	147
Revelation	148

APPENDIX
Reader's Guide
Glossary
Maps
Illustrations, Doré

NEW TESTAMENT

The Crucifixion

And Jesus said, 'Father, forgive them, for they do not know what they are doing.'
Dividing his garments among them, they cast lots.
Luke 23:34

Matthew

1 A record of the genealogy of Jesus Christ, the son of David, the son of Abraham. **2** Abraham was the father of Isaac, and Isaac the father of Jacob, and Jacob the father of Judah and his brothers, **3** and Judah was the father of Perez and Zerah by Tamar, and Perez was the father of Hezron, and Hezron the father of Ram, **4** and Ram the father of Amminadab, and Amminadab the father of Nahshon, and Nahshon the father of Salmon, **5** and Salmon the father of Boaz by Rahab, and Boaz was the father of Obed by Ruth, and Obed was the father of Jesse, **6** and Jesse the father of David the king. And David was the father of Solomon by her who had been the wife of Uriah; **7** and Solomon was the father of Rehoboam, and Rehoboam the father of Abijah, and Abijah the father of Asa; **8** and Asa the father of Jehoshaphat, and Jehoshaphat the father of Joram, and Joram the father of Uzziah, **9** and Uzziah the father of Jotham, and Jotham the father of Ahaz, and Ahaz the father of Hezekiah; **10** and Hezekiah the father of Manasseh, and Manasseh the father of Amon, and Amon the father of Josiah, **11** and Josiah the father of Jechoniah and his brothers, at the time of the exile to Babylon. **12** And after the exile to Babylon, Jechoniah was the father of Shealtiel, and Shealtiel the father of Zerubbabel, **13** and Zerubbabel the father of Abihud, and Abihud the father of Eliakim, and Eliakim the father of Azzur, **14** and Azzur the father of Zadok, and Zadok the father of Ahiam, and Ahiam the father of Elihud, **15** and Elihud the father of Eleazar, and Eleazar the father of Matthan, and Matthan the father of Jacob, **16** and Jacob the father of Joseph, the husband of Mary, from whom was born Jesus, who is called the Christ. **17** So all the generations from Abraham to David are fourteen generations; and from David to the exile to Babylon fourteen generations; and from the exile to Babylon to the Christ, fourteen generations. **18** Now the birth of Jesus Christ happened like this. His mother Mary had been engaged to Joseph, and before they came together, she was found to be with child from the Holy Spirit. **19** And Joseph, her husband, being a righteous man, and not willing to make her a public example, intended to put her away secretly. **20** But when he thought about these things, look, an angel of the Lord appeared to him in a dream, saying, "Joseph, son of David, do not be afraid to take to yourself Mary, your wife, for that which is conceived in her is of the Holy Spirit. **21** And she will bring forth a son, and you are to name him Jesus, for he will save his people from their sins." **22** Now all this has happened, that it might be fulfilled which was spoken by the Lord through the prophet, saying, **23** "Look, the virgin will conceive and bear a son, and they will call his name Immanuel;" which is translated, "God with us." **24** And Joseph arose from his sleep, and did as the angel of the Lord commanded him, and took his wife to himself; **25** and had no marital relations with her until she had brought forth a son; and he named him Jesus.

2 Now when Jesus was born in Bethlehem of Judea in the days of Herod the king, look, Magi from the east came to Jerusalem, saying, **2** "Where is he who is born King of the Jews? For we saw his star in the east, and have come to worship him." **3** And when King Herod heard it, he was troubled, and all Jerusalem with him. **4** And gathering together all the chief priests and scribes of the people, he asked them where the Christ would be born. **5** And they said to him, "In Bethlehem of Judea, for thus it is written through the prophet, **6** 'And you, Bethlehem, land of Judah, are in no way least among the rulers of Judah; for out of you will come forth a ruler who will shepherd my people, Israel.'" **7** Then Herod secretly called the Magi, and learned from them exactly what time the star appeared. **8** And he sent them to Bethlehem, and said, "Go and search diligently for the young child, and when you have found him, bring me word, so that I also may come and worship him." **9** And they, having heard the king, went their way; and look, the star which they saw in the east went before them, until it came and stood over where the young child was. **10** And when they saw the star, they rejoiced with exceedingly great joy. **11** And they came into the house and saw the young child with Mary, his mother, and they fell down and worshiped him. Then, opening their treasures, they offered to him gifts: gold, frankincense, and myrrh. **12** Being warned in a dream that they should not return to Herod, they went back to their own country another way. **13** Now when they had departed, look, an angel of the Lord appeared to Joseph in a dream, saying, "Arise and take the young child and his mother, and flee into Egypt, and stay there until I tell you, for Herod will seek the young child to destroy him." **14** And he arose and took the young child and his mother by night, and departed into Egypt, **15** and was there until the death of Herod; that it might be fulfilled which was spoken by the Lord through the prophet, saying, "Out of Egypt I called my son." **16** Then Herod, when he saw that he was mocked by the Magi, was exceedingly angry, and sent out, and killed all the male children who were in Bethlehem and in all the surrounding countryside, from two years old and under, according to the exact time which he had learned from the Magi. **17** Then that which was spoken by Jeremiah the prophet was fulfilled, saying, **18** "A voice was heard in Ramah, lamentation and weeping and great mourning, Rachel weeping for her children; and she would not be comforted, because they are no more." **19** But when Herod was dead, look, an angel of the Lord appeared in a dream to Joseph in Egypt, saying, **20** "Arise and take the young child and his mother, and go into the land of Israel, for those who sought the young child's life are dead." **21** And he arose and took the young child and his mother, and went to the land of Israel. **22** But when he heard that Archelaus was reigning over Judea in the place of his father, Herod, he was afraid to go there. Being warned in a dream, he withdrew into the region of Galilee, **23** and came and lived in a city called Nazareth; that it might be fulfilled which was spoken through the prophets, that he will be called a Nazorean.

3 And in those days John the Baptist came, preaching in the wilderness of Judea **2** and saying, "Repent, for the kingdom of heaven is near." **3** For this is he who was spoken of by Isaiah the prophet, saying, "The voice of one who calls out in the wilderness, 'Prepare the way of the Lord. Make his roads straight.'" **4** Now John himself wore clothing made of camel's hair and with a leather belt around his waist, and his food was locusts and wild honey. **5** Then people from Jerusalem, all of Judea, and all the region around the Jordan went out to him, **6** and they were baptized by him in the Jordan river, confessing their sins. **7** But when he saw many of the Pharisees and Sadducees coming for his baptism he said to them, "You offspring of vipers, who warned you to flee from the wrath to come? **8** Therefore bring forth fruit worthy of repentance, **9** and do not think to yourselves, 'We have Abraham for our father,' for I tell you that God is able to raise up children to Abraham from these stones. **10** "Even now the axe lies at the root of the trees. Therefore, every tree that does not bring forth good fruit is cut down, and cast into the fire. **11** I indeed baptize you in water for repentance, but the one who comes after me is mightier than I, whose shoes I am not worthy to carry. He will baptize you in the Holy Spirit and with fire. **12** His winnowing fork is in his hand, and he will thoroughly cleanse his threshing floor. He will gather his wheat into the barn, but the chaff he will burn up with unquenchable fire." **13** Then Jesus came from Galilee to the Jordan to John, to be baptized by him. **14** But John would have hindered him, saying, "I need to be baptized by you, and you come to me?" **15** But Jesus, answering, said to him, "Allow it to happen now, for this is the proper way for us to fulfill all righteousness." Then he allowed him. **16** And Jesus, when he was baptized, went up directly from the water; and look, the heavens were opened and he saw the Spirit of God descending as a dove, and coming on him. **17** And look, a voice out of the heavens said, "This is my beloved Son, with whom I am well pleased."

4 Then Jesus was led up by the Spirit into the wilderness to be tempted by the devil. **2** And when he had fasted forty days and forty nights, he was hungry afterward. **3** And the tempter came and said to him, "If you are the Son of God, command that these stones become bread." **4** But he answered and said, "It is written, 'Humankind cannot live by bread alone, but by every word that proceeds out of the mouth of God.'" **5** Then the devil took him into the holy city. He set him on the pinnacle of the temple, **6** and said to him, "If you are the Son of God, throw yourself down, for it is written, 'He will put his angels in charge of you.' and, 'In their hands they will lift you up, so that you will not strike your foot against a stone.'" **7** Jesus said to him, "Again, it is written, 'Do not test the Lord your God.'" **8** Again, the devil took him to a very high mountain, and showed him all the kingdoms of the world, and their glory. **9** And he said to him, "I will give you all of these things, if you will fall down and worship me." **10** Then Jesus said to him, "Go away, Satan. For it is written, 'You are to worship the Lord your God, and serve him only.'" **11** Then the devil left him, and look, angels came and served him. **12** Now when he heard that John was delivered up, he withdrew into Galilee. **13** And leaving Nazareth, he came and lived in Capernaum, which is by the sea, in the region of Zebulun and Naphtali, **14** that it might be fulfilled which was spoken through Isaiah the prophet, saying, **15** "The land of Zebulun and the land of Naphtali, toward the sea, beyond the Jordan, Galilee of the nations. **16** The people sitting in darkness have seen a great light, and those living in the land and shadow of death, on them a light has dawned." **17** From that time, Jesus began to proclaim, and to say, "Repent. For the kingdom of heaven is near." **18** And walking by the sea of Galilee, he saw two brothers: Simon, who is called Peter, and Andrew, his brother, casting a net into the sea; for they were fishermen. **19** And he said to them, "Come, follow me, and I will make you fishers of people." **20** And they immediately left their nets and followed him. **21** Going on from there, he saw two other brothers, James the son of Zebedee, and John his brother, in the boat with Zebedee their father, mending their nets, and he called them. **22** And they immediately left the boat and their father, and followed him. **23** And Jesus went about in all Galilee, teaching in their synagogues, and preaching the Good News of the Kingdom, and healing every disease and every sickness among the people. **24** And the report about him went out into all Syria, and they brought to him all who were sick, afflicted with various diseases and torments, possessed with demons, and epileptics, and paralytics; and he healed them. **25** And large crowds from Galilee, and Decapolis, and Jerusalem, and Judea, and from beyond the Jordan followed him.

5 And seeing the crowds, he went up onto the mountain, and when he had sat down, his disciples came to him. **2** Then he opened his mouth and taught them, saying, **3** "Blessed are the poor in spirit, for theirs is the kingdom of heaven. **4** Blessed are those who mourn, for they will be comforted. **5** Blessed are the gentle, for they will inherit the earth. **6** Blessed are those who hunger and thirst after righteousness, for they will be filled. **7** Blessed are the merciful, for they will obtain mercy. **8** Blessed are the pure in heart, for they will see God. **9** Blessed are the peacemakers, for they will be called the children of God. **10** Blessed are those who have been persecuted for righteousness' sake, for theirs is the kingdom of heaven. **11** "Blessed are you when they insult you, persecute you, and say all kinds of evil against you falsely, for my sake. **12** Rejoice, and be exceedingly glad, for great is your reward in heaven. For that is how they persecuted the prophets who were before you. **13** "You are the salt of the earth, but if the salt has lost its flavor, with what will it be salted? It is then good for nothing, but to be cast out and trampled under people's feet. **14** You are the light of the world. A city located on a hill cannot be hidden. **15** Neither do you light a lamp, and put it under a measuring basket, but on a stand; and it shines to all who are in the house. **16** Even so, let your light shine before people; that they may see your good works, and glorify your Father who is in heaven. **17** "Do not think that I came to destroy the Law or the Prophets. I did not come to destroy, but to fulfill. **18**

For truly, I tell you, until heaven and earth pass away, not the smallest letter or part of a letter will disappear from the Law, until all things are accomplished. **19** Therefore, whoever will break one of these least commandments, and teach others to do so, will be called least in the kingdom of heaven; but whoever will do and teach them will be called great in the kingdom of heaven. **20** For I tell you that unless your righteousness exceeds that of the scribes and Pharisees, there is no way you will enter into the kingdom of heaven. **21** "You have heard that it was said to the ancient ones, 'Do not murder;' and whoever murders will be liable to judgment. **22** But I tell you that everyone who is angry with his brother without a cause will be liable to judgment; and whoever says to his brother, 'Raqa!' will be in danger of the council; and whoever says, 'You fool!' will be in danger of the fire of Gehenna **(Geenna g1067)**. **23** "If therefore you are offering your gift at the altar, and there remember that your brother has anything against you, **24** leave your gift there before the altar, and go your way. First be reconciled to your brother, and then come and offer your gift. **25** Agree with your adversary quickly, while you are with him in the way; lest perhaps the prosecutor deliver you to the judge, and the judge to the officer, and you be cast into prison. **26** Truly I tell you, you will never get out of there until you have paid the last penny. **27** "You have heard that it was said, 'Do not commit adultery;' **28** but I tell you that everyone who looks at a woman to lust after her has committed adultery with her already in his heart. **29** And if your right eye causes you to stumble, pluck it out and throw it away from you. For it is more profitable for you that one of your members should perish, than for your whole body to be cast into Gehenna **(Geenna g1067)**. **30** And if your right hand causes you to stumble, cut it off, and throw it away from you. For it is more profitable for you that one of your members should perish, than for your whole body to be cast into Gehenna **(Geenna g1067)**. **31** "And it was said, 'Whoever divorces his wife, let him give her a certificate of divorce,' **32** but I tell you that everyone who divorces his wife, except for the cause of sexual immorality, makes her an adulteress; and whoever marries her when she is divorced commits adultery. **33** "Again you have heard that it was said to them of old time, 'Do not make false vows, but fulfill your vows to the Lord.' **34** But I tell you, do not swear at all: neither by heaven, for it is the throne of God; **35** nor by the earth, for it is the footstool of his feet; nor by Jerusalem, for it is the city of the great King. **36** Neither should you swear by your head, for you cannot make one hair white or black. **37** But let your 'Yes' be 'Yes' and your 'No' be 'No.' Whatever is more than these is of the evil one. **38** "You have heard that it was said, 'An eye for an eye, and a tooth for a tooth.' **39** But I tell you, do not set yourself against the one who is evil. But whoever strikes you on your right cheek, turn to him the other also. **40** And if anyone sues you to take away your shirt, let him have your coat also. **41** And whoever compels you to go one mile, go with him two. **42** Give to him who asks you, and do not turn away him who desires to borrow from you. **43** "You have heard that it was said, 'Love your neighbor, and hate your enemy.' **44** But I tell you, love your enemies, and pray for those who persecute you, **45** that you may be children of your Father who is in heaven. For he makes his sun to rise on the evil and the good, and sends rain on the just and the unjust. **46** For if you love those who love you, what reward do you have? Do not even the tax collectors do the same? **47** And if you only greet your brothers, what more do you do than others? Do not even the Gentiles do the same? **48** You therefore are to be perfect, as your heavenly Father is perfect.

6 "Be careful that you do not do your righteousness before people, to be seen by them, or else you have no reward from your Father who is in heaven. **2** Therefore when you practice charitable giving, do not sound a trumpet before yourself, as the hypocrites do in the synagogues and in the streets, that they may get glory from people. Truly I tell you, they have received their reward. **3** But when you practice charitable giving, do not let your left hand know what your right hand does, **4** so that your charitable giving may be in secret, then your Father who sees in secret will reward you. **5** "And when you pray, you are not to be as the hypocrites, for they love to stand and pray in the synagogues and in the corners of the streets, that they may be seen by others. Truly, I tell you, they have received their reward. **6** But you, when you pray, enter into your inner chamber, and having shut your door, pray to your Father who is in secret, and your Father who sees in secret will reward you. **7** And in praying, do not use vain repetitions, as the unbelievers do; for they think that they will be heard for their much speaking. **8** Therefore do not be like them, for your Father knows what things you need, before you ask him. **9** Therefore, you should pray this way: 'Our Father in heaven, holy be your name. **10** Let your Kingdom come. Let your will be done, on earth as it is in heaven. **11** Give us today our daily bread. **12** And forgive us our debts, as we also forgive our debtors. **13** And lead us not into temptation, but deliver us from the evil one. **14** "For if you forgive people their wrongdoing, your heavenly Father will also forgive you. **15** But if you do not forgive people, neither will your Father forgive your wrongdoing. **16** "Moreover when you fast, do not be like the hypocrites, with sad faces. For they disfigure their faces, that they may be seen by people to be fasting. Truly I tell you, they have received their reward. **17** But you, when you fast, anoint your head, and wash your face; **18** so that you are not seen by people to be fasting, but by your Father who is in secret, and your Father, who sees in secret, will reward you. **19** "Do not lay up treasures for yourselves on the earth, where moth and rust consume, and where thieves break through and steal; **20** but lay up for yourselves treasures in heaven, where neither moth nor rust consume, and where thieves do not break through and steal; **21** for where your treasure is, there your heart will be also. **22** "The lamp of the body is the eye. If therefore your eye is sound, your whole body will be full of light. **23** But if your eye is bad, your whole body will be full of darkness. If therefore the light that is in you is darkness, how great is the darkness. **24** "No one can serve two masters, for either he will hate the one and love the other; or else he will be devoted to one and despise the other. You cannot serve both God and Mammon. **25** Therefore I tell you, do not be anxious about your life, what you will eat or what you will drink; or about your body, what you will wear. Is not life more than food, and the body more than clothing? **26** See the birds of the sky, that they do not sow, neither do they reap, nor gather into barns, and your heavenly Father feeds them. Are you not of much more value than they? **27** "And which of you, by being anxious, can add one cubit to his height? **28** And why are you anxious about clothing? Consider the lilies of the field, how they grow. They do not toil, neither do they spin, **29** yet I tell you that even Solomon in all his glory was not dressed like one of these. **30** But if God so clothes the grass of the field, which today exists, and tomorrow is thrown into the oven, won't he much more clothe you, you of little faith? **31** "Therefore do not be anxious, saying, 'What will we eat?', 'What will we drink?' or, 'With what will we be clothed?' **32** For the unbelievers seek after all these things; for your heavenly Father knows that you need all these things. **33** But seek first the Kingdom and his righteousness, and all these things will be given to you as well. **34** Therefore do not be anxious for tomorrow, for tomorrow will be anxious for itself. Each day has enough trouble of its own.

7 "Do not judge, so that you won't be judged. **2** For with whatever judgment you judge, you will be judged; and with whatever measure you measure, it will be measured to you. **3** And why do you see the speck that is in your brother's eye, but do not notice the log that is in your own eye? **4** Or how will you tell your brother, 'Let me remove the speck from your eye;' and look, the log is in your own eye? **5** You hypocrite. First remove the log out of your own eye, and then you can see clearly to remove the speck out of your brother's eye. **6** "Do not give that which is holy to the dogs, neither throw your pearls before the pigs, or they will trample them under their feet and turn and tear you to pieces. **7** "Ask, and it will be given to you. Seek, and you will find. Knock, and it will be opened for you. **8** For everyone who asks receives. He who seeks finds. To him who knocks it will be opened. **9** Or who is there among you, who, if his son will ask him for bread, will give him a stone? **10** Or if he will ask for a fish, who will give him a serpent? **11** If you then, being evil, know how to give good gifts to your children, how much more will your Father who is in heaven give good things to those who ask him. **12** Therefore whatever you desire for people to do to you, so also you should do to them; for this is the Law and the Prophets. **13** "Enter in by the narrow gate; for wide is the gate and broad is the way that leads to destruction, and many are those who enter in by it. **14** How narrow is the gate, and difficult is the way that leads to life. Few are those who find it. **15** "Beware of false prophets, who come to you in sheep's clothing, but inwardly are ravening wolves. **16** By their fruits you will know them. Do you gather grapes from thorns, or figs from thistles? **17** Even so, every good tree produces good fruit; but the corrupt tree produces evil fruit. **18** A good tree cannot produce evil fruit, neither can a corrupt tree produce good fruit. **19** Every tree that does not grow good fruit is cut down, and thrown into the fire. **20** Therefore, by their fruits you will know them. **21** Not everyone who says to me, 'Lord, Lord,' will enter into the kingdom of heaven; but he who does the will of my Father who is in heaven. **22** Many will tell me in that day, 'Lord, Lord, did not we prophesy in your name, in your name cast out demons, and in your name do many mighty works?' **23** And then I will tell them, 'I never knew you. Depart from me, you who practice lawlessness.' **24** "Everyone therefore who hears these words of mine, and does them, will be compared to a wise man, who built his house on a rock. **25** And the rain came down, the floods came, and the winds blew, and beat on that house; and it did not fall, for it was founded on the rock. **26** And everyone who hears these words of mine, and does not do them will be like a foolish man, who built his house on the sand. **27** And the rain came down, the floods came, and the winds blew, and beat on that house; and it fell—and great was its fall." **28** And it happened, when Jesus had finished saying these things, that the crowds were astonished at his teaching, **29** for he taught them with authority, and not like their scribes.

8 And when he came down from the mountain, large crowds followed him. **2** And look, a leper came to him and worshiped him, saying, "Lord, if you want to, you can make me clean." **3** And he stretched out his hand, and touched him, saying, "I am willing. Be cleansed." And immediately his leprosy was cleansed. **4** And Jesus said to him, "See that you tell nobody, but go, show yourself to the priest, and offer the gift that Moses commanded, as a testimony to them." **5** And when he came into Capernaum, a centurion came to him, asking him, **6** and saying, "Lord, my servant lies in the house paralyzed, grievously tormented." **7** And he said to him, "I will come and heal him." **8** And the centurion answered, "Lord, I'm not worthy for you to come under my roof. Just say the word, and my servant will be healed. **9** For I am also a man under authority, having under myself soldiers. I tell this one, 'Go,' and he goes; and tell another, 'Come,' and he comes; and tell my servant, 'Do this,' and he does it." **10** And when Jesus heard it, he was amazed, and said to those who followed, "Truly I tell you, I have not found so great a faith with anyone in Israel. **11** And I tell you that many will come from the east and the west, and will sit down with Abraham, and Isaac, and Jacob in the kingdom of heaven, **12** but the children of the Kingdom will be thrown out into the outer darkness. There will be weeping and grinding of teeth." **13** And Jesus said to the centurion, "Go your way. Let it be done for you as you have believed." And the servant was healed in that hour. **14** And when Jesus came into Peter's house, he saw his mother-in-law lying sick with a fever. **15** So he touched her hand, and the fever left her. She got up and served him. **16** And when evening came, they brought to him many possessed with demons. He cast out the spirits with a word, and healed all who were sick; **17** that it might be fulfilled which was spoken through Isaiah the prophet, saying, "He took our infirmities, and bore our diseases." **18** Now when Jesus saw large crowds around

Matthew

him, he gave the order to depart to the other side. **19** Then a scribe came, and said to him, "Teacher, I will follow you wherever you go." **20** And Jesus said to him, "The foxes have holes, and the birds of the sky have nests, but the Son of Man has nowhere to lay his head." **21** And another of the disciples said to him, "Lord, allow me first to go and bury my father." **22** But Jesus said to him, "Follow me, and leave the dead to bury their own dead." **23** And when he got into a boat, his disciples followed him. **24** And look, a violent storm came up on the sea, so much that the boat was covered with the waves, but he was asleep. **25** They came to him, and woke him up, saying, "Save us, Lord. We are dying." **26** And he said to them, "Why are you fearful, O you of little faith?" Then he got up, rebuked the wind and the sea, and there was a great calm. **27** And the people were amazed, saying, "What kind of man is this, that even the wind and the sea obey him?" **28** And when he came to the other side, into the country of the Gadarenes, two people possessed by demons met him there, coming out of the tombs, exceedingly fierce, so that nobody could pass that way. **29** And look, they shouted, saying, "What do we have to do with you, Son of God? Have you come here to torment us before the time?" **30** Now there was a herd of many pigs feeding far away from them. **31** And the demons begged him, saying, "If you cast us out, permit us to go away into the herd of pigs." **32** And he said to them, "Go." And they came out, and went into the pigs, and look, the whole herd rushed down the cliff into the sea, and died in the water. **33** And those who fed them fled, and went away into the city, and told everything, including what happened to those who were possessed with demons. **34** And look, all the city came out to meet Jesus. And when they saw him, they pleaded with him to leave their region.

9 And he entered into a boat, and crossed over, and came into his own city. **2** And look, they brought to him a man who was paralyzed, lying on a bed. And Jesus, seeing their faith, said to the paralytic, "Son, cheer up. Your sins are forgiven." **3** And look, some of the scribes said to themselves, "This man blasphemes." **4** But Jesus, knowing their thoughts, said, "Why do you think evil in your hearts? **5** For which is easier, to say, 'Your sins are forgiven;' or to say, 'Get up, and walk?' **6** But that you may know that the Son of Man has authority on earth to forgive sins..." (then he said to the paralytic), "Get up, and take up your mat, and go up to your house." **7** And he arose and departed to his house. **8** Now when the crowds saw it, they were afraid and glorified God who had given such authority to men. **9** And as Jesus passed by from there, he saw a man called Matthew sitting at the tax collection office. He said to him, "Follow me." And he got up and followed him. **10** And it happened as he sat in the house, look, many tax collectors and sinners came and were reclining with Jesus and his disciples. **11** And when the Pharisees saw it, they said to his disciples, "Why does your Teacher eat with tax collectors and sinners?" **12** When he heard it, he said to them, "Those who are healthy have no need for a physician, but those who are sick do. **13** But you go and learn what this means: 'I desire mercy, and not sacrifice,' for I came not to call the righteous, but sinners." **14** Then John's disciples came to him, saying, "Why do we and the Pharisees fast often, but your disciples do not fast?" **15** And Jesus said to them, "Can the friends of the bridegroom mourn, as long as the bridegroom is with them? But the days will come when the bridegroom will be taken away from them, and then they will fast. **16** And no one puts a piece of unshrunk cloth on an old garment; for the patch would tear away from the garment, and a worse hole is made. **17** Neither do people put new wine into old wineskins, or else the skins would burst, and the wine be spilled, and the skins ruined. No, they put new wine into fresh wineskins, and both are preserved." **18** While he told these things to them, look, a ruler came and worshiped him, saying, "My daughter has just died, but come and lay your hand on her, and she will live." **19** And Jesus got up and followed him, as did his disciples. **20** And look, a woman who had an issue of blood for twelve years came behind him, and touched the fringe of his garment; **21** for she said within herself, "If I just touch his garment, I will be made well." **22** But Jesus, turning around and seeing her, said, "Daughter, cheer up. Your faith has made you well." And the woman was made well from that hour. **23** And when Jesus came into the ruler's house, and saw the flute players, and the crowd in noisy disorder, **24** he said, "Go away, for the girl is not dead, but asleep." And they laughed at him. **25** But when the crowd was put out, he entered in, took her by the hand, and the girl arose. **26** And the report of this went out into all that land. **27** And as Jesus passed by from there, two blind men followed him, calling out and saying, "Have mercy on us, son of David." **28** And when he had come into the house, the blind men came to him, and Jesus said to them, "Do you believe that I am able to do this?" They told him, "Yes, Lord." **29** Then he touched their eyes, saying, "According to your faith be it done to you." **30** And their eyes were opened. And Jesus strictly commanded them, saying, "See that no one knows about this." **31** But they went out and spread abroad his fame in all that land. **32** And as they went out, look, a mute man who was demon possessed was brought to him. **33** And when the demon was cast out, the mute man spoke. And the crowds were amazed, saying, "Nothing like this has ever been seen in Israel." **34** But the Pharisees said, "By the prince of the demons, he casts out demons." **35** And Jesus went about all the cities and the villages, teaching in their synagogues, and preaching the Good News of the Kingdom, and healing every disease and every sickness. **36** But when he saw the crowds, he was moved with compassion for them, because they were harassed and scattered, like sheep without a shepherd. **37** Then he said to his disciples, "The harvest indeed is plentiful, but the laborers are few. **38** Pray therefore that the Lord of the harvest will send out laborers into his harvest."

10 And he called to himself his twelve disciples, and gave them authority over unclean spirits, to cast them out, and to heal every disease and every sickness. **2** Now the names of the twelve apostles are these. The first,

Simon, who is called Peter; and Andrew his brother; and James the son of Zebedee, and John his brother; **3** Philip and Bartholomew; Thomas and Matthew the tax collector; James the son of Alphaeus, and Thaddaeus; **4** Simon the Zealot, and Judas Iscariot, who also betrayed him. **5** Jesus sent these twelve out, and commanded them, saying, "Do not go among the Gentiles, and do not enter into any city of the Samaritans. **6** Rather, go to the lost sheep of the house of Israel. **7** And as you go, proclaim, saying, 'The kingdom of heaven is near.' **8** Heal the sick, raise the dead, cleanse the lepers, cast out demons. Freely you received, freely give. **9** Do not take any gold, nor silver, nor bronze in your money belts. **10** Take no bag for your journey, neither two tunics, nor shoes, nor staff: for the laborer is worthy of his food. **11** And into whatever city or village you enter, find out who in it is worthy; and stay there until you go on. **12** And as you enter into the household, greet it. **13** And if the household is worthy, let your peace come on it, but if it is not worthy, let your peace return to you. **14** And whoever does not receive you, nor hear your words, as you leave that house or that city, shake off the dust from your feet. **15** Truly I tell you, it will be more tolerable for the land of Sodom and Gomorrah in the day of judgment than for that city. **16** "Look, I send you out as sheep in the midst of wolves, so be cunning as snakes and innocent as doves. **17** But beware of people: for they will deliver you up to councils, and in their synagogues they will scourge you. **18** Yes, and you will be brought before governors and kings for my sake, for a testimony to them and to the nations. **19** But when they deliver you over, do not be anxious how or what you will say, for it will be given you in that hour what you will say. **20** For it is not you who speak, but the Spirit of your Father who speaks in you. **21** "And brother will deliver up brother to death, and the father his child. Children will rise up against parents, and cause them to be put to death. **22** And you will be hated by all for my name's sake, but he who endures to the end will be saved. **23** But when they persecute you in one city, flee to the other. And if they persecute you in the other, flee to the next. For truly I tell you, you will not have gone through the cities of Israel before the Son of Man comes. **24** "A disciple is not above his teacher, nor a servant above his lord. **25** It is enough for the disciple that he be like his teacher, and the servant like his lord. If they have called the master of the house Beelzebul, how much more those of his household. **26** Therefore do not be afraid of them, for there is nothing covered that will not be revealed; and hidden that will not be known. **27** What I tell you in the darkness, speak in the light; and what you hear whispered in the ear, proclaim on the housetops. **28** And do not be afraid of those who kill the body, but are not able to kill the soul. Rather, fear him who is able to destroy both soul and body in Gehenna **(Geenna g1067)**. **29** "Are not two sparrows sold for an assarion coin? Not one of them falls on the ground apart from your Father's will, **30** but the very hairs of your head are all numbered. **31** Therefore do not be afraid. You are of more value than many sparrows. **32** Everyone therefore who confesses me before people, him I will also confess before my Father who is in heaven.

33 But whoever denies me before people, him I will also deny before my Father who is in heaven. **34** "Do not think that I came to send peace on the earth. I did not come to send peace, but a sword. **35** For I came to set a man at odds against his father, and a daughter against her mother, and a daughter-in-law against her mother-in-law. **36** And a person's foes will be those of his own household. **37** Whoever loves father or mother more than me is not worthy of me; and whoever loves son or daughter more than me is not worthy of me. **38** And whoever does not take his cross and follow after me, is not worthy of me. **39** Whoever seeks his life will lose it; and whoever loses his life for my sake will find it. **40** Whoever receives you receives me, and whoever receives me receives him who sent me. **41** The one who receives a prophet in the name of a prophet will receive a prophet's reward. The one who receives a righteous person in the name of a righteous person will receive a righteous person's reward. **42** And whoever gives one of these little ones just a cup of cold water to drink because he is a disciple, truly I tell you he will in no way lose his reward."

11 And it happened that when Jesus had finished directing his twelve disciples, he departed from there to teach and proclaim in their cities. **2** Now when John heard in the prison the works of the Christ, he sent [a message] by his disciples **3** and said to him, "Are you the one who is to come, or should we look for another?" **4** And Jesus answered them, "Go and tell John the things which you hear and see: **5** the blind receive their sight, the lame walk, the lepers are cleansed, the deaf hear, the dead are raised up, and the poor have good news preached to them. **6** And blessed is he who is not offended by me." **7** And as these went their way, Jesus began to say to the crowds concerning John, "What did you go out into the wilderness to see? A reed shaken by the wind? **8** But what did you go out to see? A man in soft clothing? Look, those who wear soft things are in kings' houses. **9** But what did you go out to see? A prophet? Yes, I tell you, and much more than a prophet. **10** This is the one of whom it is written, 'Look, I send my messenger ahead of you, who will prepare your way before you.' **11** Truly I tell you, among those who are born of women there has not arisen anyone greater than John the Baptist; yet he who is least in the kingdom of heaven is greater than he. **12** And from the days of John the Baptist until now, the kingdom of heaven suffers violence, and the violent take it by force. **13** For all the Prophets and the Law prophesied until John. **14** And if you are willing to receive it, this is Elijah, who is to come. **15** He who has ears to hear, let him hear. **16** "But to what should I compare this generation? It is like children sitting in the marketplaces, who call to their companions **17** and say, 'We played the flute for you, and you did not dance. We wailed in mourning, and you did not mourn.' **18** For John came neither eating nor drinking, and they say, 'He has a demon.' **19** The Son of Man came eating and drinking, and they say, 'Look, a gluttonous man and a drunkard, a friend of tax collectors and sinners.' But wisdom is justified by her children." **20** Then he began to

Matthew

denounce the cities in which most of his mighty works had been done, because they did not repent. **21** "Woe to you, Chorazin. Woe to you, Bethsaida. For if the mighty works had been done in Tyre and Sidon which were done in you, they would have repented long ago in sackcloth and ashes. **22** But I tell you, it will be more tolerable for Tyre and Sidon on the day of judgment than for you. **23** And you, Capernaum, not as far as Heaven you were exalted, but as far as Hades **(Hadēs g86)** you will descend. For if the mighty works had been done in Sodom which were done in you, it would have remained until today. **24** But I tell you that it will be more tolerable for the land of Sodom, on the day of judgment, than for you." **25** At that time, Jesus answered, "I thank you, Father, Lord of heaven and earth, that you hid these things from the wise and intelligent, and revealed them to little children. **26** Yes, Father, for so it was well-pleasing in your sight. **27** All things have been delivered to me by my Father. No one knows the Son, except the Father; neither does anyone know the Father, except the Son, and he to whom the Son desires to reveal him. **28** "Come to me, all you who labor and are heavily burdened, and I will give you rest. **29** Take my yoke upon you, and learn from me, for I am gentle and humble in heart; and you will find rest for your souls. **30** For my yoke is easy, and my burden is light."

12 At that time, Jesus went on the Sabbath day through the grain fields. His disciples were hungry and began to pluck heads of grain and to eat. **2** But the Pharisees, when they saw it, said to him, "Look, your disciples do what is not lawful to do on the Sabbath." **3** But he said to them, "Have you not read what David did, when he and his companions were hungry; **4** how he entered into the house of God, and they ate the show bread, which was not lawful for him to eat, neither for those who were with him, but only for the priests? **5** Or have you not read in the Law, that on the Sabbath day the priests in the temple profane the Sabbath and are blameless? **6** But I tell you that something greater than the temple is here. **7** But if you had known what this means, 'I desire mercy, and not sacrifice,' you would not have condemned the innocent. **8** For the Son of Man is Lord of the Sabbath." **9** And he departed from there and went into their synagogue. **10** And look, there was a man with a withered hand. They asked him, "Is it lawful to heal on the Sabbath day?" that they might accuse him. **11** And he said to them, "Which one of you who has one sheep, if it falls into a pit on the Sabbath, will not take hold of it and lift it out? **12** Of how much more value then is a person than a sheep. Therefore it is lawful to do good on the Sabbath." **13** Then he told the man, "Stretch out your hand." And he stretched it out, and it was restored whole, just like the other. **14** But the Pharisees went out, and conspired against him, how they might destroy him. **15** But Jesus, perceiving that, withdrew from there. Large crowds followed him, and he healed them all, **16** and commanded them that they should not make him known. **17** This was to fulfill what had been spoken through Isaiah the prophet, saying, **18** "Look, my servant whom I have chosen; my beloved in whom my soul delights. I will put my Spirit on him; and he will proclaim justice to the nations. **19** He will not quarrel, nor shout; nor will anyone hear his voice in the streets. **20** He won't break a bruised reed. And he won't put out a smoldering wick, until he leads justice to victory. **21** And in his name the coastlands will hope." **22** Then one possessed by a demon, blind and mute, was brought to him and he healed him, so that the mute man spoke and saw. **23** And all the crowds were amazed, and said, "Can this be the son of David?" **24** But when the Pharisees heard it, they said, "This man does not cast out demons, except by Beelzebul, the prince of the demons." **25** And knowing their thoughts, he said to them, "Every kingdom divided against itself is brought to desolation, and every city or house divided against itself will not stand. **26** And if Satan casts out Satan, he is divided against himself. How then will his kingdom stand? **27** If I by Beelzebul cast out demons, by whom do your children cast them out? Therefore they will be your judges. **28** But if I by the Spirit of God cast out demons, then the Kingdom of God has come upon you. **29** Or how can one enter into the house of the strong man, and carry off his possessions, unless he first bind the strong man? And then he will plunder his house. **30** "He who is not with me is against me, and he who does not gather with me, scatters. **31** Therefore I tell you, every sin and blasphemy will be forgiven people, but the blasphemy against the Spirit will not be forgiven. **32** And whoever speaks a word against the Son of Man, it will be forgiven him; but whoever speaks against the Holy Spirit, it will not be forgiven him, neither in this age **(aiōn g165)**, nor in the one coming. **33** "Either make the tree good, and its fruit good, or make the tree corrupt, and its fruit corrupt; for the tree is known by its fruit. **34** You offspring of vipers, how can you, being evil, speak good things? For out of the abundance of the heart, the mouth speaks. **35** The good person out of his good treasure brings out good things, and the evil person out of his evil treasure brings out evil things. **36** But I tell you that every careless word that people speak, they will give account of it in the day of judgment. **37** For by your words you will be justified, and by your words you will be condemned." **38** Then certain of the scribes and Pharisees said to him, "Teacher, we want to see a sign from you." **39** But he answered and said to them, "An evil and adulterous generation seeks after a sign, but no sign will be given it but the sign of Jonah the prophet. **40** For as Jonah was three days and three nights in the belly of the great fish, so will the Son of Man be three days and three nights in the heart of the earth. **41** The people of Nineveh will stand up in the judgment with this generation, and will condemn it, for they repented at the preaching of Jonah; and look, something greater than Jonah is here. **42** The queen of the south will rise up in the judgment with this generation, and will condemn it, for she came from a distant land to hear the wisdom of Solomon; and look, someone greater than Solomon is here. **43** But the unclean spirit, when he is gone out of the person, passes through waterless places, seeking rest, and does not find it. **44** Then he says, 'I will return into my house from which I came out,' and when he has come back, he finds it empty, swept, and put in order. **45** Then he goes, and takes with himself seven other spirits more evil than he is, and they enter in and dwell there. The last state of that person becomes worse than the first. Even so will it be also to this evil generation." **46** While he was yet speaking to the crowds, look, his mother and his brothers stood outside, seeking to speak to him. **47** Then one said to him, "Look, your mother and your brothers stand outside, seeking to speak to you." **48** But he answered him who spoke to him, "Who is my mother? Who are my brothers?" **49** And he stretched out his hand towards his disciples, and said, "Look, my mother and my brothers. **50** For whoever does the will of my Father who is in heaven, he is my brother, and sister, and mother."

13 On that day Jesus went out of the house, and sat by the seaside. **2** And large crowds gathered to him, so that he entered into a boat, and sat, and all the crowd stood on the beach. **3** And he spoke to them many things in parables, saying, "Look, a farmer went out to sow. **4** And as he sowed, some seeds fell by the roadside, and the birds came and devoured them. **5** And others fell on rocky ground, where they did not have much soil, and immediately they sprang up, because they had no depth of earth. **6** But when the sun had risen, they were scorched. Because they had no root, they withered away. **7** Others fell among thorns, and the thorns grew up and choked them. **8** Still others fell on good soil, and yielded fruit: some one hundred times as much, some sixty, and some thirty. **9** He who has ears, let him hear." **10** Then the disciples came, and said to him, "Why do you speak to them in parables?" **11** And answering, he said to them, "To you it is given to know the mysteries of the kingdom of heaven, but it is not given to them. **12** For whoever has, to him will be given, and he will have abundance, but whoever does not have, from him will be taken away even that which he has. **13** Therefore I speak to them in parables, because seeing they do not see, and hearing, they do not hear, neither do they understand. **14** And in them the prophecy of Isaiah is fulfilled, which says, 'In hearing you will hear, but will not understand, and seeing you will see, but not perceive. **15** For the heart of this people has grown dull, and their ears are sluggish in hearing, and they have closed their eyes, otherwise they might see with their eyes, and hear with their ears, and understand with their heart, and turn back, and I would heal them.' **16** "But blessed are your eyes, for they see; and your ears, for they hear. **17** For truly I tell you that many prophets and righteous people desired to see the things which you see, and did not see them; and to hear the things which you hear, and did not hear them. **18** "Hear, then, the parable of the farmer. **19** When anyone hears the word of the Kingdom, and does not understand it, the evil one comes, and snatches away that which has been sown in his heart. This is what was sown by the roadside. **20** And what was sown on the rocky places, this is he who hears the word, and immediately with joy receives it; **21** yet he has no root in himself, but endures for a while. When oppression or persecution arises because of the word, immediately he stumbles. **22** And what was sown among the thorns, this is he who hears the word, but the cares of this age **(aiōn g165)** and the deceitfulness of riches choke the word, and he becomes unfruitful. **23** And what was sown on the good ground, this is he who hears the word, and understands it, who truly bears fruit, and brings forth, some one hundred times as much, some sixty, and some thirty." **24** He set another parable before them, saying, "The kingdom of heaven is like a person who sowed good seed in his field, **25** but while everyone slept, his enemy came and sowed tares also among the wheat, and went away. **26** But when the blade sprang up and brought forth fruit, then the tares appeared also. **27** So the servants of the householder came and said to him, 'Sir, did you not sow good seed in your field? Where did these tares come from?' **28** "And he said to them, 'An enemy has done this.' "And the servants asked him, 'Then do you want us to go and gather them up?' **29** "But he said, 'No, lest perhaps while you gather up the tares, you root up the wheat with them. **30** Let both grow together until the harvest, and in the harvest time I will tell the reapers, "First, gather up the tares, and bind them in bundles to burn them; but gather the wheat into my barn."'" **31** He set another parable before them, saying, "The kingdom of heaven is like a mustard seed, which a man took, and sowed in his field; **32** which indeed is smaller than all seeds. But when it is grown, it is greater than the herbs, and becomes a tree, so that the birds of the air come and lodge in its branches." **33** He spoke another parable to them. "The kingdom of heaven is like yeast, which a woman took, and hid in three measures of meal, until it was all leavened." **34** Jesus spoke all these things in parables to the crowds; and without a parable, he did not speak to them, **35** that it might be fulfilled which was spoken through the prophet, saying, "I will open my mouth in parables; I will utter things hidden since the beginning of the world." **36** Then Jesus sent the crowds away, and went into the house. His disciples came to him, saying, "Explain to us the parable of the tares in the field." **37** And he answered them, "The one who sows the good seed is the Son of Man, **38** and the field is the world; and the good seed, these are the children of the Kingdom; and the tares are the children of the evil one, **39** And the enemy who sowed them is the devil. The harvest is the completion of the age **(aiōn g165)**, and the reapers are angels. **40** As therefore the tares are gathered up and burned with fire; so will it be at the completion of the age **(aiōn g165)**. **41** The Son of Man will send out his angels, and they will gather out of his Kingdom all things that cause stumbling, and those who do iniquity, **42** and will cast them into the furnace of fire. There will be weeping and the grinding of teeth. **43** Then the righteous will shine forth like the sun in the Kingdom of their Father. He who has ears, let him hear. **44** "The kingdom of heaven is like a treasure hidden in the field, which a man found, and hid. In his joy, he goes and sells all that he has, and buys that field. **45** "Again, the kingdom of heaven is like a man who is a merchant seeking fine pearls, **46** and having found one pearl of great price, he went and sold all that he had, and bought it. **47** "Again, the kingdom of heaven is like a dragnet, that was cast into the sea, and gathered some fish of every kind, **48** which, when it was filled, they drew up on the beach. They sat down, and gathered the good into containers, but the bad they threw away. **49** So will it be in the completion of the age **(aiōn g165)**. The angels will come and separate the wicked from among the righteous, **50** and will cast them into the furnace of fire. There will be the weeping and the grinding of teeth." **51** "Have you understood all these things?" They answered him, "Yes, Lord." **52** And he said to them, "Therefore, every scribe who has been made a disciple in the kingdom of heaven is like a man who is a householder, who brings out of his treasure new and old things." **53** And it happened that when Jesus had finished these parables, he departed from there. **54** And coming into his own country, he taught them in their synagogue, so that they were astonished, and said, "Where did this man get this wisdom, and these mighty works? **55** Is not this the carpenter's son? Is not his mother called Mary, and his brothers, James and Joseph and Simon and Judas? **56** And are not all of his sisters with us? Where then did this man get all of these things?" **57** And they were offended by him. But Jesus said to them, "A prophet is not without honor, except in his own country, and in his own house." **58** And he did not do many mighty works there because of their unbelief.

14 At that time, Herod the tetrarch heard the report concerning Jesus, **2** and said to his servants, "This is John the Baptist. He is risen from the dead. That is why these powers work in him." **3** For Herod had arrested John, and bound him, and put him in prison for the sake of Herodias, his brother Philip's wife. **4** For John said to him, "It is not lawful for you to have her." **5** And though he wanted to kill him, he feared the crowd because they regarded him as a prophet. **6** But when Herod's birthday came, the daughter of Herodias danced among them and pleased Herod. **7** Whereupon he promised with an oath to give her whatever she should ask. **8** And she, being prompted by her mother, said, "Give me here on a platter the head of John the Baptist." **9** And the king was grieved, but for the sake of his oaths, and of those who sat at the table with him, he commanded it to be given, **10** and he sent and beheaded John in the prison. **11** And his head was brought on a platter, and given to the young woman: and she brought it to her mother. **12** Then his disciples came, and took the dead body, and buried him; and they went and told Jesus. **13** Now when Jesus heard this, he withdrew from there in a boat, to a secluded place to be alone. When the crowds heard it, they followed him on foot from the cities. **14** And he went out, and he saw a large crowd, and he had compassion on them, and healed their sick. **15** Now when evening had come, the disciples came to him, saying, "This place is desolate, and the hour is already late. Send the crowds away, that they may go into the villages, and buy themselves food." **16** But Jesus said to them, "They do not need to go away. You give them something to eat." **17** And they told him, "We only have here five loaves and two fish." **18** So he said, "Bring them here to me." **19** Then he commanded the crowds to sit down on the grass; and he took the five loaves and the two fish, and looking up to heaven, he blessed, broke and gave the loaves to the disciples, and the disciples gave to the crowds. **20** And they all ate and were filled, and they took up twelve baskets full of that which remained left over from the broken pieces. **21** Now those who ate were about five thousand men, besides women and children. **22** And immediately he made the disciples get into the boat and to go ahead of him to the other side, while he sent the crowds away. **23** And after he had sent the crowds away, he went up into the mountain by himself to pray. When evening had come, he was there alone. **24** But the boat was now in the middle of the sea, battered by the waves, for the wind was against it. **25** And in the watch between three and six in the morning, he came to them, walking on the sea. **26** And when the disciples saw him walking on the sea, they were troubled, saying, "It's a ghost." and they screamed with fear. **27** But immediately Jesus spoke to them, saying "Cheer up. It is I. Do not be afraid." **28** Peter answered him and said, "Lord, if it is you, command me to come to you on the waters." **29** He said, "Come." Peter stepped down from the boat, and walked on the water and went toward Jesus. **30** But when he saw the strong wind, he was afraid, and beginning to sink, he yelled, saying, "Lord, save me." **31** Immediately Jesus stretched out his hand, took hold of him, and said to him, "You of little faith, why did you doubt?" **32** When they got up into the boat, the wind ceased. **33** Those who were in the boat worshiped him, saying, "You are truly the Son of God." **34** When they had crossed over, they came to the land of Gennesaret. **35** When the people of that place recognized him, they sent into all that surrounding region, and brought to him all who were sick, **36** and they begged him that they might just touch the fringe of his garment. And all who touched it were healed.

15 Then the Pharisees and scribes came to Jesus from Jerusalem, saying, **2** "Why do your disciples disobey the Tradition of the Elders? For they do not wash their hands when they eat bread." **3** And he answered them, "Why do you also disobey the commandment of God because of your tradition? **4** For God said, 'Honor your father and your mother,' and, 'He who speaks evil of father or mother, let him be put to death.' **5** But you say, 'Whoever may tell his father or his mother, "Whatever help you might otherwise have gotten from me is a gift devoted to God," **6** he is not to honor his father or his mother.' You have made the word of God void because of your tradition. **7** You hypocrites. Well did Isaiah prophesy of you, saying, **8** 'These people honor me with their lips; but their heart is far from me. **9** And in vain do they worship me, teaching instructions that are the commandments of humans.'" **10** He summoned the crowd, and said to them, "Hear, and understand. **11** That which enters into the mouth does not defile the man; but that which proceeds out of the mouth, this defiles the man." **12** Then the disciples came, and said to him, "Do you know that the Pharisees were offended, when they heard this saying?" **13** But he answered, "Every plant which my heavenly Father did not plant will be uprooted. **14** Leave them alone. They are blind guides of the blind. If the blind guide the blind, both will fall into a pit." **15** And answering, Peter said to him, "Explain this parable to us." **16** So he said, "Do you also still not understand? **17** Do you not understand that whatever goes into the mouth passes into the belly, and then out of the body? **18** But the things which proceed out of the mouth come out of the heart, and they defile the man. **19** For out of the heart come forth evil thoughts, murders, adulteries, sexual sins, thefts, false testimony, and blasphemies. **20** These are the things which defile the man; but to eat with unwashed hands does not defile the man." **21** Jesus went out from there, and withdrew into the region of Tyre and Sidon. **22** And look, a Canaanite woman came out from those borders, and started shouting, saying, "Have mercy on me, Lord, Son of David. My daughter is severely demonized." **23** But he did not answer her a word. His disciples came and pleaded with him, saying, "Send her away, for she keeps shouting at us." **24** But he answered, "I was not sent to anyone but the lost sheep of the house of Israel." **25** But she came and worshiped him, saying, "Lord, help me." **26** But he answered, "It is not appropriate to take the children's bread and throw it to the dogs." **27** But she said, "Yes, Lord, but even the dogs eat the crumbs which fall from their masters' table." **28** Then Jesus answered her, "Woman, great is your faith. Be it done to you even as you desire." And her daughter was healed from that hour. **29** Jesus departed there, and came near to the sea of Galilee; and he went up into the mountain, and sat there. **30** Large crowds came to him, having with them the lame, blind, mute, crippled, and many others, and they put them down at his feet; and he healed them. **31** So the crowd was amazed when they saw the mute speaking, crippled healthy, lame walking, and blind seeing—and they glorified the God of Israel. **32** Jesus summoned the disciples and said, "I have compassion on the crowd, because they continue with me now three days and have nothing to eat. I do not want to send them away fasting, or they might faint on the way." **33** Then the disciples said to him, "Where should we get so many loaves in a deserted place as to satisfy so great a crowd?" **34** Jesus said to them, "How many loaves do you have?" They said, "Seven, and a few small fish." **35** He commanded the crowd to sit down on the ground; **36** and he took the seven loaves and the fish. He gave thanks and broke them, and gave to the disciples, and the disciples to the crowds. **37** They all ate, and were filled. They took up seven baskets full of the broken pieces that were left over. **38** Those who ate were four thousand men, besides women and children. **39** Then he sent away the crowds, got into the boat, and came into the borders of Magadan.

16 The Pharisees and Sadducees came, and testing him, asked him to show them a sign from heaven. **2** But he answered and said to them, "When it is evening, you say, 'It will be fair weather, for the sky is red.' **3** In the morning, 'It will be foul weather today, for the sky is red and threatening.' You know how to discern the appearance of the sky, but you cannot discern the signs of the times.

4 An evil and adulterous generation seeks after a sign, and there will be no sign given to it, except the sign of Jonah." He left them, and departed. **5** The disciples came to the other side and had forgotten to take bread. **6** Jesus said to them, "Watch out and guard yourselves against the yeast of the Pharisees and Sadducees." **7** They reasoned among themselves, saying, "We brought no bread." **8** But Jesus, becoming aware of this, said, "You of little faith, why are you discussing among yourselves about having no bread? **9** Do you still not understand? Do you not remember the five loaves for the five thousand, and how many baskets you took up? **10** Nor the seven loaves for the four thousand, and how many baskets you took up? **11** Why is it that you do not understand that I did not speak to you concerning bread? But beware of the yeast of the Pharisees and Sadducees." **12** Then they understood that he did not tell them to beware of the yeast of bread, but of the teaching of the Pharisees and Sadducees. **13** Now when Jesus came into the parts of Caesarea Philippi, he asked his disciples, saying, "Who do people say that the Son of Man is?" **14** They said, "Some say John the Baptist, some, Elijah, and others, Jeremiah, or one of the prophets." **15** He said to them, "But who do you say that I am?" **16** Simon Peter answered, "You are the Christ, the Son of the living God." **17** And Jesus answered him, "Blessed are you, Simon Bar Jonah, for flesh and blood has not revealed this to you, but my Father who is in heaven. **18** I also tell you that you are Peter, and on this rock I will build my church, and the gates of Hades **(Hadēs g86)** will not prevail against it. **19** I will give to you the keys of the kingdom of heaven, and whatever you bind on earth will be bound in heaven, and whatever you loose on earth will be loosed in heaven." **20** Then he commanded the disciples that they should tell no one that he is the Christ. **21** From that time, Jesus began to show his disciples that he must go to Jerusalem and suffer many things from the elders, chief priests, and scribes, and be killed, and the third day be raised up. **22** Peter took him aside, and began to rebuke him, saying, "Far be it from you, Lord. This will never be done to you." **23** But he turned, and said to Peter, "Get behind me, Satan. You are a stumbling block to me, for you are not setting your mind on the things of God, but on the things of man." **24** Then Jesus said to his disciples, "If anyone desires to come after me, let him deny himself, and take up his cross, and follow me. **25** For whoever desires to save his life will lose it, and whoever will lose his life for my sake will find it. **26** For what will it profit a person, if he gains the whole world, and forfeits his life? Or what will a person give in exchange for his life? **27** For the Son of Man will come in the glory of his Father with his angels, and then he will render to everyone according to his deeds. **28** Truly I tell you, there are some standing here who will in no way taste of death, until they see the Son of Man coming in his Kingdom."

17 After six days, Jesus took with him Peter, James, and John his brother, and brought them up into a high mountain by themselves. **2** He was transfigured before them. His face shone like the sun, and his garments became as white as the light. **3** And look, Moses and Elijah appeared to them talking with him. **4** Peter answered, and said to Jesus, "Lord, it is good for us to be here. If you want, let us make three tents here: one for you, one for Moses, and one for Elijah." **5** While he was still speaking, look, a bright cloud overshadowed them. And look, a voice came out of the cloud, saying, "This is my beloved Son, in whom I am well pleased. Listen to him." **6** When the disciples heard it, they fell on their faces, and were very afraid. **7** Jesus came and touched them and said, "Get up, and do not be afraid." **8** And when they lifted up their eyes, they saw no one except Jesus alone. **9** As they were coming down from the mountain, Jesus commanded them, saying, "Do not tell anyone what you saw, until the Son of Man has risen from the dead." **10** The disciples asked him, saying, "Then why do the scribes say that Elijah must come first?" **11** And he answered and said, "Elijah indeed comes, and will restore all things, **12** but I tell you that Elijah has come already, and they did not recognize him, but did to him whatever they wanted to. Even so the Son of Man will also suffer by them." **13** Then the disciples understood that he spoke to them of John the Baptist. **14** And when they came to the crowd, a man came to him, knelt before him, **15** and said, "Lord, have mercy on my son, for he is epileptic, and suffers severely; for he often falls into the fire, and often into the water. **16** So I brought him to your disciples, and they could not cure him." **17** Jesus answered, "Faithless and perverse generation. How long will I be with you? How long will I bear with you? Bring him here to me." **18** Jesus rebuked him, the demon went out of him, and the boy was cured from that hour. **19** Then the disciples came to Jesus privately, and said, "Why weren't we able to cast it out?" **20** So he said to them, "Because of your little faith. For truly I tell you, if you have faith as a grain of mustard seed, you will tell this mountain, 'Move from here to there,' and it will move; and nothing will be impossible for you." **22** While they were gathering together in Galilee, Jesus said to them, "The Son of Man is about to be delivered up into the hands of men, **23** and they will kill him, and the third day he will be raised up." They were exceedingly sorry. **24** When they had come to Capernaum, those who collected the didrachma coins came to Peter, and said, "Does not your teacher pay the didrachma?" **25** He said, "Yes." When he came into the house, Jesus anticipated him, saying, "What do you think, Simon? From whom do the kings of the earth receive toll or tribute? From their children, or from strangers?" **26** And when he said, "From strangers." Jesus said to him, "Therefore the children are exempt. **27** But, lest we cause them to stumble, go to the sea, cast a hook, and take up the first fish that comes up. When you have opened its mouth, you will find a stater coin. Take that, and give it to them for me and you."

18
In that hour the disciples came to Jesus, saying, "Who then is greatest in the kingdom of heaven?" **2** He called a little child to himself, and set him in the midst of them, **3** and said, "Truly I tell you, unless you turn, and become as little children, you will in no way enter into the kingdom of heaven. **4** Whoever therefore humbles himself as this little child, the same is the greatest in the kingdom of heaven. **5** Whoever receives one such little child in my name receives me, **6** but whoever causes one of these little ones who believe in me to stumble, it would be better for him that a huge millstone should be hung around his neck, and that he should be sunk in the depths of the sea. **7** "Woe to the world because of stumbling blocks. For there will always be something to cause people to stumble, but woe to the person through whom the stumbling block comes. **8** If your hand or your foot causes you to stumble, cut it off and cast it from you. It is better for you to enter into life crippled or maimed, rather than having two hands or two feet to be cast into the consummate fire **(aiōnios g166)**. **9** If your eye causes you to stumble, pluck it out and cast it from you. It is better for you to enter into life with one eye, rather than having two eyes to be cast into the Gehenna **(Geenna g1067)** of fire. **10** See that you do not despise one of these little ones, for I tell you that in heaven their angels always see the face of my Father who is in heaven. **12** "What do you think? If someone has one hundred sheep, and one of them goes astray, does he not leave the ninety-nine, go to the mountains, and seek that which has gone astray? **13** If he finds it, truly I tell you, he rejoices over it more than over the ninety-nine which have not gone astray. **14** Even so it is not the will of my Father who is in heaven that one of these little ones should perish. **15** "If your brother sins against you, go, show him his fault between you and him alone. If he listens to you, you have gained back your brother. **16** But if he does not listen, take one or two more with you, that at the mouth of two or three witnesses every word may be established. **17** If he refuses to listen to them, tell it to the church. If he refuses to hear the church also, let him be to you as an unbeliever or a tax collector. **18** Truly I tell you, whatever you bind on earth will be bound in heaven, and whatever you loose on earth will be loosed in heaven. **19** Again, truly I tell you, that if two of you agree on earth concerning anything that they will ask, it will be done for them by my Father who is in heaven. **20** For where two or three are gathered together in my name, there I am in the midst of them." **21** Then Peter came to him and said, "Lord, how often can my brother sin against me, and I forgive him? Up to seven times?" **22** Jesus said to him, "I do not tell you up to seven times, but up to seventy times seven. **23** Therefore the kingdom of heaven is like a certain king, who wanted to reconcile accounts with his servants. **24** When he had begun to reconcile, one was brought to him who owed him ten thousand talents. **25** But because he could not pay, his lord commanded him to be sold, with his wife and children, and all that he had, and payment to be made. **26** The servant therefore fell down and kneeled before him, saying, 'Lord, have patience with me, and I will repay you all.' **27** The lord of that servant, being moved with compassion, released him, and forgave him the debt. **28** "But that servant went out, and found one of his fellow servants, who owed him one hundred denarii, and he grabbed him, and took him by the throat, saying, 'Pay what you owe.' **29** "So his fellow servant fell down at his feet and begged him, saying, 'Have patience with me,

and I will repay you all.' **30** He would not, but went and cast him into prison, until he should pay back that which was due. **31** So when his fellow servants saw what was done, they were exceedingly sorry, and came and told to their lord all that was done. **32** Then his lord called him in, and said to him, 'You wicked servant. I forgave you all that debt, because you begged me. **33** Should you not also have had mercy on your fellow servant, even as I had mercy on you?' **34** His lord was angry, and delivered him to the tormentors, until he should pay all that was due. **35** So my heavenly Father will also do to you, if you do not each forgive your brother his trespasses from your heart."

19 It happened when Jesus had finished these words, he departed from Galilee, and came into the borders of Judea beyond the Jordan. **2** Large crowds followed him, and he healed them there. **3** And Pharisees came to him, testing him, and saying to him, "Is it lawful for a man to divorce a wife for any reason?" **4** He answered, and said, "Have you not read that he who created them from the beginning made them male and female, **5** and said, 'For this reason a man will leave his father and mother, and be joined to his wife; and the two will become one flesh?' **6** So that they are no more two, but one flesh. What therefore God has joined together, let no one separate." **7** They asked him, "Why then did Moses command us to give her a certificate of divorce, and divorce her?" **8** He said to them, "Moses, because of the hardness of your hearts, allowed you to divorce your wives, but from the beginning it has not been so. **9** I tell you that whoever divorces his wife, except for sexual immorality, and marries another, commits adultery. And he who marries her when she is divorced commits adultery." **10** The disciples said to him, "If this is the case of a husband with a wife, it is not expedient to marry." **11** But he said to them, "Not everyone can receive this saying, but those to whom it is given. **12** For there are eunuchs who were born that way from their mother's womb, and there are eunuchs who were made eunuchs by men; and there are eunuchs who made themselves eunuchs for the kingdom of heaven's sake. He who is able to receive it, let him receive it." **13** Then little children were brought to him, that he should lay his hands on them and pray; and the disciples rebuked them. **14** But Jesus said, "Allow the little children, and do not forbid them to come to me; for the kingdom of heaven belongs to ones like these." **15** He placed his hands on them, and departed from there. **16** And look, one came to him and said, "Teacher, what good thing shall I do, that I may have consummate **(aiōnios g166)** life?" **17** He said to him, "Why do you ask me about what is good? No one is good but one. But if you want to enter into life, keep the commandments." **18** He said to him, "Which ones?" And Jesus said, "'Do not murder.' 'Do not commit adultery.' 'Do not steal.' 'Do not offer false testimony.' **19** 'Honor your father and mother.' And, 'Love your neighbor as yourself.'" **20** The young man said to him, "All these things I have kept. What do I still lack?" **21** Jesus said to him, "If you want to be perfect, go, sell what you have and give to the poor, and you will have treasure in heaven; and come, follow me." **22** But when the young man heard the saying, he went away sad, for he was one who had great possessions. **23** Jesus said to his disciples, "Truly I say to you, it is difficult for a rich person to enter the kingdom of heaven. **24** Again I tell you, it is easier for a camel to go through a needle's eye, than for a rich person to enter into the Kingdom of God." **25** When the disciples heard it, they were exceedingly astonished, saying, "Who then can be saved?" **26** Looking at them, Jesus said, "With humans this is impossible, but with God all things are possible." **27** Then Peter answered, "Look, we have left everything, and followed you. What then will we have?" **28** Jesus said to them, "Truly I tell you that you who have followed me, in the regeneration when the Son of Man will sit on the throne of his glory, you also will sit on twelve thrones, judging the twelve tribes of Israel. **29** Everyone who has left houses, or brothers, or sisters, or father, or mother, or wife, or children, or lands, for my name's sake, will receive one hundred times, and will inherit consummate **(aiōnios g166)** life. **30** But many will be last who are first; and first who are last.

20 "For the kingdom of heaven is like a landowner who went out early in the morning to hire laborers for his vineyard. **2** When he had agreed with the laborers for a denarius a day, he sent them into his vineyard. **3** He went out about nine in the morning, and saw others standing idle in the marketplace. **4** To them he said, 'You also go into the vineyard, and whatever is right I will give you.' So they went their way. **5** Again he went out about noon and at three in the afternoon, and did likewise. **6** About five that afternoon he went out, and found others standing. He said to them, 'Why do you stand here all day idle?' **7** "They said to him, 'Because no one has hired us.' "He said to them, 'You also go into the vineyard.' **8** When evening had come, the lord of the vineyard said to his manager, 'Call the laborers and pay them their wages, beginning from the last to the first.' **9** "When those who were hired at about five in the afternoon came, they each received a denarius. **10** When the first came, they supposed that they would receive more; and they likewise each received a denarius. **11** When they received it, they murmured against the master of the household, **12** saying, 'These last have spent one hour, and you have made them equal to us, who have borne the burden of the day and the scorching heat.' **13** "But he answered one of them, 'Friend, I am doing you no wrong. Did you not agree with me for a denarius? **14** Take that which is yours, and go your way. It is my desire to give to this last just as much as to you. **15** Is it not lawful for me to do what I want to with what I own? Or is your eye evil, because I am good?' **16** So the last will be first, and the first last; for many are called, but few are chosen." **17** As Jesus was going up to Jerusalem, he took the Twelve aside, and on the way he said to them, **18** "Look, we are going up to Jerusalem, and the Son of Man will be delivered to the chief priests and scribes, and they will condemn him to death, **19** and will hand him over to the Gentiles to mock, to scourge, and to crucify; and the third day he will be raised up." **20** Then the mother of the sons of Zebedee came to him with her sons, kneeling and asking a certain thing of him. **21** He said to her, "What do you want?" She said to him, "Command that these, my two sons, may sit, one on your right hand, and one on your left hand, in your Kingdom." **22** But Jesus answered and said, "You do not know what you are asking. Are you able to drink the cup that I am about to drink?" They said to him, "We are able." **23** He said to them, "You will indeed drink my cup, but to sit on my right hand and on my left hand is not mine to give; but it is for whom it has been prepared by my Father." **24** When the ten heard it, they were indignant with the two brothers. **25** But Jesus summoned them, and said, "You know that the rulers of the nations lord it over them, and their great ones exercise authority over them. **26** It will not be so among you, but whoever desires to become great among you must be your servant. **27** And whoever desires to be first among you must be your slave, **28** even as the Son of Man did not come to be served, but to serve, and to give his life as a ransom for many." **29** As they went out from Jericho, a large crowd followed him. **30** And look, two blind men sitting by the road, when they heard that Jesus was passing by, shouted, "Have mercy on us, Lord, son of David." **31** The crowd rebuked them, telling them that they should be quiet, but they shouted even more, "Have mercy on us, Lord, son of David." **32** Jesus stood still, and called them, and asked, "What do you want me to do for you?" **33** They told him, "Lord, that our eyes may be opened." **34** Jesus, being moved with compassion, touched their eyes; and immediately their eyes received their sight, and they followed him.

21

When they drew near to Jerusalem, and came to Bethphage, to the Mount of Olives, then Jesus sent two disciples, **2** saying to them, "Go into the village that is opposite you, and immediately you will find a donkey tied, and a colt with her. Untie them, and bring them to me. **3** And if anyone says anything to you, you are to say, 'Because the Lord needs them,' and he will send them at once." **4** This took place that it might be fulfilled which was spoken through the prophet, saying, **5** Say to the daughter of Zion, "Look, your King comes to you, humble, and riding on a donkey, on a colt, the foal of a donkey." **6** The disciples went, and did just as Jesus directed them, **7** and brought the donkey and the colt, and placed their clothes on them; and he sat on them. **8** A very large crowd spread their clothes on the road. Others cut branches from the trees, and spread them on the road. **9** The crowds who went before him, and who followed kept shouting, "Hosanna to the son of David. Blessed is he who comes in the name of the Lord. Hosanna in the highest." **10** When he had come into Jerusalem, all the city was stirred up, saying, "Who is this?" **11** The crowds said, "This is the prophet Jesus, from Nazareth of Galilee." **12** Jesus entered into the temple, and drove out all of those who sold and bought in the temple, and overthrew the money changers' tables and the seats of those who sold the doves. **13** He said to them, "It is written, 'My house will be called a house of prayer,' but you have made it a den of robbers." **14** The blind and the lame came to him in the temple, and he healed them. **15** But when the chief priests and the scribes saw the wonderful things that he did, and the children crying out in the temple and saying, "Hosanna to the son of David." they were indignant, **16** and said to him, "Do you hear what these are saying?" Jesus said to them, "Yes. Did you never read, 'Out of the mouth of children and infants you have prepared praise?'" **17** He left them, and went out of the city to Bethany, and lodged there. **18** Now in the morning, as he returned to the city, he was hungry. **19** Seeing a fig tree by the road, he came to it and found nothing on it but leaves. He said to it, "Let there be no fruit from you for the age **(aiōn g165)**!" Immediately the fig tree withered away. **20** When the disciples saw it, they were amazed, saying, "How did the fig tree immediately wither away?" **21** Jesus answered them, "Truly I tell you, if you have faith, and do not doubt, you will not only do what was done to the fig tree, but even if you told this mountain, 'Be taken up and cast into the sea,' it would be done. **22** All things, whatever you ask in prayer, believing, you will receive." **23** When he had come into the temple, the chief priests and the elders of the people came to him as he was teaching, and said, "By what authority do you do these things? Who gave you this authority?" **24** Jesus answered them, "I also will ask you one question, which if you tell me, I likewise will tell you by what authority I do these things. **25** The baptism of John, where was it from? From heaven or from people?" They reasoned with themselves, saying, "If we say, 'From heaven,' he will ask us, 'Why then did you not believe him?' **26** But if we say, 'From people,' we fear the crowd, for all hold John as a prophet." **27** They answered Jesus, and said, "We do not know." He also said to them, "Neither will I tell you by what authority I do these things. **28** But what do you think? A man had two sons, and he came to the first, and said, 'Son, go work today in the vineyard.' **29** He answered, 'I will not,' but afterward he changed his mind, and went. **30** And he came to the other, and said the same thing. And he answered and said, 'I go, sir,' but he did not go. **31** Which of the two did the will of his father?" They said, "The first." Jesus said to them, "Truly I tell you that the tax collectors and the prostitutes are entering into the Kingdom of God before you. **32** For John came to you in the way of righteousness, and you did not believe him, but the tax collectors and the prostitutes believed him. When you saw it, you did not even repent afterward, that you might believe him. **33** "Hear another parable. There was a landowner who planted a vineyard, set a hedge about it, dug a winepress in it, built a tower, leased it out to tenant farmers, and went on a journey. **34** When the season for the fruit drew near, he sent his servants to the tenants, to receive his fruit. **35** The tenants took his servants, beat one, killed another, and stoned another. **36** Again, he sent other servants more than the first: and they treated them the same way. **37** But afterward he sent to them his son, saying, 'They will respect my son.' **38** But the tenants, when they saw the son, said among themselves, 'This is the heir. Come, let us kill him, and have his inheritance.' **39** So they took him, and threw him out of the vineyard, and killed him. **40** When therefore the lord of the vineyard comes, what will he do to those tenants?" **41** They told him, "He will utterly destroy those evil men, and will lease out the vineyard to other tenants, who will give him the fruit in its season." **42** Jesus said to them, "Did you never read in the Scriptures, 'The stone which the builders rejected, the same was made the head of the corner. This was from the Lord. It is marvelous in our eyes?' **43** "Therefore I tell you, the Kingdom of God will be taken away from you, and will be given to a nation bringing forth its fruit. **44** He who falls on this stone will be broken to pieces; but on whomever it will fall, it will crush him." **45** When the chief priests and the Pharisees heard his parables, they perceived that he spoke about them. **46** When they sought to seize him, they feared the crowds, because they considered him to be a prophet.

22 Jesus answered and spoke again in parables to them, saying, **2** "The kingdom of heaven is like a certain king, who made a marriage feast for his son, **3** and sent out his servants to call those who were invited to the marriage feast, but they would not come. **4** Again he sent out other servants, saying, 'Tell those who are invited, "Look, I have made ready my dinner. My cattle and my fatlings are killed, and all things are ready. Come to the marriage feast."' **5** But they made light of it, and went their ways, one to his own farm, another to his merchandise, **6** and the rest grabbed his servants, and treated them shamefully, and killed them. **7** The king was enraged, and sent his armies, destroyed those murderers, and burned their city. **8** "Then he said to his servants, 'The wedding is ready, but those who were invited weren't worthy. **9** Go therefore to the intersections of the highways, and as many as you may find, invite to the marriage feast.' **10** And those servants went out into the highways, and gathered together all they found, both bad and good, and the wedding was filled with those reclining. **11** But when the king came in to see the guests, he saw there a man who did not have on wedding clothing, **12** and he said to him, 'Friend, how did you come in here not wearing wedding clothing?' He was speechless. **13** Then the king said to the servants, 'Bind him hand and foot, and throw him into the outer darkness; there is where the weeping and grinding of teeth will be.' **14** For many are called, but few chosen." **15** Then the Pharisees went and took counsel how they might entrap him in his talk. **16** They sent their disciples to him, along with the Herodians, saying, "Teacher, we know that you are honest, and teach the way of God in truth, no matter whom you teach, for you are not partial to anyone. **17** Tell us therefore, what do you think? Is it lawful to pay taxes to Caesar, or not?" **18** But Jesus perceived their wickedness, and said, "Why do you test me, you hypocrites? **19** Show me the tax money." They brought to him a denarius. **20** He asked them, "Whose is this image and inscription?" **21** They said to him, "Caesar's." Then he said to them, "Give therefore to Caesar the things that are Caesar's, and to God the things that are God's." **22** When they heard it, they were astonished, and left him, and went away. **23** On that day Sadducees came to him, the ones saying that there is no resurrection. And they asked him, **24** saying, "Teacher, Moses said, 'If a man dies, having no children, his brother is to marry his wife, and raise up offspring for his brother.' **25** Now there were with us seven brothers. The first married and died, and having no offspring, left his wife to his brother. **26** In like manner the second also, and the third, to the seventh. **27** After them all, the woman died. **28** In the resurrection therefore, whose wife will she be of the seven? For they all had her." **29** But Jesus answered them, "You are mistaken, not knowing the Scriptures, nor the power of God. **30** For in the resurrection they neither marry, nor are given in marriage, but are like the angels in heaven. **31** But concerning the resurrection of the dead, have you not read that which was spoken to you by God, saying, **32** 'I am the God of Abraham, and the God of Isaac, and the God of Jacob?' God is not the God of the dead, but of the living." **33** When the crowds heard it, they were astonished at his teaching. **34** But the Pharisees, when they heard that he had silenced the Sadducees, gathered themselves together. **35** One of them, a Law scholar, asked him a question, testing him. **36** "Teacher, which is the greatest commandment in the law?" **37** He said to him, "'You are to love the Lord your God with all your heart, with all your soul, and with all your mind.' **38** This is the great and first commandment. **39** A second likewise is this, 'You are to love your neighbor as yourself.' **40** The whole Law and the Prophets depend on these two commandments." **41** Now while the Pharisees were gathered together, Jesus asked them a question, **42** saying, "What do you think of the Christ? Whose son is he?" They said to him, "Of David." **43** He said to them, "How then does David in the Spirit call him Lord, saying, **44** 'The Lord said to my Lord, sit on my right hand, until I make your enemies the footstool of your feet'? **45** "If then David calls him Lord, how is he his son?" **46** No one was able to answer him a word, neither did anyone dare ask him any more questions from that day forth.

23 Then Jesus spoke to the crowds and to his disciples, **2** saying, "Upon the seat of Moses the Pharisees and scribes sit. **3** All which they will say unto you, observe and do; but their works do not do, because they say, and do not do. **4** For they bind heavy and hard to bear burdens, and lay them on people's shoulders; but they themselves will not lift a finger to help them. **5** But all their works they do to be seen by others. They make their tefillin broad and enlarge the fringe of their garments, **6** and love the place of honor at feasts, the best seats in the synagogues, **7** the salutations in the marketplaces, and to be called 'Rabbi' by people. **8** But you are not to be called 'Rabbi', for one is your Teacher, and all of you are brothers. **9** Call no man on the earth your father, for one is your Father, he who is in heaven. **10** Neither be called masters, for one is your master, the Christ. **11** But he who is greatest among you will be your servant. **12** Whoever exalts himself will be humbled, and whoever humbles himself will be exalted. **13** "Woe to you, scribes and Pharisees, hypocrites. For you devour the houses of widows, and for show make long prayers. Therefore you will receive greater condemnation. **14** "Woe to you, scribes and Pharisees, hypocrites. For you shut up the kingdom of heaven in front of people; for you do not enter in yourselves, neither do you allow those who are entering in to enter. **15** "Woe to you, scribes and Pharisees, hypocrites! For you travel around by sea and land to make one proselyte; and when he becomes one, you make him twice as much a son of Gehenna **(Geenna g1067)** as yourselves. **16** "Woe to you, you blind guides, who say, 'Whoever swears by the temple, it is nothing; but whoever swears by the gold of the temple, he is obligated.' **17** You blind fools. For which is greater, the gold, or the temple that sanctified the gold? **18** 'Whoever swears by the altar, it is nothing; but whoever swears by the gift that is on it, he is obligated?' **19** You blind people. For which is greater, the gift, or the altar that sanctifies the gift? **20** He therefore who swears by the altar, swears by it, and by everything on it. **21** He who swears by the temple, swears by it, and by him who dwells in it. **22** He who swears by heaven, swears by the throne of God, and by him who sits on it. **23** "Woe to you, scribes and Pharisees, hypocrites. For you tithe mint, dill, and cumin, and have left undone the weightier matters of the Law: justice, mercy, and faith. But you ought to have done these, and not to have left the other undone. **24** You blind guides, who strain out a gnat, and swallow a camel. **25** "Woe to you, scribes and Pharisees, hypocrites. For you clean the outside of the cup and the plate, but within they are full of extortion and self-indulgence. **26** You blind Pharisee, first clean the inside of the cup and the plate, so that the outside may become clean also. **27** "Woe to you, scribes and Pharisees, hypocrites. For you are like whitened tombs, which outwardly appear beautiful, but inwardly are full of dead people's bones, and of all uncleanness. **28** Even so you also outwardly appear righteous to people, but inwardly you are full of hypocrisy and iniquity. **29** "Woe to you, scribes and Pharisees, hypocrites. For you build the tombs of the prophets, and decorate the tombs of the righteous, **30** and say, 'If we had lived in the days of our fathers, we would not have been partakers with them in the blood of the prophets.' **31** Therefore you testify to yourselves that you are children of those who killed the prophets. **32** Fill up, then, the measure of your fathers. **33** You serpents, you offspring of vipers, how will you escape the judgment of Gehenna **(Geenna g1067)**? **34** Therefore, look, I send to you prophets, wise people, and scribes. Some of them you will kill and crucify; and some of them you will scourge in your synagogues, and persecute from city to city; **35** that on you may come all the righteous blood shed on the earth, from the blood of righteous Abel to the blood of Zechariah son of Berechiah, whom you killed between the sanctuary and the altar. **36** Truly I tell you, all these things will come upon this generation. **37** "Jerusalem, Jerusalem, who kills the prophets, and stones those who are sent to her. How often I would have gathered your children together, even as a hen gathers her chicks under her wings, and you would not. **38** Look, your house is left to you desolate. **39** For I tell you, you will not see me from now on, until you say, 'Blessed is he who comes in the name of the Lord.'"

24 Jesus went out from the temple, and was going on his way. His disciples came to him to show him the buildings of the temple. **2** But answering, he said to them, "Do you not see all of these things? Truly I tell you, there will not be left here one stone on another, that will not be thrown down." **3** As he sat on the Mount of Olives, the disciples came to him privately, saying, "Tell us, when will these things be? What is the sign of your coming, and of the completion of the age **(aiōn g165)**?" **4** Jesus answered them, "Be careful that no one leads you astray. **5** For many will come in my name, saying, 'I am the Christ,' and will lead many astray. **6** You will hear of wars and rumors of wars. See that you are not troubled, for this must happen, but the end is not yet. **7** For nation will rise against nation, and kingdom against kingdom; and there will be famines and plagues and earthquakes in various places. **8** But all these things are the beginning of birth pains. **9** Then they will deliver you up to oppression, and will kill you. You will be hated by all of the nations for my name's sake. **10** Then many will stumble, and will deliver up one another, and will hate one another. **11** Many false prophets will arise, and will lead many astray. **12** And because lawlessness is multiplied, the love of many will grow cold. **13** But he who endures to the end, the same will be saved. **14** This Good News of the Kingdom will be preached in the whole world for a testimony to all the nations, and then the end will come. **15** "When, therefore, you see the abomination of desolation, which was spoken of through Daniel the prophet, standing in the holy place (let the reader understand), **16** then let those who are in Judea flee to the mountains. **17** Let him who is on the housetop not go down to take out things that are in his house. **18** Let him who is in the field not return back to take his coat. **19** But woe to those who are with child and to nursing mothers in those days. **20** Pray that your flight will not be in the winter, nor on a Sabbath, **21** for then there will be great oppression, such as has not been from the beginning of the world until now, no, nor ever will be. **22** Unless those days had been shortened, no flesh would have been saved. But for the sake of the chosen ones, those days will be shortened. **23** "Then if anyone tells you, 'Look, here is the Christ,' or, 'There,' do not believe it. **24** For there will arise false messiahs, and false prophets, and they will show great signs and wonders, so as to lead astray, if possible, even the chosen ones. **25** "See, I have told you beforehand. **26** If therefore they tell you, 'Look, he is in the wilderness,' do not go out; 'Look, he is in the inner chambers,' do not believe it. **27** For as the lightning flashes from the east, and is seen even to the west, so will be the coming of the Son of Man. **28** Wherever the carcass is, there is where the vultures gather together. **29** But immediately after the oppression of those days, the sun will be darkened, the moon will not give its light, the stars will fall from heaven, and the powers of the heavens will be shaken; **30** and then the sign of the Son of Man will appear in the sky. Then all the tribes of the earth will mourn, and they will see the Son of Man coming on the clouds of the sky with power and great glory. **31** He will send out his angels with a loud trumpet call, and they will gather together his chosen ones from the four winds, from one end of the sky to the other. **32** "Now from the fig tree learn this parable. When its branch has now become tender, and puts forth its leaves, you know that the summer is near. **33** Even so you also, when you see all these things, know that it is near, even at the doors. **34** Truly I tell you, this generation will not pass away, until all these things are accomplished. **35** Heaven and earth will pass away, but my words will not pass away. **36** But no one knows of that day and hour, not even the angels of heaven, nor the Son, but my Father only. **37** "As the days of Noah were, so will be the coming of the Son of Man. **38** For as in those days before the flood they were eating and drinking, marrying and giving in marriage, until the day that Noah entered into the box-shaped vessel, **39** and they did not know until the flood came, and took them all away, so will be the coming of the Son of Man. **40** Then two men will be in the field: one will be taken and one will be left; **41** two women grinding at the mill, one will be taken and one will be left. **42** Watch therefore, for you do not know on what day your Lord comes. **43** But know this, that if the master of the house had known in what watch of the night the thief was coming, he would have watched, and would not have allowed his house to be broken into. **44** Therefore also be ready, for in an hour that you do not expect, the Son of Man will come. **45** "Who then is the faithful and wise servant, whom his lord has set over his household, to give them their food in due season? **46** Blessed is that servant whom his lord finds doing so when he comes. **47** Truly I tell you that he will set him over all that he has. **48** But if that evil servant should say in his heart, 'My lord is delayed,' **49** and begins to beat his fellow servants, and eat and drink with the drunkards, **50** the lord of that servant will come in a day when he does not expect it, and in an hour when he does not know it, **51** and will cut him in pieces, and appoint his portion with the hypocrites. There is where the weeping and grinding of teeth will be.

25

"Then the kingdom of heaven will be like ten virgins, who took their lamps, and went out to meet the bridegroom. **2** Five of them were foolish, and five were wise. **3** For the foolish, when they took their lamps, took no oil with them, **4** but the wise took oil in their vessels with their lamps. **5** Now while the bridegroom delayed, they all slumbered and slept. **6** But at midnight there was a cry, 'Look. The bridegroom. Come out to meet him.' **7** Then all those virgins arose, and trimmed their lamps. **8** The foolish said to the wise, 'Give us some of your oil, for our lamps are going out.' **9** But the wise answered, saying, 'No, there will not be enough for us and you. Go rather to those who sell, and buy for yourselves.' **10** While they went away to buy, the bridegroom came, and those who were ready went in with him to the marriage feast, and the door was shut. **11** Afterward the other virgins also came, saying, 'Lord, Lord, open to us.' **12** But he answered, 'Truly I tell you, I do not know you.' **13** Watch therefore, for you do not know the day nor the hour. **14** "For it is like a man, going on a journey, who called his own servants, and entrusted his goods to them. **15** To one he gave five talents, to another two, to another one; to each according to his own ability. Then he went on his journey. **16** Immediately the one who received the five talents went and traded with them, and made another five talents. **17** In like manner he who got the two gained another two. **18** But he who received the one went away and dug in the earth, and hid his lord's money. **19** "Now after a long time the lord of those servants came, and reconciled accounts with them. **20** And he who received the five talents came and brought another five talents, saying, 'Lord, you delivered to me five talents. See, I have gained another five talents.' **21** "His lord said to him, 'Well done, good and faithful servant. You have been faithful over a few things, I will set you over many things. Enter into the joy of your lord.' **22** "And he also who had the two talents came and said, 'Lord, you delivered to me two talents. See, I have gained another two talents.' **23** "His lord said to him, 'Well done, good and faithful servant. You have been faithful over a few things, I will set you over many things. Enter into the joy of your lord.' **24** "He also who had received the one talent came and said, 'Lord, I knew you that you are a hard man, reaping where you did not sow, and gathering where you did not scatter. **25** I was afraid, and went away and hid your talent in the earth. See, you have what is yours.' **26** "But his lord answered him, 'You wicked and slothful servant. You knew that I reap where I did not sow, and gather where I did not scatter. **27** You ought therefore to have deposited my money with the bankers, and at my coming I should have received back my own with interest. **28** Take away therefore the talent from him, and give it to him who has the ten talents. **29** For to everyone who has will be given, and he will have abundance, but from him who does not have, even that which he has will be taken away. **30** Throw out the unprofitable servant into the outer darkness, where there will be weeping and grinding of teeth.' **31** "But when the Son of Man comes in his glory, and all the angels with him, then he will sit on the throne of his glory. **32** Before him all the nations will be gathered, and he will separate them one from another, as a shepherd separates the sheep from the goats. **33** He will set the sheep on his right hand, but the goats on the left. **34** Then the King will tell those on his right hand, 'Come, blessed of my Father, inherit the Kingdom prepared for you from the foundation of the world; **35** for I was hungry, and you gave me food to eat. I was thirsty, and you gave me drink. I was a stranger, and you took me in. **36** I was naked, and you clothed me. I was sick, and you visited me. I was in prison, and you came to me.' **37** "Then the righteous will answer him, saying, 'Lord, when did we see you hungry, and feed you; or thirsty, and give you a drink? **38** When did we see you as a stranger, and take you in; or naked, and clothe you? **39** When did we see you sick, or in prison, and come to you?' **40** "The King will answer them, 'Truly I tell you, inasmuch as you did it to one of the least of these my brothers, you did it to me.' **41** Then he will say also to those on the left hand, 'Depart from me, you cursed, into the consummate (aiōnios g166) fire which is prepared for the devil and his angels; **42** for I was hungry, and you did not give me food to eat; I was thirsty, and you gave me

Matthew

no drink; **43** I was a stranger, and you did not take me in; naked, and you did not clothe me; sick, and in prison, and you did not visit me.' **44** "Then they will also answer, saying, 'Lord, when did we see you hungry, or thirsty, or a stranger, or naked, or sick, or in prison, and did not help you?' **45** "Then he will answer them, saying, 'Truly I tell you, inasmuch as you did not do it to one of the least of these, you did not do it to me.' **46** These will go away into consummate **(aiōnios g166)** punishment, but the righteous into consummate **(aiōnios g166)** life."

26 And it happened, when Jesus had finished all these words, that he said to his disciples, **2** "You know that after two days the Passover is coming, and the Son of Man will be delivered up to be crucified." **3** Then the chief priests and the scribes and the elders of the people gathered together in the court of the high priest, who was called Caiaphas. **4** They took counsel together that they might take Jesus by deceit, and kill him. **5** But they said, "Not during the feast, lest a riot occur among the people." **6** Now when Jesus was in Bethany, in the house of Simon the leper, **7** a woman came to him having an alabaster jar of very expensive ointment, and she poured it on his head as he sat at the table. **8** But when the disciples saw this, they were indignant, saying, "Why this waste? **9** For this ointment might have been sold for much, and given to the poor." **10** However, knowing this, Jesus said to them, "Why do you trouble the woman? Because she has done a good work for me. **11** For you always have the poor with you; but you do not always have me. **12** For in pouring this ointment on my body, she did it to prepare me for burial. **13** Truly I tell you, wherever this Good News is preached in the whole world, what this woman has done will also be spoken of as a memorial of her." **14** Then one of the twelve, who was called Judas Iscariot, went to the chief priests, **15** and said, "What are you willing to give me, that I should deliver him to you?" They weighed out for him thirty pieces of silver. **16** From that time he sought opportunity to betray him. **17** Now on the first day of unleavened bread, the disciples came to Jesus, saying, "Where do you want us to prepare for you to eat the Passover?" **18** He said, "Go into the city to a certain person, and tell him, 'The Teacher says, "My time is near. I will keep the Passover at your house with my disciples."'" **19** The disciples did as Jesus commanded them, and they prepared the Passover. **20** Now when evening had come, he was reclining at the table with the twelve. **21** As they were eating, he said, "Truly I tell you that one of you will betray me." **22** And they were greatly distressed, and each one began to ask him, "It is not me, is it, Lord?" **23** He answered, "He who dipped his hand with me in the dish, the same will betray me. **24** The Son of Man goes, even as it is written of him, but woe to that man through whom the Son of Man is betrayed. It would be better for that man if he had not been born." **25** Judas, who betrayed him, answered, "It is not me, is it, Rabbi?" He said to him, "You said it." **26** As they were eating, Jesus took bread, gave thanks for it, and broke it. He gave to the disciples, and said, "Take, eat; this is my body." **27** He took a cup, gave thanks, and gave to them, saying, "All of you drink it, **28** for this is my blood of the new covenant, which is poured out for many for the forgiveness of sins. **29** But I tell you that I will not drink of this fruit of the vine from now on, until that day when I drink it anew with you in my Father's Kingdom." **30** When they had sung the hymn, they went out to the Mount of Olives. **31** Then Jesus said to them, "All of you will be made to stumble because of me tonight, for it is written, 'I will strike the shepherd, and the sheep of the flock will be scattered.' **32** But after I am raised up, I will go before you into Galilee." **33** But Peter answered him, "Even if all will be made to stumble because of you, I will never be made to stumble." **34** Jesus said to him, "Truly I tell you that tonight, before the rooster crows, you will deny me three times." **35** Peter said to him, "Even if I must die with you, I will not deny you." All of the disciples also said likewise. **36** Then Jesus came with them to a place called Gethsemane, and said to his disciples, "Sit here, while I go there and pray." **37** He took with him Peter and the two sons of Zebedee, and began to be sorrowful and severely troubled. **38** Then he said to them, "My soul is exceedingly sorrowful, even to death. Stay here, and watch with me." **39** He went forward a little, fell on his face, and prayed, saying, "My Father, if it is possible, let this cup pass away from me; nevertheless, not what I desire, but what you desire." **40** He came to the disciples, and found them sleeping, and said to Peter, "What, could you not watch with me for one hour? **41** Watch and pray, that you do not enter into temptation. The spirit indeed is willing, but the flesh is weak." **42** Again, a second time he went away, and prayed, saying, "My Father, if this cannot pass away unless I drink it, your desire be done." **43** He came again and found them sleeping, for their eyes were heavy. **44** He left them again, went away, and prayed a third time, saying the same words. **45** Then he came to the disciples, and said to them, "Sleep on now, and take your rest. Look, the hour is near, and the Son of Man is betrayed into the hands of sinners. **46** Arise, let us be going. Look, he who betrays me is near." **47** While he was still speaking, look, Judas, one of the twelve, came, and with him a large crowd with swords and clubs, from the chief priests and elders of the people. **48** Now he who betrayed him gave them a sign, saying, "Whoever I kiss, he is the one. Seize him." **49** Immediately he came to Jesus, and said, "Greetings, Rabbi." and kissed him. **50** Jesus said to him, "Friend, why are you here?" Then they came and laid hands on Jesus, and took him. **51** And look, one of those who were with Jesus stretched out his hand, and drew his sword, and struck the servant of the high priest, and struck off his ear. **52** Then Jesus said to him, "Put your sword back into its place, for all those who take the sword will die by the sword. **53** Or do you think that I could not ask my Father, and he would even now send me more than twelve legions of angels? **54** How then would the Scriptures be fulfilled that it must be so?" **55** In that hour Jesus said to the crowds, "Have you come out as against a robber with swords and clubs to seize me? I sat daily in the temple teaching, and you did not arrest me. **56** But all this has happened, that the Scriptures of the prophets might be fulfilled." Then all the disciples left him, and fled. **57** Those who had taken Jesus led him away to Caiaphas the high priest, where the scribes and the elders were gathered together. **58** But Peter followed him from a distance, to the court of the high priest, and entered in and sat with the officers, to see the end. **59** Now the chief priests and the whole council sought false testimony against Jesus so they could put him to death; **60** and they found none, even though many false witnesses came forward. But afterward two came forward, **61** and said, "This man said, 'I am able to destroy the temple of God, and to build it in three days.'" **62** The high priest stood up, and said to him, "Have you no answer? What is this that these testify against you?" **63** But Jesus held his peace. The high priest answered him, "I adjure you by the living God, that you tell us whether you are the Christ, the Son of God." **64** Jesus said to him, "You have said it. Nevertheless, I tell you, after this you will see the Son of Man sitting at the right hand of Power, and coming on the clouds of the sky." **65** Then the high priest tore his clothing, saying, "He has spoken blasphemy. Why do we need any more witnesses? See, now you have heard his blasphemy. **66** What do you think?" They answered, "He is worthy of death." **67** Then they spit in his face and beat him with their fists, and some slapped him, **68** saying, "Prophesy to us, you Christ. Who hit you?" **69** Now Peter was sitting outside in the courtyard, and a servant girl came to him, saying, "You were also with Jesus, the Galilean." **70** But he denied it before them all, saying, "I do not know what you are talking about." **71** And when he had gone out onto the porch, another girl saw him, and said to those who were there, "This man also was with Jesus the Nazorean." **72** Again he denied it with an oath, "I do not know the man." **73** After a little while those who stood by came and said to Peter, "Surely you are also one of them, for your accent makes you known." **74** Then he began to curse and to swear, "I do not know the man." Immediately the rooster crowed. **75** Peter remembered the word which Jesus had said, "Before the rooster crows, you will deny me three times." He went out and wept bitterly.

27 Now when morning had come, all the chief priests and the elders of the people took counsel against Jesus to put him to death: **2** and they bound him, and led him away, and delivered him to Pilate, the governor. **3** Then Judas, who betrayed him, when he saw that Jesus was condemned, felt remorse, and returned the thirty pieces of silver to the chief priests and elders, **4** saying, "I have sinned in that I betrayed innocent blood." But they said, "What is that to us? You see to it." **5** He threw down the pieces of silver in the sanctuary, and departed. He went away and hanged himself. **6** The chief priests took the pieces of silver, and said, "It's not lawful to put them into the treasury, since it is the price of blood." **7** They took counsel, and bought the potter's field with them, to bury strangers in. **8** Therefore that field was called "The Field of Blood" to this day. **9** Then that which was spoken through Jeremiah the prophet was fulfilled, saying, "They took the thirty pieces of silver, the price of him upon whom a price had been set, whom some of the children of Israel priced, **10** and they gave them for the potter's field, as the Lord commanded me." **11** Now Jesus stood before the governor: and the governor asked him, saying, "Are you the King of the Jews?" Jesus said to him, "You say so." **12** When he was accused by the chief priests and elders, he answered nothing. **13** Then Pilate said to him, "Do you not hear how many things they testify against you?" **14** He gave him no answer, not even one word, so that the governor was greatly amazed. **15** Now at the feast the governor was accustomed to release to the crowd one prisoner, whom they desired. **16** They had then a notable prisoner, called Barabbas. **17** When therefore they were gathered together, Pilate said to them, "Whom do you want me to release to you? Barabbas, or Jesus, who is called Christ?" **18** For he knew that because of envy they had delivered him up. **19** While he was sitting on the judgment seat, his wife sent to him, saying, "Have nothing to do with that righteous man, for I have suffered many things this day in a dream because of him." **20** Now the chief priests and the elders persuaded the crowds to ask for Barabbas, and destroy Jesus. **21** But the governor answered them, "Which of the two do you want me to release to you?" They said, "Barabbas." **22** Pilate said to them, "What then should I do with Jesus, who is called Christ?" They all said, "Let him be crucified." **23** But he said, "Why? What evil has he done?" But they shouted all the louder, saying, "Let him be crucified." **24** So Pilate, seeing that nothing was being gained, but rather that a disturbance was starting, took water and he washed his hands before the crowd, saying, "I am innocent of the blood of this righteous man. You see to it." **25** All the people answered, "May his blood be on us, and on our children." **26** Then he released to them Barabbas, but Jesus he flogged and delivered to be crucified. **27** Then the governor's soldiers took Jesus into the Praetorium, and gathered the whole garrison together against him. **28** They stripped him, and put a scarlet robe on him. **29** They braided a crown of thorns and put it on his head, and a reed in his right hand; and they kneeled down before him, and mocked him, saying, "Greetings, King of the Jews." **30** They spat on him, and took the reed and struck him on the head. **31** When they had mocked him, they took the robe off of him, and put his clothes on him, and led him away to crucify him. **32** As they came out, they found a man of Cyrene, Simon by name, and they compelled him to go with them, that he might carry his cross. **33** They came to a place called "Golgotha," that is to say, "The place of a skull." **34** They gave him wine to drink mixed with gall. When he had tasted it, he would not drink. **35** When they had crucified him, they divided his clothing among themselves, casting a lot, that it might be fulfilled which was spoken by the prophet: 'They divided my clothes among themselves, and for my clothing they cast a lot.' **36** And they sat and watched him there. **37** They set up over his head the accusation against him written, "THIS IS JESUS, THE KING OF THE JEWS." **38** Then there were two robbers crucified with him, one on his right hand and one on the left. **39** Those who passed by blasphemed him, wagging their heads, **40** and saying, "You who destroy the temple, and build it in three days, save yourself. If you are the Son of God, come down from the cross." **41** Likewise the chief priests also mocking, with the scribes, and the elders, said, **42** "He saved others, but he cannot save himself. If he is the King of Israel, let him come down from the cross now, and we will believe in him. **43** He trusts in God. Let God deliver him now, if he wants him; for he said, 'I am the Son of God.'" **44** The robbers also who were crucified with him insulted him in the same way. **45** Now from noon until three in the afternoon there was darkness over all the land. **46** Then at about three in the afternoon Jesus called out with a loud voice, saying, "Eli, Eli, lema shabachthani?" That is, "My God, my God, why have you forsaken me?" **47** Some of them who stood there, when they heard it, said, "This man is calling Elijah." **48** Immediately one of them ran, and took a sponge, and filled it with vinegar, and put it on a reed, and gave him a drink. **49** The rest said, "Let him be. Let us see whether Elijah comes to save him." **50** And Jesus cried out again with a loud voice, and yielded up his spirit. **51** And look, the veil of the temple was torn in two from the top to the bottom. The earth quaked and the rocks were split. **52** The tombs were opened, and many bodies of the saints who had fallen asleep were raised; **53** and coming out of the tombs after his resurrection, they entered into the holy city and appeared to many. **54** Now the centurion, and those who were with him watching Jesus, when they saw the earthquake, and the things that were done, feared exceedingly, saying, "Truly this was the Son of God." **55** Many women were there watching from afar, who had followed Jesus from Galilee, serving him. **56** Among them were Mary Magdalene, Mary the mother of James and Joseph, and the mother of the sons of Zebedee. **57** When evening had come, a rich man from Arimathaea, named Joseph, who himself was also Jesus' disciple came. **58** This man went to Pilate, and asked for the body of Jesus. Then Pilate commanded that it be released. **59** Joseph took the body, and wrapped it in a clean linen cloth, **60** and placed it in his own new tomb, which he had cut out in the rock, and he rolled a great stone to the door of the tomb, and departed. **61** Mary Magdalene was there, and the other Mary, sitting opposite the tomb. **62** Now on the next day, which was the day after the Preparation Day, the chief priests and the Pharisees were gathered together to Pilate, **63** saying, "Sir, we remember what that deceiver said while he was still alive: 'After three days I will rise again.' **64** Command therefore that the tomb be made secure until the third day, lest perhaps his disciples come and steal him away, and tell the people, 'He is risen from the dead;' and the last deception will be worse than the first." **65** Pilate said to them, "You have a guard. Go, make it as secure as you can." **66** So they went with the guard and made the tomb secure, sealing the stone.

28 Now after the Sabbath, as it began to dawn on the first day of the week, Mary Magdalene and the other Mary came to see the tomb. **2** And look, there was a great earthquake, for an angel of the Lord descended from the sky, and came and rolled away the stone, and sat on it. **3** His appearance was like lightning, and his clothing white as snow. **4** For fear of him, the guards shook, and became like dead men. **5** The angel answered the women, "Do not be afraid, for I know that you seek Jesus, who has been crucified. **6** He is not here, for he has risen, just like he said. Come, see the place where he was lying. **7** Go quickly and tell his disciples, 'He has risen from the dead, and look, he goes before you into Galilee; there you will see him.' See, I have told you." **8** They departed quickly from the tomb, frightened yet with great joy, and ran to bring his disciples word. **9** And look, Jesus met them, saying, "Rejoice!" And they came and took hold of his feet, and worshiped him. **10** Then Jesus said to them, "Do not be afraid. Go tell my brothers that they should go into Galilee, and there they will see me." **11** Now while they were going, look, some of the guards came into the city, and told the chief priests all the things that had happened. **12** When they were assembled with the elders, and had taken counsel, they gave a large amount of silver to the soldiers, **13** saying, "Say that his disciples came by night, and stole him away while we slept. **14** If this comes to the governor's ears, we will persuade him and make you free of worry." **15** So they took the money and did as they were told. This saying was spread abroad among the Jewish people, and continues until this day. **16** But the eleven disciples went into Galilee, to the mountain where Jesus had sent them. **17** When they saw him, they bowed down to him, but some doubted. **18** Jesus came to them and spoke to them, saying, "All authority has been given to me in heaven and on earth. **19** Therefore go, and make disciples of all nations, baptizing them in the name of the Father and of the Son and of the Holy Spirit, **20** teaching them to observe all things that I commanded you. And look, I am with you every day, even to the completion of the age **(aiōn g165)**."

Mark

1 The beginning of the Good News of Jesus Christ, the Son of God. **2** As it is written in Isaiah the prophet, "Look, I send my messenger ahead of you, who will prepare your way before you. **3** The voice of one crying in the wilderness, 'Prepare the way of the Lord. Make his roads straight.'" **4** John came baptizing in the wilderness and preaching a baptism of repentance for forgiveness of sins. **5** And all the country of Judea went out to him and all those from Jerusalem, and they were baptized by him in the Jordan river, confessing their sins. **6** And John was clothed with camel's hair and a leather belt around his waist. He ate locusts and wild honey. **7** And he preached, saying, "After me comes he who is mightier than I, the strap of whose sandals I am not worthy to stoop down and loosen. **8** I baptized you in water, but he will baptize you in the Holy Spirit." **9** And it happened in those days, that Jesus came from Nazareth of Galilee, and was baptized by John in the Jordan. **10** Immediately coming up from the water, he saw the heavens parting, and the Spirit descending on him like a dove. **11** And a voice came out of the sky, "You are my beloved Son, with you I am well pleased." **12** And immediately the Spirit drove him out into the wilderness. **13** He was in the wilderness forty days tempted by Satan. He was with the wild animals; and the angels were serving him. **14** Now after John was taken into custody, Jesus came into Galilee, proclaiming the Good News of God, **15** and saying, "The time is fulfilled, and the Kingdom of God is near. Repent, and believe in the Good News." **16** And passing along by the sea of Galilee, he saw Simon and Andrew the brother of Simon casting a net into the sea, for they were fishermen. **17** Jesus said to them, "Come, follow me, and I will make you into fishers of people." **18** And immediately they left the nets, and followed him. **19** And going on a little further, he saw James the son of Zebedee, and John, his brother, who were also in the boat mending the nets. **20** And immediately he called them, and they left their father, Zebedee, in the boat with the hired servants, and went after him. **21** And they went into Capernaum, and immediately on the Sabbath day he entered into the synagogue and taught. **22** And they were astonished at his teaching, for he taught them as having authority, and not as the scribes. **23** And just then there was in their synagogue a man with an unclean spirit, and he shouted, **24** saying, "What do we have to do with you, Jesus, Nazarene? Have you come to destroy us? I know you who you are: the Holy One of God." **25** And Jesus rebuked him, saying, "Be quiet, and come out of him." **26** And the unclean spirit, convulsing him and crying with a loud voice, came out of him. **27** And they were all amazed, so that they questioned among themselves, saying, "What is this? A new teaching? For with authority he commands even the unclean spirits, and they obey him." **28** And at once the news of him went out everywhere into all the region of Galilee and its surrounding area. **29** And Immediately, when they had come out of the synagogue, they came into the house of Simon and Andrew, with James and John. **30** Now Simon's mother-in-law was sick in bed with a fever, and immediately they told him about her. **31** And he came and took her by the hand, and raised her up. The fever left her, and she served them. **32** At evening, when the sun had set, they brought to him all who were sick, and those who were possessed by demons. **33** And all the city was gathered together at the door. **34** And he healed many who were sick with various diseases, and cast out many demons. He did not allow the demons to speak, because they knew him. **35** And early in the morning, while it was still dark, he rose up and went out, and departed into a deserted place, and prayed there. **36** And Simon and those who were with him followed after him; **37** and they found him, and told him, "Everyone is looking for you." **38** And he said to them, "Let us go somewhere else into the next towns, that I may preach there also, because I came out for this reason." **39** And he went into their synagogues throughout all Galilee, preaching and casting out demons. **40** And a leper came to him, begging him, and knelt down and said to him, "If you want to, you can make me clean." **41** And being moved with compassion, he stretched out his hand, and touched him, and said to him, "I am willing. Be cleansed." **42** And immediately the leprosy departed from him, and he was made clean. **43** And he strictly warned him, and immediately sent him out, **44** and said to him, "See you say nothing to anyone, but go show yourself to the priest, and offer for your cleansing the things which Moses commanded, for a testimony to them." **45** But he went out, and began to proclaim it freely, and to spread about the matter, so that Jesus could no more openly enter into a city, but was outside in desert places: and they came to him from everywhere.

2 And when he entered again into Capernaum after some days, it was heard that he was in the house. **2** And many were gathered together, so that there was no more room, not even around the door; and he spoke the word to them. **3** And four people came, carrying a paralytic to him. **4** And when they could not bring him because of the crowd, they removed the roof above him. When they had broken it up, they let down the mat that the paralytic was lying on. **5** And Jesus, seeing their faith, said to the paralytic, "Son, your sins are forgiven you." **6** But there were some of the scribes sitting there, and reasoning in their hearts, **7** "Why does this man speak like that? He is blaspheming; who can forgive sins but God alone?" **8** And immediately Jesus, perceiving in his spirit that they so reasoned within themselves, said to them, "Why do you reason these things in your hearts? **9** Which is easier, to tell the paralytic, 'Your sins are forgiven;' or to say, 'Arise, and take up your bed, and walk?' **10** But that you may know that the Son of Man has authority on earth to forgive sins", he said to the paralytic, **11** "I tell you, arise, take up your mat, and go to your house." **12** And he arose immediately, and took up the mat, and went out in front of them all; so that they were all amazed, and glorified God, saying, "We never saw anything like this." **13** And he went out again by the seaside. All the crowd came to him, and he taught them. **14** And as he passed by, he saw

Levi, the son of Alphaeus, sitting at the tax office, and he said to him, "Follow me." And he arose and followed him. **15** It happened, that he was reclining at the table in his house, and many tax collectors and sinners sat down with Jesus and his disciples, for there were many, and they followed him. **16** And the scribes of the Pharisees, when they saw him eating with the tax collectors and sinners, said to his disciples, "Why is it that he eats and drinks with tax collectors and sinners?" **17** And when Jesus heard it, he said to them, "Those who are healthy have no need for a physician, but those who are sick. I came not to call the righteous, but sinners." **18** And John's disciples and the Pharisees were fasting, and they came and asked him, "Why do the disciples of John and those of the Pharisees fast, but your disciples do not fast?" **19** And Jesus said to them, "Can the groomsmen fast while the bridegroom is with them? As long as they have the bridegroom with them, they cannot fast. **20** But the days will come when the bridegroom will be taken away from them, and then will they fast in that day. **21** No one sews a piece of unshrunk cloth on an old garment, or else the patch shrinks and the new tears away from the old, and a worse hole is made. **22** And no one puts new wine into old wineskins, or else the wine will burst the skins, and the wine is lost, and the skins will be destroyed; but they put new wine into fresh wineskins." **23** And it happened that he was going on the Sabbath day through the grain fields, and his disciples began, as they went, to pluck the ears of grain. **24** And the Pharisees said to him, "Look, why do they do that which is not lawful on the Sabbath day?" **25** And he said to them, "Did you never read what David did, when he had need, and was hungry—he, and those who were with him? **26** How he entered into the house of God in the time of Abiathar the high priest, and ate the show bread, which is not lawful to eat except for the priests, and gave also to those who were with him?" **27** And he said to them, "The Sabbath was made for people, not people for the Sabbath. **28** Therefore the Son of Man is lord even of the Sabbath."

3 And he entered again into the synagogue, and there was a man there who had his hand withered. **2** And They watched him, whether he would heal him on the Sabbath day, that they might accuse him. **3** And he said to the man with the withered hand, "Stand up in the middle." **4** And he said to them, "Is it lawful on the Sabbath day to do good, or to do harm? To save a life, or to kill?" But they were silent. **5** And when he had looked around at them with anger, being grieved at the hardening of their hearts, he said to the man, "Stretch out your hand." He stretched it out, and his hand was restored. **6** And the Pharisees went out, and immediately conspired with the Herodians against him, how they might destroy him. **7** And Jesus withdrew to the sea with his disciples, and a large crowd followed from Galilee, and from Judea, **8** and from Jerusalem, and from Idumea, and beyond the Jordan, and those from around Tyre and Sidon. A large crowd, when they heard what great things he did, came to him. **9** And he told his disciples that a small boat should stay near him because of the crowd, so that they would not press on him. **10** For he had healed many, so that as many as had diseases pressed on him that they might touch him. **11** And the unclean spirits, whenever they saw him, fell down before him, and shouted, saying, "You are the Son of God." **12** And he sternly warned them that they should not make him known. **13** And he went up into the mountain, and called to himself those whom he wanted, and they went to him. **14** And he appointed twelve, that they might be with him, and that he might send them out to preach, **15** to have authority to heal sicknesses and to cast out demons. **16** And he appointed the twelve. And to Simon he gave the name Peter; **17** and James the son of Zebedee; and John the brother of James (and he surnamed them Boanerges which means, Sons of Thunder); **18** and Andrew, and Philip, and Bartholomew, and Matthew, and Thomas, and James the son of Alphaeus, and Thaddaeus, and Simon the Zealot; **19** and Judas Iscariot, who also betrayed him. **20** And he came into a house, and the crowd came together again, so that they could not so much as eat bread. **21** And when his family heard it, they went out to take charge of him: for they said, "He is out of his mind." **22** And the scribes who came down from Jerusalem said, "He has Beelzebul," and, "By the prince of the demons he casts out the demons." **23** And so he summoned them, and said to them in parables, "How can Satan cast out Satan? **24** And if a kingdom is divided against itself, that kingdom cannot stand. **25** And if a house is divided against itself, that house will not be able to stand. **26** And if Satan has risen up against himself, and is divided, he will not be able to stand, but has an end. **27** But no one can enter into the house of the strong man to plunder, unless he first binds the strong man; and then he will plunder his house. **28** Truly I tell you, all human sins will be forgiven, including their blasphemies with which they may blaspheme; **29** but whoever may blaspheme against the Holy Spirit has not forgiveness for the age **(aiōn g165)**, but is liable of consummate **(aiōnios g166)** sin." **30** because they said, "He has an unclean spirit." **31** And his mother and his brothers came, and standing outside, they sent to him, calling him. **32** And a crowd was sitting around him, and they told him, "Look, your mother and your brothers are outside looking for you." **33** And he answered them, saying, "Who are my mother and my brothers?" **34** And looking around at those who sat around him, he said, "Look, my mother and my brothers. **35** For whoever does the will of God, the same is my brother, and my sister, and mother."

4 And again he began to teach by the seaside. And a large crowd was gathered to him, so that he entered into a boat in the sea, and sat down. And the whole crowd was on the land by the sea. **2** And then he taught them many things in parables, and told them in his teaching, **3** "Listen. Look, the sower who went out to sow. **4** And it happened, as he sowed, some seed fell by the road, and the birds came and devoured it. **5** And others fell on the rocky ground, where it had little soil, and immediately it sprang up, because it had no depth of soil. **6** And when the sun came up, it was scorched; and because it had no root, it withered away. **7** And others fell among the thorns, and the thorns grew up, and choked it, and it yielded no fruit. **8** And others fell into the good ground, and yielded fruit, growing up and increasing; and brought forth thirty times, and sixty times, and one hundred times." **9** And he said, "Whoever has ears to hear, let him hear." **10** And when he was alone, those who were around him with the twelve asked him about the parables. **11** And he said to them, "To you has been given the mystery of the Kingdom of God, but to those who are outside, all things are done in parables, **12** that 'seeing they may see, and not perceive; and hearing they may hear, and not understand; lest perhaps they should turn and be forgiven.'" **13** And he said to them, "Do you not understand this parable? And how will you understand all of the parables? **14** The farmer sows the word. **15** And these are the ones by the road where the word is sown; and when they have heard, immediately Satan comes, and takes away the word which has been sown in them. **16** And these in a similar way are those who are sown on the rocky places, who, when they have heard the word, immediately receive it with joy. **17** And they have no root in themselves, but are short-lived. Then, when oppression or persecution arises because of the word, immediately they stumble. **18** And others are those who are sown among the thorns; these are the ones who have heard the word, **19 and the cares of this age (aiōn g165), and the deceitfulness of riches, and the lusts of other things entering in choke the word, and it becomes unfruitful. 20** And those which were sown on the good ground are those who hear the word, and accept it, and bear fruit, some thirty times, some sixty times, and some one hundred times." **21** And he said to them, "Is the lamp brought to be put under a basket or under a bed? Is it not put on a stand? **22** For there is nothing hidden, except that it should be made known; neither was anything made secret, but that it should come to light. **23** If anyone has ears to hear, let him hear." **24** And he said to them, "Consider carefully what you hear. With whatever measure you measure, it will be measured to you, and more will be given to you. **25** For whoever has, more will be given, and he who does not have, even that which he has will be taken away from him." **26** And he said, "The Kingdom of God is like someone who scatters seed on the earth, **27** and he sleeps and rises night and day, and the seed springs up and grows; he doesn't know how. **28** The earth bears fruit, first the blade, then the ear, then the full grain in the ear. **29** But when the fruit is ripe, immediately he puts forth the sickle, because the harvest has come." **30** And he said, "To what will we liken the Kingdom of God? Or with what parable will we use for it? **31** It's like a mustard seed, which, when it is sown upon the soil, though it is less than all the seeds that are upon the soil, **32** And when it is sown, grows up, and becomes greater than all the garden plants, and puts out large branches, so that the birds of the sky can lodge under its shadow." **33** And with many such parables he spoke the word to them, as they were able to hear it. **34** And he did not speak to them without a parable; but privately to his own disciples he explained everything. **35** And on that day, when evening had come, he said to them, "Let us go over to the other side." **36** And leaving the crowd, they took him with them, even as he was, in the boat. And other boats were with him. **37** And a big wind storm arose, and the waves beat into the boat, so much that the boat was already filled. **38** And he himself was in the stern, asleep on the cushion, and they woke him up, and told him, "Teacher, do you not care that we are dying?" **39** And he awoke, and rebuked the wind, and said to the sea, "Peace. Be still." And the wind ceased, and there was a great calm. **40** And he said to them, "Why are you so afraid? Do you still have no faith?" **41** And they were greatly afraid, and said to one another, "Who then is this, that even the wind and the sea obey him?"

5 And they came to the other side of the sea, into the territory of the Gerasenes. **2** And when he had come out of the boat, immediately a man with an unclean spirit met him out of the tombs. **3** He lived in the tombs, and no one could bind him any more, not even with a chain. **4** For he had been often bound with fetters and chains, and the chains had been torn apart by him, and the fetters broken in pieces. No one had the strength to tame him. **5** And always, night and day, in the tombs and in the mountains, he was crying out, and cutting himself with stones. **6** And when he saw Jesus from afar, he ran and bowed down to him, **7** and crying out with a loud voice, he said, "What have I to do with you, Jesus, you Son of the Most High God? I adjure you by God, do not torment me." **8** For he said to him, "Come out of the man, you unclean spirit." **9** And then he asked him, "What is your name?" And he replied, "My name is Legion, for we are many." **10** And he pleaded with Jesus repeatedly not to send them away out of the region. **11** Now on the mountainside there was a great herd of pigs feeding. **12** And they begged him, saying, "Send us into the pigs, that we may enter into them." **13** And he gave them permission. The unclean spirits came out and entered into the pigs; and the herd of about two thousand rushed down the steep bank into the sea, and they were drowned in the sea. **14** And those who fed them fled, and told it in the city and in the country. And the people went to see what it was that had happened. **15** And they came to Jesus, and saw him who had been possessed by demons sitting, clothed and in his right mind, even him who had the legion; and they were afraid. **16** And those who saw it declared to them how it happened to him who was possessed by demons, and about the pigs. **17** And then they began to plead with Jesus to leave their region. **18** As he was entering into the boat, he who had been possessed by demons pleaded with him that he might be with him. **19** However, Jesus did not allow him, but said to him, "Go to your house, to your own, and tell them what great things the Lord has done for you, and how he had mercy on you." **20** So he went his way, and began to proclaim in Decapolis how Jesus had done great things for him, and everyone was amazed. **21** And when Jesus had crossed back over in the boat to the other side, a large crowd was gathered to him; and he was by the sea. **22** One of the rulers of the synagogue, Jairus by name, came; and seeing him, he fell at his feet, **23** and pleaded with him repeatedly, saying, "My little daughter is at the point of death. Please come and lay your hands on her, that she may be made healthy, and live." **24** And he went with him, and a large crowd followed him, and they pressed upon him on all sides. **25** Now a woman, who had an issue of blood for twelve years, **26** and had suffered many things by many physicians, and had spent all that she had, and was no better, but rather grew worse, **27** having heard the things concerning Jesus, came up behind him in the crowd, and touched his clothes. **28** For she said, "If I just touch his clothes, I will be made well." **29** And immediately the flow of her blood was dried up, and she felt in her body that she was healed of her affliction. **30** And immediately Jesus, perceiving in himself that the power had gone out from him, turned around in the crowd, and asked, "Who touched my clothes?" **31** And his disciples said to him, "You see the crowd pressing against you, and you say, 'Who touched me?'" **32** He looked around to see her who had done this thing. **33** But the woman, fearing and trembling, knowing what had been done to her, came and fell down before him, and told him the whole truth. **34** And he said to her, "Daughter, your faith has made you well. Go in peace, and be cured of your disease." **35** While he was still speaking, people came from the synagogue ruler's house saying, "Your daughter is dead. Why bother the Teacher any more?" **36** But Jesus, overhearing the message spoken, said to the ruler of the synagogue, "Do not be afraid, only believe." **37** And he allowed no one to follow him, except Peter, James, and John the brother of James. **38** And they came to the synagogue ruler's house, and he saw an uproar, weeping, and great wailing. **39** And when he had entered in, he said to them, "Why do you make an uproar and weep? The child is not dead, but is asleep." **40** And they ridiculed him. But he, having put them all out, took the father of the child, her mother, and those who were with him, and went in where the child was. **41** And taking the child by the hand, he said to her, "Talitha koum," which translated means, "Little girl, I tell you, get up." **42** And immediately the girl rose up and walked, for she was twelve years old. And immediately they were overcome with amazement. **43** And he strictly ordered them that no one should know this, and commanded that something should be given to her to eat.

6 And he went out from there and came into his own country, and his disciples followed him. **2** And when the Sabbath had come, he began to teach in the synagogue, and many hearing him were astonished, saying, "Where did this man get these things?" and, "What is the wisdom that is given to this man, that such mighty works come about by his hands? **3** Is not this the carpenter, the son of Mary, and brother of James, Josi, Judas, and Simon? Are not his sisters here with us?" They were offended at him. **4** Jesus said to them, "A prophet is not without honor, except in his own country, and among his own relatives, and in his own house." **5** And he could do no mighty work there, except that he laid his hands on a few sick people, and healed them. **6** And he was amazed because of their unbelief. And he went around the villages teaching. **7** And he called to himself the twelve, and began to send them out two by two; and he gave them authority over the unclean spirits. **8** And he commanded them that they should take nothing for their journey, except a staff only: no bread, no pack, no money in their belts, **9** but to wear sandals, and not to put on two tunics. **10** And he said to them, "Wherever you enter into a house, stay there until you depart from there. **11** And if any place will not receive you or listen to you, as you depart from there, shake off the dust that is under your feet for a testimony against them." **12** So they went out and proclaimed that all should repent. **13** They cast out many demons, and anointed many with oil who were sick, and healed them. **14** King Herod heard this, for his name had become known, and he said, "John the Baptist has risen from the dead, and therefore these powers are at work in him." **15** But others said, "He is Elijah." Others said, "He is a prophet, like one of the prophets." **16** But Herod, when he heard this, said, "This is John, whom I beheaded. He has risen." **17** For Herod himself had sent out and arrested John, and bound him in prison for the sake of Herodias, his brother Philip's wife, for he had married her. **18** For John said to Herod, "It is not lawful for you to have your brother's wife." **19** So Herodias set herself against him, and desired to kill him, but she could not, **20** for Herod feared John, knowing that he was a righteous and holy man, and kept him safe. And when he heard him, he was very perplexed, but he heard him gladly. **21** And then a convenient day came, that Herod on his birthday gave a supper for his nobles, the high officers, and the leaders of Galilee. **22** And when the daughter of Herodias herself came in and danced, she pleased Herod and those sitting with him. The king said to the young woman, "Ask me whatever you want, and I will give it to you." **23** And he swore to her, "Whatever you ask me, I will give you, up to half of my kingdom." **24** So she went out, and said to her mother, "What should I ask?" And she said, "The head of John the baptizer." **25** And she came in immediately with haste to the king, and asked, "I want you to give me right now the head of John the Baptist on a platter." **26** And the king was exceedingly sorry, but for the sake of his oaths, and those reclining, he did not wish to refuse her. **27** So immediately the king sent out a soldier of his guard, and commanded to bring John's head, and he went and beheaded him in the prison, **28** and brought his head on a platter, and gave it to the young woman; and the young woman gave it to her mother. **29** And when his disciples heard this, they came and took up his corpse, and placed it in a tomb. **30** Then the apostles gathered themselves together to Jesus, and they told him all things, whatever they had done, and whatever they had taught. **31** And he said to them, "Come away by yourselves to an isolated place, and rest awhile." For there were many coming and going, and they had no leisure so much as to eat. **32** So they went away in the boat to an isolated place by themselves. **33** But they saw them going, and many recognized him and ran there on foot from all the cities and they arrived before them. **34** And he came out, saw a large crowd, and he had compassion on them, because they were like sheep without a shepherd, and he began to teach them many things. **35** And when it was late in the day, his disciples came to him, and said, "This place is desolate, and it is late in the day. **36** Send them away, that they may go into the surrounding country and villages, and buy themselves something to eat." **37** But he answered them, "You give them something to eat." And they said to him, "Are we to go and buy two hundred denarii worth of bread, and give them something to eat?" **38** He said to them, "How many loaves do you have? Go see." When they knew, they said, "Five, and two fish." **39** He commanded them that everyone should sit down in groups on the green grass. **40** They sat down in ranks, by hundreds and by fifties. **41** He took the five loaves and the two fish, and looking up to heaven, he blessed and broke the loaves, and he gave to his disciples to set before them, and he divided the two fish among them all. **42** They all ate, and were filled. **43** They took up twelve baskets full of broken pieces and also of the fish. **44** Those who ate the loaves were five thousand men. **45** And immediately he made his disciples get into the boat, and to go ahead to the other side, to Bethsaida, while he himself was sending the crowd away. **46** After he had taken leave of them, he went up the mountain to pray. **47** When evening had come, the boat was in the midst of the sea, and he was alone on the land. **48** He saw them distressed in rowing, for the wind was against them. In the watch between three and six in the morning he came to them, walking on the sea, and he would have passed by them, **49** but they, when they saw him walking on the sea, supposed that it was a ghost, and began to scream; **50** for they all saw him, and were troubled. But he immediately spoke with them, and said to them, "Cheer up. It is I. Do not be afraid." **51** And he got into the boat with them, and the wind ceased. And they were completely profusely astonished among themselves; **52** for they had not understood about the loaves, but their hearts were hardened. **53** When they had crossed over, they came to land at Gennesaret, and moored to the shore. **54** When they had come out of the boat, immediately the people recognized him, **55** and ran around that whole region, and began to bring those who were sick, on their mats, to where they heard he was. **56** Wherever he entered, into villages, or into cities, or into the country, they placed the sick in the marketplaces, and begged him that they might touch just the fringe of his garment; and everyone who touched him were made well.

7 Then the Pharisees, and some of the scribes gathered together to him, having come from Jerusalem. **2** Now when they saw that some of his disciples ate bread with defiled, that is, unwashed, hands, they found fault. **3** (For the Pharisees, and all Jewish people, do not eat unless they wash their hands and forearms, holding to the Tradition of the Elders. **4** They do not eat when they come from the marketplace unless they wash. And there are many other things which they have received and hold to, the washing of cups and pitchers and copper vessels and dining couches.) **5** The Pharisees and the scribes asked him, "Why do your disciples not walk according to the Tradition of the Elders, but eat their bread with unwashed hands?" **6** He said to them, "Well did Isaiah prophesy of you hypocrites, as it is written, 'This people honors me with their lips, but their heart is far from me. **7** And in vain do they worship me, teaching instructions that are the commandments of humans.' **8** "For you set aside the commandment of God, and hold tightly to human tradition." **9** He said to them, "Full well do you reject the commandment of God, that you may establish your tradition. **10** For Moses said, 'Honor your father and your mother;' and, 'Anyone who speaks evil of father or mother, let him be put to death.' **11** But you say, 'If anyone tells his father or mother, "Whatever profit you might have received from me is Corban, that is to say, given to God;"' **12** then you no longer allow him to do anything for his father or his mother, **13** making void the word of God by your tradition, which you have handed down. You do many things like this." **14** And he called the crowd to himself again, and said to them, "Hear me, all of you, and understand. **15** There is nothing from outside of the person, that going into him can defile him; but the things which proceed out of the person are what defile the person." **17** When he had entered into a house away from the crowd, his disciples asked him about the parable. **18** He said to them, "Are you thus without understanding also? Do you not perceive that whatever goes into the person from outside cannot defile him, **19** because it does not go into his heart, but into his stomach, then into the latrine, cleansing all the foods?" **20** He said, "That which proceeds out of the man, that defiles the man. **21** For from within, out of a person's heart, proceed evil thoughts, adulteries, sexual sins, murders, thefts, **22** covetings, wickedness, deceit, lustful desires, an evil eye, blasphemy, pride, and foolishness. **23** All these evil things come from within, and defile the man." **24** From there he arose, and went away into the region of Tyre and Sidon. He entered into a house, and did not want anyone to know it, but he could not escape notice. **25** But immediately a woman whose young daughter had an unclean spirit heard of him and came and fell at his feet. **26** Now the woman was a Greek, a Syrophoenician by race. She begged him that he would cast the demon out of her daughter. **27** But he said to her, "Let the children be filled first, for it is not appropriate to take the children's bread and throw it to the dogs." **28** But she answered him, "Yes, Sir. Yet even the dogs under the table eat the children's crumbs." **29** He said to her, "For this saying, go your way. The demon has gone out of your daughter." **30** And when she went away to her house, she found the child lying on the bed, the demon having left. **31** Again he departed from the borders of Tyre, and came through Sidon to the sea of Galilee, through the midst of the region of Decapolis. **32** They brought to him one who was deaf and had a speech difficulty, and they begged Jesus to lay his hand on him. **33** He took him aside from the crowd, privately, and put his fingers into his ears, and he spat, and touched his tongue. **34** Looking up to heaven, he sighed, and said to him, "Ephphatha." that is, "Be opened." **35** And his ears were opened, and the impediment of his tongue was released, and he spoke clearly. **36** He commanded them that they should tell no one, but the more he commanded them, so much the more widely they proclaimed it. **37** They were astonished beyond measure, saying, "He has done all things well. He makes even the deaf hear, and the mute speak."

8 In those days, when there was a large crowd, and they had nothing to eat, he called the disciples to himself, and said to them, **2** "I have compassion on the crowd, because they have stayed with me now three days, and have nothing to eat. **3** If I send them away fasting to their home, they will faint on the way, and some of them have come a long way." **4** His disciples answered him, "From where could one satisfy these people with bread here in a deserted place?" **5** He asked them, "How many loaves do you have?" They said, "Seven." **6** He commanded the crowd to sit down on the ground, and he took the seven loaves. Having given thanks, he broke them, and gave them to his disciples to serve, and they served the crowd. **7** They had a few small fish. Having blessed them, he said to serve these also. **8** They ate, and were filled. They took up seven baskets of broken pieces that were left over. **9** Now they were about four thousand. Then he sent them away. **10** Immediately he entered into the boat with his disciples, and came into the region of Dalmanutha. **11** The Pharisees came out and began to question him, seeking from him a sign from heaven, and testing him. **12** He sighed deeply in his spirit, and said, "Why does this generation seek a sign? Truly I tell you, no sign will be given to this generation." **13** And he left them, and got into the boat again, and went to the other side. **14** Now they forgot to take bread; and they did not have more than one loaf in the boat with them. **15** He warned them, saying, "Watch out; guard yourselves against the yeast of the Pharisees and the yeast of Herod." **16** And they began discussing among themselves that they had no bread. **17** He, perceiving it, said to them, "Why do you reason that it's because you have no bread? Do you not perceive yet, neither understand? Are your hearts hardened? **18** Having eyes, do you not see? Having ears, do you not hear? Do you not remember? **19** When I broke the five loaves among the five thousand, how many baskets full of broken pieces did you take up?" They told him, "Twelve." **20** "When the seven loaves fed the four thousand, how many baskets full of broken pieces did you take up?" And they said, "Seven." **21** He asked them, "Do you not yet understand?" **22** He came to Bethsaida. They brought a blind man to him, and begged Jesus to touch him. **23** He took hold of the blind man by the hand, and brought him out of the village. When he had spit on his eyes, and laid his hands on him, he asked him if he saw anything. **24** He looked up, and said, "I see people; they look like trees walking." **25** Then again he laid his hands on his eyes. He made him look up, and was restored, and saw everything clearly. **26** He sent him away to his house, saying, "Do not enter into the village." **27** Jesus went out, with his disciples, into the villages of Caesarea Philippi. On the way he asked his disciples, "Who do people say that I am?" **28** And they said to him, saying, "John the Baptist, and others say Elijah, but others: one of the prophets." **29** He said to them, "But who do you say that I am?" Peter answered and said to him, "You are the Christ." **30** He commanded them that they should tell no one about him. **31** He began to teach them that the Son of Man must suffer many things, and be rejected by the elders, the chief priests, and the scribes, and be killed, and after three days rise again. **32** He spoke to them openly. Peter took him, and began to rebuke him. **33** But he, turning around, and seeing his disciples, rebuked Peter, and said, "Get behind me, Satan. For you have in mind not the things of God, but the things of man." **34** He called the crowd to himself with his disciples, and said to them, "If anyone wants to come after me, let him deny himself, and take up his cross, and follow me. **35** For whoever wants to save his life will lose it; and whoever will lose his life for my sake and the sake of the Good News will save it. **36** For what does it profit a person to gain the whole world, and forfeit his soul? **37** Or what will a person give in exchange for his soul? **38** For whoever will be ashamed of me and of my words in this adulterous and sinful generation, the Son of Man also will be ashamed of him, when he comes in the glory of his Father with the holy angels."

9 He said to them, "Truly I tell you, there are some standing here who will in no way taste death until they see the Kingdom of God come with power." **2** After six days Jesus took with him Peter, James, and John, and brought them up onto a high mountain privately by themselves, and he was changed into another form in front of them. **3** His clothing became glistening, exceedingly white, such as no launderer on earth can whiten them. **4** Elijah and Moses appeared to them, and they were talking with Jesus. **5** Peter said to Jesus, "Rabbi, it is good for us to be here. Let us make three tents: one for you, one for Moses, and one for Elijah." **6** For he did not know what to answer, for they became very afraid. **7** A cloud came, overshadowing them, and a voice came out of the cloud, "This is my beloved Son. Listen to him." **8** Suddenly looking around, they saw no one with them anymore, except Jesus alone. **9** As they were coming down from the mountain, he commanded them that they should tell no one what things they had seen, until after the Son of Man had risen from the dead. **10** They kept this saying to themselves, questioning what the "rising from the dead" meant. **11** They asked him, saying, "Why do the scribes say that Elijah must come first?" **12** And he said to them, "Elijah indeed comes first, and restores all things. And why is it written of the Son of Man that he should suffer many things and be rejected? **13** But I tell you that Elijah has come, and they have also done to him whatever they wanted to, even as it is written about him." **14** And when they came to the disciples, they saw a large crowd around them, and scribes questioning them. **15** Immediately all the crowd, when they saw him, were greatly amazed, and running to him greeted him. **16** He asked them, "What are you arguing about with them?" **17** And one out of the crowd answered him, "Teacher, I brought to you my son, who has a mute spirit; **18** and wherever it seizes him, it throws him down, and he foams at the mouth, and grinds his teeth, and wastes away. I asked your disciples to cast it out, and they weren't able." **19** And answering, he said to them, "You unbelieving generation, how long must I be with you? How long must I put up with you? Bring him to me." **20** They brought him to him, and when he saw him, immediately the spirit convulsed him, and he fell on the ground, wallowing and foaming at the mouth. **21** He asked his father, "How long has it been since this has come to him?" He said, "From childhood. **22** And it has often cast him both into fire and into water, to destroy him. But if you can do anything, have compassion on us, and help us." **23** Jesus said to him, "'If you can?' All things are possible to him who believes." **24** Immediately the father of the child cried out and said, "I believe. Help my unbelief." **25** When Jesus saw that a crowd came running together, he rebuked the unclean spirit, saying to him, "You deaf and mute spirit, I command you, come out of him, and never enter him again." **26** Having screamed, and convulsed greatly, it came out of him. The boy became like one dead; so much that most of them said, "He is dead." **27** But Jesus took him by the hand, and raised him up; and he arose. **28** And when he had come into the house, his disciples asked him privately, "Why could we not cast it out?" **29** And he said to them, "This kind can come out by nothing, except by prayer and fasting." **30** They went out from there, and passed through Galilee. He did not want anyone to know it. **31** For he was teaching his disciples, and said to them, "The Son of Man is being handed over to the hands of men, and they will kill him; and when he is killed, after three days he will rise again." **32** But they did not understand the saying, and were afraid to ask him. **33** He came to Capernaum, and when he was in the house he asked them, "What were you arguing on the way?" **34** But they were silent, for they had disputed one with another on the way about who was the greatest. **35** And he sat down, and called the twelve; and he said to them, "If anyone wants to be first, he must be last of all, and servant of all." **36** He took a little child, and set him in the midst of them. Taking him in his arms, he said to them, **37** "Whoever receives one such little child in my name, receives me, and whoever receives me, does not receive me, but him who sent me." **38** John said to him, "Teacher, we saw someone casting out demons in your name; and we forbade him, because he was not following us." **39** But Jesus said, "Do not forbid him, for there is no one who will do a mighty work in my name, and be able quickly to speak evil of me. **40** For whoever is not against us is for us. **41** For whoever will give you a cup of water to drink in my name, because you belong to the Christ, truly I tell you, he will in no way lose his reward. **42** Whoever will cause one of these little ones who believe in me to stumble, it would be better for him if he was thrown into the sea with a millstone hung around his neck. **43** If your hand causes you to stumble, cut it off. It is better for you to enter into life maimed, rather than having your two hands to go into Gehenna **(Geenna g1067)**, into the unquenchable fire, **45** If your foot causes you to stumble, cut it off. It is better for you to enter into life lame, rather than having your two feet to be cast into Gehenna **(Geenna g1067)**. **47** If your eye causes you to stumble, cast it out. It is better for you to enter into God's Kingdom with one eye, rather than having two eyes to be cast into the Gehenna **(Geenna g1067)** of fire, **48** 'where their worm does not die, and the fire is not quenched.' **49** For everyone will be salted with fire, and every sacrifice will be salted with salt. **50** Salt is good, but if the salt has lost its saltiness, how can you make it salty? Have salt in yourselves, and be at peace with one another."

10 He arose from there and came into the borders of Judea and beyond the Jordan. Crowds came together to him again. As he usually did, he was again teaching them. **2** Pharisees came to him testing him, and asked him, "Is it lawful for a man to divorce his wife?" **3** He answered, "What did Moses command you?" **4** They said, "Moses allowed a certificate of divorce to be written, and to divorce her." **5** But Jesus said to them, "Because of your hardness of heart, he wrote you this commandment. **6** But from the beginning of the creation, he made them male and female. **7** For this cause a man will leave his father and mother, and will join to his wife, **8** and the two will become one flesh, so that they are no longer two, but one flesh. **9** What therefore God has joined together, let no one separate." **10** In the house, the disciples asked him again about the same matter. **11** He said to them, "Whoever divorces his wife, and marries another, commits adultery against her. **12** If she herself divorces her husband, and marries another, she commits adultery." **13** They were bringing to him little children, that he should touch them, but the disciples rebuked them. **14** But when Jesus saw it, he was moved with indignation, and said to them, "Allow the little children to come to me. Do not forbid them, for the Kingdom of God belongs to such as these. **15** Truly I tell you, whoever will not receive the Kingdom of God like a little child, he will in no way enter into it." **16** And he took them in his arms, laying his hands on them, and blessed them. **17** As he was going out into the way, one ran to him, knelt before him, and asked him, "Good Teacher, what must I do that I may inherit consummate **(aiōnios g166)** life?" **18** Jesus said to him, "Why do you call me good? No one is good except one—God. **19** You know the commandments: 'Do not commit adultery,' 'Do not murder,' 'Do not steal,' 'Do not give false testimony,' 'Do not defraud,' 'Honor your father and mother.'" **20** And he said to him, "Teacher, I have kept all these things from my youth." **21** Jesus looking at him loved him, and said to him, "One thing you lack. Go, sell whatever you have, and give to the poor, and you will have treasure in heaven; and come, follow me, taking up the cross." **22** But his face fell at that saying, and he went away sorrowful, for he was one who had great possessions. **23** Jesus looked around, and said to his disciples, "How difficult it is for those who have riches to enter into the Kingdom of God." **24** The disciples were amazed at his words. But Jesus answered again and said to them, "Children, how hard it is for those who trust in riches to enter the kingdom of God. **25** It is easier for a camel to go through a needle's eye than for a rich person to enter into the Kingdom of God." **26** They were exceedingly astonished, saying to him, "Then who can be saved?" **27** Jesus, looking at them, said, "With humans it is impossible, but not with God, for all things are possible with God." **28** Peter began to tell him, "Look, we have left everything, and have followed you." **29** Jesus said, "Truly I tell you, there is no one who has left house, or brothers, or sisters, or mother, or father, or children, or land, for my sake, and for the sake of the Good News, **30** but he will receive one hundred times more now in this time: houses, brothers, sisters, mothers, children, and land, with persecutions; and in the age **(aiōn g165)** to come, consummate **(aiōnios g166)** life. **31** But many who are first will be last; and the last first." **32** They were on the way, going up to Jerusalem; and Jesus was going in front of them, and they were amazed; and those who followed were afraid. He again took the twelve, and began to tell them the things that were going to happen to him. **33** "Look, we are going up to Jerusalem. The Son of Man will be delivered to the chief priests and the scribes. They will condemn him to death, and will deliver him to foreigners. **34** They will mock him, spit on him, scourge him, and kill him. After three days he will rise again." **35** James and John, the sons of Zebedee, came near to him, and said to him, "Teacher, we want you to do for us whatever we will ask." **36** He said to them, "What do you want me to do for you?" **37** They said to him, "Grant to us that we may sit, one at your right hand, and one at your left hand, in your glory." **38** But Jesus said to them, "You do not know what you are asking. Are you able to drink the cup that I drink, or to be baptized with the baptism that I am baptized with?" **39** And they said to him, "We are able." And Jesus said to them, "You will drink the cup I drink, and you will be baptized with the baptism that I am baptized with; **40** but to sit at my right hand and at my left hand is not mine to give, but for whom it has been prepared." **41** When the ten heard it, they began to be indignant towards James and John. **42** Jesus summoned them, and said to them, "You know that they who are recognized as rulers over the nations lord it over them, and their great ones exercise authority over them. **43** But it will not be so among you, but whoever wants to become great among you must be your servant. **44** And whoever wants to be first among you must be slave of all. **45** For the Son of Man also did not come to be served, but to serve, and to give his life as a ransom for many." **46** They came to Jericho. As he went out from Jericho, with his disciples and a large crowd, Bartimaeus, the son of Timaeus, a blind beggar, was sitting by the road. **47** When he heard that it was Jesus the Nazarene, he began to cry out, and say, "Jesus, Son of David, have mercy on me." **48** Many rebuked him, that he should be quiet, but he shouted all the louder, "Son of David, have mercy on me." **49** Jesus stood still, and said, "Call him." They called the blind man, saying to him, "Cheer up. Get up. He is calling you." **50** He, casting away his coat, jumped up, and came to Jesus. **51** Jesus asked him, "What do you want me to do for you?" The blind man said to him, "Rabboni, that I may see again." **52** Jesus said to him, "Go your way. Your faith has made you well." And immediately he received his sight, and followed him on the road.

11 When they drew near to Jerusalem, to Bethphage and Bethany, at the Mount of Olives, he sent two of his disciples, **2** and said to them, "Go your way into the village that is opposite you. Immediately as you enter into it, you will find a young donkey tied, on which no one has yet sat. Untie him, and bring him. **3** If anyone asks you, 'Why are you doing this?' say, 'Because the Lord needs it,' and he will send it back here at once." **4** They went away, and found a colt tied at the door outside in the open street, and they untied him. **5** Some of those who stood there asked them, "What are you doing, untying the young donkey?" **6** They said to them just as Jesus had said, and they let them go. **7** They brought the young donkey to Jesus, and threw their garments on it, and Jesus sat on it. **8** Many spread their garments on the way, and others spread branches which they had cut from the fields. **9** Those who went in front, and those who followed, shouted, "Hosanna. Blessed is he who comes in the name of the Lord. **10** Blessed is the kingdom of our father David. Hosanna in the highest." **11** And he entered into the temple in Jerusalem. When he had looked around at everything, it being now evening, he went out to Bethany with the twelve. **12** The next day, when they had come out from Bethany, he was hungry. **13** Seeing a fig tree afar off having leaves, he came to see if perhaps he might find anything on it. When he came to it, he found nothing but leaves, for it was not the season for figs. **14** Jesus told it, "May no one eat fruit from you again for the age **(aiōn g165)**!" and his disciples heard it. **15** They came to Jerusalem, and he entered into the temple, and began to throw out those who sold and those who bought in the temple, and overthrew the tables of the money changers, and the seats of those who sold the doves. **16** He would not allow anyone to carry a container through the temple. **17** He taught, saying to them, "Is it not written, 'My house will be called a house of prayer for all the nations?' But you have made it a den of robbers." **18** The chief priests and the scribes heard it, and sought how they might destroy him. For they feared him, because all the crowd was astonished at his teaching. **19** When evening came, they went out of the city. **20** As they passed by in the morning, they saw the fig tree withered away from the roots. **21** Peter, remembering, said to him, "Teacher, look. The fig tree which you cursed has withered away." **22** Jesus answered them, "Have faith in God. **23** Truly I tell you, whoever may tell this mountain, 'Be taken up and cast into the sea,' and does not doubt in his heart, but believes that what he says will happen, it will be done for him. **24** Therefore I tell you, whatever you ask for in prayer, believe that you have received it, and it will be yours. **25** Whenever you stand praying, forgive, if you have anything against anyone; so that your Father, who is in heaven, may also forgive you your wrongdoing. **26** But if you do not forgive, neither will your Father in heaven forgive your wrongdoing." **27** They came again to Jerusalem, and as he was walking in the temple, the chief priests, and the scribes, and the elders came to him, **28** and they began saying to him, "By what authority do you do these things? And who gave you this authority to do these things?" **29** Jesus said to them, "I will also ask

Mark

you one question. Answer me, and I will tell you by what authority I do these things. **30** The baptism of John—was it from heaven, or from people? Answer me." **31** They reasoned with themselves, saying, "If we should say, 'From heaven;' he will say, 'Why then did you not believe him?' **32** If we should say, 'From people'"—they feared the crowd, for all held John to really be a prophet. **33** They answered and said to Jesus, "We do not know." Jesus said to them, "Neither do I tell you by what authority I do these things."

12 He began to speak to them in parables. "A man planted a vineyard, put a hedge around it, dug a pit for the winepress, built a tower, rented it out to a farmer, and went on a journey. **2** When it was time, he sent a servant to the farmer to get from the farmer his share of the fruit of the vineyard. **3** They took him, beat him, and sent him away empty. **4** Again, he sent another servant to them; and they wounded him in the head, and treated him shamefully. **5** And he sent another; and they killed him; and many others, beating some, and killing some. **6** He had one left, a beloved son, he sent him last to them, saying, 'They will respect my son.' **7** But those farmers said among themselves, 'This is the heir. Come, let us kill him, and the inheritance will be ours.' **8** They took him, killed him, and cast him out of the vineyard. **9** What therefore will the lord of the vineyard do? He will come and destroy the farmers, and will give the vineyard to others. **10** Haven't you even read this Scripture: 'The stone which the builders rejected, the same was made the head of the corner. **11** This was from the Lord. It is marvelous in our eyes'?" **12** They tried to seize him, but they feared the crowd; for they perceived that he spoke the parable against them. They left him, and went away. **13** They sent some of the Pharisees and of the Herodians to him, that they might trap him with words. **14** When they had come, they asked him, "Teacher, we know that you are honest, and do not defer to anyone; for you are not partial to anyone, but truly teach the way of God. Is it lawful to pay taxes to Caesar, or not? **15** Should we pay, or should we not pay?" But he, knowing their hypocrisy, said to them, "Why do you test me? Bring me a denarius, that I may see it." **16** They brought it. He said to them, "Whose is this image and inscription?" They said to him, "Caesar's." **17** And Jesus said to them, "Render to Caesar the things that are Caesar's, and to God the things that are God's." And they were utterly amazed at him. **18** There came to him Sadducees, who say that there is no resurrection. They asked him, saying, **19** "Teacher, Moses wrote to us, 'If a man's brother dies, and leaves a wife behind him, and leaves no children, that his brother should take the wife, and raise up offspring for his brother.' **20** There were seven brothers. The first took a wife, and dying left no offspring. **21** The second took her, and died, leaving no children behind him. The third likewise; **22** and the seven left no children. Last of all the woman also died. **23** In the resurrection, when they rise, whose wife will she be of them? For the seven had her as a wife." **24** Jesus said to them, "Is not this because you are mistaken, not knowing the Scriptures, nor the power of God? **25** For when they will rise from the dead, they neither marry, nor are given in marriage, but are like angels in heaven. **26** But about the dead, that they are raised; have you not read in the book of Moses, about the bush, how God spoke to him, saying, 'I am the God of Abraham, and the God of Isaac, and the God of Jacob'? **27** He is not the God of the dead, but of the living. You are therefore badly mistaken." **28** And one of the scribes came, and heard them questioning together. Seeing that he had answered them well, asked him, "Which commandment is the greatest of all?" **29** Jesus answered, "The first is, 'Hear, Israel, the Lord our God, the Lord is one. **30** And you are to love the Lord your God with all your heart, and with all your soul, and with all your mind, and with all your strength.' **31** The second is this, 'You are to love your neighbor as yourself.' There is no other commandment greater than these." **32** The scribe said to him, "Truly, Teacher, you have said well that he is one, and there is none other but he, **33** and to love him with all the heart, and with all the understanding, and with all the soul, and with all the strength, and to love his neighbor as himself, is more important than all whole burnt offerings and sacrifices." **34** When Jesus saw that he answered wisely, he said to him, "You are not far from the Kingdom of God." No one dared ask him any question after that. **35** Jesus responded, as he taught in the temple, "How can the scribes say that the Christ is the son of David? **36** David himself said in the Holy Spirit, 'The Lord said to my Lord, "Sit at my right hand, until I make your enemies the footstool of your feet."' **37** David himself calls him Lord, so how can he be his son?" The common people heard him gladly. **38** In his teaching he said to them, "Beware of the scribes, who like to walk in long robes, and to get greetings in the marketplaces, **39** and the best seats in the synagogues, and the best places at feasts: **40** those who devour widows' houses, and for a pretense make long prayers. These will receive greater condemnation." **41** And he sat down opposite the treasury, and saw how the crowd cast money into the treasury. Many who were rich cast in much. **42** A poor widow came, and she cast in two lepta, which equal a kodrantes. **43** He called his disciples to himself, and said to them, "Truly I tell you, this poor widow gave more than all those who are giving into the treasury, **44** for they all gave out of their abundance, but she, out of her poverty, gave all that she had to live on."

13 As he went out of the temple, one of his disciples said to him, "Teacher, see what kind of stones and what kind of buildings." **2** And Jesus said to him, "Do you see these great buildings? There will not be left here one stone on another, which will not be thrown down." **3** As he sat on the Mount of Olives opposite the temple, Peter, James, John, and Andrew asked him privately, **4** "Tell us, when will these things be? What is the sign that these things are all about to be fulfilled?" **5** And Jesus began to say to them, "Be careful that no one leads you astray. **6** Many will come in my name, saying, 'I am he.' and will lead many astray. **7** "When you hear of wars and rumors of wars, do not be troubled. Such things must happen, but the end is not yet. **8** For nation will rise against nation, and

Mark

kingdom against kingdom. There will be earthquakes in various places. There will be famines. These things are the beginning of birth pains. **9** But watch yourselves, for they will deliver you up to councils. You will be beaten in synagogues. You will stand before rulers and kings for my sake, as a testimony to them. **10** The Good News must first be preached to all the nations. **11** When they lead you away and deliver you up, do not be anxious beforehand, or premeditate what you will say, but say whatever will be given you in that hour. For it is not you who speak, but the Holy Spirit. **12** "Brother will deliver up brother to death, and the father his child. Children will rise up against parents, and cause them to be put to death. **13** You will be hated by all for my name's sake, but he who endures to the end, the same will be saved. **14** But when you see the abomination of desolation, standing where it ought not (let the reader understand), then let those who are in Judea flee to the mountains, **15** and let him who is on the housetop not go down, nor enter in, to take anything out of his house. **16** Let him who is in the field not return back to take his coat. **17** But woe to those who are with child and to those who nurse babies in those days. **18** And pray that it won't be in the winter. **19** For in those days there will be oppression, such as there has not been the like from the beginning of the creation which God created until now, and never will be. **20** Unless the Lord had shortened the days, no flesh would have been saved; but for the sake of the chosen ones, whom he picked out, he shortened the days. **21** Then if anyone tells you, 'Look, here is the Christ.' or, 'Look, there.' do not believe it. **22** For there will arise false messiahs and false prophets, and will show signs and wonders, that they may lead astray, if possible, the chosen ones. **23** But you watch. "I have told you all things beforehand. **24** But in those days, after that oppression, the sun will be darkened, the moon will not give its light, **25** the stars will be falling from heaven, and the powers that are in the heavens will be shaken. **26** Then they will see the Son of Man coming in clouds with great power and glory. **27** Then he will send out his angels, and will gather together his chosen ones from the four winds, from the farthest part of the earth to the farthest part of the sky. **28** "Now from the fig tree, learn this parable. When the branch has now become tender, and puts forth its leaves, you know that the summer is near; **29** even so you also, when you see these things coming to pass, know that it is near, at the doors. **30** Truly I say to you, this generation will not pass away until all these things happen. **31** Heaven and earth will pass away, but my words will not pass away. **32** But of that day or the hour no one knows, not even the angels in heaven, nor the Son, but only the Father. **33** Watch, keep alert, and pray; for you do not know when the time is. **34** "It is like a man, traveling to another country, having left his house, and given authority to his servants, and to each one his work, and also commanded the doorkeeper to keep watch. **35** Watch therefore, for you do not know when the lord of the house is coming —at evening, or at midnight, or when the rooster crows, or in the morning; **36** lest coming suddenly he might find you sleeping. **37** What I tell you, I tell all: Watch."

14

It was now two days before the feast of the Passover and the unleavened bread, and the chief priests and the scribes sought how they might seize him by deception, and kill him. **2** For they said, "Not during the feast, because there might be a riot of the people." **3** While he was at Bethany, in the house of Simon the leper, as he was reclining, a woman came having an alabaster jar of ointment of pure nard—very costly. She broke the jar, and poured it over his head. **4** But there were some who were indignant among themselves, and saying, "Why has this ointment been wasted? **5** For this ointment might have been sold for more than three hundred denarii, and given to the poor." They grumbled against her. **6** But Jesus said, "Leave her alone. Why do you trouble her? She has done a good work for me. **7** For you always have the poor with you, and whenever you want to, you can do them good; but you will not always have me. **8** She has done what she could. She has anointed my body beforehand for the burying. **9** Truly I tell you, wherever this Good News may be preached throughout the whole world, that which this woman has done will also be spoken of for a memorial of her." **10** Judas Iscariot, who was one of the twelve, went away to the chief priests, that he might deliver him to them. **11** They, when they heard it, were glad, and promised to give him money. He sought how he might conveniently deliver him. **12** On the first day of unleavened bread, when they sacrificed the Passover lamb, his disciples asked him, "Where do you want us to go and make ready that you may eat the Passover?" **13** He sent two of his disciples, and said to them, "Go into the city, and there you will meet a man carrying a pitcher of water. Follow him, **14** and wherever he enters in, tell the master of the house, 'The Teacher says, "Where is my guest room, where I may eat the Passover with my disciples?"' **15** He will himself show you a large upper room furnished and ready. Make ready for us there." **16** The disciples went out, and came into the city, and found things as he had said to them, and they prepared the Passover. **17** When it was evening he came with the twelve. **18** And as they were reclining and eating, Jesus said, "Truly I tell you, one of you will betray me—he who eats with me." **19** And they began to be sorrowful, and to say to him one by one, "Surely not I?" And another said, "Surely not I?" **20** He said to them, "It is one of the twelve, he who dips with me in the dish. **21** For the Son of Man goes, even as it is written about him, but woe to that man by whom the Son of Man is betrayed. It would be better for that man if he had not been born." **22** As they were eating, he took bread, and when he had blessed, he broke it, and gave to them, and said, "Take; this is my body." **23** He took a cup, and when he had given thanks, he gave to them. They all drank of it. **24** He said to them, "This is my blood of the new covenant, which is poured out for many. **25** Truly I tell you, I will no more drink of the fruit of the vine, until that day when I drink it anew in the Kingdom of God." **26** When they had sung the hymn, they went out to the Mount of Olives. **27** Jesus said to them, "All of you will fall away, for it is written, 'I will strike the shepherd, and the sheep will be scattered.' **28** However, after I am raised up, I will go before you into Galilee." **29**

But Peter said to him, "Although all will be offended, yet I will not." **30** Jesus said to him, "Truly I tell you, that today, even this night, before the rooster crows twice, you will deny me three times." **31** But he insisted, "If I must die with you, I will not deny you." They all said the same thing. **32** They came to a place which was named Gethsemane. He said to his disciples, "Sit here, while I pray." **33** He took with him Peter, James, and John, and began to be greatly troubled and distressed. **34** He said to them, "My soul is exceedingly sorrowful, even to death. Stay here, and watch." **35** He went forward a little, and fell on the ground, and prayed that, if it were possible, the hour might pass away from him. **36** He said, "Abba, Father, all things are possible to you. Please remove this cup from me. However, not what I desire, but what you desire." **37** He came and found them sleeping, and said to Peter, "Simon, are you sleeping? Could you not watch one hour? **38** Watch and pray, that you may not enter into temptation. The spirit indeed is willing, but the flesh is weak." **39** Again he went away, and prayed, saying the same words. **40** Again he came and found them sleeping again, for their eyes were very heavy, and they did not know what to answer him. **41** He came the third time, and said to them, "Sleep on now, and take your rest. It is enough. The hour has come. Look, the Son of Man is betrayed into the hands of sinners. **42** Arise, let us be going. Look, he who betrays me is near." **43** Immediately, while he was still speaking, Judas, one of the twelve, came—and with him a crowd with swords and clubs, from the chief priests, the scribes, and the elders. **44** Now he who betrayed him had given them a sign, saying, "Whomever I will kiss, that is he. Seize him, and lead him away safely." **45** When he had come, immediately he came to him, and said, "Rabbi." and kissed him. **46** They laid hands on him, and seized him. **47** But a certain one of those who stood by drew his sword, and struck the servant of the high priest, and cut off his ear. **48** Jesus answered them, "Have you come out, as against a robber, with swords and clubs to seize me? **49** I was daily with you in the temple teaching, and you did not arrest me. But this is so that the Scriptures might be fulfilled." **50** They all left him, and fled. **51** And a certain young man followed him, having a linen cloth thrown around himself, over his naked body. And they grabbed him, **52** but he left the linen cloth, and fled naked. **53** They led Jesus away to the high priest. All the chief priests, the elders, and the scribes came together. **54** Peter had followed him from a distance, until he came into the court of the high priest. He was sitting with the officers, and warming himself in the light of the fire. **55** Now the chief priests and the whole council sought witnesses against Jesus to put him to death, and found none. **56** For many gave false testimony against him, and their testimony did not agree with each other. **57** Some stood up, and gave false testimony against him, saying, **58** "We heard him say, 'I will destroy this temple that is made with hands, and in three days I will build another made without hands.'" **59** Even so, their testimony did not agree. **60** The high priest stood up in the midst, and asked Jesus, "Have you no answer? What is it which these testify against you?" **61** But he stayed quiet, and answered nothing. Again the high priest asked him, "Are you the Christ, the Son of the Blessed One?" **62** And Jesus said, "I am, and you will see the Son of Man sitting at the right hand of Power, and coming with the clouds of the sky." **63** The high priest tore his clothes, and said, "What further need have we of witnesses? **64** You have heard the blasphemy. What do you think?" They all condemned him to be worthy of death. **65** Some began to spit on him, and to cover his face, and to beat him with fists, and to tell him, "Prophesy." And the officers took him and beat him. **66** Now as Peter was in the courtyard below, one of the servant girls of the high priest came, **67** and seeing Peter warming himself, she looked at him, and said, "You were also with the Nazarene, Jesus." **68** But he denied it, saying, "I neither know nor understand what you are saying." And he went out into the forecourt, and a rooster crowed. **69** And the servant girl saw him, and began again to tell those who stood by, "This is one of them." **70** But he again denied it. After a little while again those who stood by said to Peter, "You truly are one of them, for you are a Galilean, and your accent shows it." **71** But he began to curse, and to swear, "I do not know this man of whom you speak." **72** And immediately the rooster crowed the second time. Peter remembered the word, how that Jesus said to him, "Before the rooster crows twice, you will deny me three times." When he thought about that, he wept.

15 Immediately in the morning the chief priests, with the elders and scribes, and the whole council, held a consultation, and bound Jesus, and carried him away, and delivered him to Pilate. **2** Pilate asked him, "Are you the King of the Jews?" He answered, "You say so." **3** The chief priests accused him of many things. **4** Pilate again asked him, "Have you no answer? See how many things they testify against you." **5** But Jesus made no further answer, and Pilate was amazed. **6** Now at the feast he used to release to them one prisoner, whom they requested. **7** There was one called Barabbas, bound with those who had made insurrection, who in the insurrection had committed murder. **8** And the crowd went up and began to ask him to do for them according to his custom. **9** Pilate answered them, saying, "Do you want me to release to you the King of the Jews?" **10** For he perceived that for envy the chief priests had delivered him up. **11** But the chief priests stirred up the crowd, that he should release Barabbas to them instead. **12** Pilate again asked them, "What then should I do to him whom you call the King of the Jews?" **13** They shouted again, "Crucify him." **14** Pilate said to them, "Why, what evil has he done?" But they shouted all the louder, "Crucify him." **15** Pilate, wishing to please the crowd, released Barabbas to them, and handed over Jesus, when he had flogged him, to be crucified. **16** The soldiers led him away within the court, which is the Praetorium; and they called together the whole cohort. **17** They clothed him with purple, and weaving a crown of thorns, they put it on him. **18** They began to salute him, "Greetings, King of the Jews." **19** They struck his head with a reed, and spat on him, and bowing their knees, did homage to him. **20** When they had mocked him, they took the purple off of him, and put his own garments on him. They led him out to crucify him. **21** And they forced one passing by, Simon of Cyrene, coming from the country, the father of Alexander and Rufus, to go with them, that he might carry his cross. **22** And they brought him to the place called Golgotha, which is translated, "The place of a skull." **23** They offered him wine mixed with myrrh to drink, but he did not take it. **24** Crucifying him, they parted his garments among them, casting lots on them, what each should take. **25** It was nine in the morning, and they crucified him. **26** The superscription of his accusation was written over him, "THE KING OF THE JEWS." **27** With him they crucified two robbers; one on his right hand, and one on his left. **28** And the Scripture was fulfilled which says, "And he was numbered with transgressors." **29** Those who passed by blasphemed him, wagging their heads, and saying, "Ha. You who destroy the temple, and build it in three days, **30** save yourself. Come down from the cross." **31** Likewise, also the chief priests mocking among themselves with the scribes said, "He saved others. He cannot save himself. **32** Let the Christ, the King of Israel, now come down from the cross, that we may see and believe him." Those who were crucified with him insulted him. **33** Now when it was noon, there was darkness over the whole land until three in the afternoon. **34** Then at three in the afternoon Jesus called out with a loud voice, saying, "Elohi, Elohi, lema shabachthani?" which is translated, "My God, my God, why have you forsaken me?" **35** Some of those who stood by, when they heard it, said, "Look, he is calling for Elijah." **36** One ran, and filling a sponge full of vinegar, put it on a reed, and gave it to him to drink, saying, "Let him be. Let us see whether Elijah comes to take him down." **37** Jesus gave a loud cry, and gave up the spirit. **38** The veil of the temple was torn in two from the top to the bottom. **39** And when the centurion, who stood by opposite him, saw that he cried out like this and breathed his last, he said, "Truly this man was the Son of God." **40** There were also women watching from afar, among whom were both Mary Magdalene, and Mary the mother of James the younger and of Josi, and Salome; **41** who, when he was in Galilee, followed him, and served him; and many other women who came up with him to Jerusalem. **42** When evening had now come, because it was the Preparation Day, that is, the day before the Sabbath, **43** Joseph of Arimathaea, a prominent council member who also himself was looking for the Kingdom of God, came. He boldly went in to Pilate, and asked for the body of Jesus. **44** Pilate was surprised that he was already dead; and summoning the centurion, he asked him whether he had been dead long. **45** When he found out from the centurion, he granted the body to Joseph. **46** He bought a linen cloth, and taking him down, wound him in the linen cloth, and placed him in a tomb which had been cut out of a rock. He rolled a stone against the door of the tomb. **47** Mary Magdalene and Mary, the mother of Josi, saw where he was placed.

16 When the Sabbath was past, Mary Magdalene, and Mary the mother of James, and Salome, bought spices, that they might come and anoint him. **2** Very early on the first day of the week, they came to the tomb when the sun had risen. **3** They were saying among themselves, "Who will roll away the stone from the door of the tomb for us?" **4** for it was very big. Looking up, they saw that the stone was rolled back. **5** Entering into the tomb, they saw a young man sitting on the right side, dressed in a white robe, and they were amazed. **6** He said to them, "Do not be amazed. You seek Jesus, the Nazarene, who has been crucified. He has risen. He is not here. Look, the place where they put him. **7** But go, tell his disciples and Peter, 'He goes before you into Galilee. There you will see him, as he said to you.'" **8** They went out, and fled from the tomb, for trembling and astonishment had come on them. They said nothing to anyone; for they were afraid. **9** **(note: The most reliable and earliest manuscripts do not include Mark 16:9-20.)** Now when he had risen early on the first day of the week, he appeared first to Mary Magdalene, from whom he had cast out seven demons. **10** She went and told those who had been with him, as they mourned and wept. **11** When they heard that he was alive, and had been seen by her, they disbelieved. **12** And after these things he appeared in another form to two of them, as they walked on their way into the country. **13** And they went away and told it to the rest. They did not believe them, either. **14** Afterward he was revealed to the eleven themselves as they were reclining, and he rebuked them for their unbelief and hardness of heart, because they did not believe those who had seen him after he had risen. **15** And he said to them, "Go into all the world, and proclaim the Good News to the whole creation. **16** He who believes and is baptized will be saved; but he who disbelieves will be condemned. **17** And these signs will accompany those who believe: In my name they will cast out demons; they will speak with new tongues; **18** they will pick up serpents; and if they drink any deadly thing, it will not harm them; they will place their hands on the sick, and they will be made well." **19** So then the Lord Jesus, after he had spoken to them, was taken up into heaven, and sat down at the right hand of God. **20** And they went out and preached everywhere, the Lord working with them and confirming the message by the signs that followed.

Luke

1 Since many have undertaken to set in order a narrative concerning those matters which have been fulfilled among us, **2** even as those who from the beginning were eyewitnesses and servants of the word delivered them to us, **3** it seemed good to me also, having traced the course of all things accurately from the first, to write to you in order, most excellent Theophilus; **4** that you might know the certainty concerning the things in which you were instructed. **5** There was in the days of Herod, the king of Judea, a certain priest named Zechariah, of the division of Abijah. He had a wife of the daughters of Aaron, and her name was Elizabeth. **6** They were both righteous before God, walking blamelessly in all the commandments and ordinances of the Lord. **7** But they had no child, because Elizabeth was barren, and they both were well advanced in years. **8** Now it happened, while he was performing the priest's office before God in the order of his division, **9** according to the custom of the priest's office, his lot was to enter into the temple of the Lord and burn incense. **10** And the whole crowd of people were praying outside at the hour of incense. **11** An angel of the Lord appeared to him, standing on the right side of the altar of incense. **12** Zechariah was troubled when he saw him, and fear fell upon him. **13** But the angel said to him, "Do not be afraid, Zechariah, because your request has been heard, and your wife, Elizabeth, will bear you a son, and you are to name him John. **14** You will have joy and gladness; and many will rejoice at his birth. **15** For he will be great in the sight of the Lord, and he will drink no wine nor strong drink. He will be filled with the Holy Spirit, even from his mother's womb. **16** He will turn many of the children of Israel to the Lord, their God. **17** He will go before him in the spirit and power of Elijah, 'to turn the hearts of the fathers to the children,' and the disobedient to the wisdom of the just; to make ready a people prepared for the Lord." **18** Zechariah said to the angel, "How can I be sure of this? For I am an old man, and my wife is well advanced in years." **19** The angel answered him, "I am Gabriel, who stands in the presence of God. I was sent to speak to you, and to bring you this good news. **20** And look, you will be silent and not able to speak, until the day that these things will happen, because you did not believe my words, which will be fulfilled in their proper time." **21** The people were waiting for Zechariah, and they were wondering why he was delayed in the temple. **22** When he came out, he could not speak to them, and they perceived that he had seen a vision in the temple. He continued making signs to them, and remained mute. **23** It happened, when the days of his service were fulfilled, he departed to his house. **24** After these days Elizabeth, his wife, conceived, and she hid herself five months, saying, **25** "Thus has the Lord done to me in the days in which he looked at me, to take away my disgrace among people." **26** Now in the sixth month, the angel Gabriel was sent from God to a city of Galilee, named Nazareth, **27** to a virgin pledged to be married to a man whose name was Joseph, of the house of David. The virgin's name was Mary. **28** Having come in, the angel said to her, "Greetings, favored one. The Lord is with you." **29** But when she saw him, she was greatly troubled at the saying, and considered what kind of salutation this might be. **30** The angel said to her, "Do not be afraid, Mary, for you have found favor with God. **31** And look, you will conceive in your womb, and bring forth a son, and will call his name 'Jesus.' **32** He will be great, and will be called the Son of the Most High. The Lord God will give him the throne of his father, David, **33** and he will reign over the house of Jacob for the ages (aiōn g165). There will be no end to his Kingdom." **34** Mary said to the angel, "How can this be, seeing I am a virgin?" **35** The angel answered her, "The Holy Spirit will come on you, and the power of the Most High will overshadow you. Therefore also the holy one who is born will be called the Son of God. **36** And look, Elizabeth, your relative, also has conceived a son in her old age; and this is the sixth month with her who was called barren. **37** For with God nothing will be impossible." **38** And Mary said, "See, the handmaid of the Lord; be it to me according to your word." The angel departed from her. **39** Mary arose in those days and went into the hill country with haste, into a city of Judah, **40** and entered into the house of Zechariah and greeted Elizabeth. **41** It happened, when Elizabeth heard Mary's greeting, that the baby leaped in her womb, and Elizabeth was filled with the Holy Spirit. **42** She called out with a loud voice, and said, "Blessed are you among women, and blessed is the fruit of your womb. **43** Why am I so favored, that the mother of my Lord should come to me? **44** For look, when the voice of your greeting came into my ears, the baby leaped in my womb for joy. **45** Blessed is she who believed, for there will be a fulfillment of the things which have been spoken to her from the Lord." **46** Mary said, "My soul magnifies the Lord. **47** And my spirit rejoices in God my Savior, **48** for he has looked at the humble state of his servant girl. For look, from now on all generations will call me blessed. **49** For he who is mighty has done great things for me, and holy is his name. **50** His mercy is for generations of generations on those who fear him. **51** He has shown strength with his arm. He has scattered the proud in the imagination of their hearts. **52** He has put down princes from their thrones. And has exalted the lowly. **53** He has filled the hungry with good things. He has sent the rich away empty. **54** He has given help to Israel, his servant, that he might remember mercy, **55** as he spoke to our fathers, to Abraham and his offspring for the age (aiōn g165)." **56** Mary stayed with her about three months, and then returned to her house. **57** Now the time that Elizabeth should give birth was fulfilled, and she brought forth a son. **58** Her neighbors and her relatives heard that the Lord had magnified his mercy towards her, and they rejoiced with her. **59** It happened on the eighth day, that they came to circumcise the child; and they would have called him Zechariah, after the name of the father. **60** His mother answered, "Not so; but he will be called John." **61** They said to her, "There is no one among your relatives who is called by this name." **62** They made signs to his father, what he would have him called. **63** And he asked for a writing tablet, and wrote, "His name is John." And they were all amazed. **64** His mouth was opened immediately, and his tongue freed, and he spoke, blessing God. **65** Fear came on all who lived around them, and all these sayings were talked about throughout all the hill country of Judea. **66** All who heard them laid them up in their heart, saying, "What then will this child be?" The hand of the Lord was with him. **67** His father, Zechariah, was filled with the Holy Spirit, and prophesied, saying, **68** "Blessed be the Lord, the God of Israel, for he has visited and worked redemption for his people; **69** and has raised up a horn of salvation for us in the house of his servant David **70** (as he spoke by the mouth of his holy prophets who have been from the age (aiōn g165)), **71** salvation from our enemies, and from the hand of all who hate us; **72** to show mercy towards our fathers, to remember his holy covenant, **73** the oath which he spoke to Abraham, our father, **74** to grant to us that we, being delivered out of the hand of our enemies, should serve him without fear, **75** In holiness and righteousness before him all our days. **76** And you, child, will be called a prophet of the Most High, for you will go before the Lord to make ready his ways, **77** to give knowledge of salvation to his people by the forgiveness of their sins, **78** because of the tender mercy of our God, whereby the dawn from on high will visit us, **79** to shine on those who sit in darkness and the shadow of death; to guide our feet into the way of peace." **80** The child was growing, and becoming strong in spirit, and was in the desert until the day of his public appearance to Israel.

2 Now it happened in those days, that a decree went out from Caesar Augustus that all the world should be enrolled. **2** This was the first enrollment made when Quirinius was governor of Syria. **3** All went to enroll themselves, everyone to his own city. **4** Joseph also went up from Galilee, out of the city of Nazareth, into Judea, to the city of David, which is called Bethlehem, because he was of the house and family of David; **5** to enroll himself with Mary, who was pledged to be married to him, being pregnant. **6** It happened, while they were there, that the day had come that she should give birth. **7** And she gave birth to her firstborn son, and wrapped him with pieces of cloth, and placed him in a feeding trough, because there was no guest room available for them. **8** There were shepherds in the same country staying in the field, and keeping watch by night over their flock. **9** And look, an angel of the Lord stood by them, and the glory of the Lord shone around them, and they were terrified. **10** The angel said to them, "Do not be afraid, for see, I bring you good news of great joy which will be to all the people. **11** For there is born to you, this day, in the city of David, a Savior, who is Christ, the Lord. **12** This is the sign to you: you will find a baby wrapped in strips of cloth, lying in a feeding trough." **13** Suddenly, there was with the angel a multitude of the heavenly host praising God, and saying, **14** "Glory to God in the highest, and on earth peace, good will toward humankind." **15** And it happened that when the angels went away from them into the sky, the shepherds said one to another, "Let us go to Bethlehem, now, and see this thing that has happened, which the Lord has made known to us." **16** They came with haste, and found both Mary and Joseph, and the baby was lying in the feeding trough. **17** When they saw it, they made known the saying which was spoken to them about this child. **18** All who heard it wondered at the things which were spoken to them by the shepherds. **19** But Mary kept all these sayings, pondering them in her heart. **20** The shepherds returned, glorifying and praising God for all the things that they had heard and seen, just as it was told them. **21** When eight days were fulfilled to circumcise him, his name was called Jesus, which was given by the angel before he was conceived in the womb. **22** When the days of their purification according to the Law of Moses were fulfilled, they brought him up to Jerusalem, to present him to the Lord **23** (as it is written in the Law of the Lord, "Every male who opens the womb will be called holy to the Lord"), **24** and to offer a sacrifice according to that which is said in the Law of the Lord, "A pair of turtledoves, or two young pigeons." **25** And look, there was a man in Jerusalem whose name was Simeon. This man was righteous and devout, looking for the consolation of Israel, and the Holy Spirit was on him. **26** It had been revealed to him by the Holy Spirit that he should not see death before he had seen the Lord's Christ. **27** He came in the Spirit into the temple. When the parents brought in the child, Jesus, that they might do concerning him according to the requirement of the Law, **28** then he received him into his arms, and blessed God, and said, **29** "Now you are releasing your servant, Lord, according to your word, in peace; **30** for my eyes have seen your salvation, **31** which you have prepared before the face of all peoples; **32** a light for revelation to the nations, and the glory of your people Israel." **33** And his father and his mother were marveling at the things which were spoken concerning him, **34** and Simeon blessed them, and said to Mary, his mother, "Look, this child is set for the falling and the rising of many in Israel, and for a sign which is spoken against. **35** Yes, a sword will pierce through your own soul, that the thoughts of many hearts may be revealed." **36** There was one Anna, a prophetess, the daughter of Penuel, of the tribe of Asher (she was of a great age, having lived with a husband seven years from her virginity, **37** and she had been a widow for about eighty-four years), who did not depart from the temple, worshipping with fastings and petitions night and day. **38** Coming up at that very hour, she gave thanks to God, and spoke of him to all those who were looking for the redemption of Jerusalem. **39** When they had accomplished all things that were according to the Law of the Lord, they returned into Galilee, to their own city, Nazareth. **40** The child was growing, and was becoming strong, being filled with wisdom, and the grace of God was upon him. **41** His parents went every year to Jerusalem at the feast of the Passover. **42** When he was twelve years old, they went up according to the custom of the feast, **43** and when they had fulfilled the days, as they were returning, the boy Jesus stayed behind in Jerusalem. His parents did not know it, **44** but supposing him to be in the company, they went a day's journey, and they looked for him among their relatives and acquaintances. **45** When they did not find him, they returned to Jerusalem, looking for him. **46** It happened after three days they found him in the temple, sitting in the midst of the teachers, both listening to them, and asking them questions. **47** All who heard him were amazed at his understanding and his answers. **48** When they saw him, they were astonished, and his mother said to him, "Son, why have you treated us this way? Look, your father and I were anxiously looking for you." **49** He said to them, "Why were you looking for me? Did you not know that I must be doing the works of my Father?" **50** They did not understand the saying which he spoke to them. **51** And he went down with them, and came to Nazareth. He was subject to them, and his mother kept all these sayings in her heart. **52** And Jesus increased in wisdom and stature, and in favor with God and people.

3 Now in the fifteenth year of the reign of Tiberius Caesar, Pontius Pilate being governor of Judea, and Herod being tetrarch of Galilee, and his brother Philip tetrarch of the region of Ituraea and Trachonitis, and Lysanias tetrarch of Abilene, **2** in the high priesthood of Annas and Caiaphas, the word of God came to John, the son of Zechariah, in the wilderness. **3** He came into all the region around the Jordan, preaching a baptism of repentance for forgiveness of sins. **4** As it is written in the scroll of the words of Isaiah the prophet, "The voice of one crying in the wilderness, 'Prepare the way of the Lord. Make his roads straight. **5** Every valley will be filled, and every mountain and hill will be made low, and the crooked will be made straight, and the rough ways smooth. **6** And all humanity will see the salvation of God.'" **7** He said therefore to the crowds who went out to be baptized by him, "You offspring of vipers, who warned you to flee from the wrath to come? **8** Bring forth therefore fruits worthy of repentance, and do not begin to say among yourselves, 'We have Abraham for our father;' for I tell you that God is able to raise up children to Abraham from these stones. **9** Even now the axe also lies at the root of the trees. Every tree therefore that does not bring forth good fruit is cut down, and thrown into the fire." **10** The crowds asked him, "What then must we do?" **11** He answered them, "He who has two coats, let him give to him who has none. He who has food, let him do likewise." **12** Tax collectors also came to be baptized, and they said to him, "Teacher, what must we do?" **13** He said to them, "Collect no more than that which is appointed to you." **14** Soldiers also asked him, saying, "What about us? What must we do?" He said to them, "Extort from no one by violence, neither accuse anyone wrongfully. Be content with your wages." **15** As the people were in expectation, and all were wondering in their hearts concerning John, whether perhaps he was the Christ, **16** John answered them all, "I indeed baptize you with water, but he comes who is mightier than I, the strap of whose sandals I am not worthy to loosen. He will baptize you with the Holy Spirit and with fire, **17** whose winnowing fork is in his hand, to clear his threshing floor, and to gather the wheat into his barn; but he will burn up the chaff with unquenchable fire." **18** Then with many other exhortations he preached good news to the people, **19** but Herod the tetrarch, being reproved by him for Herodias, his brother's wife, and for all the evil things which Herod had done, **20** added this also to them all, that he shut up John in prison. **21** Now it happened, when all the people were baptized, Jesus also had been baptized, and was praying. The sky was opened, **22** and the Holy Spirit descended in a bodily form as a dove on him; and a voice came out of the sky, saying "You are my beloved Son. In you I am well pleased." **23** When he began, Jesus was about thirty years old, being the son, as was supposed, of Joseph, of Eli, **24** of Mattat, of Levi, of Melchi, of Jannai, of Joseph, **25** of Mattithiah, of Amos, of Nahum, of Hesli, of Naggai, **26** of Mahath, of Mattithiah, of Shimei, of Joseph, of Judah, **27** of Johanan, of Rhesa, of Zerubbabel, of Shealtiel, of Neri, **28** of Melchi, of Addi, of Cosam, of Elmodam, of Er, **29** of Josi, of Eliezer, of Jorim, of Mattat, of Levi, **30** of Simeon, of Judah, of Joseph, of Jehonan, of Eliakim, **31** of Maleah, of Menan, of Mattattah, of Nathan, of David, **32** of Jesse, of Obed, of Boaz, of Salmon, of Nahshon, **33** of Amminadab, of Ram, of Hezron, of Perez, of Judah, **34** of Jacob, of Isaac, of Abraham, of Terah, of Nahor, **35** of Serug, of Reu, of Peleg, of Eber, of Shelah, **36** of Kenan, of Arpachshad, of Shem, of Noah, of Lamech, **37** of Methuselah, of Enoch, of Jared, of Mahalalel, of Kenan, **38** of Enosh, of Seth, of Adam, of God.

4 Jesus, full of the Holy Spirit, returned from the Jordan, and was led by the Spirit into the wilderness **2** for forty days, being tempted by the devil. He ate nothing in those days. When they were completed, he was hungry. **3** The devil said to him, "If you are the Son of God, command this stone to become bread." **4** Jesus answered him, saying, "It is written, 'Humankind cannot live by bread alone.'" **5** And leading him up to a high mountain, the devil showed him all the kingdoms of the world in a moment of time. **6** The devil said to him, "I will give you all this authority, and their glory, for it has been delivered to me; and I give it to whomever I want. **7** If you therefore will worship before me, it will all be yours." **8** Jesus answered and said to him, "It is written, 'You are to worship the Lord your God, and serve him only.'" **9** He led him to Jerusalem, and set him on the pinnacle of the temple, and said to him, "If you are the Son of God, cast yourself down from here, **10** for it is written, 'He will put his angels in charge of you, to guard you;' **11** and, 'On their hands they will bear you up, lest perhaps you dash your foot against a stone.'" **12** And Jesus, answering, said to him, "It is said, 'Do not test the Lord, your God.'" **13** When the devil had completed every temptation, he departed from him until another time. **14** Jesus returned in the power of the Spirit into Galilee, and news about him spread through all the surrounding area. **15** He taught in their synagogues, being praised by all. **16** He came to Nazareth, where he had been brought up. He entered, as was his custom, into the synagogue on the Sabbath day, and stood up to read. **17** The scroll of the prophet Isaiah was handed to him, and unrolling the scroll, he found the place where it was written, **18** "The Spirit of the Lord is upon me, because he has anointed me to preach good news to the poor. He has sent me to heal the brokenhearted, to proclaim liberty to the captives, recovering of sight to the blind, to deliver those who are crushed, **19** and to proclaim the acceptable year of the Lord." **20** He closed the scroll, gave it back to the attendant, and sat down. The eyes of all in the synagogue were fastened on him. **21** He began to tell them, "Today, this Scripture has been fulfilled in your hearing." **22** All testified about him, and wondered at the gracious words which proceeded out of his mouth, and they said, "Is not this Joseph's son?" **23** He said to them, "Doubtless you will tell me this parable, 'Physician, heal yourself. Whatever we have heard done at Capernaum, do also here in your hometown.'" **24** He said, "Truly I tell you, no prophet is acceptable in his hometown. **25** But truly I tell you, there were many widows in Israel in the days of Elijah, when the sky was shut up three years and six months, when a great famine came over all the land. **26** Elijah was sent to none of them, except to Zarephath, in the land of Sidon, to a woman who was a widow. **27** There were many lepers in Israel in the time of Elisha the prophet, yet not one of them was cleansed, except Naaman, the Syrian." **28** They were all filled with wrath in the synagogue, as they heard these things. **29** They rose up, threw him out of the city, and led him to the brow of the hill that their city was built on, that they might throw him off the cliff. **30** But he, passing through the midst of them, went his way. **31** He came down to Capernaum, a city of Galilee. He was teaching them on the Sabbath day, **32** and they were astonished at his teaching, for his word was with authority. **33** In the synagogue there was a man who had a spirit of an unclean demon, and he shouted with a loud voice, **34** saying, "Ah, what have we to do with you, Jesus, Nazarene? Have you come to destroy us? I know you who you are: the Holy One of God." **35** Jesus rebuked him, saying, "Be silent, and come out of him." When the demon had thrown him down in their midst, he came out of him, having done him no harm. **36** Amazement came on all, and they spoke together, one with another, saying, "What is this word? For with authority and power he commands the unclean spirits, and they come out." **37** News about him went out into every place of the surrounding region. **38** He rose up from the synagogue, and entered into Simon's house. Now Simon's mother-in-law was suffering from a high fever, and they appealed to him about her. **39** He stood over her, and rebuked the fever; and it left her. Immediately she rose up and served them. **40** When the sun was setting, all those who had any sick with various diseases brought them to him; and he laid his hands on every one of them, and healed them. **41** Demons also came out from many, crying out, and saying, "You are the Son of God." But he rebuked them and did not allow them to speak, because they knew that he was the Christ. **42** When it was day, he departed and went into an uninhabited place, and the crowds looked for him, and came to him, and held on to him, so that he would not go away from them. **43** But he said to them, "I must proclaim the good news of the Kingdom of God to the other cities also. For this reason I have been sent." **44** And he was preaching in the synagogues of Galilee.

5 Now it happened, while the crowd pressed on him and heard the word of God, that he was standing by the lake of Gennesaret. **2** He saw two boats standing by the lake, but the fishermen had gone out of them, and were washing their nets. **3** He entered into one of the boats, which was Simon's, and asked him to put out a little from the land. He sat down and taught the crowds from the boat. **4** When he had finished speaking, he said to Simon, "Put out into the deep, and let down your nets for a catch." **5** Simon answered him, "Master, we worked all night, and took nothing; but at your word I will let down the nets." **6** When they had done this, they caught a great multitude of fish, and their net was breaking. **7** They beckoned to their partners in the other boat, that they should come and help them. They came, and filled both boats, so that they began to sink. **8** But Simon Peter, when he saw it, fell down at Jesus' knees, saying, "Depart from me, for I am a sinful man, Lord." **9** For he was amazed, and all who were with him, at the catch of fish which they had caught; **10** and so also were James and John, sons of Zebedee, who were partners with Simon. Jesus said to Simon, "Do not be afraid. From now on you will be catching people." **11** When they had brought their boats to land, they left everything, and followed him. **12** It happened, while he was in one of the cities, look, there was a man full of leprosy. When he saw Jesus, he fell on his face, and begged him, saying, "Lord, if you want to, you can make me clean." **13** And he stretched out his hand, and touched him, saying, "I am willing. Be cleansed." Immediately the leprosy left him. **14** And he commanded him, "Do not tell anyone, but go your way, and show yourself to the priest, and offer for your cleansing according to what Moses commanded, for a testimony to them." **15** But the report concerning him spread much more, and large crowds came together to hear, and to be healed of their infirmities. **16** But he withdrew himself into the desert, and prayed. **17** It happened on one of those days, that he was teaching; and there were Pharisees and teachers of the Law sitting by, who had come out of every village of Galilee, Judea, and Jerusalem. The power of the Lord was with him to heal. **18** And look, men brought a paralyzed man on a cot, and they sought to bring him in to lay before him. **19** Not finding a way to bring him in because of the crowd, they went up to the housetop, and let him down through the tiles with his cot into the midst before Jesus. **20** Seeing their faith, he said, "Man, your sins are forgiven you." **21** The scribes and the Pharisees began to reason, saying, "Who is this that speaks blasphemies? Who can forgive sins, but God alone?" **22** But Jesus, perceiving their thoughts, answered them, "Why are you reasoning so in your hearts? **23** Which is easier to say, 'Your sins are forgiven you;' or to say, 'Arise and walk?' **24** But that you may know that the Son of Man has authority on earth to forgive sins" (he said to the paralyzed man), "I tell you, arise, and take up your cot, and go to your house." **25** Immediately he rose up before them, and took up that which he was laying on, and departed to his house, glorifying God. **26** Amazement took hold on all, and they glorified God. They were filled with fear, saying, "We have seen remarkable things today." **27** After these things he went out, and saw a tax collector named Levi sitting at the tax office, and said to him, "Follow me." **28** He left everything, and rose up and followed him. **29** Levi made a great feast for him in his house. There was a large crowd of tax collectors and others who were reclining with them. **30** The Pharisees and their scribes grumbled at his disciples, saying, "Why do you eat and drink with the tax collectors and sinners?" **31** Jesus answered them, "Those who are healthy have no need for a physician, but those who are sick do. **32** I have not come to call the righteous, but sinners to repentance." **33** They said to him, "The disciples of John often fast and pray, likewise also the disciples of the Pharisees, but yours eat and drink." **34** He said to them, "Can you make the friends of the bridegroom fast, while the bridegroom is with them? **35** But the days will come when the bridegroom will be taken away from them. Then they will fast in those days." **36** He also told a parable to them. "No one having torn a piece from a new garment puts it on an old garment, or else he will tear the new, and also the piece from the new will not match the old. **37** And no one puts new wine into old wineskins, or else the new wine will burst the skins, and it will be spilled, and the skins will be destroyed. **38** But new wine must be put into fresh wineskins. **39** No one having drunk old wine desires new, for he says, 'The old is good.'"

6 Now it happened on the second chief Sabbath that he was going through the grain fields. His disciples plucked the heads of grain, and ate, rubbing them in their hands. **2** But some of the Pharisees said to them, "Why do you do that which is not lawful on the Sabbath day?" **3** Jesus, answering them, said, "Have you not read what David did when he was hungry, he, and those who were with him; **4** how he entered into the house of God, and took and ate the show bread, and gave also to those who were with him, which is not lawful to eat except for the priests alone?" **5** He said to them, "The Son of Man is lord of the Sabbath." **6** It also happened on another Sabbath that he entered into the synagogue and taught. There was a man there, and his right hand was withered. **7** The scribes and the Pharisees watched him, to see whether he would heal on the Sabbath, that they might find an accusation against him. **8** But he knew their thoughts; and he said to the man who had the withered hand, "Rise up, and stand in the middle." He arose and stood. **9** Then Jesus said to them, "I ask you, is it lawful on the Sabbath to do good, or to do harm? To save a life, or to destroy it?" **10** He looked around at them all, and said to the man, "Stretch out your hand." He did, and his hand was restored. **11** But they were filled with rage, and talked with one another about what they might do to Jesus. **12** It happened in these days, that he went out to the mountain to pray, and he continued all night in prayer to God. **13** When it was day, he called his disciples, and from them he chose twelve, whom he also named apostles: **14** Simon, whom he also named Peter, and Andrew his brother; James; John; Philip; Bartholomew; **15** Matthew; Thomas; James, the son of Alphaeus; Simon, who was called the Zealot; **16** Judas the son of James; and Judas Iscariot, who also became a traitor. **17** He came down with them, and stood on a level place, with a large crowd of his disciples, and a great number of the people from all Judea and Jerusalem, and the sea coast of Tyre and Sidon, **18** who came to hear him and to be healed of their diseases; and those who were troubled with unclean spirits were cured. **19** All the crowd sought to touch him, for power came out from him and healed them all. **20** He lifted up his eyes to his disciples, and said, "Blessed are you who are poor, for yours is the Kingdom of God. **21** Blessed are you who hunger now, for you will be filled. Blessed are you who weep now, for you will laugh. **22** Blessed are you when people hate you, and when they exclude you and insult you, and throw out your name as evil, for the Son of Man's sake. **23** Rejoice in that day, and leap for joy, for look, your reward is great in heaven, for their fathers did the same thing to the prophets. **24** "But woe to you who are rich. For you have received your consolation. **25** Woe to you, you who are full now, for you will be hungry. Woe to you who laugh now, for you will mourn and weep. **26** Woe to you when all people speak well of you, for their fathers did the same thing to the false prophets. **27** "But I tell you who hear: love your enemies, do good to those who hate you, **28** bless those who curse you, and pray for those who mistreat you. **29** To the person who strikes you on the cheek, offer the other also; and from the person who takes away your coat, do not withhold your shirt either. **30** Give to everyone who asks you, and do not ask him who takes away your goods to give them back again. **31** And as you would like people to do to you, you also do the same to them. **32** If you love those who love you, what credit is that to you? For even sinners love those who love them. **33** If you do good to those who do good to you, what credit is that to you? For even sinners do the same. **34** If you lend to those from whom you hope to receive, what credit is that to you? Even sinners lend to sinners, to receive back as much. **35** But love your enemies, and do good, and lend, expecting nothing back; and your reward will be great, and you will be children of the Most High; for he is kind toward the unthankful and evil. **36** Therefore be merciful, even as your Father is also merciful. **37** Do not judge, and you won't be judged. Do not condemn, and you won't be condemned. Forgive, and you will be forgiven. **38** "Give, and it will be given to you: good measure, pressed down, shaken together, and running over, will be poured into your lap. For with the same measure you measure it will be measured back to you." **39** He spoke a parable to them. "Can the blind guide the blind? Won't they both fall into a pit? **40** A disciple is not above his teacher, but everyone when he is fully trained will be like his teacher. **41** And why do you see the speck of chaff that is in your brother's eye, but do not notice the log that is in your own eye? **42** Or how can you tell your brother, 'Brother, let me remove the speck of chaff that is in your eye,' when you yourself do not see the log that is in your own eye? You hypocrite. First remove the log from your own eye, and then you can see clearly to remove the speck of chaff that is in your brother's eye. **43** For there is no good tree that brings forth rotten fruit; nor again a rotten tree that brings forth good fruit. **44** For each tree is known by its own fruit. For people do not gather figs from thorns, nor do they gather grapes from a bramble bush. **45** The good person out of the good treasure of his heart brings out that which is good, and the evil person out of the evil treasure brings out that which is evil, for out of the abundance of the heart, his mouth speaks. **46** "Why do you call me, 'Lord, Lord,' and do not do the things which I say? **47** Everyone who comes to me, and hears my words, and does them, I will show you who he is like. **48** He is like someone building a house, who dug and went deep, and laid a foundation on the rock. When a flood arose, the stream broke against that house, and could not shake it, because it had been well built. **49** But he who hears, and does not do, is like someone who built a house on the earth without a foundation, against which the stream broke, and immediately it fell, and the ruin of that house was great."

7 After he had finished speaking in the hearing of the people, he entered into Capernaum. **2** A certain centurion's servant, who was dear to him, was sick and at the point of death. **3** When he heard about Jesus, he sent to him Jewish elders, asking him to come and save his servant. **4** When they came to Jesus, they pleaded with him earnestly, saying, "He is worthy for you to do this for him, **5** for he loves our nation, and he built our synagogue for us." **6** Jesus went with them. When he was now not far from the house, the centurion sent friends, saying to him, "Lord, do not trouble yourself, for I am not worthy for you to come under my roof. **7** Therefore I did not even think myself worthy to come to you; but say the word, and my servant will be healed. **8** For I also am a man placed under authority, having under myself soldiers. I tell this one, 'Go.' and he goes; and to another, 'Come.' and he comes; and to my servant, 'Do this,' and he does it." **9** When Jesus heard these things, he was amazed at him, and turned and said to the crowd who followed him, "I tell you, I have not found such great faith, no, not in Israel." **10** And when those who had been sent returned to the house, they found the servant in good health. **11** It happened soon afterwards, that he went to a city called Nain; and many of his disciples, along with a large crowd, went with him. **12** And when he drew near to the gate of the city, then look, a man who was dead was carried out, the only son of his mother, and she was a widow; and a large crowd from the city was with her. **13** When the Lord saw her, he had compassion on her, and said to her, "Do not cry." **14** He came near and touched the coffin, and the bearers stood still. He said, "Young man, I tell you, arise." **15** He who was dead sat up, and began to speak. And he gave him to his mother. **16** Fear took hold of all, and they glorified God, saying, "A great prophet has arisen among us." and, "God has visited his people." **17** This report went out concerning him in the whole of Judea, and in all the surrounding region. **18** The disciples of John told him about all these things. **19** John, calling to himself two of his disciples, sent them to the Lord, saying, "Are you the one who is to come, or should we look for another?" **20** When the men had come to him, they said,

"John the Baptist has sent us to you, saying, 'Are you the one who is to come, or should we look for another?'" **21** In that hour he cured many of diseases and plagues and evil spirits; and to many who were blind he gave sight. **22** Jesus answered them, "Go and tell John the things which you have seen and heard: that the blind receive their sight, the lame walk, the lepers are cleansed, the deaf hear, the dead are raised up, and the poor have good news preached to them. **23** Blessed is he who is not offended by me." **24** When John's messengers had departed, he began to tell the crowds about John, "What did you go out into the wilderness to see? A reed shaken by the wind? **25** But what did you go out to see? A man clothed in soft clothing? Look, those who are gorgeously dressed, and live delicately, are in kings' courts. **26** But what did you go out to see? A prophet? Yes, I tell you, and much more than a prophet. **27** This is he of whom it is written, 'Look, I send my messenger ahead of you, who will prepare your way before you.' **28** "I tell you, among those who are born of women there is none greater than John, yet he who is least in the Kingdom of God is greater than he." **29** When all the people and the tax collectors heard this, they declared God to be just, having been baptized with John's baptism. **30** But the Pharisees and the Law scholars rejected the counsel of God, not being baptized by him themselves. **31** "To what then will I liken the people of this generation? What are they like? **32** They are like children who sit in the marketplace, and call one to another, saying, 'We played the flute for you, and you did not dance. We mourned, and you did not weep.' **33** For John the Baptist came neither eating bread nor drinking wine, and you say, 'He has a demon.' **34** The Son of Man has come eating and drinking, and you say, 'Look, a gluttonous man, and a drunkard; a friend of tax collectors and sinners.' **35** Wisdom is justified by all her children." **36** One of the Pharisees invited him to eat with him. He entered into the Pharisee's house, and sat at the table. **37** And look, a woman in the city who was a sinner, when she knew that he was reclining in the Pharisee's house, she brought an alabaster jar of ointment. **38** Standing behind at his feet weeping, she began to wet his feet with her tears, and she wiped them with the hair of her head, kissed his feet, and anointed them with the ointment. **39** Now when the Pharisee who had invited him saw it, he said to himself, "This man, if he were a prophet, would have perceived who and what kind of woman this is who touches him, that she is a sinner." **40** Jesus answered him, "Simon, I have something to tell you." He said, "Teacher, say on." **41** "A certain lender had two debtors. The one owed five hundred denarii, and the other fifty. **42** When they could not pay, he forgave them both. Which of them therefore will love him most?" **43** Simon answered, "He, I suppose, to whom he forgave the most." He said to him, "You have judged correctly." **44** Turning to the woman, he said to Simon, "Do you see this woman? I entered into your house, and you gave me no water for my feet, but she has wet my feet with her tears, and wiped them with her hair. **45** You gave me no kiss, but she, since the time I came in, has not ceased to kiss my feet. **46** You did not anoint my head with oil, but she has anointed my feet with ointment. **47** Therefore I tell you, her sins, which are many, are forgiven, for she loved much. But to whom little is forgiven, the same loves little." **48** He said to her, "Your sins are forgiven." **49** And those who were reclining with him began to say to themselves, "Who is this who even forgives sins?" **50** He said to the woman, "Your faith has saved you. Go in peace."

8 It happened soon afterwards, that he went about through cities and villages, proclaiming and bringing the good news of the Kingdom of God. With him were the twelve, **2** and certain women who had been healed of evil spirits and infirmities: Mary who was called Magdalene, from whom seven demons had gone out; **3** and Joanna, the wife of Chuza, Herod's steward; Susanna; and many others; who provided for them from their possessions. **4** When a large crowd came together, and people from every city were coming to him, he spoke by a parable. **5** "The farmer went out to sow his seed. As he sowed, some fell along the road, and it was trampled under foot, and the birds of the sky devoured it. **6** Other seed fell on the rock, and as soon as it grew, it withered away, because it had no moisture. **7** Other fell amid the thorns, and the thorns grew with it, and choked it. **8** Other fell into the good ground, and grew, and brought forth fruit one hundred times." As he said these things, he called out, "He who has ears to hear, let him hear." **9** Then his disciples asked him, "What does this parable mean?" **10** He said, "To you it is given to know the mysteries of the Kingdom of God, but to the rest in parables; that 'seeing they may not see, and hearing they may not understand.' **11** Now the parable is this: The seed is the word of God. **12** Those along the road are those who hear, then the devil comes, and takes away the word from their heart, that they may not believe and be saved. **13** Those on the rock are they who, when they hear, receive the word with joy; but these have no root, who believe for a while, then fall away in time of temptation. **14** That which fell among the thorns, these are those who have heard, and as they go on their way they are choked with cares, riches, and pleasures of life, and bring no fruit to maturity. **15** That in the good ground, these are such as in an honest and good heart, having heard the word, hold it tightly, and bring forth fruit with patience. **16** "No one, when he has lit a lamp, covers it with a container, or puts it under a bed; but puts it on a stand, that those who enter in may see the light. **17** For nothing is hidden, that will not be revealed; nor anything secret, that will not be known and come to light. **18** So consider carefully how you listen. For whoever has, to him will be given; and whoever does not have, from him will be taken away even that which he thinks he has." **19** His mother and brothers came to him, and they could not come near him for the crowd. **20** It was told him by some saying, "Your mother and your brothers stand outside, desiring to see you." **21** But he answered them, "My mother and my brothers are these who hear the word of God, and do it." **22** Now it happened on one of those days, that he entered into a boat, himself and his disciples, and he said to them, "Let us go over to the other side of the lake." So they launched out. **23** But as they sailed, he fell asleep. A wind storm came down on the lake, and they were taking on dangerous amounts of water. **24** So they came to him, and awoke him, saying, "Master, master, we are dying." And he awoke, and rebuked the wind and the raging of the water, and they ceased, and it was calm. **25** He said to them, "Where is your faith?" But they were terrified and astonished, saying to one another, "Who is this, then, that he commands even the winds and the water, and they obey him?" **26** They arrived at the country of the Gerasenes, which is opposite Galilee. **27** When Jesus stepped ashore, a certain man out of the city who had demons for a long time met him. He wore no clothes, and did not live in a house, but in the tombs. **28** When he saw Jesus, he shouted, and fell down before him, and with a loud voice said, "What do I have to do with you, Jesus, you Son of the Most High God? I beg you, do not torment me." **29** For Jesus was commanding the unclean spirit to come out of the man. For the unclean spirit had often seized the man. He was kept under guard, and bound with chains and fetters. Breaking the bands apart, he was driven by the demon into the desert. **30** Jesus asked him, "What is your name?" He said, "Legion," for many demons had entered into him. **31** ==They begged him that he would not command them to go into the Abyss (Abyssos g12).== **32** Now there was there a herd of many pigs feeding on the mountain, and they begged him that he would allow them to enter into those. He allowed them. **33** The demons came out from the man, and entered into the pigs, and the herd rushed down the steep bank into the lake, and were drowned. **34** When those who fed them saw what had happened, they fled, and told it in the city and in the country. **35** Then people went out to see what had happened. They came to Jesus, and found the man from whom the demons had gone out, sitting at Jesus' feet, clothed and in his right mind; and they were afraid. **36** Those who saw it told them how he who had been possessed by demons was healed. **37** All the people of the surrounding region of the Geresenes asked him to leave them, for they were very much afraid; and he entered into the boat and returned. **38** But the man from whom the demons had gone out begged him that he might go with him, but Jesus sent him away, saying, **39** "Return to your house, and declare what great things God has done for you." He went his way, proclaiming throughout the whole city what great things Jesus had done for him. **40** When Jesus returned, the crowd welcomed him, for they were all waiting for him. **41** And look, there came a man named Jairus, and he was a ruler of the synagogue. He fell down at Jesus' feet, and pleaded with him to come into his house, **42** for he had an only daughter, about twelve years of age, and she was dying. But as he went, the crowds pressed against him. **43** A woman who had a flow of blood for twelve years (who had spent all her living on physicians) and could not be healed by any, **44** came behind him, and touched the fringe of his garment, and immediately the flow of her blood stopped. **45** Jesus said, "Who touched me?" When all denied it, Peter and those with him said, "Master, the crowds press and jostle you." **46** But Jesus said, "Someone did touch me, for I perceived

Luke

that power has gone out of me." **47** When the woman saw that she was not hidden, she came trembling, and falling down before him declared to him in the presence of all the people the reason why she had touched him, and how she was healed immediately. **48** He said to her, "Daughter, your faith has made you well. Go in peace." **49** While he still spoke, one from the ruler of the synagogue's house came, saying to him, "Your daughter is dead. Do not trouble the Teacher." **50** But Jesus hearing it, answered him, "Do not be afraid. Only believe, and she will be healed." **51** When he came to the house, he did not allow anyone to enter in with him, except Peter, John, James, the father of the child, and her mother. **52** All were weeping and mourning her, but he said, "Do not weep. She is not dead, but sleeping." **53** They were ridiculing him, knowing that she was dead. **54** But he, taking her by the hand, called, saying, "Child, arise." **55** Her spirit returned, and she rose up immediately. He commanded that something be given to her to eat. **56** Her parents were amazed, but he commanded them to tell no one what had been done.

9 He called the twelve together, and gave them power and authority over all demons and to cure diseases. **2** He sent them forth to proclaim the Kingdom of God, and to heal the sick. **3** And he said to them, "Take nothing for your journey—neither staff, nor pack, nor bread, nor money; neither have two coats. **4** Into whatever house you enter, stay there, and depart from there. **5** As many as do not receive you, when you depart from that city, shake off even the dust from your feet for a testimony against them." **6** They departed, and went throughout the villages, preaching the Good News, and healing everywhere. **7** Now Herod the tetrarch heard of all that was done; and he was very perplexed, because it was said by some that John had risen from the dead, **8** and by some that Elijah had appeared, and by others that one of the old prophets had risen again. **9** Herod said, "John I beheaded, but who is this, about whom I hear such things?" He sought to see him. **10** The apostles, when they had returned, told him what things they had done. He took them, and withdrew apart to a city called Bethsaida. **11** But the crowds, perceiving it, followed him. He welcomed them, and spoke to them of the Kingdom of God, and he cured those who needed healing. **12** The day began to wear away; and the twelve came, and said to him, "Send the crowd away, that they may go into the surrounding villages and farms, and lodge, and get food, for we are here in a deserted place." **13** But he said to them, "You give them something to eat." They said, "We have no more than five loaves and two fish, unless we should go and buy food for all these people." **14** For they were about five thousand men. He said to his disciples, "Make them sit down in groups of about fifty each." **15** They did so, and made them all sit down. **16** He took the five loaves and the two fish, and looking up to the sky, he blessed them, and broke them, and gave them to the disciples to set before the crowd. **17** They ate, and were all filled. They gathered up twelve baskets of broken pieces that were left over. **18** It happened, as he was praying alone, that the disciples were with him, and he asked them, "Who do the crowds say that I am?" **19** They answered, "'John the Baptist,' but others say, 'Elijah,' and others, that one of the old prophets is risen again." **20** He said to them, "But who do you say that I am?" Peter answered, "The Christ of God." **21** But he warned them, and commanded them to tell this to no one, **22** saying, "The Son of Man must suffer many things, and be rejected by the elders, chief priests, and scribes, and be killed, and the third day be raised up." **23** He said to all, "If anyone desires to come after me, let him deny himself, take up his cross daily, and follow me. **24** For whoever desires to save his life will lose it, but whoever will lose his life for my sake, the same will save it. **25** For what does it profit a person if he gains the whole world, and loses or forfeits his own self? **26** For whoever will be ashamed of me and of my words, of him will the Son of Man be ashamed, when he comes in his glory, and the glory of the Father, and of the holy angels. **27** But I tell you the truth: There are some of those who stand here, who will in no way taste of death, until they see the Kingdom of God." **28** It happened about eight days after these sayings, that he took with him Peter, John, and James, and went up onto the mountain to pray. **29** As he was praying, the appearance of his face was altered, and his clothing became white and dazzling. **30** And look, two men were talking with him, who were Moses and Elijah, **31** who appeared in glory, and spoke of his departure, which he was about to accomplish at Jerusalem. **32** Now Peter and those who were with him were heavy with sleep, but when they were fully awake, they saw his glory, and the two men who stood with him. **33** It happened, as they were parting from him, that Peter said to Jesus, "Master, it is good for us to be here. Let us make three tents: one for you, and one for Moses, and one for Elijah," not knowing what he said. **34** While he said these things, a cloud came and overshadowed them, and they were afraid as they entered into the cloud. **35** A voice came out of the cloud, saying, "This is my Son, my Chosen One. Listen to him." **36** When the voice came, Jesus was found alone. They were silent, and told no one in those days any of the things which they had seen. **37** It happened on the next day, when they had come down from the mountain, that a large crowd met him. **38** And look, a man from the crowd called out, saying, "Teacher, I beg you to look at my son, for he is my only child. **39** And look, a spirit seizes him, and all at once he cries out, and it convulses him so that he foams, and it hardly departs from him, bruising him severely. **40** I begged your disciples to cast it out, and they could not." **41** Jesus answered, "Faithless and perverse generation, how long must I be with you and put up with you? Bring your son here." **42** While he was still coming, the demon threw him down and convulsed him violently. But Jesus rebuked the unclean spirit, and healed the boy, and gave him back to his father. **43** They were all astonished at the majesty of God. But while all were marveling at all the things which Jesus did, he said to his disciples, **44** "Let these words sink into your ears, for the Son of Man will be delivered up into the hands of men." **45** But they did not understand this saying. It was concealed from them, that they should not perceive it, and they were afraid to ask him about this saying. 46 There arose an argument among them about which of them was the greatest. 47 Jesus, knowing the reasoning of their hearts, took a little child, and set him by his side, 48 and said to them, "Whoever receives this little child in my name receives me. Whoever receives me receives him who sent me. For whoever is least among you all, this one is great." 49 John answered, "Master, we saw someone casting out demons in your name, and we forbade him, because he does not follow with us." 50 Jesus said to him, "Do not forbid him, for he who is not against you is for you." 51 It came to pass, when the days were near that he should be taken up, he intently set his face to go to Jerusalem, 52 and sent messengers before his face. They went, and entered into a village of the Samaritans, so as to prepare for him. 53 But they did not receive him, because he was traveling with his face set towards Jerusalem. 54 When his disciples, James and John, saw this, they said, "Lord, do you want us to command fire to come down from the sky, and consume them?" 55 And he turned and rebuked them, and said, "You do not realize what kind of Spirit you belong to. 56 For the Son of Man did not come to destroy people's lives, but to save them." And they went to another village. 57 As they went on the way, a certain man said to him, "I want to follow you wherever you go." 58 And Jesus said to him, "The foxes have holes, and the birds of the sky have nests, but the Son of Man has no place to lay his head." 59 He said to another, "Follow me." But he said, "Lord, allow me first to go and bury my father." 60 But Jesus said to him, "Leave the dead to bury their own dead, but you go and announce the Kingdom of God." 61 Another also said, "I want to follow you, Lord, but first allow me to bid farewell to those who are at my house." 62 But Jesus said to him, "No one, having put his hand to the plow, and looking back, is fit for the Kingdom of God."

10 Now after these things, the Lord also appointed seventy-two others, and sent them two by two ahead of him into every city and place, where he was about to come. 2 Then he said to them, "The harvest is indeed plentiful, but the laborers are few. Pray therefore to the Lord of the harvest, that he may send out laborers into his harvest. 3 Go your way. Look, I send you out as lambs among wolves. 4 Carry no money bag, nor pack, nor sandals; and greet no one on the way. 5 Into whatever house you enter, first say, 'Peace be to this house.' 6 If a peaceful person is there, your peace will rest on him; but if not, it will return to you. 7 Remain in that same house, eating and drinking the things they give, for the laborer is worthy of his wages. Do not go from house to house. 8 Into whatever city you enter, and they receive you, eat the things that are set before you. 9 Heal the sick who are in it, and tell them, 'The Kingdom of God has come near to you.' 10 But into whatever city you enter, and they do not receive you, go out into its streets and say, 11 'Even the dust from your city that clings to our feet, we wipe off against you. Nevertheless know this, that the Kingdom of God is near.' 12 I tell you, it will be more tolerable in that day for Sodom than for that city. 13 "Woe to you, Chorazin. Woe to you, Bethsaida. For if the mighty works had been done in Tyre and Sidon which were done in you, they would have repented long ago, sitting in sackcloth and ashes. 14 But it will be more tolerable for Tyre and Sidon in the judgment than for you. 15 And you, Capernaum, will you be exalted to heaven? You will be brought down to Hades (Hadēs g86). 16 Whoever listens to you listens to me, and whoever rejects you rejects me. Whoever rejects me rejects him who sent me." 17 The seventy-two returned with joy, saying, "Lord, even the demons are subject to us in your name." 18 He said to them, "I saw Satan having fallen like lightning from heaven. 19 Look, I have given you authority to tread on serpents and scorpions, and over all the power of the enemy, and nothing will in any way hurt you. 20 Nevertheless, do not rejoice in this, that the spirits are subject to you, but rejoice that your names are written in heaven." 21 In that same hour he rejoiced in the Holy Spirit, and said, "I thank you, Father, Lord of heaven and earth, that you have hidden these things from the wise and understanding, and revealed them to little children. Yes, Father, for so it was well-pleasing in your sight." 22 "All things have been delivered to me by my Father. No one knows who the Son is, except the Father, and who the Father is, except the Son, and he to whomever the Son desires to reveal him." 23 Turning to the disciples, he said privately, "Blessed are the eyes which see the things that you see, 24 for I tell you that many prophets and kings desired to see the things which you see, and did not see them, and to hear the things which you hear, and did not hear them." 25 And look, a certain Law scholar stood up and tested him, saying, "Teacher, what must I do to inherit consummate (aiōnios g166) life?" 26 He said to him, "What is written in the Law? How do you read it?" 27 He answered, "You are to love the Lord your God with all your heart, with all your soul, with all your strength, and with all your mind; and your neighbor as yourself." 28 He said to him, "You have answered correctly. Do this, and you will live." 29 But he, desiring to justify himself, asked Jesus, "Who is my neighbor?" 30 Jesus answered, "A certain man was going down from Jerusalem to Jericho, and he fell among robbers, who both stripped him and beat him, and departed, leaving him half dead. 31 By chance a certain priest was going down that way. When he saw him, he passed by on the other side. 32 In the same way a Levite also, when he came to the place, and saw him, passed by on the other side. 33 But a certain Samaritan, as he traveled, came where he was. When he saw him, he was moved with compassion, 34 came to him, and bound up his wounds, pouring on oil and wine. He set him on his own animal, and brought him to an inn, and took care of him. 35 On the next day, he took out two denarii, and gave them to the host, and said to him, 'Take care of him. Whatever you spend beyond that, I will repay you when I return.' 36 Now which of these three do you think seemed to be a neighbor to him who fell among the robbers?" 37 He said, "He who showed mercy on him." Then Jesus said to him, "Go and do likewise." 38 It happened as they went on their way, he entered into a certain village, and a certain

Luke

woman named Martha received him. **39** She had a sister called Mary, who also sat at the Lord's feet, and heard his word. **40** But Martha was distracted with much serving, and she came up to him, and said, "Lord, do you not care that my sister left me to serve alone? Ask her therefore to help me." **41** But the Lord answered and said to her, "Martha, Martha, you are anxious and troubled about many things, **42** but one thing is needed. Mary has chosen the good part, which will not be taken away from her."

11

It happened, that when he finished praying in a certain place, one of his disciples said to him, "Lord, teach us to pray, just as John also taught his disciples." **2** So he said to them, "When you pray, say, 'Our Father in heaven, holy be your name. May your kingdom come. May your will be done on earth, as it is in heaven. **3** Give us day by day our daily bread. **4** Forgive us our sins, for we ourselves also forgive everyone who is indebted to us. And lead us not into temptation, but deliver us from evil.'" **5** He said to them, "Which of you, if you go to a friend at midnight, and tell him, 'Friend, lend me three loaves of bread, **6** for a friend of mine has come to me from a journey, and I have nothing to set before him,' **7** and he from within will answer and say, 'Do not bother me. The door is now shut, and my children are with me in bed. I cannot get up and give it to you'? **8** I tell you, although he will not rise and give it to him because he is his friend, yet because of his persistence, he will get up and give him as many as he needs. **9** "I tell you, ask, and it will be given to you. Seek, and you will find. Knock, and it will be opened to you. **10** For everyone who asks receives. He who seeks finds. To him who knocks it will be opened. **11** "Which of you fathers, if your son asks for a fish, he won't give him a snake instead of a fish, will he? **12** Or if he asks for an egg, will give him a scorpion? **13** If you then, being evil, know how to give good gifts to your children, how much more will your heavenly Father give the Holy Spirit to those who ask him?" **14** He was casting out a demon, and it was mute. It happened, when the demon had gone out, the mute man spoke; and the crowds were amazed. **15** But some of them said, "He casts out demons by Beelzebul, the prince of the demons." **16** Others, testing him, sought from him a sign from heaven. **17** But he, knowing their thoughts, said to them, "Every kingdom divided against itself is brought to desolation. A house divided against itself falls. **18** If Satan also is divided against himself, how will his kingdom stand? For you say that I cast out demons by Beelzebul. **19** But if I cast out demons by Beelzebul, by whom do your children cast them out? Therefore will they be your judges. **20** But if I by the finger of God cast out demons, then the Kingdom of God has come to you. **21** "When the strong man, fully armed, guards his own dwelling, his goods are safe. **22** But when someone stronger attacks him and overcomes him, he takes from him his whole armor in which he trusted, and divides up his plunder. **23** "He that is not with me is against me. He who does not gather with me scatters. **24** The unclean spirit, when he has gone out of the person, passes through dry places, seeking rest, and finding none, he says, 'I will turn back to my house from which I came out.' **25** When he returns, he finds it swept and put in order. **26** Then he goes, and takes seven other spirits more evil than himself, and they enter in and dwell there. The last state of that person becomes worse than the first." **27** It came to pass, as he said these things, a certain woman out of the crowd lifted up her voice, and said to him, "Blessed is the womb that bore you, and the breasts which nursed you." **28** But he said, "On the contrary, blessed are those who hear the word of God, and keep it." **29** When the crowds were gathering together to him, he began to say, "This generation is an evil generation. It seeks after a sign. No sign will be given to it but the sign of Jonah. **30** For even as Jonah became a sign to the Ninevites, so will also the Son of Man be to this generation. **31** The Queen of the South will rise up in the judgment with the people of this generation, and will condemn them: for she came from a distant land to hear the wisdom of Solomon; and look, one greater than Solomon is here. **32** The people of Nineveh will stand up in the judgment with this generation, and will condemn it: for they repented at the preaching of Jonah, and look, one greater than Jonah is here. **33** "No one, when he has lit a lamp, puts it in a cellar or under a basket, but on a stand, that those who come in may see the light. **34** The lamp of the body is the eye. Therefore when your eye is good, your whole body is also full of light; but when it is bad, your body also is full of darkness. **35** Therefore see whether the light that is in you is not darkness. **36** If therefore your whole body is full of light, having no part dark, it will be wholly full of light, as when the lamp with its bright shining gives you light." **37** Now as he spoke, a Pharisee asked him to dine with him. He went in, and sat at the table. **38** When the Pharisee saw it, he was surprised that he had not first washed himself before dinner. **39** The Lord said to him, "Now you Pharisees cleanse the outside of the cup and of the platter, but your inward part is full of extortion and wickedness. **40** You foolish ones, did not he who made the outside make the inside also? **41** But give for gifts to the needy those things which are within, and see, all things will be clean to you. **42** But woe to you Pharisees. For you tithe mint and rue and every herb, but you bypass justice and the love of God. You ought to have done these, and not to have left the other undone. **43** Woe to you Pharisees. For you love the best seats in the synagogues, and the greetings in the marketplaces. **44** Woe to you. For you are like hidden graves, and the people who walk over them do not know it." **45** One of the Law scholars answered him, "Teacher, in saying this you insult us also." **46** He said, "Woe to you Law scholars also. For you load people with burdens that are difficult to carry, and you yourselves won't even lift one finger to help carry those burdens. **47** Woe to you. For you build the tombs of the prophets, and your fathers killed them. **48** So you are witnesses and consent to the works of your fathers. For they killed them, and you build their tombs. **49** Therefore also the wisdom of God said, 'I will send to them prophets and apostles; and some of them they will kill and persecute, **50** that the blood of all the prophets, which was shed from the foundation of the world, may be required of this generation; **51** from the blood of Abel to the blood of Zechariah, who perished between the altar and the sanctuary.' Yes, I tell you, it will be required of this generation. **52** Woe to you Law scholars. For you took away the key of knowledge. You did not enter in yourselves, and those who were entering in, you hindered." **53** And when he left there, the scribes and the Pharisees began to oppose him bitterly, and to provoke him to speak about many things; **54** lying in wait for him, seeking to catch him in something he might say, that they might accuse him.

12 Meanwhile, when a crowd of many thousands had gathered together, so much so that they trampled on each other, he began to tell his disciples first of all, "Beware of the yeast of the Pharisees, which is hypocrisy. **2** But there is nothing covered up, that will not be revealed, nor hidden, that will not be known. **3** Therefore whatever you have said in the darkness will be heard in the light. What you have spoken in the ear in the inner chambers will be proclaimed on the housetops. **4** "I tell you, my friends, do not be afraid of those who kill the body, and after that have no more that they can do. **5** But I will warn you whom you should fear. Fear him who after he has killed, has power to cast into Gehenna **(Geenna g1067)**. Yes, I tell you, fear him. **6** "Are not five sparrows sold for two assaria coins? Not one of them is forgotten by God. **7** But the very hairs of your head are all numbered. Therefore do not be afraid. You are of more value than many sparrows. **8** "I tell you, everyone who confesses me before people, him will the Son of Man also confess before the angels of God; **9** but the one who denies me in the presence of people will be denied in the presence of the angels of God. **10** Everyone who speaks a word against the Son of Man will be forgiven, but those who blaspheme against the Holy Spirit will not be forgiven. **11** When they bring you before the synagogues, the rulers, and the authorities, do not be anxious how or what you will answer, or what you will say; **12** for the Holy Spirit will teach you in that same hour what you must say." **13** And someone in the crowd said to him, "Teacher, tell my brother to divide the inheritance with me." **14** But he said to him, "Man, who made me a judge or an arbitrator over you?" **15** He said to them, "Beware. Keep yourselves from all covetousness, for a man's life does not consist of the abundance of the things which he possesses." **16** He spoke a parable to them, saying, "The ground of a certain rich man brought forth abundantly. **17** He reasoned within himself, saying, 'What will I do, because I do not have room to store my crops?' **18** He said, 'This is what I will do. I will pull down my barns, and build bigger ones, and there I will store all my grain and my goods. **19** I will tell my soul, "Soul, you have many goods laid up for many years. Take your ease, eat, drink, be merry."' **20** "But God said to him, 'You foolish one, tonight your soul is required of you. The things which you have prepared—whose will they be?' **21** So is he who lays up treasure for himself, and is not rich toward God." **22** He said to his disciples, "Therefore I tell you, do not be anxious for your life, what you will eat, nor yet for your body, what you will wear. **23** Life is more than food, and the body is more than clothing. **24** Consider the ravens: they do not sow, they do not reap, they have no warehouse or barn, and God feeds them. How much more valuable are you than birds. **25** Which of you by being anxious can add a cubit to his height? **26** If then you are not able to do even the least things, why are you anxious about the rest? **27** Consider the lilies, how they grow. They do not toil, neither do they spin; yet I tell you, even Solomon in all his glory was not arrayed like one of these. **28** But if this is how God clothes the grass in the field, which today exists, and tomorrow is cast into the oven, how much more will he clothe you, O you of little faith? **29** Do not seek what you will eat or what you will drink; neither be anxious. **30** For the nations of the world seek after all of these things, but your Father knows that you need these things. **31** But seek his Kingdom, and these things will be added to you. **32** Do not be afraid, little flock, for it is your Father's good pleasure to give you the Kingdom. **33** Sell that which you have, and give gifts to the needy. Make for yourselves purses which do not grow old, a treasure in the heavens that does not fail, where no thief approaches, neither moth destroys. **34** For where your treasure is, there will your heart be also. **35** "Let your waist be girded and your lamps burning. **36** Be like people watching for their lord, when he returns from the marriage feast; that, when he comes and knocks, they may immediately open to him. **37** Blessed are those servants, whom the lord will find watching when he comes. Truly I tell you, that he will dress himself, and make them recline, and will come and serve them. **38** And if he comes in the second watch, or even in the third, and finds them so, blessed are they. **39** But know this, that if the master of the house had known in what hour the thief was coming, he would have watched and not have allowed his house to be broken into. **40** Therefore be ready also, for the Son of Man is coming in an hour that you do not expect him." **41** Peter said to him, "Lord, are you telling this parable to us, or to everybody?" **42** The Lord said, "Who then is the faithful and wise steward, whom his lord will set over his household, to give them their portion of food at the right times? **43** Blessed is that servant whom his lord will find doing so when he comes. **44** Truly I tell you, that he will set him over all that he has. **45** But if that servant says in his heart, 'My lord delays his coming,' and begins to beat the menservants and the maidservants, and to eat and drink, and to be drunk, **46** then the lord of that servant will come in a day when he is not expecting him, and in an hour that he does not know, and will cut him in two, and place his portion with the unfaithful. **47** That servant, who knew his lord's will, and did not prepare, nor do what he wanted, will be beaten with many stripes, **48** but he who did not know, and did things worthy of stripes, will be beaten with few stripes. To whomever much is given, of him will much be required; and to whom much was entrusted, of him more will be asked. **49** "I came to throw fire on the earth. I wish it were already kindled. **50** But I have a baptism to be baptized with, and how distressed I am until it is accomplished. **51** Do you think that I have come to give peace in the earth? I tell you, no, but rather division. **52** For from now on, there will be five in one house divided, three against two, and two against three. **53** They will be divided, father against son, and son against father; mother against daughter, and daughter against her mother; mother-in-law against her daughter-in-law, and daughter-in-law against her mother-in-law." **54** He said to the crowds also, "When you see a cloud rising from the west, immediately you say, 'A shower is coming,' and so it happens. **55** When a south wind blows, you say, 'There will be a scorching heat,' and it happens. **56** Hypocrites. You know how to interpret the appearance of the earth and the sky, but why do you not know how to interpret this time? **57** Why do you not judge for yourselves what is right? **58** For when you are going with your adversary before the magistrate, try diligently on the way to be released from him, lest perhaps he drag you to the judge, and the judge deliver you to the officer, and the officer throw you into prison. **59** I tell you, you will by no means get out of there, until you have paid the very last penny."

13 Now there were some present at the same time who told him about the Galileans, whose blood Pilate had mixed with their sacrifices. **2** And he answered and said to them, "Do you think that these Galileans were worse sinners than all the other Galileans, because they suffered these things? **3** I tell you, no, but unless you repent, you will all perish in the same way. **4** Or those eighteen, on whom the tower in Siloam fell, and killed them; do you think that they were worse offenders than all the others who dwell in Jerusalem? **5** I tell you, no, but, unless you repent, you will all perish in the same way." **6** He spoke this parable. "A certain man had a fig tree planted in his vineyard, and he came seeking fruit on it, and found none. **7** He said to the vine dresser, 'Look, these three years I have come looking for fruit on this fig tree, and found none. Cut it down. Why does it waste the soil?' **8** He answered, 'Lord, leave it alone this year also, until I dig around it, and fertilize it. **9** And if it bears fruit next time, [fine]; but if not, you can cut it down.'" **10** He was teaching in one of the synagogues on the Sabbath day. **11** And look, a woman who had a spirit of infirmity eighteen years, and she was bent over, and could in no way straighten herself up. **12** When Jesus saw her, he called her, and said to her, "Woman, you are freed from your infirmity." **13** He laid his hands on her, and immediately she stood up straight, and glorified God. **14** The ruler of the synagogue, being indignant because Jesus had healed on the Sabbath, said to the crowd, "There are six days when work should be done Therefore come on those days and be healed, and not on the Sabbath day." **15** Therefore the Lord answered him, "You hypocrites. Does not each one of you free his ox or his donkey from the stall on the Sabbath, and lead him away to water? **16** Ought not this woman, being a daughter of Abraham, whom Satan had bound, look, eighteen years, be freed from this bondage on the Sabbath day?" **17** As he said these things, all his adversaries were disappointed, and all the crowd rejoiced for all the glorious things that were done by him. **18** Then he said, "What is the Kingdom of God like? And to what can I compare it? **19** It is like a grain of mustard seed, which a man took, and put in his own garden. It grew, and became a tree, and the birds of the sky lodged in its branches." **20** And again he said, "To what can I compare the Kingdom of God? **21** It is like yeast, which a woman took and hid in three measures of flour, until it was all leavened." **22** He went on his way through cities and villages, teaching, and traveling on to Jerusalem. **23** One said to him, "Lord, are they few who are saved?" He said to them, **24** "Strive to enter in by the narrow door, for many, I tell you, will seek to enter in, and will not be able. **25** When once the master of the house has risen up, and has shut the door, and you begin to stand outside, and to knock at the door, saying, 'Lord, open to us.' then he will answer and tell you, 'I do not know you or where you come from.' **26** Then you will begin to say, 'We ate and drank in your presence, and you taught in our streets.' **27** But he will reply, 'I do not know where you come from. Depart from me, all you workers of iniquity.' **28** There will be weeping and grinding of teeth, when you see Abraham, Isaac, Jacob, and all the prophets, in the Kingdom of God, and yourselves being thrown outside. **29** They will come from the east, west, north, and south, and will sit down in the Kingdom of God. **30** And look, there are some who are last who will be first, and there are some who are first who will be last." **31** In that same hour some Pharisees came, saying to him, "Get out of here, and go away, for Herod wants to kill you." **32** And he said to them, "Go and tell that fox, 'Look, I cast out demons and perform cures today and tomorrow, and the third day I complete my mission. **33** Nevertheless I must go on my way today and tomorrow and the next day, for it cannot be that a prophet perish outside of Jerusalem.' **34** "Jerusalem, Jerusalem, that kills the prophets, and stones those who are sent to her. How often I wanted to gather your children together, like a hen gathers her own brood under her wings, and you refused. **35** Look, your house is forsaken. And I tell you, you will not see me until you say, 'Blessed is he who comes in the name of the Lord.'"

14 And it happened, when he went into the house of one of the rulers of the Pharisees on a Sabbath to eat bread, that they were watching him. **2** And look, a certain man who had dropsy was in front of him. **3** Jesus, answering, spoke to the Law scholars and Pharisees, saying, "Is it lawful to heal on the Sabbath or not?" **4** But they were silent. He took him, and healed him, and let him go. **5** He answered them, "Which of you, if your son or an ox fell into a well, would not immediately pull him out on a Sabbath day?" **6** They could not answer him regarding these things. **7** He spoke a parable to those who were invited, when he noticed how they chose the best seats, and said to them, **8** "When you are invited by anyone to a marriage feast, do not sit in the best seat, since perhaps someone more honorable than you might be invited by him, **9** and he who invited both of you would come and tell you, 'Make room for this person.' Then you would begin, with shame, to take the lowest place. **10** But when you are invited, go and sit in the lowest place, so that when he who invited you comes, he may tell you, 'Friend, move up higher.' Then you will be honored in the presence of all who sit at the table with you. **11** For everyone who exalts himself will be humbled, and whoever humbles himself will be exalted." **12** He also said to the one who had invited him, "When you make a dinner or a supper, do not call your friends, nor your brothers, nor your kinsmen, nor rich neighbors, or perhaps they might also return the favor, and pay you back. **13** But when you make a feast, ask the poor, the maimed, the lame, or the blind; **14** and you will be blessed, because they do not have the resources to repay you. For you will be repaid in the resurrection of the righteous." **15** Now when one of those who were reclining with him heard these things, he said to him, "Blessed is he who will eat bread in the Kingdom of God." **16** But he said to him, "A certain man made a great supper, and he invited many people. **17** And he sent his servant at the hour for supper to tell those who were invited, 'Come, for everything is ready now.' **18** They all as one began to make excuses. "The first said to him, 'I have bought a field, and I must go and see it. Please have me excused.' **19** "Another said, 'I have bought five yoke of oxen, and I must go try them out. Please have me excused.' **20** "Another said, 'I have married a wife, and therefore I cannot come.' **21** "That servant came, and told his lord these things. Then the master of the house, being angry, said to his servant, 'Go out quickly into the streets and lanes of the city, and bring in the poor, maimed, blind, and lame.' **22** "The servant said, 'Lord, it is done as you commanded, and there is still room.' **23** "The lord said to the servant, 'Go out into the highways and hedges, and compel them to come in, that my house may be filled. **24** For I tell you that none of those individuals who were invited will taste of my supper.'" **25** Now large crowds were going with him. He turned and said to them, **26** "If anyone comes to me, and does not hate his own father, mother, wife, children, brothers, and sisters, yes, and his own life also, he cannot be my disciple. **27** Whoever does not bear his own cross, and come after me, cannot be my disciple. **28** For which of you, desiring to build a tower, does not first sit down and count the cost, to see if he has enough to complete it? **29** Or perhaps, when he has laid a foundation, and is not able to finish, everyone who sees begins to mock him, **30** saying, 'This man began to build, and was not able to finish.' **31** Or what king, as he goes to encounter another king in war, will not sit down first and consider whether he is able with ten thousand to meet him who comes against him with twenty thousand? **32** Or else, while the other is yet a great way off, he sends an envoy, and asks for conditions of peace. **33** So therefore whoever of you who does not renounce all that he has, he cannot be my disciple. **34** Salt is good, but if the salt becomes flat and tasteless, with what do you season it? **35** It is fit neither for the soil nor for the manure pile. It is thrown out. He who has ears to hear, let him hear."

15 Now all the tax collectors and sinners were coming close to him to hear him. **2** The Pharisees and the scribes murmured, saying, "This man welcomes sinners, and eats with them." **3** He told them this parable. **4** "Which one of you, if you had one hundred sheep, and lost one of them, would not leave the ninety-nine in the wilderness, and go after the one that was lost, until he found it? **5** When he has found it, he carries it on his shoulders, rejoicing. **6** When he comes home, he calls together his friends and his neighbors, saying to them, 'Rejoice with me, for I have found my sheep which was lost.' **7** I tell you that even so there will be more joy in heaven over one sinner who repents, than over ninety-nine righteous people who need no repentance. **8** Or what woman, if she had ten drachma coins, if she lost one drachma coin, would not light a lamp, sweep the house, and seek diligently until she found it? **9** When she has found it, she calls together her friends and neighbors, saying, 'Rejoice with me, for I have found the drachma which I had lost.' **10** Even so, I tell you, there is joy in the presence of the angels of God over one sinner repenting." **11** He said, "A certain man had two sons. **12** The younger of them said to his father, 'Father, give me my share of your property.' He divided his livelihood between them. **13** Not many days after, the younger son gathered all of this together and traveled into a far country. There he wasted his property with riotous living. **14** When he had spent all of it, there arose a severe famine in that country, and he began to be in need. **15** He went and joined himself to one of the citizens of that country, and he sent him into his fields to feed pigs. **16** And he wanted to fill himself with the carob pods that the pigs ate, but no one gave him any. **17** But when he came to himself he said, 'How many hired servants of my father's have bread enough to spare, and I'm dying here with hunger. **18** I will get up and go to my father, and will tell him, "Father, I have sinned against heaven, and in your sight. **19** I am no longer worthy to be called your son. Make me like one of your hired servants."' **20** "He arose, and came to his father. But while he was still far off, his father saw him, and was moved with compassion, and ran, and fell on his neck, and kissed him. **21** The son said to him, 'Father, I have sinned against heaven, and in your sight. I am no longer worthy to be called your son.' **22** "But the father said to his servants, 'Quickly, bring out the best robe, and put it on him. Put a ring on his hand, and shoes on his feet. **23** Bring the fattened calf, kill it, and let us eat, and celebrate; **24** for this, my son, was dead, and is alive again. He was lost, and is found.' They began to celebrate. **25** "Now his elder son was in the field. As he came near to the house, he heard music and dancing. **26** He called one of the servants to him, and asked what was going on. **27** He said to him, 'Your brother has come, and your father has killed the fattened calf, because he has received him back safe and healthy.' **28** But he was angry, and would not go in. Therefore his father came out, and pleaded with him. **29** But he answered his father, 'Look, these many years I have served you, and I never disobeyed a commandment of yours, but you never gave me a goat, that I might celebrate with my friends. **30** But when this, your son, came, who has devoured your living with prostitutes, you killed the fattened calf for him.' **31** "He said to him, 'Son, you are always with me, and all that is mine is yours. **32** But it was appropriate to celebrate and be glad, for this brother of yours was dead and is alive; and he was lost, and is found.'"

16 He also said to his disciples, "There was a certain rich man who had a manager. An accusation was made to him that this man was wasting his possessions. **2** He called him, and said to him, 'What is this that I hear about you? Give an accounting of your management, for you can no longer be manager.' **3** "The manager said within himself, 'What will I do, seeing that my lord is taking away the management position from me? I do not have strength to dig. I am ashamed to beg. **4** I know what I will do, so that when I am removed from management, they may receive me into their houses.' **5** Calling each one of his lord's debtors to him, he said to the first, 'How much do you owe to my lord?' **6** He said, 'A hundred batos of oil.' He said to him, 'Take your bill, and sit down quickly and write fifty.' **7** Then he said to another, 'How much do you owe?' He said, 'A hundred cors of wheat.' He said to him, 'Take your bill, and write eighty.' **8** "His lord commended the dishonest manager because he had done shrewdly, for the people of this age (aiōn g165) are, in their own generation, more shrewd than the people of the light. **9** I tell you, make for yourselves friends by means of unrighteous mammon, so that when it fails, they may receive you into consummate (aiōnios g166) tents. **10** He who is faithful in a very little is faithful also in much. He who is dishonest in a very little is also dishonest in much. **11** If therefore you have not been faithful in the unrighteous mammon, who will commit to your trust the true riches? **12** If you have not been faithful in that which is another's, who will give you that which is your own? **13** No servant can serve two masters, for either he will hate the one, and love the other; or else he will hold to one, and despise the other. You are not able to serve God and wealth." **14** The Pharisees, who were lovers of money, also heard all these things, and they scoffed at him. **15** He said to them, "You are those who justify yourselves in the sight of people, but God knows your hearts. For that which is exalted among people is an abomination in the sight of God. **16** The Law and the Prophets were until John. From that time the Good News of the Kingdom of God is preached, and everyone is forcing his way into it. **17** But it is easier for heaven and earth to pass away, than for one tiny stroke of a pen in the Law to become void. **18** Everyone who divorces his wife, and marries another, commits adultery. He who marries one who is divorced from a husband commits adultery. **19** "Now there was a certain rich man, and he was clothed in purple and fine linen, living in luxury every day. **20** A certain beggar, named Lazarus, was placed at his gate, full of sores, **21** and desiring to be fed with the crumbs that fell from the rich man's table. Yes, even the dogs came and licked his sores. **22** It happened that the beggar died, and that he was carried away by the angels to Abraham's bosom. The rich man also died, and was buried. **23** In Hades (Hadēs g86), he lifted up his eyes, being in torment, and saw Abraham far off, and Lazarus at his bosom. **24** He called out and said, 'Father Abraham, have mercy on me, and send Lazarus, that he may dip the tip of his finger in water, and cool my tongue. For I am in anguish in this flame.' **25** "But Abraham said, 'Son, remember that you, in your lifetime, received your good things, and Lazarus, in like manner, bad things. But now here he is comforted and you are in anguish. **26** Besides all this, between us and you there is a great gulf fixed, that those who want to pass from here to you are not able, and that none may cross over from there to us.' **27** "He said, 'I ask you therefore, father, that you would send him to my father's house; **28** for I have five brothers, that he may testify to them, so they won't also come into this place of torment.' **29** "But Abraham said to him, 'They have Moses and the Prophets. Let them listen to them.' **30** "He said, 'No, father Abraham, but if one goes to them from the dead, they will repent.' **31** "He said to him, 'If they do not listen to Moses and the Prophets, neither will they be persuaded if one rises from the dead.'"

17 He said to the disciples, "It is impossible that no occasions of stumbling should come, but woe to him through whom they come. **2** It would be better for him if a millstone were hung around his neck, and he were thrown into the sea, rather than that he should cause one of these little ones to stumble. **3** Watch yourselves. If your brother sins, rebuke him. If he repents, forgive him. **4** And if he sins against you seven times in the day, and seven times returns to you, saying, 'I repent,' you must forgive him." **5** The apostles said to the Lord, "Increase our faith." **6** The Lord said, "If you had faith like a grain of mustard seed, you would tell this mulberry tree, 'Be uprooted, and be planted in the sea,' and it would obey you. **7** But who is there among you, having a servant plowing or keeping sheep, that will say, when he comes in from the field, 'Come immediately and sit down at the table'? **8** But will he not say to him, 'Prepare my supper, clothe yourself properly, and serve me, while I eat and drink, and afterward you can eat and drink'? **9** Does he thank that servant because he did the things that were commanded? **10** Even so you also, when you have done all the things that are commanded you, say, 'We are unworthy servants. We have done our duty.'" **11** It happened as he was on his way to Jerusalem, that he was passing along the borders of Samaria and Galilee. **12** As he entered into a certain village, ten men who were lepers met him, who stood at a distance. **13** They lifted up their voices, saying, "Jesus, Master, have mercy on us." **14** When he saw them, he said to them, "Go and show yourselves to the priests." It happened that as they went, they were cleansed. **15** One of them, when he saw that he was healed, turned back, glorifying God with a loud voice. **16** He fell on his face at Jesus' feet, giving him thanks; and he was a Samaritan. **17** Jesus answered, "Weren't the ten cleansed? But where are the nine? **18** Were there none found who returned to give glory to God, except this stranger?" **19** Then he said to him, "Get up, and go your way. Your faith has healed you." **20** Being asked by the Pharisees when the Kingdom of God would come, he answered them, "The Kingdom of God does not come with observation; **21** neither will they say, 'Look, here.' or, 'Look, there.' for the Kingdom of God is within you." **22** He said to the disciples, "The days will come, when you will desire to see one of the days of the Son of Man, and you will not see it. **23** And they will tell you, 'Look, there.' or 'Look, here.' Do not go away, nor follow after them, **24** for as the lightning, when it flashes out of the one part under the sky, shines to the other part under the sky; so will the Son of Man be in his day. **25** But first, he must suffer many things and be rejected by this generation. **26** As it happened in the days of Noah, even so will it be also in the days of the Son of Man. **27** They ate, they drank, they married, they were given in marriage, until the day that Noah entered into the box-shaped vessel, and the flood came, and destroyed them all. **28** Likewise, even as it happened in the days of Lot: they ate, they drank, they bought, they sold, they planted, they built; **29** but in the day that Lot went out from Sodom, it rained fire and sulfur from the sky, and destroyed them all. **30** It will be the same way in the day that the Son of Man is revealed. **31** In that day, he who will be on the housetop, and his goods in the house, let him not go down to take them away. Let him who is in the field likewise not turn back. **32** Remember Lot's wife. **33** Whoever seeks to keep his life will lose it, but whoever loses it will preserve it. **34** I tell you, in that night there will be two people in one bed. The one will be taken, and the other will be left. **35** There will be two grinding grain together. One will be taken, and the other will be left." **37** They, answering, asked him, "Where, Lord?" He said to them, "Where the body is, there will the vultures also be gathered together."

18 He also spoke a parable to them that they must always pray, and not give up, **2** saying, "There was a judge in a certain city who did not fear God, and did not respect people. **3** A widow was in that city, and she often came to him, saying, 'Give me justice against my adversary.' **4** He would not for a while, but afterward he said to himself, 'Though I neither fear God, nor respect people, **5** yet because this widow bothers me, I will give her justice, or else she will wear me out by her continual coming.'" **6** The Lord said, "Listen to what the unrighteous judge says. **7** Won't God avenge his chosen ones, who are crying out to him day and night, and yet he exercises patience with them? **8** I tell you that he will avenge them quickly. Nevertheless, when the Son of Man comes, will he find faith on the earth?" **9** He spoke also this parable to certain people who were convinced of their own righteousness, and who despised all others. **10** "Two men went up into the temple to pray; one was a Pharisee, and the other was a tax collector. **11** The Pharisee stood and prayed to himself like this: 'God, I thank you, that I am not like other people, extortioners, unrighteous, adulterers, or even like this tax collector. **12** I fast twice a week, I give tithes of all that I get.' **13** But the tax collector, standing far away, would not even lift up his eyes to heaven, but beat his breast, saying, 'God, be merciful to me, a sinner.' **14** I tell you, this man went down to his house justified rather than the other; for everyone who exalts himself will be humbled, but he who humbles himself will be exalted." **15** Now they were also bringing their babies to him, that he might touch them. But when the disciples saw it, they rebuked them. **16** Jesus summoned them, saying, "Allow the little children to come to me, and do not hinder them, for the Kingdom of God belongs to such as these. **17** Truly, I tell you, whoever does not receive the Kingdom of God like a little child, he will in no way enter into it." **18** A certain ruler asked him, saying, "Good Teacher, what shall I do to inherit consummate **(aiōnios g166)** life?" **19** Jesus asked him, "Why do you call me good? No one is good, except one—God. **20** You know the commandments: 'Do not commit adultery,' 'Do not murder,' 'Do not steal,' 'Do not give false testimony,' 'Honor your father and your mother.'" **21** And he said, "I have kept all these things from my youth up." **22** When Jesus heard it, he said to him, "You still lack one thing. Sell all that you have, and distribute it to the poor. You will have treasure in heaven. Come, follow me." **23** But when he heard these things, he became very sad, for he was very rich. **24** And Jesus looked at him and said, "How hard it is for those who have riches to enter into the Kingdom of God. **25** For it is easier for a camel to enter in through a needle's eye, than for a rich person to enter into the Kingdom of God." **26** Those who heard it said, "Then who can be saved?" **27** But he said, "The things which are impossible with man are possible with God." **28** And Peter said, "Look, we have left our own things and followed you." **29** He said to them, "Truly I tell you, there is no one who has left house, or wife, or brothers, or parents, or children, for the Kingdom of God's sake, **30** who will not receive many times more in this time, and in the age **(aiōn g165)** to come, consummate **(aiōnios g166)** life." **31** He took the twelve aside, and said to them, "Look, we are going up to Jerusalem, and all the things that are written through the prophets concerning the Son of Man will be completed. **32** For he will be delivered up to the Gentiles, will be mocked, treated shamefully, and spit on. **33** They will scourge and kill him. On the third day, he will rise again." **34** They understood none of these things. This saying was hidden from them, and they did not understand the things that were said. **35** It happened, as he came near Jericho, a certain blind man sat by the road, begging. **36** Hearing a crowd going by, he asked what this meant. **37** They told him that Jesus of Nazareth was passing by. **38** He called out, "Jesus, Son of David, have mercy on me." **39** Those who led the way rebuked him, that he should be quiet; but he shouted all the more, "Son of David, have mercy on me." **40** Standing still, Jesus commanded him to be brought to him. When he had come near, he asked him, **41** "What do you want me to do?" He said, "Lord, that I may see again." **42** Jesus said to him, "Receive your sight. Your faith has healed you." **43** And immediately he received his sight, and followed him, glorifying God. All the people, when they saw it, praised God.

19 He entered and was passing through Jericho. **2** And look, there was a man named Zacchaeus. He was a chief tax collector, and he was rich. **3** He was trying to see who Jesus was, and could not because of the crowd, because he was short. **4** He ran on ahead, and climbed up into a sycamore tree to see him, for he was to pass that way. **5** And as he came to the place, looking up, Jesus saw him, and said to him, "Zacchaeus, hurry and come down, for today I must stay at your house." **6** He hurried, came down, and received him joyfully. **7** And when they saw it, they all murmured, saying, "He has gone in to lodge with a man who is a sinner." **8** And Zacchaeus stood and said to the Lord, "Look, Lord, half of my goods I give to the poor. If I have wrongfully exacted anything of anyone, I restore four times as much." **9** Jesus said to him, "Today, salvation has come to this house, because he also is a son of Abraham. **10** For the Son of Man came to seek and to save that which was lost." **11** As they heard these things, he went on and told a parable, because he was near Jerusalem, and they supposed that the Kingdom of God would be revealed immediately. **12** He said therefore, "A certain nobleman went into a far country to receive for himself a kingdom, and to return. **13** He called ten servants of his, and gave them ten mina coins, and told them, 'Conduct business until I come.' **14** But his citizens hated him, and sent an envoy after him, saying, 'We do not want this man to reign over us.' **15** "It happened when he had come back again, having received the kingdom, that he commanded these servants, to whom he had given the money, to be called to him, that he might know what they had gained by conducting business. **16** The first came before him, saying, 'Lord, your mina has made ten more minas.' **17** "And he said to him, 'Well done, good servant. Because you were faithful with very little, you will have authority over ten cities.' **18** "The second came, saying, 'Your mina, Lord, has made five minas.' **19** "So he said to him, 'And you are to be over five cities.' **20** Another came, saying, 'Lord, look, your mina, which I kept laid away in a handkerchief, **21** for I feared you, because you are an exacting man. You take up that which you did not lay down, and reap that which you did not sow.' **22** "He said to him, 'Out of your own mouth will I judge you, you wicked servant. You knew that I am an exacting man, taking up that which I did not lay down, and reaping that which I did not sow. **23** Then why did you not deposit my money in the bank, and at my coming, I might have earned interest on it?' **24** He said to those who stood by, 'Take the mina away from him, and give it to him who has the ten minas.' **25** "They said to him, 'Lord, he has ten minas.' **26** 'For I tell you that to everyone who has, will more be given; but from him who does not have, even that which he has will be taken away. **27** But bring those enemies of mine who did not want me to reign over them here, and kill them before me.'" **28** Having said these things, he went on ahead, going up to Jerusalem. **29** It happened, when he drew near to Bethphage and Bethany, at the mountain that is called Olivet, he sent two of the disciples, **30** saying, "Go your way into the village on the other side, in which, as you enter, you will find a colt tied, whereon no one ever yet sat. Untie it, and bring it. **31** If anyone asks you, 'Why are you untying it?' say to him: 'Because the Lord needs it.'" **32** Those who were sent went away, and found things just as he had told them. **33** As they were untying the colt, its owners said to them, "Why are you untying the colt?" **34** They said, "Because the Lord needs it." **35** They brought it to Jesus. They threw their cloaks on the colt, and set Jesus on them. **36** As he went, they spread their cloaks in the way. **37** As he was now getting near, at the descent of the Mount of Olives, the whole crowd of the disciples began to rejoice and praise God with a loud voice for all the mighty works which they had seen, **38** saying, "Blessed is the King who comes in the name of the Lord. Peace in heaven, and glory in the highest." **39** Some of the Pharisees from the crowd said to him, "Teacher, rebuke your disciples." **40** He answered them, "I tell you that if these were silent, the stones would cry out." **41** When he drew near, he saw the city and wept over it, **42** saying, "If you, even you, had known today the things that make for peace. But now, they are hidden from your eyes. **43** For the days will come on you, when your enemies will throw up a barricade against you, surround you, hem you in on every side, **44** and will dash you and your children within you to the ground. They will not leave in you one stone on another, because you did not know the time of your visitation." **45** And he entered into the temple, and began to drive out those who were selling and buying in it, **46** saying to them, "It is written, 'And my house will be a house of prayer,' but you have made it a 'den of robbers'." **47** He was teaching daily in the temple, but the chief priests and the scribes and the leaders among the people sought to destroy him. **48** They could not find what they might do, for all the people hung on to every word that he said.

20 It happened on one of those days, as he was teaching the people in the temple and preaching the Good News, that the chief priests and scribes came to him with the elders. **2** They asked him, "Tell us: by what authority do you do these things? Or who is giving you this authority?" **3** He answered them, "I also will ask you one question. Tell me: **4** the baptism of John, was it from heaven, or from man?" **5** They reasoned with themselves, saying, "If we say, 'From heaven,' he will say, 'Why did you not believe him?' **6** But if we say, 'From man,' all the people will stone us, for they are persuaded that John was a prophet." **7** They answered that they did not know where it was from. **8** Jesus said to them, "Neither will I tell you by what authority I do these things." **9** He began to tell the people this parable. "A man planted a vineyard, and rented it out to some farmers, and went on a journey for a long time. **10** At the proper season, he sent a servant to the farmers to collect his share of the fruit of the vineyard. But the farmers beat him, and sent him away empty. **11** He sent yet another servant, and they also beat him, and treated him shamefully, and sent him away empty. **12** He sent yet a third, and they also wounded him, and threw him out. **13** The lord of the vineyard said, 'What am I to do? I will send my beloved son. It may be that they will respect him.' **14** "But when the farmers saw him, they reasoned among themselves, saying, 'This is the heir. Let us kill him, that the inheritance may be ours.' **15** They threw him out of the vineyard, and killed him. What therefore will the lord of the vineyard do to them? **16** He will come and destroy these farmers, and will give the vineyard to others." When they heard it, they said, "May it never be." **17** But he looked at them, and said, "Then what is this that is written, 'The stone which the builders rejected, the same was made the chief cornerstone?' **18** Everyone who falls on that stone will be broken to pieces; but on whomever it falls, it will crush him." **19** The chief priests and the scribes sought to lay hands on him that very hour, but they feared the people—for they knew he had spoken this parable against them. **20** They watched him, and sent out spies, who pretended to be righteous, that they might trap him in something he said, so as to deliver him up to the power and authority of the governor. **21** They asked him, "Teacher, we know that you say and teach what is right, and are not partial to anyone, but truly teach the way of God. **22** Is it lawful for us to pay taxes to Caesar, or not?" **23** But he perceived their craftiness, and said to them, **24** "Show me a denarius. Whose image and inscription are on it?" They answered, "Caesar's." **25** He said to them, "Then give to Caesar the things that are Caesar's, and to God the things that are God's." **26** They weren't able to trap him in his words before the people. And amazed at his answer, they fell silent. **27** Some of the Sadducees came to him, those who deny that there is a resurrection. **28** They asked him, "Teacher, Moses wrote to us that if a man's brother dies having a wife, and he is childless, his brother should take the wife, and raise up children for his brother. **29** There were therefore seven brothers. The first took a wife, and died childless. **30** The second and **31** the third took her, and likewise the seven all left no children, and died. **32** Afterward the woman also died. **33** Therefore in the resurrection whose wife of them will she be? For the seven had her as a wife." **34** Jesus said to them, "The people of this age (aiōn g165) marry, and are given in marriage. **35** But those who are considered worthy to attain to that age (aiōn g165) and the resurrection from the dead neither marry nor are given in marriage. **36** For they cannot die any more, for they are like the angels, and are children of God, being children of the resurrection. **37** But that the dead are raised, even Moses showed at the bush, when he called the Lord 'The God of Abraham, and the God of Isaac, and the God of Jacob.' **38** Now he is not the God of the dead, but of the living, for all are alive to him." **39** Some of the scribes answered, "Teacher, you speak well." **40** They did not dare to ask him any more questions. **41** He said to them, "Why do they say that the Christ is David's son? **42** David himself says in the scroll of Psalms, 'The Lord said to my Lord, "Sit at my right hand, **43** until I make your enemies the footstool of your feet."' **44** "David therefore calls him Lord, so how is he his son?" **45** In the hearing of all the people, he said to his disciples, **46** "Beware of the scribes, who like to walk in long robes, and love greetings in the marketplaces, the best seats in the synagogues, and the best places at feasts; **47** who devour widows' houses, and for a pretense make long prayers: these will receive greater condemnation."

21 He looked up, and saw the rich people who were putting their gifts into the treasury. **2** He saw a certain poor widow casting in two lepta. **3** He said, "Truly I tell you, this poor widow put in more than all of them, **4** for all these put in gifts from their abundance, but she, out of her poverty, put in all that she had to live on." **5** As some were talking about the temple and how it was decorated with beautiful stones and gifts, he said, **6** "As for these things which you see, the days will come, in which there will not be left here one stone on another that will not be thrown down." **7** They asked him, "Teacher, so when will these things be? What is the sign that these things are about to happen?" **8** He said, "Watch out that you do not get led astray, for many will come in my name, saying, 'I am he,' and, 'The time is near.' Therefore do not follow them. **9** When you hear of wars and disturbances, do not be terrified, for these things must happen first, but the end won't come immediately." **10** Then he said to them, "Nation will rise against nation, and kingdom against kingdom. **11** There will be great earthquakes, famines, and plagues in various places. There will be terrors and great signs from heaven. **12** But before all these things, they will lay their hands on you and will persecute you, delivering you up to synagogues and prisons, bringing you before kings and governors for my name's sake. **13** It will turn out as a testimony for you. **14** Settle it therefore in your hearts not to meditate beforehand how to answer, **15** for I will give you a mouth and wisdom which all your adversaries will not be able to withstand or to contradict. **16** You will be handed over even by parents, brothers, relatives, and friends. They will cause some of you to be put to death. **17** You will be hated by all for my name's sake. **18** And not a hair of your head will perish. **19** "By your endurance you will win your lives. **20** "But when you see Jerusalem surrounded by armies, then know that its desolation is near. **21** Then let those who are in Judea flee to the mountains. Let those who are in the midst of her depart. Let those who are in the country not enter it. **22** For these are days of vengeance, that all things which are written may be fulfilled. **23** Woe to those who are pregnant and to those who nurse infants in those days. For there will be great distress in the land, and wrath to this people. **24** And they will fall by the edge of the sword and be led captive into all the nations. And Jerusalem will be trampled down by Gentile people until the times are fulfilled. And there will be times of the Gentile people. **25** And there will be signs in the sun, and moon, and stars, and on the earth distress of nations in perplexity because of the roaring of the sea and the waves; **26** people will be fainting from fear, and from expectation of the things which are coming on the world, for the powers of the heavens will be shaken. **27** Then they will see the Son of Man coming in a cloud with power and great glory. **28** But when these things begin to happen, look up, and lift up your heads, because your redemption is near." **29** He told them a parable. "See the fig tree, and all the trees. **30** When they are already budding, you see it and know by your own selves that the summer is already near. **31** Even so you also, when you see these things happening, know that the Kingdom of God is near. **32** Truly I tell you, this generation will not pass away until all things are accomplished. **33** Heaven and earth will pass away, but my words will by no means pass away. **34** "So be careful, or your hearts will be loaded down with carousing, drunkenness, and cares of this life, and that day will come on you suddenly. **35** For it will come like a snare on all those who dwell on the surface of all

Luke

the earth. **36** Therefore be watchful all the time, praying that you may be able to escape all these things that will happen, and to stand before the Son of Man." **37** Every day Jesus was teaching in the temple, and every night he would go out and spend the night on the mountain that is called Olivet. **38** All the people came early in the morning to him in the temple to hear him.

22 Now the feast of unleavened bread, which is called the Passover, drew near. **2** The chief priests and the scribes sought how they might kill him, for they feared the people. **3** Satan entered into Judas, who was called Iscariot, who was numbered with the twelve. **4** He went away, and talked with the chief priests and captains about how he might deliver him to them. **5** They were glad, and agreed to give him money. **6** He consented, and sought an opportunity to deliver him to them in the absence of the crowd. **7** The day of unleavened bread came, on which the Passover lamb must be sacrificed. **8** He sent Peter and John, saying, "Go and prepare the Passover for us, that we may eat." **9** They said to him, "Where do you want us to prepare?" **10** He said to them, "Look, when you have entered into the city, a man carrying a pitcher of water will meet you. Follow him into the house which he enters. **11** Tell the master of the house, 'The Teacher says to you, "Where is the guest room, where I may eat the Passover with my disciples?"' **12** He will show you a large, furnished upper room. Make preparations there." **13** They went, found things as he had told them, and they prepared the Passover. **14** When the hour had come, he reclined at the table, and the apostles joined him. **15** He said to them, "I have earnestly desired to eat this Passover with you before I suffer, **16** for I say to you, I will not eat of it again until it is fulfilled in the Kingdom of God." **17** He received a cup, and when he had given thanks, he said, "Take this, and share it among yourselves, **18** for I tell you, from now on I will not drink of the fruit of the vine until the Kingdom of God comes." **19** He took bread, and when he had given thanks, he broke it, and gave to them, saying, "This is my body which is given for you. Do this in remembrance of me." **20** Likewise, he took the cup after they had eaten, saying, "This cup is the new covenant in my blood, which is poured out for you. **21** But look, the hand of him who betrays me is with me on the table. **22** The Son of Man indeed goes, as it has been determined, but woe to that man through whom he is betrayed." **23** They began to question among themselves, which of them it was who would do this thing. **24** There arose also a contention among them, which of them was considered to be greatest. **25** He said to them, "The kings of the nations lord it over them, and those who have authority over them are called 'benefactors.' **26** But not so with you. But one who is the greater among you, let him become as the younger, and one who is governing, as one who serves. **27** For who is greater, one who sits at the table, or one who serves? Is it not he who sits at the table? But I am in the midst of you as one who serves. **28** But you are those who have continued with me in my trials. **29** I confer on you a kingdom, even as my Father conferred on me, **30** that you may eat and drink at my table in my kingdom, and you will sit on thrones judging the twelve tribes of Israel." **31** And the Lord said, "Simon, Simon, look, Satan asked to have you, that he might sift you as wheat, **32** but I prayed for you, that your faith would not fail. You, when once you have turned again, establish your brothers." **33** He said to him, "Lord, I am ready to go with you both to prison and to death." **34** He said, "I tell you, Peter, the rooster will by no means crow today until you deny that you know me three times." **35** He said to them, "When I sent you out without money bag, and pack, and shoes, did you lack anything?" They said, "Nothing." **36** Then he said to them, "But now, whoever has a money bag must take it, and likewise a pack. Whoever has none, must sell his cloak, and buy a sword. **37** For I tell you that this which is written must still be fulfilled in me: 'And he was numbered with transgressors.' For that which concerns me has an end." **38** They said, "Lord, look, here are two swords." He said to them, "That is enough." **39** He came out, and went, as his custom was, to the Mount of Olives. His disciples also followed him. **40** When he was at the place, he said to them, "Pray that you do not enter into temptation." **41** He was withdrawn from them about a stone's throw, and he knelt down and prayed, **42** saying, "Father, if you are willing, remove this cup from me. Nevertheless, not my will, but yours, be done." **43** And an angel from heaven appeared to him, strengthening him. **44** Being in agony he prayed more earnestly. His sweat became like great drops of blood falling down on the ground. **45** When he rose up from his prayer, he came to the disciples, and found them sleeping because of grief, **46** and said to them, "Why do you sleep? Rise and pray that you may not enter into temptation." **47** While he was still speaking, look, a crowd came, and he who was called Judas, one of the twelve, was leading them. He came near to Jesus to kiss him. **48** But Jesus said to him, "Judas, do you betray the Son of Man with a kiss?" **49** When those who were around him saw what was about to happen, they said to him, "Lord, should we strike with the sword?" **50** A certain one of them struck the servant of the high priest, and cut off his right ear. **51** But Jesus answered and said, "No more of this." Then he touched his ear and healed him. **52** Jesus said to the chief priests, captains of the temple, and elders, who had come against him, "Have you come out as against a robber, with swords and clubs? **53** When I was with you in the temple daily, you did not stretch out your hands against me. But this is your hour, and the power of darkness." **54** They seized him, and led him away, and brought him into the high priest's house. But Peter followed from a distance. **55** When they had kindled a fire in the middle of the courtyard, and had sat down together, Peter sat among them. **56** A certain servant girl saw him as he sat in the light, and looking intently at him, said, "This man also was with him." **57** But he denied it, saying, "Woman, I do not know him." **58** After a little while someone else saw him, and said, "You also are one of them." But Peter answered, "Man, I am not." **59** After about one hour passed, another confidently affirmed, saying, "Truly this man also was with him, for he is a Galilean." **60** But Peter said, "Man, I do not know what you are talking about." Immediately, while he was still speaking, a rooster crowed. **61** The Lord turned, and looked at Peter. Then Peter remembered the Lord's word, how he said to him, "Before the rooster crows today you will deny me three times." **62** And he went out, and wept bitterly. **63** The men who held Jesus mocked him and beat him. **64** And having blindfolded him, they were striking his face and kept asking him, "Prophesy, who is the one who struck you?" **65** They spoke many other things against him, insulting him. **66** As soon as it was day, the council of the elders of the people gathered together, both chief priests and scribes, and they led him away into their council, saying, **67** "If you are the Christ, tell us." But he said to them, "If I tell you, you won't believe, **68** and if I ask, you will not answer me, or let me go. **69** From now on, the Son of Man will be seated at the right hand of the power of God." **70** They all said, "Are you then the Son of God?" He said to them, "You say that I am." **71** They said, "Why do we need any more witness? For we ourselves have heard from his own mouth."

23 The whole company of them rose up and brought him before Pilate. **2** They began to accuse him, saying, "We found this man subverting our nation, forbidding paying taxes to Caesar, and saying that he himself is the Christ, a king." **3** Pilate asked him, "Are you the King of the Jews?" He answered him, "You say so." **4** Pilate said to the chief priests and the crowds, "I find no basis for a charge against this man." **5** But they insisted, saying, "He stirs up the people, teaching throughout all Judea, beginning from Galilee even to this place." **6** But when Pilate heard it, he asked if the man was a Galilean. **7** When he found out that he was in Herod's jurisdiction, he sent him to Herod, who was also in Jerusalem during those days. **8** Now when Herod saw Jesus, he was exceedingly glad, for he had wanted to see him for a long time, because he had heard about him. He hoped to see some miracle done by him. **9** He questioned him with many words, but he gave no answers. **10** The chief priests and the scribes stood, vehemently accusing him. **11** Herod with his soldiers treated him with contempt and mocked him. Dressing him in luxurious clothing, they sent him back to Pilate. **12** Herod and Pilate became friends with each other that very day, for before that they were enemies with each other. **13** Pilate called together the chief priests and the rulers and the people, **14** and said to them, "You brought this man to me as one that subverts the people, and see, I have examined him before you, and found no basis for a charge against this man concerning those things of which you accuse him. **15** Neither has Herod, for he sent him back to us, and see, nothing worthy of death has been done by him. **16** I will therefore chastise him and release him." **17** (Now he had to release one prisoner to them at the feast.) **18** But they all shouted out together, saying, "Away with this man. Release to us Barabbas!" **19** (one who was thrown into prison for a certain revolt in the city, and for murder.) **20** Then Pilate spoke to them again, wanting to release Jesus, **21** but they shouted, saying, "Crucify. Crucify him." **22** He said to them the third time, "Why? What evil has this man done? I have found no capital crime in him. I will therefore chastise him and release him." **23** But they were urgent with loud voices, asking that he might be crucified. And their voices, and those of the chief priests, prevailed. **24** Pilate decreed that what they asked for should be done. **25** He released him who had been thrown into prison for insurrection and murder, for whom they asked, but he delivered Jesus up to their will. **26** When they led him away, they grabbed one Simon of Cyrene, coming from the country, and placed on him the cross, to carry it after Jesus. **27** A large crowd of the people followed him, including women who also mourned and lamented him. **28** But Jesus, turning to them, said, "Daughters of Jerusalem, do not weep for me, but weep for yourselves and for your children. **29** For look, the days are coming in which they will say, 'Blessed are the barren, the wombs that never bore, and the breasts that never nursed.' **30** Then they will begin to say to the mountains, 'Fall on us,' and to the hills, 'Cover us.' **31** For if they do these things in the green tree, what will be done in the dry?" **32** There were also others, two criminals, led with him to be put to death. **33** When they came to the place that is called The Skull, they crucified him there with the criminals, one on the right and the other on the left. **34** And Jesus said, "Father, forgive them, for they do not know what they are doing." Dividing his garments among them, they cast lots. **35** The people stood watching. The rulers also scoffed at him, saying, "He saved others. Let him save himself, if this is the Christ of God, his Chosen One." **36** The soldiers also mocked him, coming to him and offering him vinegar, **37** and saying, "If you are the King of the Jews, save yourself." **38** An inscription was also written above him: "THIS IS THE KING OF THE JEWS." **39** One of the criminals who hung there insulted him, saying, "Are you not the Christ? Save yourself and us." **40** But the other answered, and rebuking him said, "Do you not even fear God, seeing you are under the same condemnation? **41** And we indeed justly, for we receive the due reward for our deeds; but this man has done nothing wrong." **42** And he said, "Jesus, remember me when you come into your Kingdom." **43** And he said to him, "Assuredly I tell you, today you will be with me in Paradise." **44** And it was now about noon, and darkness came over the whole land until three in the afternoon, **45** for the sun's light failed. And the veil of the temple was torn in two. **46** And Jesus, crying with a loud voice, said, "Father, into your hands I commit my spirit." Having said this, he breathed his last. **47** When the centurion saw what was done, he glorified God, saying, "Certainly this was a righteous man." **48** All the crowds that came together to see this, when they saw the things that were done, returned home beating their breasts. **49** All his acquaintances, and the women who followed with him from Galilee, stood at a distance, watching these things. **50** And look, a man named Joseph, who was a member of the council, a good and righteous man **51** (he had not consented to their counsel and deed), from Arimathaea, a city of the Judeans, who was also waiting for the Kingdom of God: **52** this man went to Pilate, and asked for the body of Jesus. **53** He took it down, and wrapped it in a linen cloth, and placed him in a tomb that was cut in stone, where no one had ever been placed. **54** It was the day of the Preparation, and the Sabbath was drawing near. **55** The women, who had come with him out of Galilee, followed after, and saw the tomb, and how his body was placed. **56** They returned, and prepared spices and ointments. On the Sabbath they rested according to the commandment.

24 But on the first day of the week, at early dawn, they came to the tomb, bringing the spices which they had prepared. **2** They found the stone rolled away from the tomb. **3** They entered in, and did not find the body of the Lord Jesus. **4** It happened, while they were greatly perplexed about this, look, two men stood by them in dazzling clothing. **5** Becoming terrified, they bowed their faces down to the earth. They said to them, "Why do you seek the living among the dead? **6** He is not here, but is risen. Remember what he told you when he was still in Galilee, **7** saying that the Son of Man must be delivered up into the hands of sinful men, and be crucified, and the third day rise again?" **8** Then they remembered his words. **9** And returning from the tomb, they told all these things to the eleven and to all the rest. **10** Now they were Mary Magdalene and Joanna and Mary the mother of James and the other women with them who told these things to the apostles. **11** These words seemed to them to be nonsense, and they did not believe them. **12** But Peter got up and ran to the tomb. Stooping and looking in, he saw the strips of linen by themselves, and he departed to his home, wondering what had happened. **13** And look, two of them were going that very day to a village named Emmaus, which was about seven miles from Jerusalem. **14** They talked with each other about all of these things which had happened. **15** It happened, while they talked and questioned together, that Jesus himself came near, and went with them. **16** But their eyes were kept from recognizing him. **17** And he said to them, "What are these words that you are exchanging with each other as you walk?" And they stood still, looking sad. **18** One of them, named Cleopas, answered him, "Are you the only stranger in Jerusalem who does not know the things which have happened there in these days?" **19** He said to them, "What things?" They said to him, "The things concerning Jesus, the Nazarene, a man who was a prophet mighty in deed and word before God and all the people; **20** and how the chief priests and our rulers delivered him up to be condemned to death, and crucified him. **21** But we were hoping that it was he who would redeem Israel. Yes, and besides all this, it is now the third day since these things happened. **22** Also, certain women of our company amazed us, having arrived early at the tomb; **23** and when they did not find his body, they came saying that they had also seen a vision of angels, who said that he was alive. **24** Some of us went to the tomb, and found it just like the women had said, but they did not see him." **25** Then he said to them, "O foolish ones, and slow of heart to believe in all that the prophets have spoken. **26** Did not the Christ have to suffer these things and to enter into his glory?" **27** Beginning from Moses and from all the prophets, he explained to them in all the Scriptures the things concerning himself. **28** They drew near to the village, where they were going, and he acted like he would go further. **29** They urged him, saying, "Stay with us, for it is almost evening, and the day is almost over." He went in to stay with them. **30** It happened, that when he had sat down at the table with them, he took the bread and gave thanks. Breaking it, he gave to them. **31** Their eyes were opened, and they recognized him, and he vanished out of their sight. **32** And they said to one another, "Weren't our hearts burning within us, while he spoke to us along the way, and while he opened the Scriptures to us?" **33** They rose up that very hour, returned to Jerusalem, and found the eleven gathered together, and those who were with them, **34** saying, "The Lord is risen indeed, and has appeared to Simon." **35** They related the things that happened along the way, and how he was recognized by them in the breaking of the bread. **36** As they said these things, Jesus himself stood among them, and said to them, "Peace be to you." **37** But they were terrified and filled with fear, and supposed that they had seen a spirit. **38** He said to them, "Why are you troubled? Why do doubts arise in your hearts? **39** See my hands and my feet, that it is truly me. Touch me and see, for a spirit does not have flesh and bones, as you see that I have." **40** When he had said this, he showed them his hands and his feet. **41** While they still did not believe for joy, and wondered, he said to them, "Do you have anything here to eat?" **42** And they gave him a piece of a broiled fish. **43** And he took it and ate in front of them. **44** And he said to them, "This is what I told you, while I was still with you, that all things which are written in the Law of Moses, the Prophets, and the Psalms, concerning me must be fulfilled." **45** Then he opened their minds, that they might understand the Scriptures. **46** He said to them, "Thus it is written, for the Christ to suffer and to rise from the dead the third day, **47** and that repentance leading to forgiveness of sins should be preached in his name to all the nations, beginning at Jerusalem. **48** You are witnesses of these things. **49** And look, I send forth the promise of my Father on you. But wait in the city until you are clothed with power from on high." **50** He led them out as far as Bethany, and he lifted up his hands, and blessed them. **51** It happened, while he blessed them, that he departed from them, and was carried up into heaven. **52** They worshiped him, and returned to Jerusalem with great joy, **53** and were continually in the temple, praising and blessing God.

John

1 In the beginning was the Word, and the Word was with God, and the Word was God. **2** He was in the beginning with God. **3** All things were made through him, and apart from him nothing was made that has been made. **4** In him was life, and the life was the light of humanity. **5** And the light shines in the darkness, and the darkness hasn't overcome it. **6** There came a man, sent from God, whose name was John. **7** He came as a witness to testify about the light, that all might believe through him. **8** He was not the light, but was sent that he might testify about the light. **9** The true light that enlightens everyone was coming into the world. **10** He was in the world, and the world was made through him, but the world did not recognize him. **11** He came to his own, and those who were his own did not receive him. **12** But as many as received him, to them he gave the right to become God's children, to those who believe in his name, **13** who were born not of blood, nor of the will of the flesh, nor of the will of man, but of God. **14** And the Word became flesh and lived among us, and we saw his glory, such glory as of the one and only of the Father, full of grace and truth. **15** John testified about him and shouted out, saying, "This was the one of whom I said, 'He who comes after me has surpassed me, for he was before me.'" **16** For of his fullness we all received, and grace upon grace. **17** For the Law was given through Moses, grace and truth came through Jesus Christ. **18** No one has seen God at any time. The only Son, who is at the Father's side, has made him known. **19** And this is John's testimony, when the Jewish leaders sent priests and Levites from Jerusalem to ask him, "Who are you?" **20** And he confessed, and did not deny, but he confessed, "I am not the Christ." **21** And they asked him, "What then? Are you Elijah?" And he said, "I am not." "Are you the Prophet?" And he answered, "No." **22** They said therefore to him, "Who are you? Give us an answer to take back to those who sent us. What do you say about yourself?" **23** He said, "I am the voice of one crying in the wilderness, 'Make straight the way of the Lord,' as Isaiah the prophet said." **24** (Now they had been sent from the Pharisees.) **25** And they asked him, "Why then do you baptize, if you are not the Christ, nor Elijah, nor the Prophet?" **26** John answered them, saying, "I baptize in water, but among you stands one whom you do not know. **27** He is the one who comes after me, whose sandal strap I'm not worthy to loosen." **28** These things were done in Bethany across the Jordan, where John was baptizing. **29** The next day, he saw Jesus coming to him, and said, "Look, the Lamb of God, who takes away the sin of the world. **30** This is he of whom I said, 'After me comes a man who ranks ahead of me, because he existed before me.' **31** I did not know him, but for this reason I came baptizing in water: that he would be revealed to Israel." **32** And John testified, saying, "I saw the Spirit descending like a dove out of heaven, and it remained on him. **33** And I did not recognize him, but he who sent me to baptize in water, he said to me, 'On whomever you will see the Spirit descending, and remaining on him, this is he who baptizes in the Holy Spirit.' **34** And I have seen and have testified that this is the Chosen One of God." **35** Again, the next day, John was standing with two of his disciples, **36** and he looked at Jesus as he walked, and said, "Look, the Lamb of God." **37** And the two disciples heard him say this, and they followed Jesus. **38** And Jesus turned and saw them following, and said to them, "What are you looking for?" They said to him, "Rabbi" (which translated means Teacher), "where are you staying?" **39** He said to them, "Come, and you will see." They came and saw where he was staying, and they stayed with him that day. It was about four in the afternoon. **40** One of the two who heard John, and followed him, was Andrew, Simon Peter's brother. **41** He first found his own brother, Simon, and said to him, "We have found the Messiah." (which is translated, Christ). **42** He brought him to Jesus. Jesus looked at him, and said, "You are Simon the son of John. You will be called Cephas" (which is translated, Peter). **43** On the next day, he was determined to go out into Galilee, and he found Philip. And Jesus said to him, "Follow me." **44** Now Philip was from Bethsaida, of the city of Andrew and Peter. **45** Philip found Nathanael, and said to him, "We have found him of whom Moses in the Law and the Prophets wrote: Jesus of Nazareth, the son of Joseph." **46** And Nathanael said to him, "Can any good thing come out of Nazareth?" Philip said to him, "Come and see." **47** Jesus saw Nathanael coming to him, and said about him, "Look, a true Israelite in whom there is no deceit." **48** Nathanael said to him, "How do you know me?" Jesus answered him, "Before Philip called you, when you were under the fig tree, I saw you." **49** Nathanael answered him, "Rabbi, you are the Son of God. You are King of Israel." **50** Jesus answered him, "Because I told you, 'I saw you underneath the fig tree,' do you believe? You will see greater things than these." **51** And he said to him, "Truly, truly, I tell you, you will see heaven opened, and the angels of God ascending and descending on the Son of Man."

2 And the third day there was a wedding in Cana of Galilee, and the mother of Jesus was there. **2** Now Jesus also was invited, with his disciples, to the wedding. **3** And when the wine ran out, Jesus' mother said to him, "They have no wine." **4** Jesus said to her, "Woman, what does that have to do with you and me? My hour has not yet come." **5** His mother said to the servants, "Whatever he says to you, do it." **6** Now there were six stone water jars set there after the Jewish manner of purifying, containing two or three metretes apiece. **7** Jesus said to them, "Fill the water jars with water." They filled them up to the brim. **8** He said to them, "Now draw some out, and take it to the ruler of the feast." So they took it. **9** When the ruler of the feast tasted the water now become wine, and did not know where it came from (but the servants who had drawn the water knew), the ruler of the feast called the bridegroom, **10** and said to him, "Everyone serves the good wine first, and when the guests have drunk freely, then that which is worse. You have kept the good wine until now." **11** This beginning of his signs Jesus did in Cana of Galilee, and revealed his glory; and his disciples believed in him. **12** After this, he went down to Capernaum, he, and his mother and brothers, and his disciples; and they stayed there a few days. **13** The Jewish Passover was near, and Jesus went up to Jerusalem. **14** And he found in the temple those who sold oxen, sheep, and doves, and the money changers sitting. **15** And he made a whip of cords, and threw all out of the temple, both the sheep and the oxen; and he poured out the changers' money, and overthrew their tables. **16** To those who sold the doves, he said, "Take these things out of here. Do not make my Father's house a marketplace." **17** His disciples remembered that it was written, "Zeal for your house will consume me." **18** The Jewish leaders therefore answered him, "What sign do you show us, seeing that you do these things?" **19** Jesus answered them, "Destroy this temple, and in three days I will raise it up." **20** The Jewish leaders therefore said, "It has taken forty-six years to build this temple, and will you raise it up in three days?" **21** But he spoke of the temple of his body. **22** When therefore he was raised from the dead, his disciples remembered that he said this, and they believed the Scripture, and the word which Jesus had said. **23** Now when he was in Jerusalem at the Passover, during the feast, many believed in his name, after seeing his signs which he did. **24** But Jesus did not trust himself to them, because he knew everyone, **25** and because he did not need anyone to testify concerning man; for he himself knew what was in man.

3 Now there was a man of the Pharisees named Nicodemus, a ruler of the Jewish people. **2** This man came to him at night, and said to him, "Rabbi, we know that you are a teacher come from God, for no one can do these signs that you do, unless God is with him." **3** Jesus answered him, "Truly, truly, I tell you, unless one is born again he cannot see the Kingdom of God." **4** Nicodemus said to him, "How can anyone be born when he is old? Can he enter a second time into his mother's womb, and be born?" **5** Jesus answered, "Truly, truly, I tell you, unless one is born of water and Spirit he cannot enter into the Kingdom of God. **6** That which is born of the flesh is flesh. That which is born of the Spirit is spirit. **7** Do not be surprised that I said to you, 'You must be born again.' **8** The wind blows where it wants to, and you hear its sound, but do not know where it comes from and where it is going. So is everyone who is born of the Spirit." **9** Nicodemus answered and said to him, "How can these things be?" **10** Jesus answered him, "Are you the teacher of Israel, and do not understand these things? **11** Truly, truly, I tell you, we speak that which we know, and testify of that which we have seen, but you do not accept our testimony. **12** If I told you earthly things and you do not believe, how will you believe if I tell you heavenly things? **13** And no one has ascended into heaven, but he who descended out of heaven, the Son of Man, who is in heaven. **14** And as Moses lifted up the serpent in the wilderness, even so must the Son of Man be lifted up, **15** that whoever believes in him may have consummate (aiōnios g166) life. **16** For God so loved the world, that he gave his only begotten Son, that whoever believes in him should not perish, but have consummate (aiōnios g166) life. **17** For God did not send his Son into the world to judge the world, but that the world should be saved through him. **18** The one who believes in him is not judged, but the one who does not believe has been judged already, because he has not believed in the name of the only Son of God. **19** This is the judgment, that the light has come into the world, and people loved the darkness rather than the light, because their works were evil. **20** For everyone who does evil hates the light, and does not come to the light, so that his works will not be exposed. **21** But the one who does the truth comes to the light, that his works may be revealed, that they have been done in God." **22** After these things, Jesus came with his disciples into the land of Judea. He stayed there with them, and baptized. **23** Now John also was baptizing in Aenon near Salim, because there was much water there. They came, and were baptized. **24** For John was not yet thrown into prison. **25** Now a dispute arose between John's disciples with a Jew about purification. **26** And they came to John, and said to him, "Rabbi, he who was with you beyond the Jordan, to whom you have testified, look, he is baptizing, and everyone is coming to him." **27** John answered, "No one can receive anything, unless it has been given to him from heaven. **28** You yourselves bear me witness that I said, 'I am not the Christ,' but, 'I have been sent before him.' **29** He who has the bride is the bridegroom; but the friend of the bridegroom, who stands and hears him, rejoices greatly because of the bridegroom's voice. So this joy of mine is now complete. **30** He must increase, but I must decrease. **31** He who comes from above is above all. He who is from the earth belongs to the earth, and speaks of the earth. He who comes from heaven is above all. **32** What he has seen and heard, of that he testifies; and no one receives his witness. **33** He who has received his witness has set his seal to this, that God is true. **34** For he whom God has sent speaks the words of God; for he does not give the Spirit by measure. **35** The Father loves the Son, and has given all things into his hand. **36** One who believes in the Son has consummate (aiōnios g166) life, but one who disobeys the Son will not see life, but the wrath of God remains on him."

4 Therefore when Jesus knew that the Pharisees had heard, "Jesus is making and baptizing more disciples than John" **2** (although Jesus himself did not baptize, but his disciples), **3** he left Judea, and departed again into Galilee. **4** He needed to pass through Samaria. **5** So he came to a city of Samaria, called Sychar, near the parcel of ground that Jacob gave to his son, Joseph. **6** Jacob's well was there. Jesus therefore, being tired from his journey, sat down by the well. It was about the sixth hour. **7** A woman of Samaria came to draw water. Jesus said to her, "Give me a drink." **8** For his disciples had gone away into the city to buy food. **9** The Samaritan woman therefore said to him, "How can you, being a Jew, ask for a drink from me, a Samaritan woman?" (For Jews have no dealings with Samaritans.) **10** Jesus answered her, "If you knew the gift of God, and who it is who says to you, 'Give me a drink,' you would have asked him, and he would have given you living water." **11** The woman said to him, "Sir, you have nothing to draw with, and the well is deep. From where do you get that living water? **12** Are you greater than our father, Jacob, who gave us the well, and drank of it himself, as did his children, and his livestock?" **13** Jesus answered her, "Everyone who drinks of this water will thirst again, **14** but whoever drinks of the water that I will give him by no means will thirst for the age (aiōn g165); but the water that I will give him will become in him a well of water springing up to consummate (aiōnios g166) life." **15** The woman said to him, "Sir, give me this water, so that I do not get thirsty, neither come all the way here to draw." **16** He said to her, "Go, call your husband, and come here." **17** The woman answered and said to him, "I have no husband." Jesus said to her, "You said well, 'I have no husband,' **18** for you have had five husbands; and he whom you now have is not your husband. This you have said truly." **19** The woman said to him, "Sir, I perceive that you are a prophet. **20** Our fathers worshiped in this mountain, and you say that in Jerusalem is the place where people ought to worship." **21** Jesus said to her, "Woman, believe me, the hour comes, when neither in this mountain, nor in Jerusalem, will you worship the Father. **22** You worship that which you do not know. We worship that which we know; for salvation is from the Jews. **23** But the hour comes, and now is, when the true worshippers will worship the Father in spirit and truth, for the Father seeks such to be his worshippers. **24** God is spirit, and those who worship him must worship in spirit and truth." **25** The woman said to him, "I know that Messiah comes," (he who is called Christ). "When he has come, he will declare to us all things." **26** Jesus said to her, "I am he, the one who speaks to you." **27** At this, his disciples came. They were surprised that he was speaking with a woman; yet no one said, "What are you looking for?" or, "Why do you speak with her?" **28** So the woman left her water pot, and went away into the city, and said to the people, **29** "Come, see a man who told me everything that I did. Can this be the Christ?" **30** They went out of the city, and were coming to him. **31** In the meanwhile, the disciples urged him, saying, "Rabbi, eat." **32** But he said to them, "I have food to eat that you do not know about." **33** The disciples therefore said one to another, "Has anyone brought him something to eat?" **34** Jesus said to them, "My food is to do the will of him who sent me, and to accomplish his work. **35** Do you not say, 'There are yet four months until the harvest?' Look, I tell you, lift up your eyes and see the fields, that they are white for harvest already. **36** He who reaps receives wages and gathers fruit to consummate (aiōnios g166) life; that both he who sows and he who reaps may rejoice together. **37** For in this the saying is true, 'One sows, and another reaps.' **38** I sent you to reap that for which you have not labored. Others have labored, and you have entered into their labor." **39** From that city many of the Samaritans believed in him because of the word of the woman, who testified, "He told me everything that I did." **40** So when the Samaritans came to him, they asked him to stay with them. He stayed there two days. **41** Many more believed because of his word. **42** They said to the woman, "Now we believe, not because of your speaking; for we have heard for ourselves, and know that this is indeed the Savior of the world." **43** After the two days he went out from there and went into Galilee. **44** For Jesus himself testified that a prophet has no honor in his own country. **45** So when he came into Galilee, the Galileans received him, having seen all the things that he did in Jerusalem at the feast, for they also went to the feast. **46** Jesus came therefore again to Cana of Galilee, where he made the water into wine. There was a certain nobleman whose son was sick at Capernaum. **47** When he heard that Jesus had come out of Judea into Galilee, he went to him, and pleaded with him that he would come down and heal his son, for he was close to death. **48** Jesus therefore said to him, "Unless you see signs and wonders, you will in no way believe." **49** The nobleman said to him, "Sir, come down before my child dies." **50** Jesus said to him, "Go your way. Your son lives." The man believed the word that Jesus spoke to him, and he went his way. **51** As he was now going down, his servants met him, saying that his son was alive. **52** So he inquired of them the hour when he began to get better. They said therefore to him, "Yesterday at one in the afternoon, the fever left him." **53** So the father knew that it was at that hour in which Jesus said to him, "Your son lives." He believed, as did his whole house. **54** This is again the second sign that Jesus did, having come out of Judea into Galilee.

5 After these things, there was a Jewish festival, and Jesus went up to Jerusalem. **2** Now in Jerusalem by the sheep area there is a pool, which is called in Hebrew, "Beth Hesda," having five porches. **3** In these lay a multitude of those who were sick, blind, lame, or paralyzed. **5** A certain man was there, who had been sick for thirty-eight years. **6** When Jesus saw him lying there, and knew that he had been sick for a long time, he asked him, "Do you want to be made well?" **7** The sick man answered him, "Sir, I have no one to put me into the pool when the water is stirred up, but while I'm coming, another steps down before me." **8** Jesus said to him, "Arise, take up your mat, and walk." **9** Immediately, the man was made well, and took up his mat and walked. Now it was the Sabbath on that day. **10** So the Jewish leaders said to him who was cured, "It is the Sabbath. It is not lawful for you to carry the mat." **11** But he answered them, "The one who made me well, that one said to me, 'Take up your mat, and walk.'" **12** Then they asked him, "Who is the man who said to you to pick it up and walk?" **13** But the one who was healed did not know who it was, for Jesus had withdrawn, a crowd being in the place. **14** Afterward Jesus found him in the temple, and said to him, "See, you are made well. Sin no more, so that nothing worse happens to you." **15** The man went away, and told the Jewish leaders that it was Jesus who had made him well. **16** For this cause the Jewish leaders persecuted Jesus, because he did these things on the Sabbath. **17** But he answered them, "My Father is still working, so I am working, too." **18** For this cause therefore the Jewish leaders sought all the more to kill him,

John

because he not only broke the Sabbath, but also called God his own Father, making himself equal with God. **19** Jesus therefore answered them, "Truly, truly, I tell you, the Son can do nothing of himself, but what he sees the Father doing. For whatever things he does, these the Son also does likewise. **20** For the Father loves the Son, and shows him all things that he himself does. He will show him greater works than these, so that you may marvel. **21** For as the Father raises the dead and gives them life, even so the Son also gives life to whom he desires. **22** For the Father judges no one, but he has given all judgment to the Son, **23** that all may honor the Son, even as they honor the Father. Whoever does not honor the Son does not honor the Father who sent him. **24** "Truly, truly, I tell you, he who hears my word and believes him who sent me has consummate **(aiōnios g166)** life, and does not come into judgment, but has passed out of death into life. **25** Truly, truly, I tell you, the hour comes, and now is, when the dead will hear the Son of God's voice; and those who hear will live. **26** For as the Father has life in himself, even so he gave to the Son also to have life in himself. **27** He also gave him authority to execute judgment, because he is the Son of Man. **28** Do not be amazed at this, for the hour comes, in which all that are in the tombs will hear his voice, **29** and will come out; those who have done good, to the resurrection of life; and those who have done evil, to the resurrection of judgment. **30** I can of myself do nothing. As I hear, I judge, and my judgment is righteous; because I do not seek my own will, but the will of the One who sent me. **31** "If I testify about myself, my witness is not valid. **32** It is another who testifies about me. I know that the testimony which he testifies about me is true. **33** You have sent to John, and he has testified to the truth. **34** But the testimony which I receive is not from man. However, I say these things that you may be saved. **35** He was the burning and shining lamp, and you were willing to rejoice for a while in his light. **36** But the testimony which I have is greater than that of John, for the works which the Father gave me to accomplish, the very works that I do, testify about me, that the Father has sent me. **37** The Father himself, who sent me, has testified about me. You have neither heard his voice at any time, nor seen his form. **38** You do not have his word living in you; because you do not believe him whom he sent. **39** You search the Scriptures, because you think that in them you have consummate **(aiōnios g166)** life; and these are they which testify about me. **40** But you are unwilling to come to me so that you may have life. **41** I do not receive glory from people. **42** But I know you, that you do not have God's love in yourselves. **43** I have come in my Father's name, and you do not receive me. If another comes in his own name, you will receive him. **44** How can you believe, who receive glory from one another, and you do not seek the glory that comes from the only God? **45** "Do not think that I will accuse you to the Father. There is one who accuses you, even Moses, on whom you have set your hope. **46** For if you believed Moses, you would believe me; for he wrote about me. **47** But if you do not believe his writings, how will you believe my words?"

6 After these things, Jesus went away to the other side of the sea of Galilee, which is also called the Sea of Tiberias. **2** A large crowd followed him, because they saw the signs which he did on those who were sick. **3** Jesus went up into the mountain, and he sat there with his disciples. **4** Now the Passover, the Jewish festival, was near. **5** Jesus therefore lifting up his eyes, and seeing that a large crowd was coming to him, said to Philip, "Where are we to buy bread, that these may eat?" **6** This he said to test him, for he himself knew what he would do. **7** Philip answered him, "Two hundred denarii worth of bread is not sufficient for them, that everyone of them may receive a little." **8** One of his disciples, Andrew, Simon Peter's brother, said to him, **9** "There is a boy here who has five barley loaves and two fish, but what are these among so many?" **10** Jesus said, "Have the people sit down." Now there was much grass in that place. So the men sat down, in number about five thousand. **11** Jesus took the loaves; and having given thanks, he distributed to the disciples, and the disciples to those who were sitting down; likewise also of the fish as much as they desired. **12** When they were filled, he said to his disciples, "Gather up the broken pieces which are left over, that nothing be lost." **13** So they gathered them up, and filled twelve baskets with broken pieces from the five barley loaves, which were left over by those who had eaten. **14** When therefore the people saw the sign which he did, they said, "This is truly the Prophet who comes into the world." **15** Jesus therefore, perceiving that they were about to come and take him by force, to make him king, withdrew again to the mountain by himself. **16** When evening came, his disciples went down to the sea, **17** and they entered into the boat, and were going over the sea to Capernaum. It was now dark, and Jesus had not come to them. **18** The sea was tossed by a great wind blowing. **19** When therefore they had rowed about three or four miles, they saw Jesus walking on the sea, and drawing near to the boat; and they were afraid. **20** But he said to them, "It is I. Do not be afraid." **21** They were willing therefore to receive him into the boat. Immediately the boat was at the land where they were going. **22** On the next day, the crowd that stood on the other side of the sea saw that there was no other boat there, except one, and that Jesus had not entered with his disciples into the boat, but his disciples had gone away alone. **23** Other boats from Tiberias came near to the place where they ate the bread after the Lord had given thanks. **24** When the crowd therefore saw that Jesus was not there, nor his disciples, they themselves got into the boats, and came to Capernaum, seeking Jesus. **25** When they found him on the other side of the sea, they asked him, "Rabbi, when did you come here?" **26** Jesus answered them, "Truly, truly, I tell you, you seek me, not because you saw signs, but because you ate of the loaves, and were filled. **27** Do not work for the food which perishes, but for the food which remains for consummate **(aiōnios g166)** life, which the Son of Man will give to you. For God the Father has sealed him." **28** They said therefore to him, "What must we do, that we may work the works of God?" **29** Jesus answered them, "This is the work of God, that you believe in him whom he has sent." **30** They said therefore to him, "What then do you do for a sign, that we may see, and believe you? What work do you do? **31** Our fathers ate the manna in the wilderness. As it is written, 'He gave them bread out of heaven to eat.'" **32** Jesus therefore said to them, "Truly, truly, I tell you, it was not Moses who gave you the bread out of heaven, but my Father gives you the true bread out of heaven. **33** For the bread of God is that which comes down out of heaven, and gives life to the world." **34** They said therefore to him, "Lord, always give us this bread." **35** Jesus said to them, "I am the bread of life. He who comes to me will not be hungry, and he who believes in me will never be thirsty. **36** But I told you that you have seen me, and yet you do not believe. **37** All those whom the Father gives me will come to me. Him who comes to me I will in no way throw out. **38** For I have come down from heaven, not to do my own will, but the will of him who sent me. **39** This is the will of him who sent me, that of all he has given to me I should lose nothing, but should raise him up at the last day. **40** This is the will of my Father, that everyone who sees the Son, and believes in him, should have consummate (**aiōnios g166**) life; and I will raise him up at the last day." **41** The Jewish people therefore murmured concerning him, because he said, "I am the bread which came down out of heaven." **42** They said, "Is not this Jesus, the son of Joseph, whose father and mother we know? How then does he say, 'I have come down out of heaven?'" **43** Therefore Jesus answered them, "Do not murmur among yourselves. **44** No one can come to me unless the Father who sent me draws him, and I will raise him up in the last day. **45** It is written in the Prophets, 'And they will all be taught by God.' Therefore everyone who hears and learns from the Father comes to me. **46** Not that anyone has seen the Father, except he who is from God. He has seen the Father. **47** Truly, truly, I tell you, he who believes in me has consummate (**aiōnios g166**) life. **48** I am the bread of life. **49** Your fathers ate the manna in the wilderness, and they died. **50** This is the bread which comes down out of heaven, that anyone may eat of it and not die. **51** I am the living bread which came down out of heaven. If anyone eats of this bread, he will live in this age (**aiōn g165**). Indeed, the bread which I will give for the life of the world is my flesh." **52** The Jews therefore argued with one another, saying, "How can this one give us flesh to eat?" **53** Jesus therefore said to them, "Truly I tell you, unless you eat the flesh of the Son of Man and drink his blood, you do not have life in yourselves. **54** He who eats my flesh and drinks my blood has consummate (**aiōnios g166**) life, and I will raise him up at the last day. **55** For my flesh is food indeed, and my blood is drink indeed. **56** He who eats my flesh and drinks my blood lives in me, and I in him. **57** As the living Father sent me, and I live because of the Father; so he who feeds on me, he will also live because of me. **58** This is the bread which came down out of heaven—not as our fathers ate, and died. He who eats this bread will live in this age (**aiōn g165**)." **59** He said these things in the synagogue, as he taught in Capernaum. **60** Therefore many of his disciples, when they heard this, said, "This is a hard saying. Who can listen to it?" **61** But Jesus knowing in himself that his disciples murmured at this, said to them, "Does this cause you to stumble? **62** Then what if you would see the Son of Man ascending to where he was before? **63** It is the spirit who gives life. The flesh profits nothing. The words that I speak to you are spirit, and are life. **64** But there are some of you who do not believe." For Jesus knew from the beginning who they were who did not believe, and who it was who would betray him. **65** He said, "For this cause have I said to you that no one can come to me, unless it is given to him by the Father." **66** At this, many of his disciples went back, and walked no more with him. **67** Jesus said therefore to the twelve, "You do not also want to go away, do you?" **68** Simon Peter answered him, "Lord, to whom would we go? You have the words of consummate (**aiōnios g166**) life. **69** We have come to believe and know that you are the Holy One of God." **70** Jesus answered them, "Did I not choose you, the twelve, and one of you is a devil?" **71** Now he spoke of Judas, the son of Simon Iscariot, for it was he who would betray him, being one of the twelve.

7

After these things, Jesus was walking in Galilee, for he would not walk in Judea, because the Jewish leaders sought to kill him. **2** Now the Jewish festival, the Feast of Tabernacles, was near. **3** So his brothers said to him, "Depart from here, and go into Judea, that your disciples also may see your works that you are doing. **4** For no one does anything in secret when he himself seeks to be known openly. If you do these things, show yourself to the world." **5** For even his brothers did not believe in him. **6** Jesus therefore said to them, "My time has not yet come, but your time is always ready. **7** The world cannot hate you, but it hates me, because I testify about it, that its works are evil. **8** You go up to the feast. I am not yet going up to this feast, because my time is not yet fulfilled." **9** Having said these things to them, he stayed in Galilee. **10** But when his brothers had gone up to the feast, then he also went up, not publicly, but as it were in secret. **11** The Jewish leaders therefore sought him at the feast, and said, "Where is he?" **12** There was much murmuring among the crowds concerning him. Some said, "He is a good man." Others said, "Not so, but he leads the crowd astray." **13** Yet no one spoke openly of him for fear of the Jewish leaders. **14** But when it was now the midst of the feast, Jesus went up into the temple and taught. **15** Then the Jewish leaders were astonished, saying, "How does this man know such writings, having never been educated?" **16** Jesus therefore answered them, "My teaching is not mine, but his who sent me. **17** If anyone desires to do his will, he will know about the teaching, whether it is from God, or if I am speaking from myself. **18** He who speaks from himself seeks his own glory, but he who seeks the glory of him who sent him is true, and no unrighteousness is in him. **19** Did not Moses give you the Law, and yet none of you keeps the Law? Why do you seek to kill me?" **20** The crowd answered, "You have a demon. Who seeks to kill you?" **21** Jesus answered them, "I did one work, and you are all amazed. **22** Moses has given you circumcision (not that it is of Moses, but of the fathers), and on the Sabbath

John

you circumcise a boy. **23** If a boy receives circumcision on the Sabbath, that the Law of Moses may not be broken, are you angry with me, because I made a man completely healthy on the Sabbath? **24** Do not judge according to appearance, but judge righteous judgment." **25** Therefore some of them of Jerusalem said, "Is not this he whom they seek to kill? **26** Look, he speaks openly, and they say nothing to him. Can it be that the rulers indeed know that this is the Christ? **27** However we know where this man comes from, but when the Christ comes, no one will know where he comes from." **28** Jesus therefore called out in the temple, teaching and saying, "You both know me, and know where I am from. I have not come of myself, but he who sent me is true, whom you do not know. **29** I know him, because I am from him, and he sent me." **30** They sought therefore to take him; but no one laid a hand on him, because his hour had not yet come. **31** But many in the crowd believed in him. They said, "When the Christ comes, he won't do more signs than those which this man has done, will he?" **32** The Pharisees heard the crowd murmuring these things concerning him, and the chief priests and the Pharisees sent officers to arrest him. **33** Then Jesus said, "I will be with you a little while longer, then I go to him who sent me. **34** You will seek me, and won't find me; and where I am, you cannot come." **35** The Jewish leaders therefore said among themselves, "Where will this man go that we won't find him? Will he go to the Diaspora among the Greeks, and teach the Greeks? **36** What is this word that he said, 'You will seek me, and won't find me; and where I am, you cannot come'?" **37** Now on the last and greatest day of the feast, Jesus stood and said in a loud voice, "If anyone is thirsty, let him come to me and drink. **38** He who believes in me, as the Scripture has said, from within him will flow rivers of living water." **39** But he said this about the Spirit, which those believing in him were to receive. For the Spirit was not yet given, because Jesus was not yet glorified. **40** Some of the crowd therefore, when they heard these words, said, "This is truly the Prophet." **41** Others said, "This is the Christ." But some said, "What, does the Christ come out of Galilee? **42** Hasn't the Scripture said that the Christ comes of the offspring of David, and from Bethlehem, the village where David was?" **43** So there arose a division in the crowd because of him. **44** Some of them would have arrested him, but no one laid hands on him. **45** The officers therefore came to the chief priests and Pharisees, and they said to them, "Why did you not bring him?" **46** The officers answered, "No one ever spoke like this man." **47** The Pharisees therefore answered them, "You are not also led astray, are you? **48** Have any of the rulers believed in him, or of the Pharisees? **49** But this crowd that does not know the Law is accursed." **50** Nicodemus (he who came to him before, being one of them) said to them, **51** "Does our Law judge a man, unless it first hears from him personally and knows what he does?" **52** They answered him, "Are you also from Galilee? Search, and see that no prophet comes from Galilee." **53** Then everyone went to his own house,

8 but Jesus went to the Mount of Olives. **2** Now very early in the morning, he came again into the temple, and all the people came to him, and he sat down and taught them. **3** Then the scribes and the Pharisees brought a woman taken in adultery, and having set her in the midst, **4** they said to him, "Teacher, we found this woman in adultery, in the very act. **5** Now in the Law, Moses commanded us to stone such. So what do you say?" **6** Now they said this to test him, that they might have something to accuse him of. But Jesus stooped down, and wrote on the ground with his finger. **7** But when they continued asking him, he looked up and said to them, "He who is without sin among you, let him throw the first stone at her." **8** Again he stooped down, and with his finger wrote on the ground. **9** But when they heard it, they went out one by one, beginning from the oldest, even to the last, and he was left alone with the woman where she was, in the middle. **10** Then Jesus, standing up, said to her, "Woman, where are they? Did no one condemn you?" **11** And she said, "No one, Lord." And Jesus said, "Neither do I condemn you. Go, and sin no more." **12** Again, therefore, Jesus spoke to them, saying, "I am the light of the world. He who follows me will not walk in the darkness, but will have the light of life." **13** The Pharisees therefore said to him, "You testify about yourself. Your testimony is not valid." **14** Jesus answered them, "Even if I testify about myself, my testimony is true, for I know where I came from, and where I am going; but you do not know where I came from, or where I am going. **15** You judge according to the flesh. I judge no one. **16** Even if I do judge, my judgment is true, for I am not alone, but I am with the Father who sent me. **17** It's also written in your Law that the testimony of two people is valid. **18** I am one who testifies about myself, and the Father who sent me testifies about me." **19** They said therefore to him, "Where is your Father?" Jesus answered, "You know neither me, nor my Father. If you knew me, you would know my Father also." **20** Jesus spoke these words in the treasury, as he taught in the temple. Yet no one arrested him, because his hour had not yet come. **21** Jesus said therefore again to them, "I am going away, and you will seek me, and you will die in your sins. Where I go, you cannot come." **22** The Jewish leaders therefore said, "Will he kill himself, that he says, 'Where I am going, you cannot come?'" **23** He said to them, "You are from beneath. I am from above. You are of this world. I am not of this world. **24** I said therefore to you that you will die in your sins; for unless you believe that I am he, you will die in your sins." **25** They said therefore to him, "Who are you?" Jesus said to them, "Just what I have been saying to you from the beginning. **26** I have many things to speak and to judge concerning you. However he who sent me is true; and the things which I heard from him, these I say to the world." **27** They did not understand that he spoke to them about the Father. **28** Jesus therefore said to them, "When you have lifted up the Son of Man, then you will know that I am he, and I do nothing of myself, but as the Father taught me, I say these things. **29** He who sent me is with me. The Father hasn't left me alone, for I always do the things that are pleasing to him." **30** As he spoke these things, many believed in him. **31** Jesus therefore said to those Judeans who had believed him, "If you remain in my word, then you are truly my disciples. **32** You will know the truth, and the truth will make you free." **33** They answered him, "We are Abraham's descendants, and have never been in bondage to anyone. How can you say, 'You will be made free?'" **34** Jesus answered them, "Truly I tell you, everyone who commits sin is the slave of sin. **35** A slave does not live in the house for life (aiōn g165). A son remains for a lifetime (aiōn g165). **36** So if the Son sets you free, you will be free indeed. **37** I know that you are Abraham's descendants, yet you seek to kill me, because my word finds no place in you. **38** I say the things which I have seen with my Father; and you also do the things which you have heard from your father." **39** They answered him, "Our father is Abraham." Jesus said to them, "If you were Abraham's children, you would do the works of Abraham. **40** But now you seek to kill me, a man who has told you the truth, which I heard from God. Abraham did not do this. **41** You do the works of your father." They said to him, "We were not born of sexual immorality. We have one Father, God." **42** Therefore Jesus said to them, "If God were your father, you would love me, for I came out and have come from God. For I have not come of myself, but he sent me. **43** Why do you not understand my speech? Because you cannot hear my word. **44** You are of your father, the devil, and you want to do the desires of your father. He was a murderer from the beginning, and does not stand in the truth, because there is no truth in him. When he speaks a lie, he speaks on his own; for he is a liar, and its father. **45** But because I tell the truth, you do not believe me. **46** Which of you convicts me of sin? If I tell the truth, why do you not believe me? **47** He who is of God hears the words of God. For this cause you do not hear, because you are not of God." **48** Then the Judeans answered him, "Do not we say well that you are a Samaritan, and have a demon?" **49** Jesus answered, "I do not have a demon, but I honor my Father, and you dishonor me. **50** But I do not seek my own glory. There is one who seeks and judges. **51** Truly, truly, I tell you, if a person keeps my word, he will never see death in this age (aiōn g165)." **52** Then the Jews said to him, "Now we know that you have a demon. Abraham died, as did the prophets; and you say, 'If a man keeps my word, he will never taste of death in this age (aiōn g165).' **53** Are you greater than our father, Abraham, who died? The prophets died. Who do you make yourself out to be?" **54** Jesus answered, "If I glorify myself, my glory is nothing. It is my Father who glorifies me, of whom you say 'He is our God.' **55** You have not known him, but I know him. If I said, 'I do not know him,' I would be like you, a liar. But I know him, and keep his word. **56** Your father Abraham rejoiced to see my day. He saw it, and was glad." **57** The Judeans therefore said to him, "You are not yet fifty years old, and have you seen Abraham?" **58** Jesus said to them, "Truly, truly, I tell you, before Abraham came into existence, I AM." **59** Therefore they took up stones to throw at him, but Jesus was concealed, and went out of the temple.

9 And as he passed by, he saw a man blind from birth. **2** And his disciples asked him, "Rabbi, who sinned, this man or his parents, that he was born blind?" **3** Jesus answered, "Neither did this man sin, nor his parents; but, that the works of God might be revealed in him. **4** We must work the works of him who sent me, while it is day. The night is coming, when no one can work. **5** While I am in the world, I am the light of the world." **6** When he had said this, he spat on the ground, made mud with the saliva, anointed the blind man's eyes with the mud, **7** and said to him, "Go, wash in the pool of Siloam" (which means "Sent"). So he went away, washed, and came back seeing. **8** The neighbors therefore, and those who saw that he was a beggar before, said, "Is this not the one who used to sit and beg?" **9** Some said, "It is he." Others said, "He looks like him." He said, "I am he." **10** They therefore were asking him, "How were your eyes opened?" **11** He answered, "A man called Jesus made mud, anointed my eyes, and said to me, 'Go to Siloam, and wash.' So I went away and washed, and I received sight." **12** Then they asked him, "Where is he?" He said, "I do not know." **13** They brought him who had been blind to the Pharisees. **14** Now it was a Sabbath on the day when Jesus made the mud and opened his eyes. **15** Again therefore the Pharisees also asked him how he received his sight. He said to them, "He put mud on my eyes, I washed, and I see." **16** Some therefore of the Pharisees said, "This man is not from God, because he does not keep the Sabbath." Others said, "How can a man who is a sinner do such signs?" There was division among them. **17** Therefore they asked the blind man again, "What do you say about him, because he opened your eyes?" He said, "He is a prophet." **18** The Jewish leaders therefore did not believe concerning him, that he had been blind, and had received his sight, until they called the parents of him who had received his sight, **19** and asked them, "Is this your son, who you say was born blind? How then does he now see?" **20** His parents answered them, "We know that this is our son, and that he was born blind; **21** but how he now sees, we do not know; or who opened his eyes, we do not know. He is of age. Ask him. He will speak for himself." **22** His parents said these things because they feared the Jewish leaders; for the Jewish leaders had already agreed that if anyone would confess him as the Christ, he would be put out of the synagogue. **23** Therefore his parents said, "He is of age. Ask him." **24** So they called the man who was blind a second time, and said to him, "Give glory to God. We know that this man is a sinner." **25** He therefore answered, "I do not know if he is a sinner. One thing I do know: that though I was blind, now I see." **26** They said to him, "What did he do to you? How did he open your eyes?" **27** He answered them, "I told you already, and you did not listen. Why do you want to hear it again? You do not also want to become his disciples, do you?" **28** They insulted him and said, "You are his disciple, but we are disciples of Moses. **29** We know that God has spoken to Moses. But as for this man, we do not know where he comes from." **30** The man answered them, "How amazing. You do not know where he comes from, yet he opened my

John

eyes. **31** We know that God does not listen to sinners, but if anyone is a worshipper of God, and does his will, he listens to him. **32** From the age **(aiōn g165)** it has never been heard of that anyone opened the eyes of someone born blind. **33** If this man were not from God, he could do nothing." **34** They answered him, "You were altogether born in sins, and do you teach us?" They threw him out. **35** Jesus heard that they had thrown him out, and finding him, he said, "Do you believe in the Son of Man?" **36** He answered, "Who is he, Lord, that I may believe in him?" **37** Jesus said to him, "You have both seen him, and it is he who speaks with you." **38** He said, "Lord, I believe." and he worshiped him. **39** Jesus said, "I came into this world for judgment, that those who do not see may see; and that those who see may become blind." **40** Those of the Pharisees who were with him heard these things, and said to him, "Are we also blind?" **41** Jesus said to them, "If you were blind, you would have no sin; but since you say, 'We see,' your sin remains.

10 "Truly, truly, I tell you, one who does not enter by the door into the sheep fold, but climbs up some other way, the same is a thief and a robber. **2** But one who enters in by the door is the shepherd of the sheep. **3** The gatekeeper opens the gate for him, and the sheep listen to his voice. He calls his own sheep by name, and leads them out. **4** Whenever he brings out his own sheep, he goes before them, and the sheep follow him, for they know his voice. **5** They will by no means follow a stranger, but will flee from him; for they do not know the voice of strangers." **6** Jesus spoke this parable to them, but they did not understand what he was telling them. **7** Jesus therefore said to them again, "Truly, truly, I tell you, I am the sheep's door. **8** All who came before me are thieves and robbers, but the sheep did not listen to them. **9** I am the door. If anyone enters in by me, he will be saved, and will go in and go out, and will find pasture. **10** The thief only comes to steal, kill, and destroy. I came that they may have life, and may have it abundantly. **11** I am the good shepherd. The good shepherd lays down his life for the sheep. **12** He who is a hired hand and not a shepherd, who does not own the sheep, sees the wolf coming and leaves the sheep and runs away; and the wolf snatches them and scatters them. **13** And the hired hand flees because he is a hired hand and the sheep means nothing to him. **14** I am the good shepherd. I know my own, and my own know me; **15** even as the Father knows me, and I know the Father. I lay down my life for the sheep. **16** I have other sheep, which are not of this fold. I must bring them also, and they will hear my voice. They will become one flock with one shepherd. **17** Therefore the Father loves me, because I lay down my life, that I may take it again. **18** No one takes it away from me, but I lay it down by myself. I have power to lay it down, and I have power to take it again. I received this commandment from my Father." **19** A division arose again among the Jewish people because of these words. **20** Many of them said, "He has a demon, and is insane. Why do you listen to him?" **21** Others said, "These are not the sayings of one possessed by a demon. It is not possible for a demon to open the eyes of the blind, is it?" **22** At that time Hanukkah took place in Jerusalem. **23** It was winter, and Jesus was walking in the temple, in Solomon's porch. **24** The Jewish leaders therefore came around him and said to him, "How long will you keep us in suspense? If you are the Christ, tell us plainly." **25** Jesus answered them, "I told you, and you do not believe. The works that I do in my Father's name, these testify about me. **26** But you do not believe, because you are not of my sheep. **27** As I said to you, my sheep hear my voice, and I know them, and they follow me. **28** I give consummate **(aiōnios g166)** life to them. By no means will they perish in this age **(aiōn g165)**, and no one will snatch them out of my hand. **29** My Father, who has given them to me, is greater than all. No one is able to snatch them out of the Father's hand. **30** I and the Father are one." **31** Therefore the Jewish leaders took up stones again to stone him. **32** Jesus answered them, "I have shown you many good works from the Father. For which of those works do you stone me?" **33** The Jewish leaders answered him, "We do not stone you for a good work, but for blasphemy: because you, being a man, make yourself God." **34** Jesus answered them, "Is it not written in your law, 'I said, you are gods?' **35** If he called them gods, to whom the word of God came (and the Scripture cannot be broken), **36** do you say of him whom the Father sanctified and sent into the world, 'You blaspheme,' because I said, 'I am the Son of God?' **37** If I do not do the works of my Father, do not believe me. **38** But if I do them, though you do not believe me, believe the works; that you may know and understand that the Father is in me, and I in the Father." **39** Now they sought again to seize him, and he went out of their hand. **40** He went away again beyond the Jordan into the place where John was baptizing at first, and there he stayed. **41** Many came to him. They said, "John indeed did no sign, but everything that John said about this man is true." **42** And many believed in him there.

11 Now a certain man was sick, Lazarus from Bethany, of the village of Mary and her sister, Martha. **2** It was that Mary who had anointed the Lord with ointment, and wiped his feet with her hair, whose brother, Lazarus, was sick. **3** The sisters therefore sent to him, saying, "Lord, look, the one you love is sick." **4** But when Jesus heard it, he said, "This sickness is not to death, but for the glory of God, that God's Son may be glorified by it." **5** Now Jesus loved Martha, and her sister, and Lazarus. **6** When therefore he heard that he was sick, he stayed two days in the place where he was. **7** Then after this he said to the disciples, "Let us go into Judea again." **8** The disciples told him, "Rabbi, the Jewish leaders were just trying to stone you, and are you going there again?" **9** Jesus answered, "Are there not twelve hours of daylight? If anyone walks in the day, he does not stumble, because he sees the light of this world. **10** But if anyone walks in the night, he stumbles, because the light is not in him." **11** He said these things, and after that, he said to them, "Our friend, Lazarus, has fallen asleep, but I am going so that I may awake him out of sleep." **12** Then the disciples said to him, "Lord, if he has fallen asleep, he will recover." **13** Now Jesus had spoken of his death, but they thought that he spoke of taking rest in sleep. **14** So Jesus said to them plainly then, "Lazarus is dead. **15** I am glad for your sakes that I was not there, so that you may believe. Nevertheless, let us go to him." **16** Thomas therefore, who is called Didymus, said to his fellow disciples, "Let us go also, that we may die with him." **17** So when Jesus came, he found that he had been in the tomb four days already. **18** Now Bethany was near Jerusalem, about two miles away. **19** Many of the Jewish people had come to Martha and Mary, to console them concerning their brother. **20** Then when Martha heard that Jesus was coming, she went and met him, but Mary stayed in the house. **21** Therefore Martha said to Jesus, "Lord, if you would have been here, my brother would not have died. **22** Even now I know that whatever you ask of God, God will give you." **23** Jesus said to her, "Your brother will rise again." **24** Martha said to him, "I know that he will rise again in the resurrection at the last day." **25** Jesus said to her, "I am the resurrection and the life. He who believes in me will still live, even if he dies. **26** Whoever lives and believes in me will never die in this age (aiōn g165). Do you believe this?" **27** She said to him, "Yes, Lord. I have come to believe that you are the Christ, the Son of God, he who comes into the world." **28** And when she had said this, she went away, and called Mary, her sister, secretly, saying, "The Teacher is here, and is calling you." **29** When she heard this, she arose quickly, and went to him. **30** Now Jesus had not yet come into the village, but was still in the place where Martha met him. **31** Then the Judeans who were with her in the house, and were consoling her, when they saw Mary, that she rose up quickly and went out, followed her, supposing that she was going to the tomb to weep there. **32** Therefore when Mary came to where Jesus was, and saw him, she fell down at his feet, saying to him, "Lord, if you would have been here, my brother would not have died." **33** When Jesus therefore saw her weeping, and the Judeans weeping who came with her, he was deeply moved in spirit and was troubled, **34** and said, "Where have you put him?" They told him, "Lord, come and see." **35** Jesus wept. **36** The Judeans therefore said, "See how he loved him." **37** But some of them said, "Could not this man, who opened the eyes of him who was blind, have also kept this man from dying?" **38** So Jesus, deeply moved again, came to the tomb. Now it was a cave, and a stone lay against it. **39** Jesus said, "Take away the stone." Martha, the sister of the dead man, said to him, "Lord, by this time there is a stench, for he has been dead four days." **40** Jesus said to her, "Did I not tell you that if you believed, you would see God's glory?" **41** So they took away the stone. And Jesus lifted up his eyes, and said, "Father, I thank you that you listened to me. **42** I know that you always listen to me, but because of the crowd that stands around I said this, that they may believe that you sent me." **43** When he had said this, he shouted with a loud voice, "Lazarus, come out." **44** The man who had died came out, bound hand and foot with wrappings, and his face was wrapped around with a cloth. Jesus said to them, "Free him, and let him go."

45 Therefore many of the Judeans, who came to Mary and had seen the things which he did, believed in him. **46** But some of them went away to the Pharisees, and told them the things which Jesus had done. **47** The chief priests therefore and the Pharisees gathered a council, and said, "What are we doing? For this man does many signs. **48** If we leave him alone like this, everyone will believe in him, and the Romans will come and take away both our place and our nation." **49** But a certain one of them, Caiaphas, being high priest that year, said to them, "You know nothing at all, **50** nor do you consider that it is advantageous for you that one man should die for the people, and that the whole nation not perish." **51** Now he did not say this of himself, but being high priest that year, he prophesied that Jesus would die for the nation, **52** and not for the nation only, but that he might also gather together into one the children of God who are scattered abroad. **53** So from that day on they plotted to kill him. **54** Jesus therefore walked no more openly among the Judeans, but departed from there into the country near the wilderness, to a city called Ephraim; and stayed there with his disciples. **55** Now the Jewish Passover was near, and many went up from the country to Jerusalem before the Passover, to purify themselves. **56** Then they sought for Jesus and spoke one with another, as they stood in the temple, "What do you think—that he is not coming to the feast at all?" **57** Now the chief priests and the Pharisees had given orders that if anyone knew where he was, he should report it, that they might arrest him.

12 Then six days before the Passover, Jesus came to Bethany, where Lazarus was, whom Jesus raised from the dead. **2** So they prepared a dinner for him there; and Martha served, but Lazarus was one of those reclining at the table with him. **3** Mary, therefore, took a pound of ointment of pure nard, very precious, and anointed the feet of Jesus, and wiped his feet with her hair. And the house was filled with the fragrance of the ointment. **4** Then Judas Iscariot, one of his disciples, who would betray him, said, **5** "Why was this ointment not sold for three hundred denarii, and given to the poor?" **6** Now he said this, not because he cared for the poor, but because he was a thief, and having the money box, used to steal what was put into it. **7** But Jesus said, "Leave her alone, that she may keep this for the day of my burial. **8** For you always have the poor with you, but you do not always have me." **9** A large crowd therefore of the Judeans learned that he was there, and they came, not for Jesus' sake only, but that they might see Lazarus also, whom he had raised from the dead. **10** But the chief priests plotted to kill Lazarus also, **11** because on account of him many of the Jewish people went away and believed in Jesus. **12** On the next day the large crowd that had come to the feast heard that Jesus was coming to Jerusalem, **13** they took the branches of the palm trees, and went out to meet him, and were shouting, "Hosanna. Blessed is he who comes in the name of the Lord, the King of Israel." **14** And Jesus, having found a young donkey, sat on it. As it is written, **15** "Do not be afraid, daughter of Zion. Look, your King comes, sitting on a donkey's colt." **16** His disciples did not understand these things at first, but when Jesus was glorified, then they remembered that these things were written about him, and that they had done these things to him. **17** The crowd therefore that was with him when he called Lazarus out of the tomb, and raised him from the dead, was testifying about it. **18** For this cause also the crowd went and met him, because they heard that he had done this sign. **19** The Pharisees therefore said among themselves, "See how you accomplish nothing. Look, the whole world has gone after him." **20** Now there were certain Greeks among those that went up to worship at the feast. **21** These, therefore, came to Philip, who was from Bethsaida of Galilee, and asked him, saying, "Sir, we want to see Jesus." **22** Philip came and told Andrew, and in turn, Andrew came with Philip, and they told Jesus. **23** And Jesus answered them, "The time has come for the Son of Man to be glorified. **24** Truly, truly, I tell you, unless a grain of wheat falls into the earth and dies, it remains by itself alone. But if it dies, it bears much fruit. **25** He who loves his life will lose it. He who hates his life in this world will keep it for consummate (**aiōnios g166**) life. **26** If anyone serves me, let him follow me; and where I am, there will my servant also be. If anyone serves me, the Father will honor him. **27** "Now my soul is troubled. And what should I say? 'Father, save me from this hour?' But for this cause I came to this hour. **28** Father, glorify your name." Then there came a voice out of the sky, saying, "I have both glorified it, and will glorify it again." **29** The crowd therefore, who stood by and heard it, said that it had thundered. Others said, "An angel has spoken to him." **30** Jesus answered, "This voice hasn't come for my sake, but for your sakes. **31** Now is the judgment of this world. Now the prince of this world will be cast out. **32** And I, if I am lifted up from the earth, will draw everyone to myself." **33** But he said this, signifying by what kind of death he should die. **34** The crowd answered him, "We have heard out of the law that the Messiah remains for this age (**aiōn g165**). How do you say, 'The Son of Man must be lifted up?' Who is this Son of Man?" **35** Jesus therefore said to them, "Yet a little while the light is with you. Walk while you have the light, that darkness does not overtake you. He who walks in the darkness does not know where he is going. **36** While you have the light, believe in the light, that you may become children of light." Jesus said these things, and he departed and hid himself from them. **37** But though he had done so many signs before them, yet they did not believe in him, **38** that the word of Isaiah the prophet might be fulfilled, which he spoke, "Lord, who has believed our report, and to whom has the arm of the Lord been revealed?" **39** For this cause they could not believe, for Isaiah said again, **40** He has blinded their eyes and hardened their heart, lest they should see with their eyes, and understand with their heart, and turn, and I would heal them. **41** Isaiah said these things because he saw his glory, and spoke of him. **42** Nevertheless even of the rulers many believed in him, but because of the Pharisees they did not confess it, so that they would not be put out of the synagogue, **43** for they loved praise from people more than praise from God. **44** Then Jesus shouted out and said, "Whoever believes in me, believes not in me, but in him who sent me. **45** And he who sees me sees him who sent me. **46** I have come as a light into the world, that whoever believes in me may not remain in the darkness. **47** And if anyone hears my words and does not keep them, I do not judge him. For I came not to judge the world, but to save the world. **48** He who rejects me, and does not accept my words, has one who judges him. The word that I spoke will judge him on the last day. **49** For I spoke not from myself, but the Father who sent me, he gave me a commandment, what I should say, and what I should speak. **50** I know that his commandment is consummate (**aiōnios g166**) life. The things therefore which I speak, even as the Father has said to me, so I speak."

13 Now before the feast of the Passover, Jesus, knowing that his time had come that he would depart from this world to the Father, having loved his own who were in the world, he loved them to the end. **2** And during the meal, the devil had already put into the heart of Judas Iscariot, Simon's son, to betray him. **3** Because he knew that the Father had given all things into his hands, and that he came forth from God, and was going to God, **4** arose from the meal, and removed his outer garments. He took a towel, and wrapped a towel around his waist. **5** Then he poured water into the basin, and began to wash the disciples' feet, and to wipe them with the towel that was wrapped around him. **6** Then he came to Simon Peter. He said to him, "Lord, do you wash my feet?" **7** Jesus answered him, "You do not know what I am doing now, but you will understand later." **8** Peter said to him, "You will never wash my feet in this lifetime (**aiōn g165**)!" Jesus answered him, "If I do not wash you, you have no part with me." **9** Simon Peter said to him, "Lord, not my feet only, but also my hands and my head." **10** Jesus said to him, "Someone who has bathed only needs to have his feet washed, but is completely clean. You are clean, but not all of you." **11** For he knew him who would betray him, therefore he said, "You are not all clean." **12** So when he had washed their feet, put his outer garment back on, and sat down again, he said to them, "Do you know what I have done to you? **13** You call me, 'Teacher' and 'Lord.' You say so correctly, for so I am. **14** If I then, the Lord and the Teacher, have washed your feet, you also ought to wash one another's feet. **15** For I have given you an example, that you also should do as I have done to you. **16** Truly, truly, I tell you, a servant is not greater than his master, neither one who is sent greater than he who sent him. **17** If you know these things, blessed are you if you do them. **18** I do not speak concerning all of you. I know whom I have chosen. But that the Scripture may be fulfilled, 'He who ate my bread has lifted up his heel against me.' **19** I am telling you this now before it happens, so that when it does happen you may believe that I am he. **20** Truly, truly, I tell you, he who receives whomever I send, receives me; and he who receives me, receives him who sent me." **21** When Jesus had said this, he was troubled in spirit, and testified, "Truly, truly, I tell you that one of you will betray me." **22** The disciples looked at one another, perplexed about whom he spoke. **23** One of his disciples, whom Jesus loved, was reclining against Jesus' chest. **24** Simon Peter therefore motioned to him to inquire who it was he was talking about. **25** He, leaning back, as he was, on Jesus' chest, asked him, "Lord, who is it?" **26** Jesus therefore answered, "It is he to whom I will give this piece of bread when I have dipped it." So when he had dipped the piece of bread, he gave it to Judas, the son of Simon Iscariot. **27** After the piece of bread, then Satan entered into him. Then Jesus said to him, "What you do, do quickly." **28** Now none of those reclining knew why he said this to him. **29** For some thought, because Judas had the money box, that Jesus said to him, "Buy what things we need for the feast," or that he should give something to the poor. **30** Therefore, having received the piece of bread, he went out immediately; and it was night. **31** When he had gone out, Jesus said, "Now the Son of Man has been glorified, and God has been glorified in him. **32** If God has been glorified in him, God will also glorify him in himself, and he will glorify him at once. **33** Little children, I will be with you a little while longer. You will seek me, and as I said to the Jewish leaders, 'Where I am going, you cannot come,' so now I tell you. **34** A new commandment I give to you, that you love one another. Just as I have loved you, you also must love one another. **35** By this everyone will know that you are my disciples, if you have love for one another." **36** Simon Peter said to him, "Lord, where are you going?" Jesus answered, "Where I am going, you cannot follow now, but you will follow afterwards." **37** Peter said to him, "Lord, why can I not follow you now? I will lay down my life for you." **38** Jesus answered him, "Will you lay down your life for me? Truly, truly, I tell you, the rooster won't crow until you have denied me three times.

14 "Do not let your heart be troubled. Believe in God. Believe also in me. **2** In my Father's house are many mansions. If it weren't so, I would have told you; for I go to prepare a place for you. **3** And if I go and prepare a place for you, I will come again, and will receive you to myself; that where I am, you may be there also. **4** And you know the way where I am going." **5** Thomas said to him, "Lord, we do not know where you are going. How can we know the way?" **6** Jesus said to him, "I am the way, the truth, and the life. No one comes to the Father except through me. **7** If you know me, you will know my Father also. From now on you do know him and have seen him." **8** Philip said to him, "Lord, show us the Father, and that will be enough for us." **9** Jesus said to him, "Have I been with you all this time, and still you do not know me, Philip? He who has seen me has seen the Father. How can you say, 'Show us the Father?' **10** Do you not believe that I am in the Father, and the Father is in me? The words that I say to you I do not speak from myself; but the Father who lives in me does his works. **11** Believe me that I am in the Father, and the Father is in me; or else believe because of the works themselves. **12** Truly, truly, I tell you, he who believes in me, the works that I do, he will do also; and he will do greater works than these, because I am going to the Father. **13** And whatever you ask in my name, this I will do, that the Father may be glorified in the Son. **14** If you ask me anything in my name, I will do it. **15** If you love me, you will keep my commandments. **16** I will pray to the Father, and he will give you another Comforter, that he may be with you in this age **(aiōn g165)**: **17** the Spirit of truth, whom the world cannot receive; because it neither sees him nor knows him; but you know him, for he lives with you, and will be in you. **18** I will not leave you orphans. I will come to you. **19** Yet a little while, and the world will see me no more; but you will see me. Because I live, you will live also. **20** In that day you will know that I am in my Father, and you in me, and I in you. **21** The one who has my commandments and keeps them is the one who loves me. And the one who loves me will be loved by my Father, and I will love him, and will reveal myself to him." **22** Judas (not Iscariot) said to him, "Lord, what has happened that you are about to reveal yourself to us, and not to the world?" **23** Jesus answered and said to him, "If anyone loves me, he will keep my word; and my Father will love him, and we will come to him and make our dwelling place with him. **24** He who does not love me does not keep my words. The word which you hear is not mine, but the Father's who sent me. **25** All this I have spoken to you while I am still with you. **26** But the Helper, the Holy Spirit, whom the Father will send in my name, he will teach you all things, and will remind you of all that I said to you. **27** Peace I leave with you. My peace I give to you. I do not give to you as the world gives. Do not let your heart be troubled, neither let it be afraid. **28** You heard how I told you, 'I am going away, and I will come to you.' If you loved me, you would rejoice that I am going to the Father; for the Father is greater than I. **29** Now I have told you before it happens so that, when it happens, you may believe. **30** I will not speak with you much longer, for the ruler of this world is coming, and he has no hold on me. **31** But that the world may know that I love the Father, and as the Father commanded me, so I do. Arise, let us go from here.

15 "I am the true vine, and my Father is the gardener. **2** Every branch in me that does not bear fruit, he takes away. Every branch that bears fruit, he prunes, that it may bear more fruit. **3** You are already clean because of the word which I have spoken to you. **4** Remain in me, and I in you. As the branch cannot bear fruit by itself, unless it remains in the vine, so neither can you, unless you remain in me. **5** I am the vine. You are the branches. He who remains in me, and I in him, the same bears much fruit, for apart from me you can do nothing. **6** If anyone does not remain in me, he is thrown out as a branch, and withers; and they gather them, throw them into the fire, and they are burned. **7** If you remain in me, and my words remain in you, ask whatever you desire, and it will be done for you. **8** "In this is my Father glorified, that you bear much fruit and so prove to be my disciples. **9** Even as the Father has loved me, I also have loved you. Remain in my love. **10** If you keep my commandments, you will remain in my love; even as I have kept my Father's commandments, and remain in his love. **11** I have spoken these things to you, that my joy may be in you, and that your joy may be made full. **12** "This is my commandment, that you love one another, even as I have loved you. **13** Greater love has no one than this, that someone lays down his life for his friends. **14** You are my friends, if you do whatever I command you. **15** No longer do I call you servants, for the servant does not know what his master is doing. But I have called you friends, for everything that I heard from my Father I have made known to you. **16** You did not choose me, but I chose you, and appointed you, that you should go and bear fruit, and that your fruit should remain; that whatever you will ask of the Father in my name, he may give it to you. **17** "I command these things to you, that you may love one another. **18** If the world hates you, you know that it has hated me before it hated you. **19** If you were of the world, the world would love its own. But because you are not of the world, since I chose you out of the world, therefore the world hates you. **20** Remember the word that I said to you: 'A servant is not greater than his master.' If they persecuted me, they will also persecute you. If they kept my word, they will keep yours also. **21** But all these things will they do to you because of my name, because they do not know him who sent me. **22** If I had not come and spoken to them, they would not have had sin; but now they have no excuse for their sin. **23** He who hates me hates my Father also. **24** If I had not done among them the works which no one else did, they would not have had sin. But now have they seen and also hated both me and my Father. **25** But this happened so that the word may be fulfilled which is written in their law, 'They hated me without a cause.' **26** "When the Helper has come, whom I will send to you from the Father, the Spirit of truth, who proceeds from the Father, he will testify about me. **27** And you will also testify, because you have been with me from the beginning.

16 "I have said all these things to you so that you may be kept from stumbling. **2** They will put you out of the synagogues, but an hour is coming when whoever kills you will think that he is offering a service to God. **3** They will do these things because they have not known the Father or me. **4** But I have told you these things, so that when their hour comes, you may remember that I told you about them. I did not tell you these things from the beginning, because I was with you. **5** But now I am going to him who sent me, and none of you asks me, 'Where are you going?' **6** But because I have told you these things, sorrow has filled your heart. **7** Nevertheless I tell you the truth: It is to your advantage that I go away, for if I do not go away, the Helper won't come to you. But if I go, I will send him to you. **8** When he has come, he will convict the world about sin, and about righteousness, and about judgment; **9** about sin, because they do not believe in me; **10** about righteousness, because I am going to the Father, and you won't see me any more; **11** about judgment, because the prince of this world has been judged. **12** "I have yet many things to tell you, but you cannot bear them now. **13** However when he, the Spirit of truth, has come, he will guide you into all truth, for he will not speak on his own; but whatever he hears he will speak, and he will declare to you things that are coming. **14** He will glorify me, for he will take from what is mine, and will declare it to you. **15** All things that the Father has are mine; that is why I said that he takes of mine, and will declare it to you. **16** A little while, and you will no longer see me. Again a little while, and you will see me." **17** Some of his disciples therefore said to one another, "What is this that he says to us, 'A little while, and you won't see me, and again a little while, and you will see me;' and, 'Because I go to the Father?'" **18** They said therefore, "What is this that he says, 'A little while?' We do not know what he is saying." **19** Jesus knew that they wanted to ask him, so he said to them, "Do you inquire among yourselves concerning this, that I said, 'A little while, and you won't see me, and again a little while, and you will see me?' **20** Truly, truly, I tell you, that you will weep and lament, but the world will rejoice. You will be sorrowful, but your sorrow will be turned into joy. **21** A woman, when she gives birth, has pain, because her time has come. But when she has delivered the child, she does not remember the anguish any more, for the joy that a human being is born into the world. **22** Therefore you have sorrow now, but I will see you again, and your heart will rejoice, and no one will take your joy away from you. **23** "And in that day you will ask nothing of me. Truly, truly I tell you, whatever you may ask of the Father in my name, he will give it to you. **24** Until now, you have asked nothing in my name. Ask, and you will receive, that your joy may be made full. **25** I have spoken these things to you in figures of speech. The hour is coming when I will no more speak to you in figures of speech, but will tell you plainly about the Father. **26** In that day you will ask in my name, and I am not saying to you that I will ask the Father on your behalf, **27** for the Father himself loves you, because you have loved me, and have believed that I came forth from God. **28** I came forth from the Father and have come into the world. Again, I leave the world, and go to the Father." **29** His disciples said to him, "Look, now you are speaking plainly and not in any figure of speech. **30** Now we know that you know all things and do not need anyone to question you. By this we believe that you came forth from God." **31** Jesus answered them, "Do you now believe? **32** Look, the time is coming, and has come, that you will be scattered, everyone to his own place, and you will leave me alone. But I am not alone, because the Father is with me. **33** I have told you these things, that in me you may have peace. In the world you have oppression; but cheer up. I have overcome the world."

17 Jesus said these things, and lifting up his eyes to heaven, he said, "Father, the time has come. Glorify your Son, that your Son may also glorify you; **2** even as you gave him authority over all flesh, so he will give consummate **(aiōnios g166)** life to all whom you have given him. **3** This is consummate **(aiōnios g166)** life, that they may know you, the only true God, and him whom you sent, Jesus Christ. **4** I glorified you on the earth. I have accomplished the work which you have given me to do. **5** Now, Father, glorify me with your own self with the glory which I had with you before the world existed. **6** I revealed your name to the people whom you have given me out of the world. They were yours, and you have given them to me. They have kept your word. **7** Now they have known that all things whatever you have given me are from you, **8** for the words which you have given me I have given to them, and they received them, and knew for sure that I came forth from you, and they have believed that you sent me. **9** I pray for them. I do not pray for the world, but for those whom you have given me, for they are yours. **10** All things that are mine are yours, and yours are mine, and I am glorified in them. **11** I am no more in the world, but these are in the world, and I am coming to you. Holy Father, keep them through your name which you have given me, that they may be one, even as we are. **12** While I was with them, I kept them in your name which you have given me, and I guarded them, and not one of them perished, except the son of destruction, that the Scripture might be fulfilled. **13** But now I come to you, and I say these things in the world, that they may have my joy made full in themselves. **14** I have given them your word. The world hated them, because they are not of the world, even as I am not of the world. **15** I pray not that you would take them from the world, but that you would keep them from the evil one. **16** They are not of the world even as I am not of the world. **17** Sanctify them in the truth. Your word is truth. **18** As you sent me into the world, even so I have sent them into the world. **19** For their sakes I sanctify myself, that they themselves also may be sanctified in truth. **20** Not for these only do I pray, but for those also who believe in me through their word, **21** that they may all be one; even as you, Father, are in me, and I in you, that they also may be in us; that the world may believe that you sent me. **22** The glory which you have given me, I have given to them; that they may be one, even as we are one; **23** I in them, and you in me, that they may be perfected into one; that the world may know that you sent me, and loved them, even as you loved me. **24** Father, I desire that they also whom you have given me be with me where I am, that they may see my glory, which you have given me, for you loved me before the foundation of the world. **25** Righteous Father, the world hasn't known you, but I knew you; and these knew that you sent me. **26** I made known to them your name, and will make it known; that the love with which you loved me may be in them, and I in them."

18 When Jesus had spoken these words, he went out with his disciples over the wadi of the Kidron, where there was a garden, into which he and his disciples entered. **2** Now Judas, who betrayed him, also knew the place, for Jesus often met there with his disciples. **3** Judas then, having taken a detachment of soldiers and officers from the chief priests and the Pharisees, came there with lanterns, torches, and weapons. **4** Jesus therefore, knowing all the things that were happening to him, went forth, and said to them, "Who are you looking for?" **5** They answered him, "Jesus the Nazorean." Jesus said to them, "I AM." Judas also, who betrayed him, was standing with them. **6** When therefore he said to them, "I AM," they went backward, and fell to the ground. **7** Again therefore he asked them, "Who are you looking for?" They said, "Jesus the Nazorean." **8** Jesus answered, "I told you that I AM. If therefore you seek me, let these go their way," **9** that the word might be fulfilled which he spoke, "Of those whom you have given me, I have lost none." **10** Simon Peter therefore, having a sword, drew it, and struck the high priest's servant, and cut off his right ear. The servant's name was Malchus. **11** Jesus therefore said to Peter, "Put the sword into its sheath. Am I not to drink the cup which the Father has given me?" **12** So the detachment, the commanding officer, and the officers of the Jewish leaders, seized Jesus and bound him, **13** and led him to Annas first, for he was father-in-law to Caiaphas, who was high priest that year. **14** Now it was Caiaphas who advised the Jewish leaders that it was expedient that one man should perish for the people. **15** Simon Peter followed Jesus, as did another disciple. Now that disciple was known to the high priest, and entered in with Jesus into the court of the high priest; **16** but Peter was standing at the door outside. So the other disciple, who was known to the high priest, went out and spoke to her who kept the door, and brought in Peter. **17** Then the maid who kept the door said to Peter, "Are you also one of this man's disciples?" He said, "I am not." **18** Now the servants and the officers were standing there, having made a fire of coals, for it was cold. They were warming themselves. Peter was with them, standing and warming himself. **19** The high priest therefore asked Jesus about his disciples, and about his teaching. **20** Jesus answered him, "I spoke openly to the world. I always taught in synagogues, and in the temple, where all the Jewish people come together. I said nothing in secret. **21** Why do you ask me? Ask those who have heard what I spoke to them; surely they know what I said." **22** When he had said this, one of the officers standing by slapped Jesus with his hand, saying, "Do you answer the high priest like that?" **23** Jesus answered him, "If I have spoken evil, testify of the evil; but if well, why do you beat me?" **24** Annas sent him bound to Caiaphas, the high priest. **25** Now Simon Peter was standing and warming himself. They said therefore to him, "You are not also one of his disciples, are you?" He denied it, and said, "I am not." **26** One of the servants of the high priest, being a relative of him whose ear Peter had cut off, said, "Did I not see you in the garden with him?" **27** Peter therefore denied it again, and immediately the rooster crowed. **28** They led Jesus therefore from Caiaphas into the Praetorium. It was early, and they themselves did not enter into the Praetorium, that they might not be defiled, but might eat the Passover. **29** Pilate therefore went out to them, and said, "What accusation do you bring against this man?" **30** They answered him, "If this man weren't an evildoer, we would not have delivered him up to you." **31** Pilate therefore said to them, "Take him yourselves, and judge him according to your law." Therefore the Jewish leaders said to him, "It is not lawful for us to put anyone to death," **32** that the word of Jesus might be fulfilled, which he spoke, signifying by what kind of death he should die. **33** Pilate therefore entered again into the Praetorium, called Jesus, and said to him, "Are you the King of the Jews?" **34** Jesus answered him, "Do you say this by yourself, or did others tell you about me?" **35** Pilate answered, "I'm not a Jew, am I? Your own nation and the chief priests delivered you to me. What have you done?" **36** Jesus answered, "My Kingdom is not of this world. If my Kingdom were of this world, then my servants would fight, that I would not be delivered to the Jewish leaders. But now my Kingdom is not from here." **37** Pilate therefore said to him, "Are you a king then?" Jesus answered, "You say that I am a king. For this reason I have been born, and for this reason I have come into the world, that I should testify to the truth. Everyone who is of the truth listens to my voice." **38** Pilate said to him, "What is truth?" When he had said this, he went out again to the Jewish leaders, and said to them, "I find no basis for a charge against him. **39** But you have a custom, that I should release someone to you at the Passover. Therefore do you want me to release to you the King of the Jews?" **40** Then they shouted again, saying, "Not this man, but Barabbas." Now Barabbas was a robber.

19 So Pilate then took Jesus, and flogged him. **2** The soldiers twisted thorns into a crown, and put it on his head, and dressed him in a purple garment. **3** And they kept coming up to him and saying, "Greetings, King of the Jews." and they struck him with their hands. **4** Then Pilate went out again, and said to them, "Look, I am bringing him out to you, that you may know that I find no basis for a charge against him." **5** Then Jesus came out, wearing the crown of thorns and the purple garment. Pilate said to them, "Look, here is the man." **6** When therefore the chief priests and the officers saw him, they shouted, saying, "Crucify. Crucify." Pilate said to them, "Take him yourselves, and crucify him, for I find no basis for a charge against him." **7** The Jewish leaders answered him, "We have a law, and by that law he ought to die, because he made himself the Son of God." **8** When therefore Pilate heard this saying, he was more afraid. **9** He entered into the Praetorium again, and said to Jesus, "Where are you from?" But Jesus gave him no answer. **10** Pilate therefore said to him, "Are you not speaking to me? Do you not know that I have power to release you, and have power to crucify you?" **11** Jesus answered, "You would have no power at all against me, unless it were given to you from above. Therefore he who delivered me to you has greater sin." **12** At this, Pilate was seeking to release him, but the Jewish leaders shouted, saying, "If you release this man, you are not Caesar's friend. Everyone who makes himself a king speaks against Caesar." **13** When Pilate therefore heard these words, he brought Jesus out, and sat down on the judgment seat at a place called "The Pavement," but in Hebrew, "Gabbatha." **14** Now it was the Preparation Day of the Passover, at about noon. He said to the Jewish leaders, "Look, here is your King." **15** They shouted, "Away with him. Away with him. Crucify him." Pilate said to them, "Should I crucify your King?" The chief priests answered, "We have no king but Caesar." **16** So then he delivered him to them to be crucified. So they took Jesus. **17** And he went out, carrying the cross himself, to the place called "The Place of a Skull," which is called in Hebrew, "Golgotha," **18** where they crucified him, and with him two others, on either side one, and Jesus in the middle. **19** Pilate wrote a title also, and put it on the cross. There was written, "JESUS THE NAZOREAN, THE KING OF THE JEWS." **20** Therefore many Jews read this title, for the place where Jesus was crucified was near the city; and it was written in Hebrew, in Latin, and in Greek. **21** The chief priests of the Jewish people therefore said to Pilate, "Do not write, 'The King of the Jews,' but, 'he said, I am King of the Jews.'" **22** Pilate answered, "What I have written, I have written." **23** Then the soldiers, when they had crucified Jesus, took his clothes and made four parts, to every soldier a part; and also the tunic. Now the tunic was without seam, woven from the top throughout. **24** Then they said to one another, "Let us not tear it, but cast lots for it to decide whose it will be," that the Scripture might be fulfilled, which says, "They divided my clothes among themselves, and for my clothing they cast a lot." Therefore the soldiers did these things. **25** But there were standing by the cross of Jesus his mother, and his mother's sister, Mary the wife of Cleopas, and Mary Magdalene. **26** Therefore when Jesus saw his mother, and the disciple whom he loved standing there, he said to his mother, "Woman, look, your son." **27** Then he said to the disciple, "Look, your mother." From that hour, the disciple took her to his own home. **28** After this, Jesus, knowing that all things were now finished, that the Scripture might be fulfilled, said, "I am thirsty." **29** Now a vessel full of vinegar was set there; so they put a sponge full of the vinegar on hyssop, and held it at his mouth. **30** When Jesus therefore had received the vinegar, he said, "It is finished." He bowed his head, and gave up his spirit. **31** Therefore the Jewish leaders, because it was the Preparation Day, so that the bodies would not remain on the cross on the Sabbath (for that Sabbath was a special one), asked of Pilate that their legs might be broken, and that they might be taken away. **32** Therefore the soldiers came, and broke the legs of the first, and of the other who was crucified with him; **33** but when they came to Jesus, and saw that he was already dead, they did not break his legs. **34** However one of the soldiers pierced his side with a spear, and immediately blood and water came out. **35** He who has seen has testified, and his testimony is true. He knows that he tells the truth, that you may believe. **36** For these things happened, that the Scripture might be fulfilled, "A bone of him will not be broken." **37** Again another Scripture says, "They will look on him whom they pierced." **38** After these things, Joseph of Arimathaea, being a disciple of Jesus, but secretly for fear of the Jewish leaders, asked of Pilate that he might take away the body of Jesus. Pilate gave him permission. He came therefore and took away his body. **39** Nicodemus, who at first came to Jesus by night, also came bringing a mixture of myrrh and aloes, about seventy-five pounds. **40** So they took the body of Jesus, and bound it in linen cloths with the spices, according to Jewish burial practice. **41** Now in the place where he was crucified there was a garden. In the garden was a new tomb in which no one had ever yet been placed. 42 Then because of the Jewish Preparation Day (for the tomb was nearby) they put Jesus there.

20 Now on the first day of the week, Mary Magdalene went early, while it was still dark, to the tomb, and saw the stone taken away from the tomb. 2 Therefore she ran and came to Simon Peter, and to the other disciple whom Jesus loved, and said to them, "They have taken away the Lord out of the tomb, and we do not know where they have put him." 3 Therefore Peter and the other disciple went out, and they went toward the tomb. 4 They both ran together. The other disciple outran Peter, and came to the tomb first. 5 Stooping and looking in, he saw the linen cloths lying, yet he did not enter in. 6 Then Simon Peter came, following him, and entered into the tomb. He saw the linen cloths lying, 7 and the cloth that had been on his head, not lying with the linen cloths, but rolled up in a place by itself. 8 So then the other disciple who came first to the tomb also entered in, and he saw and believed. 9 For as yet they did not know the Scripture, that he must rise from the dead. 10 So the disciples went away again to their own homes. 11 But Mary was standing outside at the tomb weeping. So, as she wept, she stooped and looked into the tomb, 12 and she saw two angels in white sitting, one at the head, and one at the feet, where the body of Jesus had lain. 13 They told her, "Woman, why are you weeping?" She said to them, "Because they have taken away my Lord, and I do not know where they have put him." 14 When she had said this, she turned around and saw Jesus standing, and did not know that it was Jesus. 15 Jesus said to her, "Woman, why are you weeping? Who are you looking for?" She, supposing him to be the gardener, said to him, "Sir, if you have carried him away, tell me where you have put him, and I will take him away." 16 Jesus said to her, "Mary." She turned and said to him in Hebrew, "Rabboni." which is to say, "Teacher." 17 Jesus said to her, "Do not touch me, for I have not yet ascended to the Father; but go to my brothers, and tell them, 'I am ascending to my Father and your Father, to my God and your God.'" 18 Mary Magdalene came and told the disciples, "I have seen the lord," and that he had said these things to her. 19 When therefore it was evening, on that day, the first day of the week, and when the doors were locked where the disciples were, for fear of the Jewish leaders, Jesus came and stood in the midst, and said to them, "Peace be to you." 20 When he had said this, he showed them his hands and his side. The disciples therefore were glad when they saw the Lord. 21 Jesus therefore said to them again, "Peace be to you. As the Father has sent me, even so I send you." 22 When he had said this, he breathed on them, and said to them, "Receive the Holy Spirit. 23 Whoever's sins you forgive, they are forgiven them. Whoever's sins you retain, they have been retained." 24 But Thomas, one of the twelve, called Didymus, was not with them when Jesus came. 25 The other disciples therefore said to him, "We have seen the Lord." But he said to them, "Unless I see in his hands the mark of the nails, and put my finger into the mark of the nails, and put my hand into his side, I will not believe." 26 After eight days again his disciples were inside, and Thomas was with them. Jesus came, the doors being locked, and stood in the midst, and said, "Peace be to you." 27 Then he said to Thomas, "Put your finger here, and observe my hands. Reach out your hand, and put it into my side; and do not be unbelieving, but believing." 28 Thomas answered and said to him, "My Lord and my God." 29 Jesus said to him, "Because you have seen me, you have believed. Blessed are those who have not seen, and have believed." 30 Therefore Jesus did many other signs in the presence of his disciples, which are not written in this book; 31 but these are written, that you may believe that Jesus is the Christ, the Son of God, and that believing you may have life in his name.

21 After these things, Jesus revealed himself again to the disciples at the sea of Tiberias. He revealed himself this way. 2 Simon Peter, Thomas called Didymus, Nathanael of Cana in Galilee, and the sons of Zebedee, and two others of his disciples were together. 3 Simon Peter said to them, "I'm going fishing." They told him, "We are also coming with you." They went out, and entered into the boat. That night, they caught nothing. 4 But when day had already come, Jesus stood on the beach, yet the disciples did not know that it was Jesus. 5 Jesus therefore said to them, "Children, have you anything to eat?" They answered him, "No." 6 He said to them, "Cast the net on the right side of the boat, and you will find some." They cast it therefore, and now they weren't able to draw it in for the multitude of fish. 7 That disciple therefore whom Jesus loved said to Peter, "It's the Lord." So when Simon Peter heard that it was the Lord, he wrapped his coat around him (for he was naked), and threw himself into the sea. 8 But the other disciples came in the little boat (for they were not far from the land, but about one hundred yards away), dragging the net full of fish. 9 So when they got out on the land, they saw a fire of coals there, and fish placed on it, and bread. 10 Jesus said to them, "Bring some of the fish which you have just caught." 11 Simon Peter went up, and drew the net to land, full of great fish, one hundred fifty-three; and even though there were so many, the net was not torn. 12 Jesus said to them, "Come and eat breakfast." None of the disciples dared inquire of him, "Who are you?" knowing that it was the Lord. 13 Then Jesus came and took the bread, gave it to them, and the fish likewise. 14 This is now the third time that Jesus was revealed to his disciples, after he had risen from the dead. 15 So when they had eaten their breakfast, Jesus said to Simon Peter, "Simon, son of John, do you love me more than these?" He said to him, "Yes, Lord; you know that I love you." He said to him, "Feed my lambs." 16 He said to him again a second time, "Simon, son of John, do you love me?" He said to him, "Yes, Lord; you know that I love you." He said to him, "Tend my sheep." 17 He said to him the third time, "Simon, son of John, do you love me?" Peter was grieved because he asked him the third time, "Do you love me?" And he said to him, "Lord, you know everything. You know that I love you." Jesus said to him, "Feed my sheep. 18 Truly I tell you, when you were young, you dressed yourself, and walked where you wanted to. But when you are old, you will stretch out your hands, and another will dress you, and carry you where you do not want to go." **19** Now he said this, signifying by what kind of death he would glorify God. When he had said this, he said to him, "Follow me." **20** Then Peter, turning around, saw a disciple following. This was the disciple whom Jesus sincerely loved, the one who had also leaned on Jesus' chest at the evening meal and asked, "Lord, who is going to betray You?" **21** Peter seeing him, said to Jesus, "Lord, what about this man?" **22** Jesus said to him, "If I desire that he stay until I come, what is that to you? You follow me." **23** This saying therefore went out among the brothers, that this disciple would not die. Yet Jesus did not say to him that he would not die, but, "If I desire that he stay until I come, what is that to you?" **24** This is the disciple who testifies about these things, and wrote these things. We know that his witness is true. **25** There are also many other things which Jesus did, which if they would all be written, I suppose that even the world itself would not have room for the books that would be written.

Acts

1 The first account I wrote, Theophilus, concerned all that Jesus began both to do and to teach, **2** until the day in which he was received up, after he had given commandment through the Holy Spirit to the apostles whom he had chosen. **3** To these he also showed himself alive after he suffered, by many proofs, appearing to them over a period of forty days, and speaking about God's Kingdom. **4** Being assembled together with them, he commanded them, "Do not depart from Jerusalem, but wait for the promise of the Father, which you heard from me. **5** For John indeed baptized in water, but you will be baptized in the Holy Spirit not many days from now." **6** Therefore, when they had come together, they asked him, "Lord, are you now restoring the kingdom to Israel?" **7** He said to them, "It is not for you to know times or seasons which the Father has set within his own authority. **8** But you will receive power when the Holy Spirit has come upon you. You will be my witnesses in Jerusalem, in all Judea and Samaria, and to the farthest part of the earth." **9** When he had said these things, as they were looking, he was taken up, and a cloud took him out of their sight. **10** While they were looking steadfastly into the sky as he went, look, two men stood by them in white clothing, **11** who also said, "You men of Galilee, why do you stand looking into the sky? This Jesus, who was received up from you into the sky will come back in the same way as you saw him going into the sky." **12** Then they returned to Jerusalem from the mountain called Olivet, which is near Jerusalem, a Sabbath day's journey away. **13** When they had come in, they went up into the upper room, where they were staying; that is Peter, John, James, Andrew, Philip, Thomas, Bartholomew, Matthew, James the son of Alphaeus, Simon the Zealot, and Judas the son of James. **14** All these with one accord continued steadfastly in prayer, along with the women, and Mary the mother of Jesus, and with his brothers. **15** In these days, Peter stood up in the midst of the brothers (and the number of names was about one hundred twenty), and said, **16** "Brothers, it was necessary that this Scripture should be fulfilled, which the Holy Spirit spoke before by the mouth of David concerning Judas, who was guide to those who took Jesus. **17** For he was numbered with us, and received his portion in this ministry. **18** Now this man obtained a field with the reward for his wickedness, and falling headfirst his body burst open, and all his intestines gushed out. **19** It became known to everyone who lived in Jerusalem that in their language that field was called 'Hakel-Dema,' that is, 'The field of blood.' **20** For it is written in the scroll of Psalms, 'Let his habitation be made desolate, and let no one dwell in it;' and, 'Let another take his office.' **21** "Of the men therefore who have accompanied us all the time that the Lord Jesus went in and out among us, **22** beginning from the baptism of John, to the day that he was received up from us, of these one must become a witness with us of his resurrection." **23** They put forward two, Joseph called Barsabbas, who was surnamed Justus, and Matthias. **24** They prayed, and said, "You, Lord, who know the hearts of all people, show which one of these two you have chosen **25** to take part in this ministry and office of apostle from which Judas fell away, that he might go to his own place." **26** They drew lots for them, and the lot fell on Matthias, and he was numbered with the eleven apostles.

2 Now when the day of Pentecost had come, they were all together in one place. **2** Suddenly there came from the sky a sound like the rushing of a mighty wind, and it filled all the house where they were sitting. **3** Tongues like fire appeared and were distributed to them, and one sat on each of them. **4** They were all filled with the Holy Spirit, and began to speak with other tongues, as the Spirit gave them the ability to speak. **5** Now there were dwelling in Jerusalem Jews, devout people from every nation under the sky. **6** When this sound was heard, the crowd came together, and were bewildered, because everyone heard them speaking in his own language. **7** They were all amazed and marveled, saying, "Look, are not all these who speak Galileans? **8** How do we hear, everyone in our own native language? **9** Parthians, Medes, Elamites, and people from Mesopotamia, Judea, Cappadocia, Pontus, Asia, **10** Phrygia, Pamphylia, Egypt, the parts of Libya around Cyrene, visitors from Rome, both Jews and proselytes, **11** Cretans and Arabians: we hear them speaking in our tongues the mighty works of God." **12** They were all amazed, and were perplexed, saying one to another, "What does this mean?" **13** Others, mocking, said, "They are filled with new wine." **14** But Peter, standing up with the eleven, lifted up his voice, and spoke out to them, "You men of Judea, and all you who live in Jerusalem, let this be known to you, and listen to my words. **15** For these are not drunk, as you suppose, seeing it is only nine in the morning. **16** But this is what has been spoken through the prophet Joel: **17** 'And it will be in the last days, says God, that I will pour out my Spirit on all flesh; and your sons and your daughters will prophesy, and your young men will see visions, and your old men will dream dreams. **18** And even on my servants, both men and women, I will pour out my Spirit in those days, and they will prophesy. **19** And I will show wonders in the sky above, and signs on the earth beneath; blood, and fire, and billows of smoke. **20** The sun will be turned into darkness, and the moon into blood, before the great and glorious day of the Lord comes. **21** And it will be that whoever will call on the name of the Lord will be saved.' **22** "Men of Israel, hear these words. Jesus the Nazorean, a man approved by God to you by mighty works and wonders and signs which God did by him in the midst of you, even as you yourselves know, **23** him, being delivered up by the determined counsel and foreknowledge of God, by the hand of lawless men, crucified and killed; **24** whom God raised up, having freed him from the pains of death, because it was not possible that he should be held by it. **25** For David says concerning him, 'I saw the Lord always before me, for he is at my right hand, that I should not be shaken. **26** Therefore my heart was glad, and my tongue rejoiced, and moreover my flesh also will dwell in hope; **27** because you will not abandon my soul in Hades **(Hadēs g86)**, neither will you allow your Holy One to see decay. **28** You made known to me the paths of life. You will make me full of joy in your presence.' **29** "Brothers, I may tell you freely of the patriarch David, that he both died and was buried, and his tomb is with us to this day. **30** Therefore, being a prophet, and knowing that God had sworn with an oath to him that one of his descendants would sit on his throne, **31** he foreseeing this spoke about the resurrection of the Christ, that neither was he left in Hades **(Hadēs g86)**, nor did his flesh see decay. **32** This Jesus God raised up, to which we all are witnesses. **33** Being therefore exalted by the right hand of God, and having received from the Father the promise of the Holy Spirit, he has poured out this, which you see and hear. **34** For David did not ascend into the heavens, but he says himself, 'The Lord said to my Lord, "Sit by my right hand, **35** until I make your enemies a footstool for your feet."' **36** "Let all the house of Israel therefore know certainly that God has made him both Lord and Christ, this Jesus whom you crucified." **37** Now when they heard this, they were cut to the heart, and said to Peter and the rest of the apostles, "Brothers, what should we do?" **38** Peter said to them, "Repent, and be baptized, every one of you, in the name of Jesus Christ for the forgiveness of your sins, and you will receive the gift of the Holy Spirit. **39** For to you is the promise, and to your children, and to all who are far off, even as many as the Lord our God will call to himself." **40** With many other words he testified, and exhorted them, saying, "Save yourselves from this crooked generation." **41** Then those who received his word were baptized. There were added that day about three thousand souls. **42** They continued steadfastly in the apostles' teaching and fellowship, in the breaking of bread, and prayer. **43** Fear came on every soul, and many wonders and signs were done through the apostles. **44** All who believed were together, and had all things in common. **45** They sold their possessions and goods, and distributed them to all, according as anyone had need. **46** Day by day, continuing steadfastly with one accord in the temple, and breaking bread at home, they took their food with gladness and singleness of heart, **47** praising God, and having favor with all the people. The Lord added to their number day by day those who were being saved.

3 Now Peter and John were going up into the temple at the hour of prayer, at three in the afternoon. **2** A certain man who was lame from his mother's womb was being carried, whom they put daily at the gate of the temple which is called Beautiful, to ask gifts for the needy of those who entered into the temple. **3** Seeing Peter and John about to go into the temple, he asked to receive gifts for the needy. **4** Peter, fastening his eyes on him, with John, said, "Look at us." **5** He listened to them, expecting to receive something from them. **6** But Peter said, "Silver and gold have I none, but what I have, that I give you. In the name of Jesus Christ the Nazorean, get up and walk." **7** He took him by the right hand, and raised him up. Immediately his feet and his ankle bones received strength. **8** Leaping up, he stood, and began to walk. He entered with them into the temple, walking, leaping, and praising God. **9** All the people saw him walking and praising God. **10** They recognized him, that it was he who used to sit begging for gifts for the needy at the Beautiful Gate of the temple. They were filled with wonder and amazement at what had happened to him. **11** And as he held on to Peter and John, all the people ran together to them in the porch that is called Solomon's, greatly wondering. **12** When Peter saw it, he responded to the people, "You men of Israel, why are you amazed at this? Why do you fasten your eyes on us, as though by our own power or godliness we had made him walk? **13** The God of Abraham, Isaac, and Jacob, the God of our fathers, has glorified his Servant Jesus, whom you delivered up, and denied in the presence of Pilate, when he had determined to release him. **14** But you denied the Holy and Righteous One, and asked for a man who was a murderer to be granted to you, **15** and killed the Originator of life, whom God raised from the dead, to which we are witnesses. **16** By faith in his name, his name has made this man strong, whom you see and know. Yes, the faith which is through him has given him this perfect soundness in the presence of you all. **17** "Now, brothers, I know that you did this in ignorance, as did also your rulers. **18** But the things which God announced by the mouth of all his prophets, that the Christ should suffer, he thus fulfilled. **19** "Repent therefore, and turn again, that your sins may be blotted out, so that there may come times of refreshing from the presence of the Lord, **20** and that he may send Jesus, the Christ who was ordained for you before, **21** whom heaven must receive until the times of restoration of all things, which God spoke from the age **(aiōn g165)** by the mouth of his holy prophets. **22** For Moses indeed said to the fathers, 'The Lord your God will raise up a prophet for you from among your brothers, like me. You must listen to him in all things whatever he says to you. **23** It will be, that every soul that will not listen to that prophet will be utterly destroyed from among the people.' **24** Yes, and all the prophets from Samuel and those who followed after, as many as have spoken, they also told of these days. **25** You are the children of the prophets, and of the covenant which God made with our fathers, saying to Abraham, 'And through your offspring all the families of the earth will be blessed.' **26** God, having raised up his Servant, sent him to you first, to bless you, in turning away everyone of you from your wickedness."

4 As they spoke to the people, the priests and the captain of the temple and the Sadducees came to them, **2** being upset because they taught the people and proclaimed in Jesus the resurrection from the dead. **3** They laid hands on them, and put them in custody until the next day, for it was now evening. **4** But many of those who heard the word believed, and the number of the men came to be about five thousand. **5** It happened in the morning, that their rulers, elders, and scribes were gathered together in Jerusalem. **6** Annas the high priest was there, with Caiaphas, John, Alexander, and as many as were relatives of the high priest. **7** When they had stood them in the middle of them, they inquired, "By what power, or in what name, have you done this?" **8** Then Peter, filled with the Holy Spirit, said to them, "Rulers of the people, and elders, **9** if we are examined today concerning a good deed done to a crippled man, by what means this man has been healed, **10** be it known to you all, and to all the children of Israel, that in the name of Jesus Christ the Nazorean, whom you crucified, whom God raised from the dead, in him does this man stand here before you whole. **11** This one is the stone which was regarded as worthless by you, the builders, which has become the head of the corner. **12** And there is salvation in no one else, for there is no other name under heaven that is given among people by which we must be saved." **13** Now when they saw the boldness of Peter and John, and had perceived that they were unlearned and ignorant men, they were amazed. They recognized that they had been with Jesus. **14** Seeing the man who was healed standing with them, they could say nothing against it. **15** But when they had commanded them to go aside out of the council, they conferred among themselves, **16** saying, "What should we do with these men? Because indeed a notable miracle has been done through them, as can be plainly seen by all who dwell in Jerusalem, and we cannot deny it. **17** But so this does not spread any further among the people, let us severely threaten them, that from now on they do not speak to anyone in this name." **18** They called them, and commanded them not to speak at all nor teach in the name of Jesus. **19** But Peter and John answered them, "Whether it is right in the sight of God to listen to you rather than to God, judge for yourselves, **20** for we cannot help telling the things which we saw and heard." **21** When they had further threatened them, they let them go, finding no way to punish them, because of the people; for everyone glorified God for that which was done. **22** For the man on whom this miracle of healing was performed was more than forty years old. **23** Being let go, they came to their own company, and reported all that the chief priests and the elders had said to them. **24** When they heard it, they lifted up their voice to God with one accord, and said, "Lord, you are the God who made the heaven and the earth and the sea, and all that is in them. **25** You said through the Holy Spirit, through the mouth of our father David your servant: 'Why do the nations rage, and the peoples plot in vain? **26** The kings of the earth take a stand, and the rulers take council together, against the Lord, and against his Christ.' **27** "For truly, in this city against your holy servant, Jesus, whom you anointed, both Herod and Pontius Pilate, with the Gentiles and the people of Israel, were gathered together **28** to do whatever your hand and your council foreordained to happen. **29** Now, Lord, look at their threats, and grant to your servants to speak your word with all boldness, **30** while you stretch out your hand to heal; and that signs and wonders may be done through the name of your holy Servant Jesus." **31** When they had prayed, the place was shaken where they were gathered together. They were all filled with the Holy Spirit, and they spoke the word of God with boldness. **32** And the full number of those who believed were of one heart and soul. Not one of them claimed that anything of the things which he possessed was his own, but they had all things in common. **33** With great power, the apostles gave their testimony of the resurrection of the Lord Jesus. Great grace was on them all. **34** For neither was there among them any who lacked, for as many as were owners of lands or houses sold them, and brought the proceeds of the things that were sold, **35** and put them at the apostles' feet, and distribution was made to each, according as anyone had need. **36** Joseph, who by the apostles was surnamed Barnabas (which is translated, Son of Encouragement), a Levite, a native of Cyprus by birth, **37** having a field, sold it, and brought the money and put it at the apostles' feet.

5 But a certain man named Ananias, with Sappirah, his wife, sold a possession, **2** and kept back part of the price, his wife also being aware of it, and brought a certain part, and put it at the apostles' feet. **3** But Peter said, "Ananias, why has Satan filled your heart to lie to the Holy Spirit, and to keep back part of the price of the land? **4** While you kept it, did not it remain your own? After it was sold, was not it in your power? How is it that you have conceived this thing in your heart? You have not lied to people, but to God." **5** Ananias, hearing these words, fell down and died. Great fear came on all who heard it. **6** The young men arose and wrapped him up, and they carried him out and buried him. **7** About three hours later, his wife, not knowing what had happened, came in. **8** Peter answered her, "Tell me whether you sold the land for so much." She said, "Yes, for so much." **9** But Peter asked her, "How is it that you have agreed together to tempt the Spirit of the Lord? Look, the feet of those who have buried your husband are at the door, and they will carry you out." **10** She fell down immediately at his feet, and died. The young men came in and found her dead, and they carried her out and buried her by her husband. **11** Great fear came on the whole church, and on all who heard these things. **12** By the hands of the apostles many signs and wonders were done among the people. They were all with one accord in Solomon's porch. **13** None of the rest dared to join them, however the people honored them. **14** More believers were added to the Lord, crowds of both men and women. **15** They even carried out the sick into the streets, and put them on cots and mats, so that as Peter came by at the least his shadow would fall on some of them. **16** Crowds also came together from the cities around Jerusalem, bringing sick people, and those who were tormented by unclean spirits: and they were all healed. **17** But the high priest rose up, and all those who were with him (which is the sect of the Sadducees), and they were filled with jealousy, **18** and laid hands on the apostles, and put them in public custody. **19** But an angel of the Lord opened the prison doors by night, and brought them out, and said, **20** "Go stand and speak in the temple to the people all the words of this life." **21** When they heard this, they entered into the temple about daybreak, and taught. But the high priest came, and those who were with him, and called the council together, and all the senate of the children of Israel, and sent to the prison to have them brought. **22** But the officers who came did not find them in

Acts

the prison. They returned and reported, **23** "We found the prison shut and locked, and the guards standing before the doors, but when we opened them, we found no one inside." **24** Now when the captain of the temple, and the chief priests heard these words, they were very perplexed about them and what might become of this. **25** One came and told them, "Look, the men whom you put in prison are in the temple, standing and teaching the people." **26** Then the captain went with the officers, and brought them without violence, for they were afraid that the people might stone them. **27** When they had brought them, they set them before the council. The high priest questioned them, **28** saying, "Did we not strictly command you not to teach in this name? And look, you have filled Jerusalem with your teaching, and intend to bring this man's blood on us." **29** But Peter and the apostles answered, "We must obey God rather than people. **30** The God of our fathers raised up Jesus, whom you killed, hanging him on a tree. **31** God exalted him with his right hand to be a Leader and a Savior, to give repentance to Israel, and forgiveness of sins. **32** We are witnesses of these things; and so also is the Holy Spirit, whom God has given to those who obey him." **33** But they, when they heard this, were cut to the heart, and wanted to kill them. **34** But one stood up in the council, a Pharisee named Gamaliel, a teacher of the Law, honored by all the people, and commanded to put the men out for a little while. **35** He said to them, "You men of Israel, be careful concerning these men, what you are about to do. **36** For before these days Todah rose up, making himself out to be somebody; to whom a number of men, about four hundred, joined themselves: who was slain; and all, as many as obeyed him, were dispersed, and came to nothing. **37** After this man, Judas of Galilee rose up in the days of the enrollment, and drew away some people after him. He also perished, and all, as many as obeyed him, were scattered abroad. **38** Now I tell you, withdraw from these men, and leave them alone. For if this counsel or this work is of human origin, it will be overthrown. **39** But if it is of God, you will not be able to overthrow them, and you would be found even to be fighting against God." **40** They agreed with him. Summoning the apostles, they beat them and commanded them not to speak in the name of Jesus, and let them go. **41** They therefore departed from the presence of the council, rejoicing that they were counted worthy to suffer dishonor for the Name. **42** Every day, in the temple and at home, they never stopped teaching and proclaiming that Jesus is the Christ.

6 Now in those days, when the number of the disciples was multiplying, a complaint arose from the Hellenists against the Hebrews, because their widows were neglected in the daily service. **2** So the twelve summoned the full number of the disciples and said, "It is not appropriate for us to forsake the word of God and serve tables. **3** Therefore select from among you, brothers, seven men of good report, full of the Spirit and of wisdom, whom we may appoint over this business. **4** But we will continue steadfastly in prayer and in the ministry of the word." **5** And these words pleased the whole gathering. They chose Stephen, a man full of faith and of the Holy Spirit, Philip, Prochorus, Nicanor, Timon, Parmenas, and Nicolaus, a proselyte of Antioch; **6** whom they set before the apostles. When they had prayed, they laid their hands on them. **7** The word of God increased and the number of the disciples multiplied greatly in Jerusalem; and a large group of the priests were obedient to the faith. **8** Stephen, full of grace and power, performed great wonders and signs among the people. **9** But some of those who were of the synagogue called "The Libertines," and of the Cyrenians, of the Alexandrians, and of those of Cilicia and Asia arose, disputing with Stephen. **10** They weren't able to withstand the wisdom and the Spirit by which he spoke. **11** Then they secretly induced men to say, "We have heard him speak blasphemous words against Moses and God." **12** They stirred up the people, the elders, and the scribes, and came against him and seized him, and brought him in to the council, **13** and set up false witnesses who said, "This man never stops speaking blasphemous words against this holy place and the Law. **14** For we have heard him say that this Jesus the Nazorean will destroy this place, and will change the customs which Moses delivered to us." **15** All who sat in the council, fastening their eyes on him, saw his face like it was the face of an angel.

7 The high priest said, "Are these things so?" **2** He said, "Brothers and fathers, listen. The God of glory appeared to our father Abraham, when he was in Mesopotamia, before he lived in Haran, **3** and said to him, 'Go out from your land and from your relatives, and come into a land which I will show you.' **4** Then he came out of the land of the Kasdim, and lived in Haran. From there, after his father died, he moved him into this land, where you are now living. **5** He gave him no inheritance in it, no, not so much as to set his foot on. He promised that he would give it to him for a possession, and to his descendants after him, when he still had no child. **6** God spoke in this way, that his 'descendants would live as foreigners in a strange land, and that they would be enslaved and oppressed for four hundred years. **7** But I will judge the nation to which they will be in bondage,' said God, 'and after that will they come out, and serve me in this place.' **8** He gave him the covenant of circumcision. So Abraham became the father of Isaac, and circumcised him the eighth day. Isaac became the father of Jacob, and Jacob became the father of the twelve patriarchs. **9** "The patriarchs, moved with jealousy against Joseph, sold him into Egypt; and God was with him, **10** and delivered him out of all his afflictions, and gave him favor and wisdom before Pharaoh, king of Egypt. He made him governor over Egypt and all his house. **11** Now a famine came over all Egypt and Canaan, and great affliction, and our fathers found no food. **12** But when Jacob heard that there was grain in Egypt, he sent out our fathers the first time. **13** On the second time Joseph was made known to his brothers, and Joseph's family became known to Pharaoh. **14** Then Joseph sent, and summoned Jacob, his father, and all his relatives, seventy-five souls. **15** Jacob went down into Egypt, and he died, himself and our fathers, **16** and they were brought back to Shechem, and placed in the tomb that Abraham bought for a price in silver from the children of Hamor in Shechem. **17** "But as the time of the promise came close which God had made to Abraham, the people grew and multiplied in Egypt, **18** until 'there arose a different king over Egypt, who did not know Joseph.' **19** The same took advantage of our race, and mistreated our fathers, and forced them to throw out their babies, so that they would not stay alive. **20** At that time Moses was born, and was exceedingly handsome. He was nourished three months in his father's house. **21** When he was thrown out, Pharaoh's daughter took him up, and reared him as her own son. **22** Moses was instructed in all the wisdom of the Egyptians. He was mighty in his words and works. **23** But when he was forty years old, it came into his heart to visit his brothers, the children of Israel. **24** Seeing one of them suffer wrong, he defended him, and avenged him who was oppressed, striking the Egyptian. **25** He supposed that his brothers understood that God, by his hand, was giving them deliverance; but they did not understand. **26** "The day following, he appeared to them as they fought, and urged them to be at peace again, saying, 'Men, you are brothers. Why do you wrong one another?' **27** But he who did his neighbor wrong pushed him away, saying, 'Who made you a ruler and a judge over us? **28** Do you want to kill me, as you killed the Egyptian yesterday?' **29** Moses fled at this saying, and became a stranger in the land of Midian, where he became the father of two sons. **30** "When forty years were fulfilled, an angel appeared to him in the wilderness of Mount Sinai, in a flame of fire in a bush. **31** When Moses saw it, he wondered at the sight. As he came close to see, a voice of the Lord came, **32** 'I am the God of your fathers, the God of Abraham, and of Isaac, and of Jacob.' Moses trembled, and dared not look. **33** The Lord said to him, 'Take your sandals off of your feet, for the place where you stand is holy ground. **34** I have surely seen the affliction of my people that is in Egypt, and have heard their groaning. I have come down to deliver them. Now come, I will send you to Egypt.' **35** "This Moses, whom they refused, saying, 'Who made you a ruler and a judge?'—God has sent him as both a ruler and a deliverer by the hand of the angel who appeared to him in the bush. **36** This man led them out, having worked wonders and signs in Egypt, in the Red Sea, and in the wilderness for forty years. **37** This is that Moses, who said to the children of Israel, 'God will raise up a prophet for you from among your brothers, like me.' **38** This is he who was in the assembly in the wilderness with the angel that spoke to him on Mount Sinai, and with our fathers, who received words of life to give to us, **39** to whom our fathers would not be obedient, but rejected him, and turned back in their hearts to Egypt, **40** saying to Aaron, 'Make us gods that will go before us, for as for this Moses, who led us out of the land of Egypt, we do not know what has become of him.' **41** They made a calf in those days, and brought a sacrifice to the idol, and rejoiced in the works of their hands. **42** But God turned, and gave them over to worship the host of heaven, as it is written in the book of the prophets, 'Did you offer to me sacrifices and offerings forty years in the wilderness, O house of Israel? **43** You took up the tabernacle of Moloch, and the star of your god Rephan, the images that you made to worship them. Therefore I will exile you beyond Babylon.' **44** "Our fathers had the tabernacle of the testimony in the wilderness, even as he who spoke to Moses commanded him to make it according to the pattern that he had seen; **45** which also our fathers, in their turn, brought in with Joshua when they entered into the possession of the nations, whom God drove out before the face of our fathers, to the days of David, **46** who found favor in the sight of God, and asked to find a habitation for the God of Jacob. **47** But Solomon built him a house. **48** However, the Most High does not dwell in temples made with hands, as the prophet says, **49** 'Heaven is my throne, and the earth a footstool for my feet. What kind of house will you build me?' says the Lord; 'or what is the place of my rest? **50** Did not my hand make all these things?' **51** "You stiff-necked and uncircumcised in heart and ears, you always resist the Holy Spirit. As your fathers did, so you do. **52** Which of the prophets did not your fathers persecute? They killed those who foretold the coming of the Righteous One, of whom you have now become betrayers and murderers. **53** You received the Law as it was ordained by angels, and did not keep it." **54** Now when they heard these things, they were cut to the heart, and they gnashed at him with their teeth. **55** But he, being full of the Holy Spirit, looked up steadfastly into heaven, and saw the glory of God, and Jesus standing on the right hand of God, **56** And he said, "Look, I see the heavens opened, and the Son of Man standing at the right hand of God." **57** But they shouted out with a loud voice, and stopped their ears, and rushed at him with one accord. **58** They threw him out of the city, and stoned him. The witnesses placed their garments at the feet of a young man named Saul. **59** They stoned Stephen as he called out, saying, "Lord Jesus, receive my spirit." **60** He kneeled down, and shouted out, "Lord, do not hold this sin against them." When he had said this, he fell asleep.

8 Saul was consenting to his death. A great persecution arose against the church which was in Jerusalem in that day. They were all scattered abroad throughout the regions of Judea and Samaria, except for the apostles. **2** Devout men buried Stephen, and lamented greatly over him. **3** But Saul ravaged the church, entering into every house, and dragged both men and women off to prison. **4** Therefore those who were scattered abroad went around proclaiming the word. **5** And Philip went down to the city of Samaria, and proclaimed to them the Christ. **6** The crowds listened with one accord to the things that were spoken by Philip, when they heard and saw the signs which he did. **7** For unclean spirits came out of many of those who had them. They came out, crying with a loud voice. Many who had been paralyzed and lame were healed. **8** There was great joy in that city. **9** But there was a certain man, Simon by name, who used to practice sorcery in the city, and amazed the people of Samaria, making himself out to be some great one, **10** to whom they all listened, from the least to the greatest, saying, "This man is that power of God which is called Great." **11** They listened to him, because for a long time he had amazed them with his sorceries. **12** But when they believed Philip as he preached good news concerning the Kingdom of God and the name of Jesus Christ, they were baptized, both men and women. **13** Simon himself also believed. Being baptized, he continued with Philip. Seeing signs and great miracles occurring, he was amazed. **14** Now when the apostles who were at Jerusalem heard that Samaria had received the word of God, they sent Peter and John to them, **15** who, when they had come down, prayed for them, that they might receive the Holy Spirit; **16** for he had not yet fallen upon any of them. They had only been baptized in the name of the Lord Jesus. **17** Then they laid their hands on them, and they received the Holy Spirit. **18** Now when Simon saw that the Holy Spirit was given through the laying on of the apostles' hands, he offered them money, **19** saying, "Give me also this power, that whomever I lay my hands on may receive the Holy Spirit." **20** But Peter said to him, "May your silver perish with you, because you thought you could obtain the gift of God with money. **21** You have neither part nor lot in this matter, for your heart is not right before God. **22** Repent therefore of this, your wickedness, and ask the Lord if perhaps the thought of your heart may be forgiven you. **23** For I see that you are in the gall of bitterness and in the bondage of iniquity." **24** Simon answered, "Pray for me to the Lord, that none of the things which you have spoken happen to me." **25** They therefore, when they had testified and spoken the word of the Lord, returned to Jerusalem, and preached the Good News to many villages of the Samaritans. **26** But an angel of the Lord spoke to Philip, saying, "Arise, and go toward the south to the way that goes down from Jerusalem to Gaza. This is a desert." **27** And he arose and went. And look, there was a man from Ethiopia, a eunuch of great authority under Kandake, the queen of the Ethiopians, who was in charge over all her treasure. He had come to Jerusalem to worship, **28** and he was returning. And sitting in his chariot, he was reading the prophet Isaiah. **29** And the Spirit said to Philip, "Go and join up with that chariot." **30** And running near, Philip heard him reading the prophet Isaiah, and said, "Do you understand what you are reading?" **31** He said, "How can I, unless someone explains it to me?" So he invited Philip to come up and sit with him. **32** Now the passage of the Scripture which he was reading was this, "He was led like a sheep to the slaughter, and like a lamb before its shearer is silent, so he does not open his mouth. **33** In his humiliation his justice was taken away. Who will declare his generation? For his life is taken from the earth." **34** The eunuch answered Philip, "Who is the prophet talking about? About himself, or about someone else?" **35** Philip opened his mouth, and beginning from this Scripture, preached to him Jesus. **36** As they went on the way, they came to some water, and the eunuch said, "Look, here is water. What is keeping me from being baptized?" **37** And he said, "If you believe with all your heart, you may." And he answered and said, "I believe that Jesus Christ is the Son of God." **38** He commanded the chariot to stand still, and they both went down into the water, both Philip and the eunuch, and he baptized him. **39** When they came up out of the water, the Spirit of the Lord caught Philip away, and the eunuch did not see him any more, for he went on his way rejoicing. **40** But Philip was found at Azotus. Passing through, he preached the Good News to all the cities, until he came to Caesarea.

9 But Saul, still breathing threats and slaughter against the disciples of the Lord, went to the high priest, **2** and asked for letters from him to the synagogues of Damascus, that if he found any who were of the Way, whether men or women, he might bring them bound to Jerusalem. **3** As he traveled, it happened that he got close to Damascus, and suddenly a light from the sky shone around him. **4** And he fell to the ground, and heard a voice saying to him, "Saul, Saul, why do you persecute me?" **5** And he said, "Who are you, Lord?" And he said, "I am Jesus, whom you are persecuting. **6** But rise up, and enter into the city, and you will be told what you must do." **7** The men who traveled with him stood speechless, hearing the sound, but seeing no one. **8** Saul arose from the ground, but when he opened his eyes he could not see anything. They led him by the hand, and brought him into Damascus. **9** He was without sight for three days, and neither ate nor drank. **10** Now there was a certain disciple at Damascus named Ananias. The Lord said to him in a vision, "Ananias." And he said, "Look, it's me, Lord." **11** The Lord said to him, "Arise, and go to the street which is called Straight, and inquire in the house of Judas for one named Saul, a man of Tarsus. For look, he is praying, **12** and in a vision he has seen a man named Ananias coming in, and laying his hands on him, that he might receive his sight." **13** But Ananias answered, "Lord, I have heard from many about this man, how much evil he did to your saints at Jerusalem. **14** Here he has authority from the chief priests to bind all who call on your name." **15** But the Lord said to him, "Go your way, for he is my chosen vessel to bear my name before the nations and kings, and the children of Israel. **16** For I will show him how many things he must suffer for my name's sake." **17** Ananias departed, and entered into the house. Laying his hands on him, he said, "Brother Saul, the Lord, who appeared to you on the road by which you came, has sent me, that you may receive your sight, and be filled with the Holy Spirit." **18** Immediately something like scales fell from his eyes, and he received his sight. He arose and was baptized. **19** He took food and was strengthened. He stayed several days with the disciples who were at Damascus. **20** Immediately in the synagogues he proclaimed Jesus, that he is the Son of God. **21** All who heard him were amazed, and said, "Is not this he who in Jerusalem made havoc of those who called on this name? And he had come here intending to bring them bound before the chief priests." **22** But Saul increased more in strength, and confounded the Jews who lived at Damascus, proving that this is the Christ. **23** When many days were fulfilled, the Jews conspired together to kill him, **24** but their plot became known to Saul. They watched the gates both day and night that they might kill him, **25** but his disciples took him by night, and let him down through the wall, lowering him in a basket. **26** When Saul had come to Jerusalem, he tried to join himself to the disciples; but they were all afraid of him, not believing that he was a disciple. **27** But Barnabas took him, and brought him to the apostles, and declared to them how he had seen the Lord in the way, and that he had spoken to him, and how at Damascus he had preached boldly in the name of Jesus. **28** He was with them coming in and going out in Jerusalem, speaking boldly in the name of the Lord. **29** He spoke and disputed against the Hellenists, but they were seeking to kill him. **30** When the brothers knew it, they brought him down to Caesarea, and sent him off to Tarsus. **31** So the church throughout all Judea and Galilee and Samaria had peace, and were built up. They were multiplied, walking in the fear of the Lord and in the comfort of the Holy Spirit. **32** It happened, as Peter went throughout all those parts, he came down also to the saints who lived at Lydda. **33** There he found a certain man named Aeneas, who had been bedridden for eight years, because he was paralyzed. **34** Peter said to him, "Aeneas, Jesus Christ heals you. Get up and make your bed." Immediately he arose. **35** All who lived at Lydda and in Sharon saw him, and they turned to the Lord. **36** Now there was at Joppa a certain disciple named Tabitha (which when translated, means Dorcas). This woman was full of good works and acts of mercy which she did. **37** It happened in those days that she fell sick, and died. When they had washed her, they placed her in an upper chamber. **38** As Lydda was near Joppa, the disciples, hearing that Peter was there, sent two men to him, imploring him not to delay in coming to us. **39** Peter got up and went with them. When he had come, they brought him into the upper chamber. All the widows stood by him weeping, and showing the coats and garments which Dorcas had made while she was with them. **40** Peter put them all out, and kneeled down and prayed. Turning to the body, he said, "Tabitha, get up." She opened her eyes, and when she saw Peter, she sat up. **41** He gave her his hand, and raised her up. Calling the saints and widows, he presented her alive. **42** And it became known throughout all Joppa, and many believed in the Lord. **43** It happened, that he stayed many days in Joppa with one Simon, a tanner.

10 Now there was a certain man in Caesarea, Cornelius by name, a centurion of what was called the Italian Regiment, **2** a devout man, and one who feared God with all his house, who gave gifts for the needy generously to the people, and always prayed to God. **3** At about three in the afternoon, he clearly saw in a vision an angel of God coming to him, and saying to him, "Cornelius." **4** He, fastening his eyes on him, and being frightened, said, "What is it, Lord?" He said to him, "Your prayers and your gifts to the needy have gone up for a memorial before God. **5** Now send men to Joppa, and bring one Simon who is surnamed Peter. **6** He lodges with one Simon, a tanner, whose house is by the seaside." **7** When the angel who spoke to him had departed, he called two of his household servants and a devout soldier of those who waited on him continually. **8** Having explained everything to them, he sent them to Joppa. **9** Now on the next day as they were on their journey, and got close to the city, Peter went up on the housetop to pray at about noon. **10** He became hungry and desired to eat, but while they were preparing, he fell into a trance. **11** He saw heaven opened and a certain container descending to him, like a great sheet let down by four corners on the earth, **12** in which were all kinds of four-footed animals of the earth, crawling creatures and birds of the sky. **13** A voice came to him, "Rise, Peter, kill and eat." **14** But Peter said, "Not so, Lord; for I have never eaten anything that is common or unclean." **15** A voice came to him again the second time, "What God has cleansed, you must not call unclean." **16** This was done three times, and immediately the vessel was received up into heaven. **17** Now while Peter was very perplexed within himself what the vision which he had seen might mean, look, the men who were sent by Cornelius, having made inquiry for Simon's house, stood before the gate, **18** and called and asked whether Simon, who was surnamed Peter, was lodging there. **19** While Peter was pondering the vision, the Spirit said to him, "Look, three men seek you. **20** But arise, get down, and go with them, doubting nothing; for I have sent them." **21** And Peter went down to the men, and said, "Look, I am the one whom you seek. Why have you come?" **22** They said, "Cornelius, a centurion, a righteous man and one who fears God, and well spoken of by all the Jewish nation, was directed by a holy angel to invite you to his house, and to listen to what you say." **23** So he called them in and lodged them. On the next day he arose and went out with them, and some of the brothers from Joppa accompanied him. **24** On the next day he entered into Caesarea. Cornelius was waiting for them, having called together his relatives and his near friends. **25** When it happened that Peter entered, Cornelius met him, fell down at his feet, and worshiped him. **26** But Peter raised him up, saying, "Stand up. I myself am also a man." **27** And as he talked with him, he went in and found many gathered together. **28** He said to them, "You yourselves know how it is an unlawful thing for a man who is a Jew to join himself or come to one of another nation, but God has shown me that I should not call any man unholy or unclean. **29** Therefore also I came without complaint when I was sent for. I ask therefore, why did you send for me?" **30** Cornelius said, "Four days ago until this hour, at three in the afternoon, I was praying in my house, and look, a man stood before me in bright clothing, **31** and said, 'Cornelius, your prayer is heard, and your gifts to the needy are remembered in the sight of God. **32** Send therefore to Joppa, and summon Simon, who is surnamed Peter. He lodges in the house of Simon, a tanner, by the seaside.' **33** Therefore I sent to you at once, and it was good of you to come. Now therefore we are all here present in the sight of God to hear all things that have been commanded you by the Lord." **34** And Peter opened his mouth and said, "Truly I perceive that God does not show favoritism; **35** but in every nation he who fears him and works righteousness is acceptable to him. **36** The word which he sent to the children of Israel, preaching good news of peace through Jesus Christ—he is Lord of all— **37** that spoken word you yourselves know, which was proclaimed throughout all Judea, beginning from Galilee, after the baptism which John preached; **38** even Jesus of Nazareth, how God anointed him with the Holy Spirit and with power, who went about doing good and healing all who were oppressed by the devil, for God was with him. **39** We are witnesses of everything he did both in the land of the Jews and in Jerusalem, whom they also killed by hanging on a tree. **40** God raised him up the third day, and gave him to be revealed, **41** not to all the people, but to witnesses who were chosen before by God, to us, who ate and drank with him after he rose from the dead. **42** He commanded us to proclaim to the people and to testify that this is he who is appointed by God as the Judge of the living and the dead. **43** All the prophets testify about him, that through his name everyone who believes in him receives forgiveness of sins." **44** While Peter was still speaking these words, the Holy Spirit fell on all those who heard the word. **45** They of the circumcision who believed were amazed, as many as came with Peter, because the gift of the Holy Spirit was also poured out on the Gentile people. **46** For they heard them speaking in other tongues and magnifying God. Then Peter answered, **47** "Can anyone withhold the water, that these who have received the Holy Spirit as well as we should not be baptized?" **48** He commanded them to be baptized in the name of Jesus Christ. Then they asked him to stay some days.

11 Now the apostles and the brothers who were in Judea heard that the Gentile people had also received the word of God. **2** When Peter had come up to Jerusalem, those who were of the circumcision contended with him, **3** saying, "You went in to uncircumcised men, and ate with them." **4** But Peter began, and explained to them in order, saying, **5** "I was in the city of Joppa praying, and in a trance I saw a vision: a certain container descending, like it was a great sheet let down from heaven by four corners. It came as far as me. **6** When I had looked intently at it, I considered, and saw the four-footed animals of the earth, wild animals, crawling creatures, and birds of the sky. **7** I also heard a voice saying to me, 'Rise, Peter, kill and eat.' **8** But I said, 'Not so, Lord, for nothing unholy or unclean has ever entered into my mouth.' **9** But a voice answered the second time out of heaven, 'What God has cleansed, do not call unclean.' **10** This was done three times, and all were drawn up again into heaven. **11** And look, immediately three men stood before the house where we were, having been sent from Caesarea to me. **12** The Spirit told me to go with them, without discriminating. These six brothers also accompanied me, and we entered into the man's house. **13** He told us how he had seen the angel standing in his house, and saying to him, 'Send to Joppa, and get Simon, whose surname is Peter, **14** who will speak to you words by which you will be saved, you and all your house.' **15** As I began to speak, the Holy Spirit fell on them, even as on us at the beginning. **16** I remembered the word of the Lord, how he said, 'John indeed baptized in water, but you will be baptized in the Holy Spirit.' **17** If then God gave to them the same gift as us, when we believed in the Lord Jesus Christ, who was I, that I could withstand God?" **18** When they heard these things, they held their peace, and glorified God, saying, "Then God has also granted to the Gentiles repentance to life." **19** They therefore who were scattered abroad by the oppression that arose about Stephen traveled as far as Phoenicia, Cyprus, and Antioch, speaking the word to no one except to Jews only. **20** But there were some of them, men of Cyprus and Cyrene, who, when they had come to Antioch, spoke to the Greeks, proclaiming the good news of the Lord Jesus. **21** The hand of the Lord was with them, and a great number believed and turned to the Lord. **22** And the report concerning them was heard by the church in Jerusalem, so they sent Barnabas to Antioch, **23** who, when he had come, and had seen the grace of God, was glad. He exhorted them all, that with purpose of heart they should remain true to the Lord. **24** For he was a good man, and full of the Holy Spirit and of faith, and many people were added to the Lord. **25** Barnabas went out to Tarsus to look for Saul. **26** When he had found him, he brought him to Antioch. It happened, that for a whole year they were gathered together with the church, and taught many people. The disciples were first called Christians in Antioch. **27** Now in these days, prophets came down from Jerusalem to Antioch. **28** One of them named Agabus stood up, and indicated by the Spirit that there should be a great famine all over the world, which also happened in the days of Claudius. **29** As any of the disciples had plenty, each determined to send relief to the brothers who lived in Judea; **30** which they also did, sending it to the elders by the hands of Barnabas and Saul.

12 Now about that time, Herod the king stretched out his hands to oppress some of the church. **2** He killed James, the brother of John, with the sword. **3** When he saw that it pleased the Jewish people, he proceeded to seize Peter also. This was during the days of unleavened bread. **4** When he had arrested him, he put him in prison, and delivered him to four squads of four soldiers each to guard him, intending to bring him out to the people after the Passover. **5** Peter therefore was kept in the prison, but constant prayer was made by the church to God for him. **6** The same night when Herod was about to bring him out, Peter was sleeping between two soldiers, bound with two chains. Guards in front of the door kept the prison. **7** And look, an angel of the Lord stood by him, and a light shone in the cell. He struck Peter on the side, and woke him up, saying, "Stand up quickly." His chains fell off from his hands. **8** The angel said to him, "Get dressed and put on your sandals." He did so. He said to him, "Put on your cloak, and follow me." **9** And he went out and followed him. He did not know that what was being done by the angel was real, but thought he saw a vision. **10** When they were past the first and the second guard, they came to the iron gate that leads into the city, which opened to them by itself. They went out, and went down one street, and immediately the angel departed from him. **11** When Peter had come to himself, he said, "Now I truly know that the Lord has sent out his angel and delivered me out of the hand of Herod, and from everything the Jewish people were expecting." **12** Thinking about that, he came to the house of Mary, the mother of John whose surname was Mark, where many were gathered together and were praying. **13** And when Peter knocked at the door of the gate, a servant girl named Rhoda came to answer. **14** When she recognized Peter's voice, she did not open the gate for joy, but ran in, and reported that Peter was standing in front of the gate. **15** They said to her, "You are crazy." But she insisted that it was so. They said, "It is his angel." **16** But Peter continued knocking. When they had opened, they saw him, and were amazed. **17** But he, beckoning to them with his hand to be silent, declared to them how the Lord had brought him out of the prison. He said, "Tell these things to James, and to the brothers." Then he departed, and went to another place. **18** Now as soon as it was day, there was no small stir among the soldiers about what had become of Peter. **19** When Herod had sought for him, and did not find him, he examined the guards, and commanded that they should be put to death. He went down from Judea to Caesarea, and stayed there. **20** Now Herod was very angry with the people of Tyre and Sidon. They came with one accord to him, and, having made Blastus, the king's personal aide, their friend, they asked for peace, because their country depended on the king's country for food. **21** On an appointed day, Herod dressed himself in royal clothing, and sat on the throne, and gave a speech to them. **22** But the crowd shouted, "The voice of a god, and not of a man." **23** Immediately an angel of the Lord struck him, because he did not give God the glory, and he was eaten by worms and died. **24** But the word of God grew and multiplied. **25** Barnabas and Saul returned to Jerusalem, when they had fulfilled their service, also taking with them John whose surname was Mark.

13 Now in the church that was at Antioch there were some prophets and teachers: Barnabas, Simeon who was called Niger, Lucius of Cyrene, Manaen the foster brother of Herod the tetrarch, and Saul. **2** As they served the Lord and fasted, the Holy Spirit said, "Separate Barnabas and Saul for me, for the work to which I have called them." **3** Then, when they had fasted and prayed and laid their hands on them, they sent them away. **4** So, being sent out by the Holy Spirit, they went down to Seleucia. From there they sailed to Cyprus. **5** When they were at Salamis, they proclaimed the word of God in the Jewish synagogues. They had also John as their attendant. **6** When they had gone through the whole island as far as Paphos, they found a certain man, a sorcerer, a false prophet, a Jew, whose name was Bar-Jesus, **7** who was with the proconsul, Sergius Paulus, a man of understanding. This man summoned Barnabas and Saul, and sought to hear the word of God. **8** But Elymas the sorcerer (for so is his name by interpretation) withstood them, seeking to turn aside the proconsul from the faith. **9** But Saul, who is also called Paul, filled with the Holy Spirit, fastened his eyes on him, **10** and said, "Full of all deceit and all fraud, you son of the devil, you enemy of all righteousness, will you not cease to pervert the right ways of the Lord? **11** Now, look, the hand of the Lord is on you, and you will be blind, unable to see the sun for a time." Immediately a mist and darkness fell on him. He went around seeking someone to lead him by the hand. **12** Then the proconsul, when he saw what was done, believed, being astonished at the teaching of the Lord. **13** Now Paul and his company set sail from Paphos, and came to Perga in Pamphylia, and John departed from them and returned to Jerusalem. **14** But they, passing on from Perga, came to Antioch of Pisidia. They went into the synagogue on the Sabbath day, and sat down. **15** After the reading of the Law and the Prophets, the rulers of the synagogue sent to them, saying, "Brothers, if you have any word of exhortation for the people, speak." **16** Paul stood up, and beckoning with his hand said, "Men of Israel, and you who fear God, listen. **17** The God of this people Israel chose our fathers, and exalted the people when they stayed as foreigners in the land of Egypt, and with an uplifted arm, he led them out of it. **18** For a period of about forty years he put up with them in the wilderness. **19** When he had destroyed seven nations in the land of Canaan, he gave them their land as an inheritance. **20** All this took about four hundred and fifty years. And after these things he gave them judges, until Samuel the prophet. **21** Afterward they asked for a king, and God gave to them Saul the son of Kish, a man of the tribe of Benjamin, for forty years. **22** When he had removed him, he raised up David to be their king, to whom he also testified, 'I have found David the son of Jesse, a man after my heart, who will do all my will.' **23** From this man's offspring, according to his promise, God has brought to Israel a Savior, Jesus, **24** before his coming, when John had first preached the baptism of repentance to all the people of Israel. **25** As John was fulfilling his course, he said, 'What do you suppose that I am? I am not he. But look, one comes after me the sandals of whose feet I am not worthy to untie.' **26** Brothers, children of the stock of Abraham, and those among you who fear God, the word of this salvation is sent out to us. **27** For those who dwell in Jerusalem, and their rulers, because they did not know him, nor the voices of the prophets which are read every Sabbath, fulfilled them by condemning him. **28** Though they found no cause for death, they still asked Pilate to have him killed. **29** When they had fulfilled all things that were written about him, they took him down from the tree, and placed him in a tomb. **30** But God raised him from the dead, **31** and he was seen for many days by those who came up with him from Galilee to Jerusalem, who are his witnesses to the people. **32** We bring you good news of the promise made to the fathers, **33** that God has fulfilled for us the children in that he raised up Jesus. As it is also written in the second psalm, 'You are my Son. Today I have become your Father.' **34** "Concerning that he raised him up from the dead, now no more to return to corruption, he has spoken thus: 'I will give to you the faithful sacred things of David.' **35** Therefore he says also in another psalm, 'You will not allow your Holy One to see decay.' **36** For David, after he had in his own generation served the counsel of God, fell asleep, and was placed with his fathers, and saw decay. **37** But he whom God raised up

Acts

saw no decay. **38** Be it known to you therefore, brothers, that through this man is proclaimed to you forgiveness of sins, **39** and by him everyone who believes is justified from all things, from which you could not be justified by the Law of Moses. **40** So beware, lest what is said in the Prophets should come about: **41** 'Look, you scoffers, and be amazed, and perish; for I am working a work in your days, a work which you will not believe, if one tells it to you.'" **42** So when they went out they urged them to speak about these things on the next Sabbath. **43** Now when the synagogue broke up, many of the Jews and of the devout proselytes followed Paul and Barnabas; who, speaking to them, urged them to continue in the grace of God. **44** The next Sabbath almost the whole city was gathered together to hear the word of the Lord. **45** But when the Jews saw the crowds, they were filled with jealousy, and contradicted the things which were spoken by Paul, and reviled him. **46** Paul and Barnabas spoke out boldly, and said, "It was necessary that God's word should be spoken to you first. Since indeed you pushed it away, and judge yourselves unworthy of consummate **(aiōnios g166)** life, look, we turn to the Gentiles. **47** For so has the Lord commanded us, saying, 'I have set you as a light to the nations, that you may bring salvation to the farthest part of the earth.'" **48** As the Gentiles heard this, they were glad, and glorified the word of the Lord, and as many as were appointed to consummate **(aiōnios g166)** life believed. **49** The Lord's word was spread abroad throughout all the region. **50** But the Jews stirred up the devout and prominent women and the chief men of the city, and stirred up a persecution against Paul and Barnabas, and threw them out of their borders. **51** But they shook off the dust of their feet against them, and came to Iconium. **52** The disciples were filled with joy with the Holy Spirit.

14 It happened in Iconium that they entered together into the Jewish synagogue, and so spoke that a great number of both of Jews and of Greeks believed. **2** But the disbelieving Jews stirred up and embittered the souls of the Gentile people against the brothers. **3** Therefore they stayed there a long time, speaking boldly in the Lord, who testified to the word of his grace, granting signs and wonders to be done by their hands. **4** But the population of the city was divided. Some sided with the Jews, and some with the apostles. **5** When some of both the Gentile people and the Jews, with their rulers, made a violent attempt to mistreat and stone them, **6** they became aware of it, and fled to the cities of Lycaonia, Lystra, Derbe, and the surrounding region. **7** There they preached the Good News. **8** At Lystra a certain man sat, without strength in his feet, a cripple from his mother's womb, who never had walked. **9** He was listening to Paul speaking, who, fastening eyes on him, and seeing that he had faith to be made whole, **10** said with a loud voice, "Stand upright on your feet." He leaped up and walked. **11** When the crowd saw what Paul had done, they lifted up their voice, saying in the language of Lycaonia, "The gods have come down to us in human form." **12** They called Barnabas "Jupiter," and Paul "Mercury," because he was the chief speaker. **13** The priest of Jupiter, whose temple was in front of their city, brought oxen and garlands to the gates, and would have made a sacrifice along with the crowds. **14** But when the apostles, Barnabas and Paul, heard of it, they tore their clothes, and sprang into the crowd, crying out, **15** "Men, why are you doing these things? We also are men of like passions with you, and bring you good news, that you should turn from these vain things to the living God, who made the sky and the earth and the sea, and all that is in them; **16** who in the generations gone by allowed all the nations to walk in their own ways. **17** Yet he did not leave himself without witness, in that he did good and gave you rains from the sky and fruitful seasons, filling your hearts with food and gladness." **18** Even saying these things, they hardly stopped the crowds from making a sacrifice to them. **19** But some Jews from Antioch and Iconium came there, and having persuaded the crowds, they stoned Paul, and dragged him out of the city, supposing that he was dead. **20** But as the disciples stood around him, he rose up, and entered into the city. On the next day he went out with Barnabas to Derbe. **21** When they had preached the Good News to that city, and had made many disciples, they returned to Lystra, Iconium, and Antioch, **22** confirming the souls of the disciples, exhorting them to continue in the faith, and that through many afflictions we must enter into the Kingdom of God. **23** When they had appointed elders for them in every church, and had prayed with fasting, they commended them to the Lord, on whom they had believed. **24** They passed through Pisidia, and came to Pamphylia. **25** When they had spoken the word in Perga, they went down to Attalia. **26** From there they sailed to Antioch, from where they had been committed to the grace of God for the work which they had fulfilled. **27** When they had arrived, and had gathered the church together, they reported all the things that God had done with them, and that he had opened a door of faith to the nations. **28** They stayed there with the disciples for a long time.

15 Some men came down from Judea and taught the brothers, "Unless you are circumcised after the custom of Moses, you cannot be saved." **2** Therefore when Paul and Barnabas had no small discord and discussion with them, they appointed Paul and Barnabas, and some others of them, to go up to Jerusalem to the apostles and elders about this question. **3** They, being sent on their way by the church, passed through both Phoenicia and Samaria, describing in detail the conversion of the Gentile people. They caused great joy to all the brothers. **4** When they had come to Jerusalem, they were received by the church and the apostles and the elders, and they reported all things that God had done with them. **5** But some of the sect of the Pharisees who believed rose up, saying, "It is necessary to circumcise them, and to command them to keep the Law of Moses." **6** The apostles and the elders were gathered together to see about this matter. **7** When there had been much discussion, Peter rose up and said to them, "Brothers, you know that a good while ago God made a choice among you, that by my mouth the nations should hear the word of the Good News, and believe. **8**

God, who knows the heart, testified about them, giving them the Holy Spirit, just like he did to us. **9** He made no distinction between us and them, cleansing their hearts by faith. **10** Now therefore why do you tempt God, that you should put a yoke on the neck of the disciples which neither our fathers nor we were able to bear? **11** But we believe that we are saved through the grace of the Lord Jesus, just as they are." **12** And all the people kept quiet, and they listened to Barnabas and Paul reporting what signs and wonders God had done among the nations through them. **13** After they were silent, James answered, "Brothers, listen to me. **14** Simeon has reported how God first visited the nations, to take out of them a people for his name. **15** This agrees with the words of the prophets. As it is written, **16** 'After these things I will return; and I will rebuild the tabernacle of David that has fallen, and I will rebuild its ruins, and I will restore it, **17** that the rest of humanity may seek after the Lord, and all the nations who are called by my name, says the Lord, who makes these things **18** known from the age **(aiōn g165)**. **19** "Therefore my judgment is that we do not trouble those from among the Gentile people who turn to God, **20** but that we write to them that they abstain from things defiled by idols, from sexual immorality, from what is strangled, and from blood. **21** For Moses from generations of old has in every city those who proclaim him, being read in the synagogues every Sabbath." **22** Then it seemed good to the apostles and the elders, with the whole church, to choose men out of their company, and send them to Antioch with Paul and Barnabas: Judas called Barsabbas, and Silas, chief men among the brothers. **23** They wrote these things by their hand: "The apostles, the elders, and the brothers, to the Gentile brothers who are in Antioch, Syria, and Cilicia: greetings. **24** Because we have heard that some who went out from us have troubled you with words, unsettling your souls; to whom we gave no commandment; **25** it seemed good to us, having come to one accord, to choose out men and send them to you with our beloved Barnabas and Paul, **26** who have risked their lives for the name of our Lord Jesus Christ. **27** We have sent therefore Judas and Silas, who themselves will also tell you the same things by word of mouth. **28** For it seemed good to the Holy Spirit, and to us, to lay no greater burden on you than these necessary things: **29** that you abstain from things sacrificed to idols, from blood, from things strangled, and from sexual immorality, from which if you keep yourselves, it will be well with you. Farewell." **30** So, when they were sent off, they came to Antioch, and having gathered the congregation together, they delivered the letter. **31** When they had read it, they rejoiced over the encouragement. **32** Judas and Silas, also being prophets themselves, encouraged the brothers with many words, and strengthened them. **33** After they had spent some time there, they were sent back with greetings from the brothers to those that had sent them forth. **34** However, Silas decided to remain there. **35** And Paul and Barnabas stayed in Antioch, teaching and proclaiming the word of the Lord, with many others also. **36** After some days Paul said to Barnabas, "Let us return now and visit our brothers in every city in which we proclaimed the word of the Lord, to see how they are doing." **37** Barnabas planned to take John, who was called Mark, with them also. **38** But Paul did not think that it was a good idea to take with them someone who had withdrawn from them in Pamphylia, and did not go with them to do the work. **39** Then the contention grew so sharp that they separated from each other. Barnabas took Mark with him, and sailed away to Cyprus, **40** but Paul chose Silas, and went out, being commended by the brothers to the grace of the Lord. **41** He went through Syria and Cilicia, strengthening the churches.

16 He came to Derbe and Lystra. And look, a certain disciple was there, named Timothy, the son of a Jewish woman who believed; but his father was a Greek. **2** The brothers who were at Lystra and Iconium gave a good testimony about him. **3** Paul wanted to have him go out with him, and he took and circumcised him because of the Jews who were in those parts; for they all knew that his father was a Greek. **4** As they went on their way through the cities, they delivered the decrees to them to keep which had been ordained by the apostles and elders who were at Jerusalem. **5** So the churches were strengthened in the faith, and increased in number daily. **6** When they had gone through the region of Phrygia and Galatia, they were forbidden by the Holy Spirit to speak the word in Asia. **7** When they had come opposite Mysia, they tried to go into Bithynia, but the Spirit of Jesus did not allow them. **8** Passing by Mysia, they came down to Troas. **9** A vision appeared to Paul in the night. There was a man of Macedonia standing, begging him, and saying, "Come over into Macedonia and help us." **10** When he had seen the vision, immediately we sought to go out to Macedonia, concluding that the Lord had called us to proclaim the Good News to them. **11** Then, setting sail from Troas, we made a straight course to Samothrace, and the day following to Neapolis; **12** and from there to Philippi, which is a principle city of that district of Macedonia, a colony. We were staying some days in this city. **13** On the Sabbath day we went forth outside of the gate by a riverside, where we supposed there was a place of prayer, and we sat down, and spoke to the women who had come together. **14** A certain woman named Lydia, a seller of purple, of the city of Thyatira, one who worshiped God, heard us; whose heart the Lord opened to listen to the things which were spoken by Paul. **15** When she and her household were baptized, she urged us, saying, "If you have judged me to be faithful to the Lord, come into my house, and stay." So she persuaded us. **16** It happened, as we were going to prayer, that a certain girl having a spirit of Python met us, who brought her masters much gain by fortune telling. **17** She followed Paul and us, shouting, "These men are servants of the Most High God, who proclaim to you the way of salvation." **18** She was doing this for many days. But Paul, becoming greatly annoyed, turned and said to the spirit, "I command you in the name of Jesus Christ to come out of her." And it came out at once. **19** But when her masters saw that the hope of their gain was gone, they seized Paul and Silas, and

Acts

dragged them into the marketplace before the rulers. **20** When they had brought them to the magistrates, they said, "These men, being Jews, are agitating our city, **21** and set forth customs which it is not lawful for us to accept or to observe, being Romans." **22** The crowd rose up together against them, and the magistrates tore their clothes off of them, and commanded them to be beaten with rods. **23** When they had laid many stripes on them, they threw them into prison, charging the jailer to keep them safely, **24** who, having received such a command, threw them into the inner prison, and secured their feet in the stocks. **25** But about midnight Paul and Silas were praying and singing hymns to God, and the prisoners were listening to them. **26** Suddenly there was a great earthquake, so that the foundations of the prison were shaken; and immediately all the doors were opened, and everyone's bonds were loosened. **27** The jailer, being roused out of sleep and seeing the prison doors open, drew his sword and was about to kill himself, supposing that the prisoners had escaped. **28** But Paul shouted loudly, saying, "Do not harm yourself, for we are all here." **29** He called for lights and sprang in, and, fell down trembling before Paul and Silas, **30** and brought them out and said, "Sirs, what must I do to be saved?" **31** They said, "Believe in the Lord Jesus, and you will be saved, you and your household." **32** They spoke the word of the Lord to him, and to all who were in his house. **33** He took them the same hour of the night, and washed their stripes, and was immediately baptized, he and all his household. **34** He brought them up into his house, and set food before them, and rejoiced greatly, with all his household, having believed in God. **35** But when it was day, the magistrates sent the sergeants, saying, "Let those men go." **36** The jailer reported these words to Paul, saying, "The magistrates have sent to let you go; now therefore come out, and go in peace." **37** But Paul said to them, "They have beaten us publicly, without a trial, men who are Romans, and have cast us into prison. Do they now release us secretly? No indeed. Let them come themselves and bring us out." **38** The sergeants reported these words to the magistrates, and they were afraid when they heard that they were Romans, **39** and they came and apologized to them. When they had brought them out, they asked them to depart from the city. **40** They went out of the prison, and entered into Lydia's house. When they had seen the brothers, they encouraged them, and departed.

17 Now when they had passed through Amphipolis and Apollonia, they came to Thessalonica, where there was a Jewish synagogue. **2** Paul, as was his custom, went in to them, and for three Sabbath days reasoned with them from the Scriptures, **3** explaining and demonstrating that the Christ had to suffer and rise again from the dead, and saying, "This Jesus, whom I proclaim to you, is the Christ." **4** Some of them were persuaded, and joined Paul and Silas, as did a large number of the devout Greeks, and not a few of the prominent women. **5** But the Jews, being moved with jealousy, took along some wicked men from the marketplace, and gathering a crowd, set the city in an uproar. Assaulting the house of Jason, they sought to bring them out to the people. **6** When they did not find them, they dragged Jason and certain brothers before the rulers of the city, crying, "These who have turned the world upside down have come here also, **7** whom Jason has received. These all act contrary to the decrees of Caesar, saying that there is another king, Jesus." **8** The crowd and the rulers of the city were troubled when they heard these things. **9** When they had taken security from Jason and the rest, they let them go. **10** The brothers immediately sent Paul and Silas away by night to Beroea. When they arrived, they went into the Jewish synagogue. **11** Now these were more noble than those in Thessalonica, in that they received the word with all readiness of the mind, examining the Scriptures daily to see whether these things were so. **12** Many of them therefore believed; also of the prominent Greek women, and not a few men. **13** But when the Jews of Thessalonica had knowledge that the word of God was proclaimed by Paul at Beroea also, they came there likewise, inciting and disturbing the crowds. **14** Then the brothers immediately sent out Paul to go as far as to the sea, and Silas and Timothy still stayed there. **15** But those who escorted Paul brought him as far as Athens. Receiving a commandment to Silas and Timothy that they should come to him very quickly, they departed. **16** Now while Paul waited for them at Athens, his spirit was provoked within him as he saw the city full of idols. **17** So he reasoned in the synagogue with the Jews and the devout persons, and in the marketplace every day with those who met him. **18** Some of the Epicurean and Stoic philosophers also were conversing with him. Some said, "What does this babbler want to say?" Others said, "He seems to be advocating foreign deities," because he preached Jesus and the resurrection. **19** They took hold of him, and brought him to the Areopagus, saying, "May we know what this new teaching is, which is spoken by you? **20** For you bring certain strange things to our ears. We want to know therefore what these things mean." **21** Now all the Athenians and the strangers living there spent their time in nothing else, but either to tell or to hear some new thing. **22** Paul stood in the middle of the Areopagus, and said, "You men of Athens, I perceive that you are very religious in all things. **23** For as I passed along, and observed the objects of your worship, I found also an altar with this inscription: 'TO AN UNKNOWN GOD.' What therefore you worship in ignorance, this I announce to you. **24** The God who made the world and all things in it, he, being Lord of heaven and earth, does not dwell in temples made with hands, **25** neither is he served by human hands, as though he needed anything, seeing he himself gives to all life and breath, and all things. **26** He made from one blood every nation of the human race to dwell on all the surface of the earth, having determined appointed seasons, and the boundaries of their dwellings, **27** that they should seek God, if perhaps they might reach out for him and find him, though he is not far from each one of us. **28** 'For in him we live, and move, and have our being.' As some of your own poets have said, 'For we are also his offspring.' **29** Being then the offspring of God, we ought not to think that the Divine Nature is like gold, or silver, or stone, engraved by human art and design. **30** The times of ignorance therefore God overlooked. But now he commands that all people everywhere should repent, **31** because he has appointed a day in which he will judge the world in righteousness by the man whom he has ordained; of which he has given assurance to everyone by raising him from the dead." **32** Now when they heard of the resurrection of the dead, some mocked; but others said, "We want to hear you again concerning this." **33** Thus Paul went out from among them. **34** But some people joined with him, and believed, among whom also was Dionysius the Areopagite, and a woman named Damaris, and others with them.

18 After these things Paul departed from Athens, and came to Corinth. **2** He found a certain Jew named Aquila, a man of Pontus by race, who had recently come from Italy, with his wife Priscilla, because Claudius had commanded all the Jews to depart from Rome. He came to them, **3** and because he practiced the same trade, he lived with them and worked, for by trade they were tent makers. **4** He reasoned in the synagogue every Sabbath, and persuaded Jews and Greeks. **5** But when Silas and Timothy came down from Macedonia, Paul was compelled by the word, testifying to the Jews that Jesus was the Christ. **6** When they opposed him and blasphemed, he shook out his clothing and said to them, "Your blood be on your own heads. I am clean. From now on, I will go to the Gentile people." **7** He departed there, and went into the house of a certain man named Titius Justus, one who worshiped God, whose house was next door to the synagogue. **8** Crispus, the ruler of the synagogue, believed in the Lord with all his house. Many of the Corinthians, when they heard, believed and were baptized. **9** The Lord said to Paul in the night by a vision, "Do not be afraid, but speak and do not be silent; **10** for I am with you, and no one will attack you to harm you, for I have many people in this city." **11** He lived there a year and six months, teaching the word of God among them. **12** But when Gallio was proconsul of Achaia, the Jews with one accord rose up against Paul and brought him before the judgment seat, **13** saying, "This one persuades people to worship God contrary to the law." **14** But when Paul was about to open his mouth, Gallio said to the Jews, "If indeed it were a matter of wrong or of wicked crime, you Jews, it would be reasonable that I should bear with you; **15** but if they are questions about words and names and your own law, look to it yourselves. For I do not want to be a judge of these matters." **16** He drove them from the judgment seat. **17** Then they all took hold of Sosthenes, the ruler of the synagogue, and beat him before the judgment seat. But none of these things were of concern to Gallio. **18** Paul, having stayed after this many more days, took his leave of the brothers, and sailed from there for Syria, together with Priscilla and Aquila. He shaved his head in Cenchreae, for he had a vow. **19** They came to Ephesus, and he left them there; but he himself entered into the synagogue, and reasoned with the Jews. **20** When they asked him to stay a longer time, he declined; **21** but taking his leave of them, and saying, "I will return again to you if God wills," he set sail from Ephesus. **22** When he had landed at Caesarea, he went up and greeted the church, and went down to Antioch. **23** Having spent some time there, he departed, and went through the region of Galatia, and Phrygia, in order, strengthening all the disciples. **24** Now a certain Jew named Apollos, an Alexandrian by race, an eloquent man, came to Ephesus. He was mighty in the Scriptures. **25** This man had been instructed in the way of the Lord; and being fervent in spirit, he spoke and taught accurately the things concerning Jesus, although he knew only the baptism of John. **26** He began to speak boldly in the synagogue. But when Priscilla and Aquila heard him, they took him aside, and explained to him the way of God more accurately. **27** When he had determined to pass over into Achaia, the brothers encouraged him, and wrote to the disciples to receive him. When he had come, he greatly helped those who had believed through grace; **28** for he powerfully refuted the Jews, publicly showing by the Scriptures that Jesus was the Christ.

19 It happened that, while Apollos was at Corinth, Paul, having passed through the upper country, came to Ephesus, and found certain disciples. **2** He said to them, "Did you receive the Holy Spirit when you believed?" They said to him, "No, we have not even heard that there is a Holy Spirit." **3** He said, "Into what then were you baptized?" They said, "Into John's baptism." **4** Paul said, "John indeed baptized with the baptism of repentance, saying to the people that they should believe in the one who would come after him, that is, in Jesus." **5** When they heard this, they were baptized in the name of the Lord Jesus. **6** When Paul had laid his hands on them, the Holy Spirit came on them, and they spoke with other tongues and prophesied. **7** They were about twelve men in all. **8** He entered into the synagogue, and spoke boldly for a period of three months, reasoning and persuading about the things concerning the Kingdom of God. **9** But when some were hardened and disobedient, speaking evil of the Way before the crowd, he departed from them, and separated the disciples, reasoning daily in the school of Tyrannus. **10** This continued for two years, so that all those who lived in Asia heard the word of the Lord Jesus, both Jews and Greeks. **11** God worked special miracles by the hands of Paul, **12** so that even handkerchiefs or aprons were carried away from his body to the sick, and the evil spirits went out. **13** But some of the itinerant Jews, exorcists, took on themselves to invoke over those who had the evil spirits the name of the Lord Jesus, saying, "I adjure you by Jesus whom Paul preaches." **14** There were seven sons of one Sceva, a Jewish chief priest, who did this. **15** The evil spirit answered, "Jesus I know, and Paul I know, but who are you?" **16** The man in whom the evil spirit was leaped on them, and overpowered them all, and prevailed against them, so that they fled out of that house naked and wounded. **17** This became known to all, both Jews and Greeks, who lived at Ephesus. Fear fell on them all, and the name of the Lord Jesus was magnified. **18** Many also of those who had believed came, confessing, and declaring their deeds. **19** Many of those who practiced

Acts

magical arts brought their books together and burned them in the sight of all. They counted the price of them, and found it to be fifty thousand pieces of silver. **20** So the word of the Lord was growing and becoming mighty. **21** Now after these things had ended, Paul determined in the spirit, when he had passed through Macedonia and Achaia, to go to Jerusalem, saying, "After I have been there, I must also see Rome." **22** Having sent into Macedonia two of those who served him, Timothy and Erastus, he himself stayed in Asia for a while. **23** About that time there arose no small stir concerning the Way. **24** For a certain man named Demetrius, a silversmith, who made silver shrines of Artemis, brought no little business to the craftsmen, **25** whom he gathered together, with the workmen of like occupation, and said, "Sirs, you know that by this business we have our wealth. **26** You see and hear, that not at Ephesus alone, but almost throughout all Asia, this Paul has persuaded and turned away many people, saying that they are no gods, that are made with hands. **27** Not only is there danger that this our trade come into disrepute; but also that the temple of the great goddess Artemis will be counted as nothing, and that she should even be deposed from her magnificence, whom all Asia and the world worships." **28** When they heard this they were filled with anger, and began to shout, saying, "Great is Artemis of the Ephesians." **29** The city was filled with confusion, and they rushed with one accord into the theater, having seized Gaius and Aristarchus, Macedonians, Paul's companions in travel. **30** When Paul wanted to enter in to the people, the disciples did not allow him. **31** And also some of the Asiarchs, who were his friends, sent to him and urged him not to venture into the theater. **32** Some therefore shouted one thing, and some another, for the assembly was in confusion. Most of them did not know why they had come together. **33** They brought Alexander out of the crowd, the Jews putting him forward. Alexander beckoned with his hand, and would have made a defense to the people. **34** But when they perceived that he was a Jew, all with one voice for a time of about two hours shouted, "Great is Artemis of the Ephesians." **35** When the town clerk had quieted the crowd, he said, "You men of Ephesus, is there anyone who does not know that the city of the Ephesians is temple keeper of the great Artemis, and of the image which fell down from Zeus? **36** Seeing then that these things cannot be denied, you ought to be quiet, and to do nothing rash. **37** For you have brought these men here, who are neither robbers of temples nor blasphemers of our goddess. **38** If therefore Demetrius and the craftsmen who are with him have a matter against anyone, the courts are open, and there are proconsuls. Let them press charges against one another. **39** But if you seek anything further, it will be settled in the regular assembly. **40** For indeed we are in danger of being accused concerning this day's riot, there being no cause. Concerning it, we would not be able to give an account of this commotion." **41** When he had thus spoken, he dismissed the assembly.

20 After the uproar had ceased, Paul sent for the disciples and, after encouraging them, took leave of them, and departed to go into Macedonia. **2** When he had gone through those parts, and had encouraged them with many words, he came into Greece. **3** When he had spent three months there, and a plot was made against him by Jews as he was about to set sail for Syria, he determined to return through Macedonia. **4** He was accompanied by Sopater son of Pyrrhus of Beroea; Aristarchus and Secundus of the Thessalonians; Gaius of Derbe; Timothy; and Tychicus and Trophimus of Asia. **5** But these had gone ahead, and were waiting for us at Troas. **6** We sailed away from Philippi after the days of Unleavened Bread, and came to them at Troas in five days, where we stayed seven days. **7** On the first day of the week, when we were gathered together to break bread, Paul talked with them, intending to depart on the next day, and continued his speech until midnight. **8** There were many lights in the upper chamber where we were gathered together. **9** A certain young man named Eutychus sat in the window, weighed down with deep sleep. As Paul spoke still longer, being weighed down by his sleep, he fell down from the third story, and was taken up dead. **10** Paul went down, and fell upon him, and embracing him said, "Do not be troubled, for his life is in him." **11** When he had gone up, and had broken bread, and eaten, and had talked with them a long while, even until break of day, he departed. **12** They brought the boy in alive, and were greatly comforted. **13** But we who went ahead to the ship set sail for Assos, intending to take Paul aboard there, for he had so arranged, intending himself to go by land. **14** When he met us at Assos, we took him aboard, and came to Mitylene. **15** Sailing from there, we came the following day opposite Chios. The next day we landed at Samos, and the day after we came to Miletus. **16** For Paul had determined to sail past Ephesus, that he might not have to spend time in Asia; for he was hastening, if it were possible for him, to be in Jerusalem on the day of Pentecost. **17** From Miletus he sent to Ephesus, and called to himself the elders of the church. **18** When they had come to him, he said to them, "You yourselves know, from the first day that I set foot in Asia, how I was with you all the time, **19** serving the Lord with all humility, with many tears, and with trials which happened to me by the plots of the Jews; **20** how I did not hold back from declaring to you anything that was profitable, and teaching you publicly and from house to house, **21** testifying both to Jews and to Greeks repentance toward God, and faith toward our Lord Jesus. **22** And now, look, compelled by the Spirit, I am going to Jerusalem, not knowing what will happen to me there; **23** except that the Holy Spirit testifies in every city, saying that bonds and afflictions wait for me. **24** But I make my life an account of nothing precious to myself, so that I may finish my race, and the ministry which I received from the Lord Jesus, to fully testify to the Good News of the grace of God. **25** "And now, look, I know that you all, among whom I went about proclaiming the Kingdom, will see my face no more. **26** Therefore I testify to you today that I am innocent of everyone's blood, **27** for I did not hold back from declaring to you the whole counsel of God. **28** Watch out for yourselves and to all the flock, in which the Holy Spirit has made you overseers, to shepherd the church of God which he purchased with his own blood. **29** For I know that after my departure, vicious wolves will enter in among you, not sparing the flock. **30** Men will arise from among your own selves, speaking perverse things, to draw away the disciples after them. **31** Therefore watch, remembering that for a period of three years I did not cease to admonish everyone night and day with tears. **32** Now I entrust you to God, and to the word of his grace, which is able to build up, and to give you the inheritance among all those who are sanctified. **33** I coveted no one's silver, or gold, or clothing. **34** You yourselves know that these hands served my necessities, and those who were with me. **35** In all things I gave you an example, that so laboring you ought to help the weak, and to remember the words of the Lord Jesus, that he himself said, 'It is more blessed to give than to receive.'" **36** When he had spoken these things, he knelt down and prayed with them all. **37** They all wept a lot, and fell on Paul's neck and kissed him, **38** sorrowing most of all because of the word which he had spoken, that they should see his face no more. And they accompanied him to the ship.

21 When it happened that we had parted from them and had set sail, we came with a straight course to Cos, and the next day to Rhodes, and from there to Patara. **2** Having found a ship crossing over to Phoenicia, we went aboard, and set sail. **3** When we had come in sight of Cyprus, leaving it on the left hand, we sailed to Syria, and landed at Tyre, for there the ship was to unload her cargo. **4** Having found the disciples, we stayed there seven days. These said to Paul through the Spirit, that he should not go up to Jerusalem. **5** When it happened that we had accomplished the days, we departed and went on our journey. They all, with wives and children, brought us on our way until we were out of the city. Kneeling down on the beach, we prayed. **6** After saying goodbye to each other, we went on board the ship, and they returned home again. **7** When we had finished the voyage from Tyre, we arrived at Ptolemais. We greeted the brothers, and stayed with them one day. **8** On the next day, we departed and came to Caesarea. We entered into the house of Philip the evangelist, who was one of the seven, and stayed with him. **9** Now this man had four virgin daughters who prophesied. **10** As we stayed there some days, a certain prophet named Agabus came down from Judea. **11** Coming to us, and taking Paul's belt, he bound his own feet and hands, and said, "Thus says the Holy Spirit: 'So will the Jews in Jerusalem bind the man who owns this belt, and will deliver him into the hands of Gentile people.'" **12** When we heard these things, both we and the people of that place urged him not to go up to Jerusalem. **13** Then Paul answered, "What are you doing, weeping and breaking my heart? For I am ready not only to be bound, but also to die at Jerusalem for the name of the Lord Jesus." **14** When he would not be persuaded, we ceased, saying, "The Lord's will be done." **15** After these days we took up our baggage and went up to Jerusalem. **16** Some of the disciples from Caesarea also went with us, bringing one Mnason of Cyprus, an early disciple, with whom we would stay. **17** When we had come to Jerusalem, the brothers received us gladly. **18** The day following, Paul went in with us to James; and all the elders were present. **19** When he had greeted them, he reported one by one the things which God had worked among the Gentile people through his ministry. **20** They, when they heard it, glorified God. They said to him, "You see, brother, how many thousands there are among the Jews of those who have believed, and they are all zealous for the Law. **21** They have been informed about you, that you teach all the Jews who are among the Gentiles to forsake Moses, telling them not to circumcise their children neither to walk after the customs. **22** What then? The multitude must certainly meet. They will hear that you have come. **23** Therefore do what we tell you. We have four men who have taken a vow. **24** Take them, and purify yourself with them, and pay their expenses for them, that they may shave their heads. Then all will know that there is no truth in the things that they have been informed about you, but that you yourself also walk keeping the Law. **25** But concerning the Gentile who believe, we have written our decision that they should keep themselves from food offered to idols, from blood, from strangled things, and from sexual immorality." **26** Then Paul took the men, and the next day, purified himself and went with them into the temple, declaring the fulfillment of the days of purification, until the offering was offered for every one of them. **27** When the seven days were almost completed, the Jews from Asia, when they saw him in the temple, stirred up all the crowd and laid hands on him, **28** crying out, "Men of Israel, help. This is the man who teaches all men everywhere against the people, and the Law, and this place. Moreover, he also brought Greeks into the temple, and has defiled this holy place." **29** For they had previously seen Trophimus, the Ephesian, with him in the city, and they supposed that Paul had brought him into the temple. **30** All the city was moved, and the people ran together. They seized Paul and dragged him out of the temple. Immediately the doors were shut. **31** As they were trying to kill him, news came up to the commanding officer of the regiment that all Jerusalem was in an uproar. **32** Immediately he took soldiers and centurions, and ran down to them. They, when they saw the chief captain and the soldiers, stopped beating Paul. **33** Then the commanding officer came near, arrested him, commanded him to be bound with two chains, and inquired who he was and what he had done. **34** Some shouted one thing, and some another, among the crowd. When he could not find out the truth because of the noise, he commanded him to be brought into the barracks. **35** When he came to the stairs, it happened that he was carried by the soldiers because of the violence of the crowd; **36** for the crowd of the people followed after, crying out, "Away with him." **37** As Paul was about to be brought into the barracks, he asked the commanding officer, "May I speak something to you?" He said, "Do you know Greek? **38** Are you not then the Egyptian, who before these days stirred up to sedition and led out into the wilderness the four thousand men of the Assassins?" **39** But Paul said, "I am a Jew, from Tarsus in

Cilicia, a citizen of no insignificant city. I beg you, allow me to speak to the people." **40** When he had given him permission, Paul, standing on the stairs, beckoned with his hand to the people. When there was a great silence, he spoke to them in the Hebrew language, saying,

22 "Brothers and fathers, listen to the defense which I now make to you." **2** When they heard that he spoke to them in the Hebrew language, they were even more quiet. He said, **3** "I am indeed a Jew, born in Tarsus of Cilicia, but brought up in this city at the feet of Gamaliel, instructed according to the strict manner of the Law of our fathers, being zealous for God, even as you all are this day. **4** I persecuted this Way to the death, binding and delivering into prisons both men and women. **5** As also the high priest and all the council of the elders testify, from whom also I received letters to the brothers, and traveled to Damascus to bring them also who were there to Jerusalem in bonds to be punished. **6** It happened that, as I made my journey, and came close to Damascus, about noon, suddenly there shone from the sky a great light around me. **7** I fell to the ground, and heard a voice saying to me, 'Saul, Saul, why are you persecuting me?' **8** I answered, 'Who are you, Lord?' He said to me, 'I am Jesus the Nazorean, whom you persecute.' **9** "Those who were with me indeed saw the light, and were afraid, but they did not understand the voice of him who spoke to me. **10** I said, 'What should I do, Lord?' The Lord said to me, 'Arise, and go into Damascus. There you will be told about all things which are appointed for you to do.' **11** When I could not see for the glory of that light, being led by the hand of those who were with me, I came into Damascus. **12** One Ananias, a devout man according to the Law, well reported of by all the Jews who lived in Damascus, **13** came to me, and standing by me said to me, 'Brother Saul, receive your sight.' In that very hour I looked up at him. **14** He said, 'The God of our fathers has appointed you to know his will, and to see the Righteous One, and to hear a voice from his mouth. **15** For you will be a witness for him to all people of what you have seen and heard. **16** Now why do you wait? Arise, be baptized, and wash away your sins, calling on his name.' **17** "It happened that, when I had returned to Jerusalem, and while I prayed in the temple, I fell into a trance, **18** and saw him saying to me, 'Hurry and get out of Jerusalem quickly, because they will not receive testimony concerning me from you.' **19** I said, 'Lord, they themselves know that I imprisoned and beat in every synagogue those who believed in you. **20** When the blood of Stephen, your witness, was shed, I also was standing by, and guarding the cloaks of those who killed him.' **21** "He said to me, 'Depart, for I will send you out far from here to Gentile people.'" **22** They listened to him until he said that; then they lifted up their voice, and said, "Rid the earth of this fellow, for he is not fit to live." **23** As they yelled, and threw off their cloaks, and threw dust into the air, **24** the commanding officer commanded him to be brought into the barracks, ordering him to be examined by scourging, that he might know for what crime they yelled at him like that. **25** When they had tied him up with thongs, Paul asked the centurion who stood by, "Is it lawful for you to scourge a man who is a Roman, and not found guilty?" **26** When the centurion heard it, he went to the commanding officer and told him, "What are you about to do? For this man is a Roman." **27** The commanding officer came and asked him, "Tell me, are you a Roman?" He said, "Yes." **28** The commanding officer answered, "I bought my citizenship for a great price." Paul said, "But I was born a Roman." **29** Immediately those who were about to examine him departed from him, and the commanding officer also was afraid when he realized that he was a Roman, because he had bound him. **30** But on the next day, desiring to know the truth about why he was accused by the Jews, he freed him, and commanded the chief priests and all the council to come together, and brought Paul down and set him before them.

23 Paul, looking steadfastly at the council, said, "Brothers, I have lived before God in all good conscience until this day." **2** The high priest, Ananias, commanded those who stood by him to strike him on the mouth. **3** Then Paul said to him, "God will strike you, you whitewashed wall. Do you sit to judge me according to the Law, and command me to be struck contrary to the law?" **4** Those who stood by said, "Do you malign God's high priest?" **5** Paul said, "I did not know, brothers, that he was high priest. For it is written, 'You must not speak evil of a ruler of your people.'" **6** But when Paul perceived that the one part were Sadducees and the other Pharisees, he shouted in the council, "Men and brothers, I am a Pharisee, a son of Pharisees. Concerning the hope and resurrection of the dead I am being judged." **7** When he had said this, an argument arose between the Pharisees and Sadducees, and the assembly was divided. **8** For the Sadducees say that there is no resurrection, nor angel, nor spirit; but the Pharisees confess all of these. **9** A great clamor arose, and some of the scribes of the Pharisees part stood up, and contended, saying, "We find no evil in this man. What if a spirit spoke to him, or an angel?" **10** When a great argument arose, the commanding officer, fearing that Paul would be torn in pieces by them, commanded the soldiers to go down and take him by force from among them, and bring him into the barracks. **11** The following night, the Lord stood by him, and said, "Cheer up, for as you have testified about me at Jerusalem, so you must testify also at Rome." **12** When it was day, the Jews formed a conspiracy, and bound themselves under a curse, saying that they would neither eat nor drink until they had killed Paul. **13** There were more than forty people who had made this conspiracy. **14** They came to the chief priests and the elders, and said, "We have bound ourselves under a great curse, to taste nothing until we have killed Paul. **15** Now therefore, you with the council inform the commanding officer that he should bring him down to you, as though you were going to judge his case more exactly. We are ready to kill him before he comes near." **16** But Paul's sister's son heard of their lying in wait, and he came and entered into the barracks and told Paul. **17** Paul summoned one of the centurions, and said, "Bring this young man to the commanding officer, for he has something to tell him." **18** So he took him, and brought him to the commanding officer, and said, "Paul, the prisoner, summoned me and asked me to bring this young man to you, who has something to tell you." **19** The commanding officer took him by the hand, and going aside, asked him privately, "What is it that you have to tell me?" **20** And he said, "The Jews have agreed to ask you to bring Paul down to the council tomorrow, as though they intended to inquire somewhat more thoroughly concerning him. **21** Therefore do not yield to them, for more than forty men lie in wait for him, who have bound themselves under a curse neither to eat nor to drink until they have killed him. Now they are ready, looking for the promise from you." **22** So the commanding officer let the young man go, charging him, "Tell no one that you have revealed these things to me." **23** He called to himself two of the centurions, and said, "Prepare two hundred soldiers to go as far as Caesarea, with seventy horsemen, and two hundred spearmen, at nine tonight." **24** He asked them to provide animals, that they might set Paul on one, and bring him safely to Felix the governor. **25** He wrote a letter like this: **26** "Claudius Lysias to the most excellent governor Felix: Greetings. **27** "This man was seized by the Jews, and was about to be killed by them, when I came with the soldiers and rescued him, having learned that he was a Roman. **28** Desiring to know the cause why they accused him, I brought him down to their council. **29** I found him to be accused about questions of their law, but not to be charged with anything worthy of death or of imprisonment. **30** When I was told that there would be a plot against the man, I sent him to you immediately, charging his accusers also to bring their accusations against him before you. Farewell." **31** So the soldiers, carrying out their orders, took Paul and brought him by night to Antipatris. **32** But on the next day they left the horsemen to go with him, and returned to the barracks. **33** When they came to Caesarea and delivered the letter to the governor, they also presented Paul to him. **34** When the governor had read it, he asked what province he was from. When he understood that he was from Cilicia, he said, **35** "I will hear you fully when your accusers also arrive." He commanded that he be kept in Herod's palace.

24 After five days, the high priest, Ananias, came down with certain elders and an orator, one Tertullus. They informed the governor against Paul. **2** When he was called, Tertullus began to accuse him, saying, "Seeing that by you we enjoy much peace, and that by your foresight reforms are coming to this nation, **3** we accept it in all ways and in all places, most excellent Felix, with all thankfulness. **4** But, that I do not delay you, I entreat you to bear with us and hear a few words. **5** For we have found this man to be a plague, an instigator of insurrections among all the Jews throughout the world, and a ringleader of the sect of the Nazarenes. **6** He even tried to profane the temple, and we arrested him. And we would have judged him according to our law, **7** but the chief captain Lysias came, and with great violence took him away out of our hands, **8** commanding his accusers to come to you. By examining him yourself you may ascertain all these things of which we accuse him." **9** The Jews also joined in the attack, affirming that these things were so. **10** When the governor had beckoned to him to speak, Paul answered, "Because I know that you have been a judge of this nation for many years, I cheerfully make my defense, **11** seeing that you can recognize that it is not more than twelve days since I went up to worship at Jerusalem. **12** In the temple they did not find me disputing with anyone or stirring up a crowd, either in the synagogues, or in the city. **13** Nor can they prove to you the things of which they now accuse me. **14** But this I confess to you, that after the Way, which they call a sect, so I serve the God of our fathers, believing all things which are according to the Law, and which are written in the Prophets; **15** having hope toward God, which these also themselves look for, that there will be a resurrection, both of the just and unjust. **16** This being so, I also do my best to always have a clear conscience toward God and people. **17** Now after some years, I came to bring gifts for the needy to my nation, and offerings; **18** amid which certain Jews from Asia found me purified in the temple, not with a mob, nor with turmoil. **19** They ought to have been here before you, and to make accusation, if they had anything against me. **20** Or else let these men themselves say what injustice they found in me when I stood before the council, **21** unless it is for this one thing that I shouted out standing among them, 'Concerning the resurrection of the dead I am being judged before you today.'" **22** But Felix, having more exact knowledge concerning the Way, deferred them, saying, "When Lysias, the commanding officer, comes down, I will decide your case." **23** He ordered the centurion that he should be kept in custody, and should have some privileges, and not to forbid any of his friends to serve him or to visit him. **24** But after some days, Felix came with Drusilla, his wife, who was Jewish, and sent for Paul, and heard him concerning the faith in Christ Jesus. **25** As he reasoned about righteousness, self-control, and the judgment to come, Felix was terrified, and answered, "Go your way for this time, and when it is convenient for me, I will summon you." **26** Meanwhile, he also hoped that money would be given to him by Paul. Therefore also he sent for him more often, and talked with him. **27** But when two years were fulfilled, Felix was succeeded by Porcius Festus, and desiring to gain favor with the Jews, Felix left Paul in bonds.

25 Festus therefore, having come into the province, after three days went up to Jerusalem from Caesarea. **2** Then the high priest and the principal men of the Jews informed him against Paul, and they urged him, **3** asking a favor against him, that he would summon him to Jerusalem; plotting to kill him on the way. **4** However Festus answered that Paul should be kept in custody at Caesarea, and that he himself was about to depart shortly. **5** "Let them therefore," he said, "that are in power among you go down with me, and if there is anything wrong in the man, let them accuse him." **6** When he had stayed among them more than eight or ten days, he went down to Caesarea, and on the next day he sat on the judgment seat, and commanded

Paul to be brought. **7** When he had come, the Jews who had come down from Jerusalem stood around him, bringing against him many and grievous charges which they could not prove, **8** while he said in his defense, "Neither against the law of the Jews, nor against the temple, nor against Caesar, have I sinned at all." **9** But Festus, desiring to gain favor with the Jews, answered Paul and said, "Are you willing to go up to Jerusalem, and be judged by me there concerning these things?" **10** But Paul said, "I am standing before Caesar's judgment seat, where I ought to be tried. I have done no wrong to the Jews, as you also know very well. **11** For if I have done wrong, and have committed anything worthy of death, I do not refuse to die; but if none of those things is true that they accuse me of, no one can give me up to them. I appeal to Caesar." **12** Then Festus, when he had conferred with the council, answered, "You have appealed to Caesar. To Caesar you will go." **13** Now when some days had passed, Agrippa the King and Bernice arrived at Caesarea, and greeted Festus. **14** As they stayed there many days, Festus laid Paul's case before the king, saying, "There is a certain man left a prisoner by Felix; **15** about whom, when I was at Jerusalem, the chief priests and the Jewish elders informed me, asking for a sentence against him. **16** To whom I answered that it is not the custom of the Romans to give up anyone to destruction before the accused has met the accusers face to face, and has had opportunity to make his defense against the charge. **17** When therefore they had come together here, I did not delay, but on the next day sat on the judgment seat, and commanded the man to be brought. **18** Concerning whom, when the accusers stood up, they brought no charge of such things as I supposed; **19** but had certain questions against him about their own religion, and about one Jesus, who was dead, whom Paul affirmed to be alive. **20** Being perplexed how to inquire concerning these things, I asked whether he was willing to go to Jerusalem and there be judged concerning these matters. **21** But when Paul had appealed to be kept for the decision of the emperor, I commanded him to be kept until I could send him to Caesar." **22** Agrippa said to Festus, "I also would like to hear the man myself." "Tomorrow," he said, "you will hear him." **23** So on the next day, when Agrippa and Bernice had come with great pomp, and they had entered into the place of hearing with the commanding officers and principal men of the city, at the command of Festus, Paul was brought in. **24** And Festus said, "King Agrippa, and all people who are here present with us, you see this man, about whom the whole assembly of the Jews petitioned me, both at Jerusalem and here, crying that he ought not to live any longer. **25** But when I found that he had committed nothing worthy of death, and as he himself appealed to the emperor I determined to send him. **26** Of whom I have no certain thing to write to my lord. Therefore I have brought him forth before you, and especially before you, King Agrippa, that, after examination, I may have something to write. **27** For it seems to me unreasonable, in sending a prisoner, not to also specify the charges against him."

26 Agrippa said to Paul, "You may speak for yourself." Then Paul stretched out his hand, and made his defense. **2** "I think myself happy, King Agrippa, that I am to make my defense before you this day concerning all the things that I am accused by the Jews, **3** especially because you are expert in all customs and questions which are among Jews. Therefore I beg you to hear me patiently. **4** "Indeed, all Jews know my way of life from my youth up, which was from the beginning among my own nation and at Jerusalem; **5** having known me from the first, if they are willing to testify, that after the strictest sect of our religion I lived a Pharisee. **6** Now I stand here to be judged for the hope of the promise made by God to our fathers, **7** which our twelve tribes, earnestly serving night and day, hope to attain. Concerning this hope I am accused by the Jews, O King. **8** Why is it judged incredible with you, if God does raise the dead? **9** "In fact, I thought to myself that I ought to do many things against the name of Jesus the Nazorean. **10** This I also did in Jerusalem. I both shut up many of the saints in prisons, having received authority from the chief priests, and when they were put to death I gave my vote against them. **11** Punishing them often in all the synagogues, I tried to make them blaspheme. Being exceedingly enraged against them, I persecuted them even to foreign cities. **12** "Whereupon as I traveled to Damascus with the authority and commission from the chief priests, **13** at noon, O King, I saw on the way a light from the sky, brighter than the sun, shining around me and those who traveled with me. **14** When we had all fallen to the earth, I heard a voice saying to me in the Hebrew language, 'Saul, Saul, why are you persecuting me? It is hard for you to kick against the goads.' **15** "I said, 'Who are you, Lord?' "He said, 'I am Jesus, whom you are persecuting. **16** But arise, and stand on your feet, for I have appeared to you for this purpose: to appoint you a servant and a witness both of the things which you have seen me, and of the things which I will reveal to you; **17** delivering you from the people, and from the Gentile people, to whom I send you, **18** to open their eyes, that they may turn from darkness to light and from the power of Satan to God, that they may receive forgiveness of sins and an inheritance among those who are sanctified by faith in me.' **19** "Therefore, King Agrippa, I was not disobedient to the heavenly vision, **20** but declared first to them of Damascus, at Jerusalem, and throughout all the country of Judea, and also to the Gentiles, that they should repent and turn to God, doing works worthy of repentance. **21** For this reason Jews seized me in the temple, and tried to kill me. **22** Having therefore obtained the help that is from God, I stand to this day testifying both to small and great, saying nothing but what the Prophets and Moses said would happen, **23** how the Christ would suffer, and how, by the resurrection of the dead, he would be first to proclaim light both to these people and to Gentile people." **24** As he thus made his defense, Festus said with a loud voice, "Paul, you are crazy. Your great learning is driving you insane." **25** But he said, "I am not crazy, most excellent Festus, but boldly declare words of truth and reasonableness. **26** For the king knows of these things, to whom also I speak freely.

For I am persuaded that none of these things is hidden from him, for this has not been done in a corner. **27** King Agrippa, do you believe the prophets? I know that you believe." **28** Agrippa said to Paul, "With a little persuasion are you trying to make me a Christian?" **29** Paul said, "I pray to God, that whether with little or with much, not only you, but also all that hear me this day, might become such as I am, except for these bonds." **30** The king rose up with the governor, and Bernice, and those who sat with them. **31** When they had withdrawn, they spoke one to another, saying, "This man does nothing worthy of death or of bonds." **32** Agrippa said to Festus, "This man might have been set free if he had not appealed to Caesar."

27 When it was determined that we should sail for Italy, they delivered Paul and certain other prisoners to a centurion named Julius, of the Augustan band. **2** Embarking in a ship from Adramyttium, which was about to sail to places on the coast of Asia, we put to sea; Aristarchus, a Macedonian of Thessalonica, being with us. **3** The next day, we landed at Sidon. Julius treated Paul kindly, and gave him permission to go to his friends and refresh himself. **4** Putting to sea from there, we sailed under the lee of Cyprus, because the winds were contrary. **5** When we had sailed across the sea which is off Cilicia and Pamphylia, we came to Myra, a city of Lycia. **6** There the centurion found a ship of Alexandria sailing for Italy, and he put us on board. **7** When we had sailed slowly many days, and had come with difficulty opposite Cnidus, the wind not allowing us further, we sailed under the lee of Crete, opposite Salmone. **8** With difficulty sailing along it we came to a certain place called Fair Havens, near the city of Lasea. **9** When much time had passed and the voyage was now dangerous, because the Fast had now already gone by, Paul admonished them, **10** and said to them, "Sirs, I perceive that the voyage will be with injury and much loss, not only of the cargo and the ship, but also of our lives." **11** But the centurion gave more heed to the master and to the owner of the ship than to those things which were spoken by Paul. **12** Because the haven was not suitable to winter in, the majority advised going to sea from there, if by any means they could reach Phoenix, and winter there, which is a port of Crete, looking northeast and southeast. **13** When the south wind blew softly, supposing that they had obtained their purpose, they weighed anchor and sailed along Crete, close to shore. **14** But before long, a stormy wind beat down from shore, which is called Euraquilo. **15** When the ship was caught, and could not face the wind, we gave way to it, and were driven along. **16** Running under the lee of a small island called Cauda, we were able, with difficulty, to secure the boat. **17** After they had hoisted it up, they used cables to help reinforce the ship. Fearing that they would run aground on the Syrtis, they lowered the sea anchor, and so were driven along. **18** As we labored exceedingly with the storm, the next day they began to throw things overboard. **19** On the third day, they threw out the ship's tackle with their own hands. **20** When neither sun nor stars shone on us for many days, and no small storm pressed on us, all hope that we would be saved was now taken away. **21** When they had been long without food, Paul stood up in the middle of them, and said, "Sirs, you should have listened to me, and not have set sail from Crete, and have gotten this injury and loss. **22** Now I exhort you to cheer up, for there will be no loss of life among you, but only of the ship. **23** For there stood by me this night an angel, belonging to the God whose I am and whom I serve, **24** saying, 'Do not be afraid, Paul. You must stand before Caesar. And look, God has granted you all those who sail with you.' **25** Therefore, sirs, cheer up. For I believe God, that it will be just as it has been spoken to me. **26** But we must run aground on a certain island." **27** But when the fourteenth night had come, as we were driven back and forth in the Adriatic Sea, about midnight the sailors surmised that they were drawing near to some land. **28** They took soundings, and found twenty fathoms. After a little while, they took soundings again, and found fifteen fathoms. **29** Fearing that we would run aground on rocky ground, they let go four anchors from the stern, and wished for daylight. **30** As the sailors were trying to flee out of the ship, and had lowered the boat into the sea, pretending that they would lay out anchors from the bow, **31** Paul said to the centurion and to the soldiers, "Unless these stay in the ship, you cannot be saved." **32** Then the soldiers cut away the ropes of the boat, and let it fall off. **33** While the day was coming on, Paul urged them all to take some food, saying, "This day is the fourteenth day that you wait and continue fasting, having taken nothing. **34** Therefore I urge you to take some food, for this is for your preservation; for not a hair will perish from any of your heads." **35** When he had said this, and had taken bread, he gave thanks to God in the presence of all, and he broke it, and began to eat. **36** Then they all cheered up, and they also took food. **37** In all, we were two hundred seventy-six souls on the ship. **38** When they had eaten enough, they lightened the ship, throwing out the wheat into the sea. **39** When it was day, they did not recognize the land, but they noticed a certain bay with a beach, and they decided to try to drive the ship onto it. **40** Casting off the anchors, they left them in the sea, at the same time untying the rudder ropes. Hoisting up the foresail to the wind, they made for the beach. **41** But coming to a place where two seas met, they ran the vessel aground. The bow struck and remained immovable, but the stern began to break up by the violence of the waves. **42** The soldiers' counsel was to kill the prisoners, so that none of them would swim out and escape. **43** But the centurion, desiring to save Paul, stopped them from their purpose, and commanded that those who could swim should throw themselves overboard first to go toward the land; **44** and the rest should follow, some on planks, and some on other things from the ship. So it happened that they all escaped safely to the land.

28 When we had escaped, then we learned that the island was called Malta. **2** The natives showed us uncommon kindness; for they kindled a fire, and received us all, because of the present rain, and because of the cold. **3** But when Paul had gathered a bundle of sticks and placed them on the fire, a viper came out because of the heat, and fastened on his hand. **4** When the natives saw the creature hanging from his hand, they said one to another, "No doubt this man is a murderer, whom, though he has escaped from the sea, yet Justice has not allowed to live." **5** However he shook off the creature into the fire, and was not harmed. **6** But they expected that he would have swollen or fallen down dead suddenly, but when they watched for a long time and saw nothing bad happen to him, they changed their minds, and said that he was a god. **7** Now in the neighborhood of that place were lands belonging to the chief official of the island, named Publius, who received us, and courteously entertained us for three days. **8** It happened that the father of Publius lay sick of fever and dysentery. Paul entered in to him, prayed, and laying his hands on him, healed him. **9** Then when this was done, the rest also who had diseases in the island came, and were cured. **10** They also honored us with many honors, and when we sailed, they put on board the things that we needed. **11** After three months, we set sail in a ship of Alexandria which had wintered in the island, whose sign was "The Twin Brothers." **12** Touching at Syracuse, we stayed there three days. **13** From there we cast off and arrived at Rhegium. After one day, a south wind sprang up, and on the second day we came to Puteoli, **14** where we found brothers, and were entreated to stay with them for seven days. So we came to Rome. **15** From there the brothers, when they heard of us, came to meet us as far as The Market of Appius and The Three Taverns. When Paul saw them, he thanked God, and took courage. **16** When we entered into Rome, Paul was allowed to stay by himself with the soldier who guarded him. **17** It happened that after three days Paul called together those who were the Jewish leaders. When they had come together, he said to them, "I, brothers, though I had done nothing against the people, or the customs of our fathers, still was delivered prisoner from Jerusalem into the hands of the Romans, **18** who, when they had examined me, desired to set me free, because there was no cause of death in me. **19** But when the Jews spoke against it, I was forced to appeal to Caesar, not that I had anything about which to accuse my nation. **20** For this cause therefore I asked to see you and to speak with you. For because of the hope of Israel I am bound with this chain." **21** They said to him, "We neither received letters from Judea concerning you, nor did any of the brothers come here and report or speak any evil of you. **22** But we desire to hear from you what you think. For, as concerning this sect, it is known to us that everywhere it is spoken against." **23** When they had appointed him a day, many people came to him at his lodging. He explained to them, testifying about the Kingdom of God, and persuading them concerning Jesus, both from the Law of Moses and from the Prophets, from morning until evening. **24** Some believed the things which were spoken, and some disbelieved. **25** When they did not agree among themselves, they departed after Paul had spoken one word, "The Holy Spirit spoke rightly through Isaiah, the prophet, to your fathers, **26** saying, 'Go to this people, and say, in hearing, you will hear, but will in no way understand. In seeing, you will see, but will in no way perceive. **27** For this people's heart has grown callous. Their ears are dull of hearing. Their eyes they have closed. Lest they should see with their eyes, hear with their ears, understand with their heart, and would turn again, and I would heal them.' **28** "Be it known therefore to you, that the salvation of God is sent to the nations. They will also listen." **29** And when he had said these words, the Jews departed, having a great dispute among themselves. **30** And Paul stayed two whole years in his own rented house, and received all who were coming to him, **31** proclaiming the Kingdom of God, and teaching the things concerning the Lord Jesus Christ with all boldness, without hindrance.

Romans

1 Paul, a servant of Christ Jesus, called to be an apostle, set apart for the Good News of God, **2** which he promised before through his prophets in the holy Scriptures, **3** concerning his Son, who was born of the offspring of David according to the flesh, **4** who was declared to be the Son of God with power, according to the Spirit of holiness, by the resurrection from the dead, Jesus Christ our Lord, **5** through whom we received grace and the office of apostle, for obedience of faith among all the nations, for his name's sake; **6** among whom you are also called to belong to Jesus Christ; **7** to all who are in Rome, loved by God, called to be saints: Grace to you and peace from God our Father and the Lord Jesus Christ. **8** First, I thank my God through Jesus Christ for all of you, because your faith is proclaimed throughout the whole world. **9** For God is my witness, whom I serve in my spirit in the Good News of his Son, how I constantly mention you **10** always in my prayers, requesting, if by any means now at last I may succeed by the will of God to come to you. **11** For I long to see you, that I may impart to you some spiritual gift to strengthen you; **12** that is, that you and I may be mutually encouraged by each other's faith, both yours and mine. **13** Now I do not desire to have you unaware, brothers, that I often planned to come to you, and was hindered so far, that I might have some fruit among you also, even as among the other Gentile people. **14** I have an obligation both to Greeks and to barbarians, both to the wise and to the foolish. **15** So, for my part, I am eager to preach the Good News to you also who are in Rome. **16** For I am not ashamed of the Good News, for it is the power of God for salvation for everyone who believes; for the Jew first, and also for the Greek. **17** For in it is revealed God's righteousness from faith to faith. As it is written, "But the righteous will live by faith." **18** For the wrath of God is revealed from heaven against all ungodliness and unrighteousness of people, who suppress the truth by unrighteousness, **19** because what can be known about God is plain to them, because God has shown it to them. **20** For since the creation of the world his invisible attributes, his eternal **(aïdios g126)** power and divine nature, have been clearly seen, being understood from what has been made. So they are without excuse. **21** Because, although they knew God, they did not glorify him as God or give him thanks, but their thinking became nonsense, and their foolish heart was darkened. **22** Claiming to be wise, they became fools, **23** and traded the glory of the incorruptible God for images resembling corruptible man, and of birds, and four-footed animals, and crawling creatures. **24** Therefore God also abandoned them in the lusts of their hearts to impurity, to the degrading of their bodies among themselves, **25** who exchanged the truth of God for a lie, and worshiped and served the creature rather than the Creator, who is blessed for the ages **(aiōn g165)**. Amen. **26** For this reason, God abandoned them to their degrading passions. For their women exchanged natural relations for that which is contrary to nature. **27** Likewise also the men, giving up natural relations with women, burned in their lust toward one another, men with men, committing what is shameful, and receiving in themselves the due penalty of their error. **28** Even as they refused to have God in their knowledge, God abandoned them to a reprobate mind, to do those things which are not right; **29** being filled with all unrighteousness, sexual immorality, wickedness, covetousness, maliciousness; full of envy, murder, strife, deceit, evil habits, secret slanderers, **30** slanderers, haters of God, insolent, arrogant, boastful, inventors of evil things, disobedient to parents, **31** foolish, promise-breakers, heartless, unforgiving, unmerciful; **32** who, knowing the ordinance of God, that those who practice such things are worthy of death, not only do the same, but also approve of those who practice them.

2 Therefore you are without excuse, everyone of you who passes judgment. For in that which you judge another, you condemn yourself. For you who judge practice the same things. **2** Now we know that the judgment of God is in accordance with truth against those who practice such things. **3** And do you think this, you who judge those who practice such things, and do the same, that you will escape the judgment of God? **4** Or do you despise the riches of his goodness, forbearance, and patience, not knowing that the goodness of God leads you to repentance? **5** But according to your hardness and unrepentant heart you are storing up for yourself wrath in the day of wrath and revelation of the righteous judgment of God; **6** who "will pay back to everyone according to their works:" **7** to those who by perseverance in good works seek glory and honor and incorruptibility, for consummate **(aiōnios g166)** life; **8** But to those who are self-seeking, and do not obey the truth, but obey wickedness -- wrath and anger, **9** affliction and distress, on every human being who does evil, to the Jew first, and also to the Greek. **10** But glory, honor, and peace for everyone who does good, to the Jew first, and also to the Greek. **11** For there is no partiality with God. **12** For as many as have sinned without the law will also perish without the law. As many as have sinned under the law will be judged by the law. **13** For it is not the hearers of the law who are righteous before God, but the doers of the law will be justified. **14** For when the Gentiles who do not have the law do by nature the things of the law, these, not having the law, are a law to themselves, **15** since they show the work of the law written on their hearts, their conscience bearing witness, and their thoughts either accusing or defending them, **16** in the day when God will judge the secrets of people, according to my Good News, by Christ Jesus. **17** But if you call yourself a Jew, and rely on the law, and boast in God, **18** and know his will, and approve the things that are excellent, being instructed out of the law, **19** and are confident that you yourself are a guide of the blind, a light to those who are in darkness, **20** a corrector of the foolish, a teacher of children, having in the law the embodiment of knowledge and truth. **21** You therefore who teach another, do you not teach yourself? You who preach against stealing, do you steal? **22** You who say that one should not commit adultery, do you commit adultery? You who detest idols, do you rob temples? 23 You who boast in the law, do you, by disobeying the law, dishonor God? 24 For because of you the name of God is blasphemed among the nations, just as it is written. 25 For circumcision indeed profits, if you are a doer of the law, but if you are a transgressor of the law, your circumcision has become uncircumcision. 26 If therefore the uncircumcised keep the requirements of the law, won't his uncircumcision be counted as circumcision? 27 Won't the uncircumcision which is by nature, if it fulfills the law, judge you, who with the letter and circumcision are a transgressor of the law? 28 For he is not a Jew who is one outwardly, neither is that circumcision which is outward in the flesh; 29 but he is a Jew who is one inwardly, and circumcision is that of the heart, by the Spirit, not in the letter; whose praise is not from people, but from God.

3 Then what advantage does the Jew have? Or what is the profit of circumcision? 2 Much in every way. Because first of all, they were entrusted with the oracles of God. 3 For what if some were without faith? Will their lack of faith nullify the faithfulness of God? 4 Absolutely not. Let God be found true, but every human being a liar. As it is written, "That you may be justified in your words, and prevail when you judge." 5 But if our unrighteousness commends the righteousness of God, what will we say? Is God unrighteous who inflicts wrath? (I am speaking in human terms). 6 Absolutely not. For then how will God judge the world? 7 For if the truth of God through my lie abounded to his glory, why am I also still judged as a sinner? 8 And Why not (as we are slanderously reported, and as some affirm that we say), "Let us do evil, that good may come?" Their condemnation is just. 9 What then? Are we better than they? No, in no way. For we previously warned both Jews and Greeks, that they are all under sin. 10 As it is written, "There is no one righteous; no, not one." 11 "There is no one who understands. There is no one who seeks after God. 12 They have all turned aside. They have together become unprofitable. There is no one who does good, there is not even one." 13 "Their throat is an open tomb. With their tongues they have used deceit." "Viper's poison is under their lips;" 14 "Whose mouth is full of cursing and bitterness." 15 "Their feet are swift to shed blood. 16 Destruction and calamity are in their paths. 17 The way of peace, they have not known." 18 "There is no fear of God before their eyes." 19 Now we know that whatever things the law says, it speaks to those who are under the law, that every mouth may be closed, and all the world may be brought under the judgment of God. 20 Because by the works of the law, no flesh will be justified in his sight. For through the law comes the knowledge of sin. 21 But now apart from the law, a righteousness of God has been revealed, being testified by the Law and the Prophets; 22 even the righteousness of God through faith in Jesus Christ to all and upon all who believe. For there is no distinction, 23 for all have sinned, and fall short of the glory of God; 24 being justified freely by his grace through the redemption that is in Christ Jesus; 25 whom God set forth whom God displayed publicly as a mercy seat, through faith in his blood, for a demonstration of his righteousness, because in God's forbearance he had passed over the sins previously committed; 26 to demonstrate his righteousness at this present time, so that he would be just, and the justifier of him who has faith in Jesus. 27 Where then is the boasting? It is excluded. By what manner of law? Of works? No, but by a law of faith. 28 For we maintain that one is justified by faith apart from the works of the law. 29 Or is God for Jews only? Is he not the God of the Gentiles also? Yes, of the Gentiles also, 30 since indeed there is one God who will justify the circumcised by faith, and the uncircumcised through faith. 31 Do we then nullify the law through faith? Absolutely not. No, we establish the law.

4 What then will we say that Abraham, our forefather, has found according to the flesh? 2 For if Abraham was justified by works, he has something to boast about, but not before God. 3 For what does the Scripture say? "And Abraham believed God, and it was credited to him as righteousness." 4 Now to the one who works, the pay is not counted as a gift, but as an obligation. 5 But to him who does not work, but believes in him who justifies the ungodly, his faith is credited as righteousness. 6 Even as David also pronounces blessing on the one to whom God counts righteousness apart from works, 7 "Happy are those whose lawless deeds are forgiven, and whose sins are covered. 8 Happy is the one whom the Lord will not charge with sin." 9 Is this blessing then pronounced on the circumcised, or on the uncircumcised also? For we say that faith was credited to Abraham as righteousness. 10 How then was it credited? When he was in circumcision, or in uncircumcision? Not in circumcision, but in uncircumcision. 11 He received the sign of circumcision, a seal of the righteousness of the faith which he had while he was in uncircumcision, so that he might be the father of all those who believe, though they be in uncircumcision, that righteousness might also be credited to them. 12 The father of circumcision to those who not only are of the circumcision, but who also walk in the steps of that faith of our father Abraham, which he had in uncircumcision. 13 For the promise to Abraham and to his descendants that he should be heir of the world was not through the law, but through the righteousness of faith. 14 For if those who are of the law are heirs, faith is made void, and the promise is made of no effect. 15 For the law works wrath, for where there is no law, neither is there disobedience. 16 For this cause it is of faith, that it may be according to grace, to the end that the promise may be sure to all the descendants, not to that only which is of the law, but to that also which is of the faith of Abraham, who is the father of us all. 17 As it is written, "I have made you a father of many nations." This is in the presence of him whom he believed: God, who gives life to the dead, and calls the things that are not, as though they were. 18 Who hoped in spite of hopeless circumstances, with the result that he might become the father of many nations, according to that which had been spoken, "so will your descendants be." 19 And not being weak in faith, he considered his own body,

Romans

which was as good as dead (he being about a hundred years old), and the deadness of Sarah's womb. **20** Yet, looking to the promise of God, he did not waver through unbelief, but grew strong through faith, giving glory to God, **21** and being fully assured that what he had promised, he was able also to perform. **22** And therefore "it was credited to him as righteousness." **23** Now it was not written that it was credited to him for his sake alone, **24** but for our sake also, to whom it will be credited, who believe in him who raised Jesus our Lord from the dead, **25** who was delivered up for our trespasses, and was raised for our justification.

5 Being therefore justified by faith, we have peace with God through our Lord Jesus Christ; **2** through whom we also have our access by faith into this grace in which we stand, and we rejoice in hope of the glory of God. **3** Not only this, but we also rejoice in our sufferings, knowing that suffering works perseverance; **4** and perseverance, proven character; and proven character, hope: **5** and hope does not disappoint us, because God's love has been poured out into our hearts through the Holy Spirit who was given to us. **6** For while we were yet weak, at the right time Christ died for the ungodly. **7** For rarely does one die for the righteous. Yet perhaps for a good person someone might dare to die. **8** But God commends his own love toward us, in that while we were yet sinners, Christ died for us. **9** Much more then, being now justified by his blood, we will be saved from God's wrath through him. **10** For if, while we were enemies, we were reconciled to God through the death of his Son, much more, being reconciled, we will be saved by his life. **11** Not only so, but we also rejoice in God through our Lord Jesus Christ, through whom we have now received the reconciliation. **12** Therefore, as sin entered into the world through one man, and death through sin; and so death passed to all people, because all sinned. **13** For until the law, sin was in the world; but sin is not charged when there is no law. **14** Nevertheless death reigned from Adam until Moses, even over those whose sins weren't like Adam's disobedience, who is a foreshadowing of him who was to come. **15** But the free gift is not like the trespass. For if by the trespass of the one the many died, much more did the grace of God, and the gift by the grace of the one man, Jesus Christ, abound to the many. **16** The gift is not as through one who sinned: for the judgment came by one to condemnation, but the free gift came of many trespasses to justification. **17** For if by the trespass of the one, death reigned through the one; so much more will those who receive the abundance of grace and of the gift of righteousness reign in life through the one, Jesus Christ. **18** So then as through one trespass, all people were condemned; even so through one act of righteousness, all people were justified to life. **19** For as through the one man's disobedience many were made sinners, even so through the obedience of the one, many will be made righteous. **20** The law came in besides, that the trespass might abound; but where sin abounded, grace abounded more exceedingly; **21** that as sin reigned in death, even so grace might reign through righteousness to consummate (aiōnios g166) life through Jesus Christ our Lord.

6 What should we say then? Should we continue in sin, that grace may abound? **2** Absolutely not. We who died to sin, how could we live in it any longer? **3** Or do you not know that all we who were baptized into Christ Jesus were baptized into his death? **4** We were buried therefore with him through baptism to death, that just like Christ was raised from the dead through the glory of the Father, so we also might walk in newness of life. **5** For if we have become united with him in the likeness of his death, we will also be part of his resurrection; **6** knowing this, that our old self was crucified with him, that the body of sin might be done away with, so that we would no longer be in bondage to sin. **7** For he who has died has been freed from sin. **8** But if we died with Christ, we believe that we will also live with him; **9** knowing that Christ, being raised from the dead, dies no more. Death no more has dominion over him. **10** For the death that he died, he died to sin one time; but the life that he lives, he lives to God. **11** In the same way, consider yourselves dead to sin, but alive to God in Christ Jesus. **12** Therefore do not let sin reign in your mortal body, that you should obey it in its lusts. **13** Neither present your members to sin as instruments of unrighteousness, but present yourselves to God, as alive from the dead, and your members as instruments of righteousness to God. **14** For sin will not have dominion over you. For you are not under law, but under grace. **15** What then? Should we sin because we are not under law, but under grace? Absolutely not. **16** Do you not know that when you present yourselves to someone as obedient slaves, you are slaves of the one whom you obey, whether of sin, which leads to death, or of obedience, which leads to righteousness? **17** But thanks be to God, that, whereas you were slaves of sin, you became obedient from the heart to that form of teaching to which you were entrusted. **18** Being made free from sin, you became slaves of righteousness. **19** I speak in human terms because of the weakness of your flesh, for as you presented your members as slaves to uncleanness and to wickedness upon wickedness, even so now present your members as slaves to righteousness for sanctification. **20** For when you were slaves of sin, you were free in regard to righteousness. **21** What fruit then did you have at that time in the things of which you are now ashamed? For the end of those things is death. **22** But now, having been freed from sin and having been enslaved to God, you have your fruit of sanctification and the result, consummate (aiōnios g166) life. **23** For the wages of sin is death, but the free gift of God is consummate (aiōnios g166) life in Christ Jesus our Lord.

7 Or do you not know, brothers (for I speak to those who know the law), that the law has authority over a person for as long as he lives? **2** For the married woman is bound by law to her husband as long as he lives. But if her husband dies, she is released from the law concerning the husband. **3** So then if, while the husband lives, she is joined to another man, she is called an adulteress. But if

Romans

the husband dies, she is free from the law, so that she is not an adulteress, though she is joined to another man. **4** Therefore, my brothers, you also were made dead to the law through the body of Christ, that you would be joined to another, to him who was raised from the dead, that we may bear fruit to God. **5** For when we were in the flesh, the sinful passions which were through the law, worked in our members to bring forth fruit for death. **6** But now we have been released from the law, having died to that which held us captive, so that we serve in newness of the Spirit, and not in oldness of the letter. **7** What should we say then? Is the law sin? Absolutely not. However, I would not have known sin, except through the law. For I would not have known covetousness, unless the law had said, "Do not covet." **8** But sin, taking opportunity through the commandment, produced in me all kinds of covetousness. For apart from the law, sin is dead. **9** I was alive apart from the law once, but when the commandment came, sin became alive, and I died. **10** The commandment, which was for life, this I found to be for death; **11** for sin, taking the opportunity through the commandment, deceived me, and through it killed me. **12** Therefore the law indeed is holy, and the commandment holy, and righteous, and good. **13** Did that which is good, then, become death to me? Absolutely not. But sin, that it might be shown to be sin, by working death to me through that which is good; that through the commandment sin might become exceeding sinful. **14** For we know that the law is spiritual, but I am fleshly, sold under sin. **15** For I do not know what I am doing. For I do not practice what I desire to do; but what I hate, that I do. **16** But if I do what I do not want to do, I agree with the law that it is good. **17** So now it is no more I that do it, but sin which dwells in me. **18** For I know that in me, that is, in my flesh, dwells no good thing. For the desire is present in me, but the doing of the good is not. **19** For the good which I desire, I do not do; but the evil which I do not desire, that I practice. **20** But if what I do not desire, that I do, it is no more I that do it, but sin which dwells in me. **21** I find then the law, that, to me, while I desire to do good, evil is present. **22** For I delight in God's law in my inner being, **23** but I see a different law in my members, warring against the law of my mind, and bringing me into captivity under the law of sin which is in my members. **24** What a wretched man I am. Who will deliver me out of the body of this death? **25** Thanks be to God through Jesus Christ, our Lord. So then with the mind, I myself serve God's law, but with the flesh, the sin's law.

8 There is therefore now no condemnation to those who are in Christ Jesus. **2** For the law of the Spirit of life in Christ Jesus has set you free from the law of sin and of death. **3** For what the law could not do, in that it was weak through the flesh, God did, sending his own Son in the likeness of sinful flesh and for sin, he condemned sin in the flesh; **4** so that the requirement of the law might be fulfilled in us, who do not walk according to the flesh but according to the Spirit. **5** For those who live according to the flesh set their minds on the things of the flesh, but those who live according to the Spirit, the things of the Spirit. **6** For the mind set on the flesh is death, but the mind set on the Spirit is life and peace; **7** because the mind set on the flesh is hostile towards God, for it does not submit to God's law; indeed, it cannot. **8** And those who are in the flesh cannot please God. **9** But you are not in the flesh but in the Spirit, if it is so that the Spirit of God dwells in you. But if anyone does not have the Spirit of Christ, he does not belong to him. **10** And if Christ is in you, the body is dead because of sin, but the Spirit gives life because of righteousness. **11** But if the Spirit of him who raised up Jesus from the dead dwells in you, he who raised up Christ from the dead will also give life to your mortal bodies through his Spirit who dwells in you. **12** So then, brothers, we have no obligation to the flesh, to live after the flesh. **13** For if you live after the flesh, you must die; but if by the Spirit you put to death the deeds of the body, you will live. **14** For as many as are led by the Spirit of God, these are children of God. **15** For you did not receive the spirit of bondage again to fear, but you received the Spirit of adoption, by whom we cry, "Abba. Father." **16** The Spirit himself testifies with our spirit that we are children of God; **17** and if children, then heirs; heirs of God and fellow heirs with Christ; if indeed we suffer with him, that we may also be glorified with him. **18** For I consider that the sufferings of this present time are not worthy to be compared with the glory which will be revealed to us. **19** For the creation waits with eager expectation for the children of God to be revealed. **20** For the creation was subjected to futility, not of its own will, but because of him who subjected it, in hope **21** that the creation itself also will be delivered from the bondage of decay into the glorious freedom of the children of God. **22** For we know that the whole creation groans and suffers with labor pains together until now. **23** And not only this, but ourselves also, who have the first fruits of the Spirit, even we ourselves groan within ourselves, waiting for adoption, the redemption of our body. **24** For we were saved in hope, but hope that is seen is not hope. For who hopes for that which he sees? **25** But if we hope for that which we do not see, we wait for it with patience. **26** And in the same way, the Spirit also helps our weaknesses, for we do not know how to pray as we ought. But the Spirit himself makes intercession for us with inexpressible groanings. **27** And he who searches the hearts knows what is on the Spirit's mind, because he makes intercession for the saints in accordance with God. **28** And we know that all things work together for good for those who love God, to those who are called according to his purpose. **29** For whom he foreknew, he also predestined to be conformed to the image of his Son, that he might be the firstborn among many brothers. **30** Whom he predestined, those he also called. Whom he called, those he also justified. Whom he justified, those he also glorified. **31** What then are we to say about these things? If God is for us, who can be against us? **32** He who did not spare his own Son, but delivered him up for us all, how would he not also with him freely give us all things? **33** Who could bring a charge against God's chosen ones? It is God who justifies. **34** Who is he who condemns? It is Christ who died, and more than that, who was raised, who is at the right hand of God, who also makes intercession for us. **35** Who will separate us from the love of Christ? Could oppression, or anguish, or persecution, or famine, or nakedness, or danger, or sword? **36** Even as it is written, "For your sake we are killed all day long. We were regarded as sheep to be slaughtered." **37** No, in all these things, we are more than conquerors through him who loved us. **38** For I am persuaded, that neither death, nor life, nor angels, nor rulers, nor things present, nor things to come, nor powers, **39** nor height, nor depth, nor any other created thing, will be able to separate us from the love of God, which is in Christ Jesus our Lord.

9 I tell the truth in Christ. I am not lying, my conscience testifying with me in the Holy Spirit, **2** that I have great sorrow and unceasing anguish in my heart. **3** For I could wish that I myself were accursed from Christ for my brothers' sake, my physical relatives according to the flesh, **4** who are Israelites; whose is the adoption, and the glory, and the covenants, and the giving of the law, and the service, and the promises; **5** of whom are the fathers, and from whom is the Christ according to the flesh, the one over all, God, blessed for the ages (**aiōn g165**). Amen. **6** But it is not as though the word of God has come to nothing. For they are not all Israel, that are of Israel. **7** Neither, because they are Abraham's descendants, are they all children. But, "In Isaac will your descendants be called." **8** That is, it is not the children of the flesh who are children of God, but the children of the promise are counted as descendants. **9** For this is what the promise said, "At the appointed time I will come, and Sarah will have a son." **10** And not only that, but Rebekah also had conceived by one, our father Isaac. **11** For being not yet born, neither having done anything good or bad, that the purpose of God according to election might stand, not of works, but of him who calls, **12** it was said to her, "The elder will serve the younger." **13** Even as it is written, "Jacob I loved, but Esau I hated." **14** What should we say then? Is there unrighteousness with God? Absolutely not. **15** For he said to Moses, "I will have mercy on whom I have mercy, and I will have compassion on whom I have compassion." **16** So then it is not of him who wills, nor of him who runs, but of God who has mercy. **17** For the Scripture says to Pharaoh, "For this very purpose I caused you to be raised up, that I might show in you my power, and that my name might be proclaimed in all the earth." **18** So then, he has mercy on whom he desires, and he hardens whom he desires. **19** You will say then to me, "Why does he still find fault? For who withstands his will?" **20** But who indeed are you, a human being, to reply against God? Will the thing formed ask him who formed it, "Why did you make me like this?" **21** Or hasn't the potter a right over the clay, from the same lump to make one part a vessel for honor, and another for dishonor? **22** What if God, willing to show his wrath, and to make his power known, endured with much patience vessels of wrath made for destruction, **23** and that he might make known the riches of his glory on vessels of mercy, which he prepared beforehand for glory, **24** us, whom he also called, not from the Jews only, but also from the Gentiles? **25** As he says also in Hosea, "I will call them which were not my people 'my people,' and her who was not loved, 'loved.'" **26** "It will be that in the place where it was said to them, 'You are not my people,' There they will be called 'children of the living God.'" **27** And Isaiah cries out concerning Israel, "Though the number of the children of Israel are as the sand of the sea, the remnant will be kept safe. **28** For he will fulfill the word and decisively in righteousness; because the Lord will carry out the word decisively on the earth." **29** As Isaiah has said before, "Unless the Lord of hosts had left us a few survivors, we would have become like Sodom, and would have been made like Gomorrah." **30** What should we say then? That the Gentiles, who did not follow after righteousness, attained to righteousness, even the righteousness which is of faith; **31** but Israel, following after a law of righteousness, did not arrive at that law. **32** Why? Because they did not seek it by faith, but as it were by works. They stumbled over the stumbling stone; **33** even as it is written, "Look, I am laying in Zion a stumbling stone and a rock to trip over; and whoever believes in him will not be put to shame."

10 Brothers, my heart's desire and my prayer to God is for them, that they may be saved. **2** For I testify about them that they have a zeal for God, but not according to knowledge. **3** For being ignorant of God's righteousness, and seeking to establish their own righteousness, they did not subject themselves to the righteousness of God. **4** For Christ is the end of the law for righteousness to everyone who believes. **5** For Moses writes about the righteousness of the law, "The one who does them will live by them." **6** But the righteousness which is of faith says this, "Do not say in your heart, 'Who will go up into heaven?' (that is, to bring Christ down); **7** or, 'Who will descend into the Abyss (**Abyssos g12**)?' (that is, to bring Christ up from the dead.)" **8** But what does it say? "The word is near you, in your mouth, and in your heart;" that is, the word of faith, which we proclaim: **9** that if you acknowledge with your mouth that Jesus is Lord, and believe in your heart that God raised him from the dead, you will be saved. **10** For with the heart one believes, resulting in righteousness, and with the mouth acknowledgement is made, resulting in salvation. **11** For the Scripture says, "Whoever believes in him will not be put to shame." **12** For there is no distinction between Jew and Greek; for the same Lord of all is rich to all who call on him. **13** For, "Whoever will call on the name of the Lord will be saved." **14** How then will they call on him in whom they have not believed? How will they believe in him whom they have not heard? And how will they hear without someone preaching? **15** And how will they preach unless they are sent? As it is written: "How beautiful are the feet of those who bring good news of peace, who bring good news of good things." **16** But they did not all listen to the Good News. For Isaiah says, "Lord, who has believed our report?" **17** So faith comes by hearing, and hearing by the word of Christ. **18** But I ask, isn't it rather that they did not hear? On the contrary, "Their voice has gone out to all the earth, their words to the farthest parts of the world." **19**

But I ask, did not Israel know? First Moses says, "I will provoke you to jealousy with that which is not a people. I will make you angry with a foolish nation." 20 Isaiah is very bold, and says, "I was found by those who did not seek me. I was revealed to those who did not ask for me." 21 But as to Israel he says, "All day long I have stretched out my hands to a disobedient and obstinate people."

11 I ask then, has God rejected his people? Absolutely not. For I also am an Israelite, a descendant of Abraham, of the tribe of Benjamin. 2 God did not reject his people, which he foreknew. Or do you not know what the Scripture says about Elijah? How he pleads with God against Israel: 3 "Lord, they have killed your prophets, they have broken down your altars; and I am left alone, and they seek my life." 4 But how does God answer him? "I have kept for myself seven thousand people, who have not bowed the knee to Baal." 5 Even so then at this present time also there is a remnant according to the election of grace. 6 And if by grace, then it is no longer of works; otherwise grace is no longer grace. 7 What then? That which Israel seeks for, that he did not obtain, but the chosen ones obtained it, and the rest were hardened. 8 According as it is written, God gave them a spirit of stupor, eyes that they should not see, and ears that they should not hear, to this very day. 9 David says, "Let their table be made a snare, and a trap, and a stumbling block, and a retribution to them. 10 Let their eyes be darkened, so that they can't see, and their backs be bent continually." 11 I ask then, did they stumble that they might fall? Absolutely not. But by their fall salvation has come to the Gentiles, to provoke them to jealousy. 12 Now if their fall is the riches of the world, and their loss the riches of the Gentiles; how much more their fullness? 13 For I speak to you who are the Gentiles. Since then as I am an apostle to the Gentiles, I glorify my ministry; 14 if by any means I may provoke to jealousy those who are my flesh, and may save some of them. 15 For if the rejection of them is the reconciling of the world, what would their acceptance be, but life from the dead? 16 If the first fruit is holy, so is the lump. If the root is holy, so are the branches. 17 But if some of the branches were broken off, and you, being a wild olive, were grafted in among them, and became partaker with them of the rich root of the olive tree; 18 do not boast over the branches. But if you boast, it is not you who support the root, but the root supports you. 19 You will say then, "Branches were broken off, that I might be grafted in." 20 True; by their unbelief they were broken off, and you stand by your faith. Do not be conceited, but fear; 21 for if God did not spare the natural branches, neither will he spare you. 22 See then the goodness and severity of God. Toward those who fell, severity; but toward you, goodness, if you continue in his goodness; otherwise you also will be cut off. 23 They also, if they do not continue in their unbelief, will be grafted in, for God is able to graft them in again. 24 For if you were cut out of that which is by nature a wild olive tree, and were grafted contrary to nature into a good olive tree, how much more will these, which are the natural branches, be grafted into their own olive tree? 25 For I do not desire you to be ignorant, brothers, of this mystery, so that you won't be wise in your own conceits, that a partial hardening has happened to Israel, until the fullness of the Gentiles has come in, 26 and so all Israel will be saved. Even as it is written, "There will come out of Zion the Deliverer, and he will turn away ungodliness from Jacob. 27 This is my covenant to them, when I will take away their sins." 28 Concerning the Good News, they are enemies for your sake. But concerning the election, they are loved for the fathers' sake. 29 For the gifts and the calling of God are irrevocable. 30 For as you in time past were disobedient to God, but now have obtained mercy by their disobedience, 31 even so these also have now been disobedient, that by the mercy shown to you they may now also obtain mercy. 32 For God has shut up all to disobedience, that he might have mercy on all. 33 Oh the depth of the riches both of the wisdom and the knowledge of God. How unsearchable are his judgments, and his ways past tracing out. 34 For "Who has known the mind of the Lord, or who has been his counselor?" 35 "Or who has first given to him, and it will be repaid to him again?" 36 For of him, and through him, and to him are all things. To him be the glory for the ages **(aiōn g165)**! Amen.

12 Therefore I urge you, brothers, by the mercies of God, to present your bodies a living sacrifice, holy, acceptable to God, which is your reasonable service. 2 And do not be conformed to this age **(aiōn g165)**, but be transformed by the renewing of your mind, so that you may prove what is the good, well-pleasing, and perfect will of God. 3 For I say, through the grace that was given me, to everyone among you, not to think of himself more highly than he ought to think; but to think reasonably, as God has apportioned to each person a measure of faith. 4 For even as we have many members in one body, and all the members do not have the same function, 5 so we, who are many, are one body in Christ, and individually members one of another. 6 Having gifts differing according to the grace that was given to us, if prophecy, let us prophesy according to the proportion of our faith; 7 or service, let us give ourselves to service; or he who teaches, to his teaching; 8 or he who exhorts, to his exhorting: he who gives, let him do it with liberality; he who rules, with diligence; he who shows mercy, with cheerfulness. 9 Let love be without hypocrisy. Abhor that which is evil. Cling to that which is good. 10 In love of the brothers be tenderly affectionate one to another; outdo one another in showing honor; 11 not lagging in diligence; fervent in spirit; serving the Lord; 12 rejoicing in hope; enduring in troubles; continuing steadfastly in prayer; 13 contributing to the needs of the saints; given to hospitality. 14 Bless those who persecute you; bless, and do not curse. 15 Rejoice with those who rejoice. Weep with those who weep. 16 Be of the same mind one toward another. Do not be arrogant, but associate with the humble. Do not be wise in your own conceits. 17 Repay no one evil for evil. Respect what is honorable in the sight of all people. 18 If it is possible, as much as it is up to you, be at peace with all people. 19 Do not seek revenge yourselves, beloved, but leave room for the wrath. For it is written, "Vengeance belongs to me; I will repay, says the Lord." 20 Therefore "If your enemy is hungry, feed him. If he is thirsty, give him a drink; for by doing this you will heap coals of fire on his head." 21 Do not be overcome by evil, but overcome evil with good.

13 Let every person be subject to the governing authorities, for there is no authority except from God, and those that exist are appointed by God. 2 Therefore he who resists the authority, withstands the ordinance of God; and those who withstand will receive to themselves judgment. 3 For rulers are not a terror to the good work, but to the evil. Do you desire to have no fear of the authority? Do that which is good, and you will have praise from the same, 4 for he is a servant of God to you for good. But if you do that which is evil, be afraid, for he does not bear the sword in vain; for he is a servant of God, an avenger for wrath to him who does evil. 5 Therefore you need to be in subjection, not only because of the wrath, but also for conscience' sake. 6 For this reason you also pay taxes, for they are servants of God's service, attending continually on this very thing. 7 Give therefore to everyone what you owe: taxes to whom taxes are due; customs to whom customs; respect to whom respect; honor to whom honor. 8 Owe no one anything, except to love one another; for he who loves his neighbor has fulfilled the law. 9 For the commandments, "Do not commit adultery," "Do not murder," "Do not steal," "Do not give false testimony," "Do not covet," and whatever other commandments there are, are all summed up in this saying, namely, "You are to love your neighbor as yourself." 10 Love does not harm a neighbor. Love therefore is the fulfillment of the law. 11 Do this, knowing the time, that it is already time for you to awaken out of sleep, for salvation is now nearer to us than when we first believed. 12 The night is far gone, and the day is near. Let us therefore throw off the works of darkness, and let us put on the armor of light. 13 Let us walk decently, as in the daytime; not in carousing and drunkenness, not in sexual immorality and lustful acts, and not in dissension and jealousy. 14 But put on the Lord Jesus Christ, and make no provision for the flesh, for its lusts.

14 Now accept one who is weak in faith, but not for disputes over opinions. 2 One person has faith to eat all things, but the one who is weak eats only vegetables. 3 Do not let the one who eats despise the one who does not eat. Do not let the one who does not eat judge the one who eats, for God has accepted him. 4 Who are you who judge another's servant? To his own lord he stands or falls. Yes, he will be made to stand, for the Lord has power to make him stand. 5 One esteems one day as more important; and another one esteems every day alike. Let each one be fully convinced in his own mind. 6 The one who observes the day, observes it to the Lord; and the one who does not observe the day, he does not observe it to the Lord. The one who eats, he eats to the Lord; since he gives thanks to God. And the one who does not eat, he does not eat to the Lord, and gives thanks to God. 7 For none of us lives to himself, and none dies to himself. 8 For if we live, we live to the Lord. Or if we die, we die to the Lord. If therefore we live or die, we are the Lord's. 9 For to this end Christ died, and lived again, that he might be Lord of both the dead and the living. 10 But you, why do you judge your brother? Or you again, why do you despise your brother? For we will all stand before the judgment seat of God. 11 For it is written, "'As I live,' says the Lord, 'to me every knee will bow. Every tongue will confess to God.'" 12 So then each one of us will give account of himself to God. 13 Therefore let us not judge one another any more, but judge this rather, not to put a stumbling block in a brother's way, or an occasion for falling. 14 I know, and am persuaded in the Lord Jesus, that nothing is unclean of itself; except that to him who considers anything to be unclean, to him it is unclean. 15 Yet if because of food your brother is grieved, you walk no longer in love. Do not destroy with your food him for whom Christ died. 16 Then do not let your good be slandered, 17 for the Kingdom of God is not eating and drinking, but righteousness, peace, and joy in the Holy Spirit. 18 For he who serves Christ in these things is acceptable to God and approved by people. 19 So then, let us follow after things which make for peace, and things by which we may build one another up. 20 Do not overthrow God's work for food's sake. All things indeed are clean, however it is evil for anyone who creates a stumbling block by eating. 21 It is good to not eat meat, drink wine, or do anything by which your brother stumbles, or is offended, or is made weak. 22 Do you have faith? Have it to yourself before God. Happy is he who does not judge himself in that which he approves. 23 But he who doubts is condemned if he eats, because it is not of faith; and whatever is not of faith is sin.

15 Now we who are strong ought to bear the weaknesses of the weak, and not to please ourselves. 2 Let each one of us please his neighbor for that which is good, to be building him up. 3 For even Christ did not please himself. But, as it is written, "The insults of those who insult you fell on me." 4 For whatever things were written before were written for our instruction, that through patience and through encouragement of the Scriptures we might have hope. 5 Now the God of patience and of encouragement grant you to be of the same mind one with another according to Christ Jesus, 6 that with one accord you may with one mouth glorify the God and Father of our Lord Jesus Christ. 7 Therefore accept one another, even as Christ also accepted you, to the glory of God. 8 Now I say that Christ has been made a servant of the circumcision for the truth of God, that he might confirm the promises given to the fathers, 9 and that the Gentiles might glorify God for his mercy. As it is written, "therefore I will give praise to you among the Gentiles, and sing to your name." 10 Again he says, "Rejoice, you nations, with his people." 11 Again, "Praise the Lord, all you nations. Let all the peoples praise him." 12 Again, Isaiah says, "There will be the root of Jesse, he who arises to rule over the peoples; in him will the nations hope." 13 Now may the God of hope fill you with all joy and peace in believing, that you may abound in hope, in the power of the Holy Spirit. **14** I myself am also persuaded about you, my brothers, that you yourselves are full of goodness, filled with all knowledge, able also to admonish others. **15** But I write the more boldly to you in part, as reminding you, because of the grace that was given to me by God, **16** that I should be a servant of Christ Jesus to the Gentiles, serving as a priest the Good News of God, that the offering up of the Gentiles might be made acceptable, sanctified by the Holy Spirit. **17** I have therefore my boasting in Christ Jesus in things pertaining to God. **18** For I will not dare to speak of any things except those which Christ worked through me, for the obedience of the Gentiles, by word and deed, **19** in the power of signs and wonders, in the power of the Spirit of God; so that from Jerusalem, and around as far as to Illyricum, I have fully preached the Good News of Christ; **20** yes, making it my aim to proclaim the Good News, not where Christ was already named, that I might not build on another's foundation. **21** But, as it is written, "Those who were not told about him, they will see, and those who have not heard, they will understand." **22** Therefore also I was hindered these many times from coming to you, **23** but now, no longer having any place in these regions, and having these many years a longing to come to you, **24** whenever I journey to Spain I will come to you. For I hope to see you on my journey, and to be helped on my way there by you, if first I may enjoy your company for a while. **25** But now, I say, I am going to Jerusalem, serving the saints. **26** For it has been the good pleasure of Macedonia and Achaia to make a certain contribution for the poor among the saints who are at Jerusalem. **27** Yes, it has been their good pleasure, and they are their debtors. For if the Gentile people have been made partakers of their spiritual things, they owe it to them also to serve them in fleshly things. **28** When therefore I have accomplished this, and have sealed to them this fruit, I will go on by way of you to Spain. **29** I know that, when I come to you, I will come in the fullness of the blessing of Christ. **30** Now I appeal to you, brothers, by our Lord Jesus Christ, and by the love of the Spirit, that you strive together with me in your prayers to God for me, **31** that I may be delivered from those who are disobedient in Judea, and that my service which I have for Jerusalem may be acceptable to the saints; **32** that I may come to you in joy through the will of God, and together with you, find rest. **33** Now the God of peace be with you all. Amen.

16 I commend to you Phoebe, our sister, who is a servant of the church that is at Cenchreae, **2** that you receive her in the Lord, in a way worthy of the saints, and that you assist her in whatever matter she may need from you, for she herself also has been a helper of many, and of my own self. **3** Greet Prisca and Aquila, my fellow workers in Christ Jesus, **4** who for my life, laid down their own necks; to whom not only I give thanks, but also all the churches of the Gentile people. **5** Greet the church that is in their house. Greet Epaenetus, my beloved, who is the first fruits of Asia to Christ. **6** Greet Mary, who labored much for you. **7** Greet Andronicus and Junia, my compatriots and my fellow prisoners, who are notable among the apostles, who also were in Christ before me. **8** Greet Ampliatus, my beloved in the Lord. **9** Greet Urbanus, our fellow worker in Christ, and Stachys, my beloved. **10** Greet Apelles, the approved in Christ. Greet those who are of the household of Aristobulus. **11** Greet Herodion, my kinsman. Greet them of the household of Narcissus, who are in the Lord. **12** Greet Tryphaena and Tryphosa, who labor in the Lord. Greet Persis, the beloved, who labored much in the Lord. **13** Greet Rufus, the chosen in the Lord, and his mother and mine. **14** Greet Asyncritus, Phlegon, Hermes, Patrobas, Hermas, and the brothers who are with them. **15** Greet Philologus and Julia, Nereus and his sister, and Olympas, and all the saints who are with them. **16** Greet one another with a holy kiss. The churches of Christ greet you. **17** Now I appeal to you, brothers, look out for those who are causing the divisions and occasions of stumbling, contrary to the doctrine which you learned, and turn away from them. **18** For those who are such do not serve our Lord Christ, but their own belly; and by their smooth and flattering speech, they deceive the hearts of the innocent. **19** For your obedience has become known to all. I rejoice therefore over you. But I desire to have you wise in that which is good, but innocent in that which is evil. **20** And the God of peace will quickly crush Satan under your feet. The grace of our Lord Jesus Christ be with you. **21** Timothy, my fellow worker, greets you, as do Lucius, Jason, and Sosipater, my relatives. **22** I, Tertius, who write the letter, greet you in the Lord. **23** Gaius, my host and host of the whole church, greets you. Erastus, the treasurer of the city, greets you, as does Quartus, the brother. **25** Now to him who is able to establish you according to my Good News and the proclamation of Jesus Christ, according to the revelation of the mystery which has been kept secret in the times of the ages (aiōnios g166), **26** but now is revealed, and by the Scriptures of the prophets, according to the commandment of the consummate (aiōnios g166) God, is made known for obedience of faith to all the nations; **27** to the only wise God, through Jesus Christ, to whom be the glory for the ages (aiōn g165) of the ages (aiōn g165)! Amen.

1 Corinthians

1 Paul, called to be an apostle of Christ Jesus by the will of God, and our brother Sosthenes, **2** to the church of God which is at Corinth, to those who are sanctified in Christ Jesus, called to be saints, with all who call on the name of our Lord Jesus Christ in every place, both theirs and ours: **3** Grace to you and peace from God our Father and the Lord Jesus Christ. **4** I always thank my God concerning you, for the grace of God which was given you in Christ Jesus; **5** that in everything you were enriched in him, in all speech and all knowledge; **6** even as the testimony of Christ was confirmed in you: **7** so that you are not lacking in any gift, as you wait for the revelation of our Lord Jesus Christ; **8** who will also strengthen you to the end, blameless in the day of our Lord Jesus Christ. **9** God is faithful, through whom you were called into the fellowship of his Son, Jesus Christ, our Lord. **10** Now I appeal to you, brothers, through the name of our Lord, Jesus Christ, that you all speak the same thing and that there be no divisions among you, but that you be perfected together in the same mind and in the same judgment. **11** For it has been reported to me concerning you, my brothers, by those who are from Chloe's household, that there are contentions among you. **12** Now I mean this, that each one of you says, "I follow Paul," "I follow Apollos," "I follow Cephas," and, "I follow Christ." **13** Is Christ divided? Was Paul crucified for you? Or were you baptized into the name of Paul? **14** I thank God that I baptized none of you, except Crispus and Gaius, **15** so that no one should say that you had been baptized into my own name. **16** (Now I also baptized the household of Stephanas; beyond that, I do not know whether I baptized any other.) **17** For Christ sent me not to baptize, but to proclaim the Good News—not in wisdom of words, so that the cross of the Christ would not be made void. **18** For the message about the cross is foolishness to those who are perishing, but to us who are being saved it is the power of God. **19** For it is written, "I will destroy the wisdom of the wise, and the discernment of the discerning I will nullify." **20** Where is the wise? Where is the scribe? Where is the disputer of this age (aiōn g165)? Has not God made foolish the wisdom of the world? **21** For seeing that in the wisdom of God, the world through its wisdom did not know God, it was God's good pleasure through the foolishness of the preaching to save those who believe. **22** For Jews ask for signs, and Greeks seek after wisdom, **23** but we preach Christ crucified, a stumbling block to Jews and foolishness to the Gentiles, **24** but to those who are called, both Jews and Greeks, Christ is the power of God and the wisdom of God. **25** Because the foolishness of God is wiser than man's, and the weakness of God is stronger than man's. **26** For consider your calling, brothers, that not many were wise from a human perspective, not many mighty, not many of noble birth. **27** But God chose the foolish of the world to shame the wise. And God chose the weak of the world to shame the strong. **28** And God chose the lowly of the world, and the despised, what is considered to be nothing, to bring to nothing what is considered to be something, **29** that no flesh might boast before God. **30** And because of him you are in Christ Jesus, who became for us wisdom from God, and righteousness and sanctification and redemption, **31** so that, as it is written, "Let him who boasts, boast in the Lord."

2 When I came to you, brothers, I did not come with superiority of speech or wisdom, proclaiming to you the mystery of God. **2** For I determined not to know anything among you, except Jesus Christ, and him crucified. **3** When I was with you, I was weak and afraid and I shook. **4** My speech and my preaching were not in persuasive words of wisdom, but in demonstration of the Spirit and of power, **5** that your faith would not rest on human wisdom, but on the power of God. **6** We speak wisdom, however, among those who are mature, yet a wisdom not of this age (aiōn g165) nor of the rulers of this age (aiōn g165) who are coming to nothing. **7** But we speak God's wisdom in a mystery, the wisdom that has been hidden, which God foreordained before the ages (aiōn g165) for our glory, **8** which none of the rulers of this age (aiōn g165) has known. For had they known it, they would not have crucified the Lord of glory. **9** But as it is written, No eye has seen, and no ear has heard, and no mind has imagined the things which God has prepared for those who love him. **10** But to us God revealed it through the Spirit. For the Spirit searches all things, even the deep things of God. **11** For what person knows the things of a person except the spirit of the person that is in him? So also, no one knows the things of God except the Spirit of God. **12** But we received, not the spirit of the world, but the Spirit which is from God, that we might know the things that were freely given to us by God. **13** And we speak of these things, not with words taught by human wisdom, but with those taught by the Spirit, comparing spiritual things with spiritual things. **14** Now the natural person does not receive the things of the Spirit of God, for they are foolishness to him, and he cannot understand them, because they are spiritually discerned. **15** But he who is spiritual discerns all things, and he himself is judged by no one. **16** For, "Who has known the mind of the Lord? Who will instruct him?" But we have the mind of Christ.

3 And I, brothers, could not address you as spiritual, but as fleshly, as infants in Christ. **2** I fed you with milk, not solid food, for you weren't yet ready. And even now you are still not ready, **3** for you are still fleshly. For insofar as there is jealousy and strife among you, are you not fleshly, and living by human standards? **4** For when one says, "I follow Paul," and another, "I follow Apollos," are you not merely human? **5** What then is Apollos? And what is Paul? Servants through whom you believed, and each as the Lord gave to him. **6** I planted. Apollos watered. But God made it grow. **7** So then neither he who plants is anything, nor he who waters, but God who makes it grow. **8** Now he who plants and he who waters are the same, but each will receive his own reward according to his own labor. **9** For we are God's fellow workers. You are God's field, God's building. **10** According to the grace of God which was given to me, as a wise master builder I laid a foundation, and another builds on it. But let each one be careful how he builds on it. **11** For no one can lay any other foundation than that which has been laid, which is Jesus Christ. **12** But if anyone builds on the foundation with gold, silver, costly stones, wood, hay, or straw; **13** each man's work will be revealed. For the Day will declare it, because it is revealed in fire; and the fire itself will test what sort of work each man's work is. **14** If any man's work remains which he built on it, he will receive a reward. **15** If any man's work is burned, he will suffer loss, but he himself will be saved, but as through fire. **16** Do you not know that you are a temple of God, and that God's Spirit lives in you? **17** If anyone destroys the temple of God, God will destroy him; for God's temple is holy, which you are. **18** Let no one deceive himself. If anyone thinks that he is wise among you in this age **(aiōn g165)**, let him become a fool, that he may become wise. **19** For the wisdom of this world is foolishness with God. For it is written, "He traps the wise in their craftiness." **20** And again, "The Lord knows the thoughts of the wise, that they are futile." **21** Therefore let no one boast about people. For all things are yours, **22** whether Paul, or Apollos, or Cephas, or the world, or life, or death, or things present, or things to come. All are yours, **23** and you are Christ's, and Christ is God's.

4 So a person should consider us as Christ's servants, and stewards of God's mysteries. **2** Here, moreover, it is required of stewards, that they be found faithful. **3** But with me it is a very small thing that I should be judged by you, or by man's judgment. Yes, I do not judge my own self. **4** For I know nothing against myself. Yet I am not justified by this, but he who judges me is the Lord. **5** Therefore judge nothing before the time, until the Lord comes, who will both bring to light the hidden things of darkness, and reveal the counsels of the hearts. Then each one will get his praise from God. **6** Now these things, brothers, I have in a figure transferred to myself and Apollos for your sakes, that in us you might learn not to go beyond the things which are written, that none of you be puffed up against one another. **7** For who makes you different? And what do you have that you did not receive? But if you did receive it, why do you boast as if you had not received it? **8** You are already filled. You have already become rich. You have come to reign without us. Yes, and I wish that you did reign, that we also might reign with you. **9** For, I think that God has displayed us, the apostles, last of all, like men sentenced to death. For we are made a spectacle to the world, both to angels and people. **10** We are fools for Christ's sake, but you are wise in Christ. We are weak, but you are strong. You have honor, but we have dishonor. **11** Even to this present hour we hunger, thirst, are naked, are beaten, and have no certain dwelling place. **12** We toil, working with our own hands. When people curse us, we bless. Being persecuted, we endure. **13** Being defamed, we entreat. We are made as the filth of the world, the dirt wiped off by all, even until now. **14** I do not write these things to shame you, but to admonish you as my beloved children. **15** For though you have ten thousand tutors in Christ, yet not many fathers. For in Christ Jesus, I became your father through the Good News. **16** I appeal to you therefore, be imitators of me. **17** Because of this I have sent Timothy to you, who is my beloved and faithful child in the Lord, who will remind you of my ways which are in Christ, even as I teach everywhere in every church. **18** Now some are puffed up, as though I were not coming to you. **19** But I will come to you shortly, if the Lord is willing. And I will know, not the word of those who are puffed up, but the power. **20** For the Kingdom of God is not in word, but in power. **21** What do you want? Should I come to you with a rod, or in love and a spirit of gentleness?

5 It is actually reported that there is sexual immorality among you, and such sexual immorality as is not even among the nations, that one has his father's wife. **2** You are puffed up, and did not rather mourn, that he who had done this deed might be removed from among you. **3** For I most certainly, as being absent in body but present in spirit, have already, as though I were present, judged him who has done this thing. **4** In the name of our Lord Jesus, you being gathered together, and my spirit, with the power of our Lord Jesus, **5** are to deliver such a one to Satan for the destruction of the flesh, that the spirit may be saved in the day of the Lord. **6** Your boasting is not good. Do you not know that a little yeast leavens the whole lump? **7** Purge out the old yeast, that you may be a new lump, even as you are unleavened. For indeed Christ, our Passover, has been sacrificed for us. **8** Therefore let us keep the feast, not with old yeast, neither with the yeast of malice and wickedness, but with the unleavened bread of sincerity and truth. **9** I wrote to you in my letter to have no company with sexual sinners; **10** yet not at all meaning with the sexual sinners of this world, or with the covetous and extortioners, or with idolaters; for then you would have to leave the world. **11** But as it is, I wrote to you not to associate with anyone who is called a brother who is a sexual sinner, or covetous, or an idolater, or a slanderer, or a drunkard, or an extortioner. Do not even eat with such a person. **12** For what have I to do with also judging those who are outside? Do you not judge those who are within? **13** But those who are outside, God judges. "Put away the wicked man from among yourselves."

6 If any of you has a dispute against another, does he dare go to court before the unrighteous, instead of the saints? **2** Do you not know that the saints will judge the world? And if the world is judged by you, are you unworthy to judge the smallest matters? **3** Do you not know that we will judge angels? How much more, things that pertain to this life? **4** If then, you have to judge things pertaining to this life, do you set them to judge who have no standing in the church? **5** I say this to move you to shame. Is not there even one wise person among you who would be able to decide between his brothers? **6** But brother goes to law with brother, and that before unbelievers. **7** Actually, it is already a defeat for you, that you have lawsuits among yourselves. Why not rather be wronged? Why not rather be cheated? **8** No, but you yourselves do wrong, and cheat, and that against your brothers. **9** Or do you not know that the unrighteous will not inherit the Kingdom of God? Do not be deceived. Neither the sexually immoral, nor idolaters, nor adulterers, nor effeminate, nor men who have sexual relations with men, **10** nor thieves, nor covetous, nor drunkards, nor slanderers, nor swindlers, will inherit the Kingdom of God. **11** Such were some of you, but you were washed. But you were sanctified. But you were justified in the name of the Lord Jesus Christ, and in the Spirit of our God. **12** "All things are lawful for me," but not all things are expedient. "All things are lawful for me," but I will not be brought under the power of anything. **13** "Foods for the belly, and the belly for foods," but God will bring to nothing both it and them. But the body is not for sexual immorality, but for the Lord; and the Lord for the body. **14** Now God raised up the Lord, and will also raise us up by his power. **15** Do you not know that your bodies are members of Christ? Should I then take the members of Christ, and make them members of a prostitute? Absolutely not. **16** Or do you not know that he who is joined to a prostitute is one body? For he says, "The two will become one flesh." **17** But he who is joined to the Lord is one spirit. **18** Flee sexual immorality. "Every sin that a person does is outside the body," but he who commits sexual immorality sins against his own body. **19** Or do you not know that your body is a temple of the Holy Spirit which is in you, which you have from God? You are not your own, **20** for you were bought with a price. Therefore glorify God in your body.

7 Now concerning the things about which you wrote: it is good for a man not to touch a woman. **2** But, because of sexual immoralities, let each man have his own wife, and let each woman have her own husband. **3** Let the husband fulfill his marital duty to his wife, and likewise also the wife to her husband. **4** The wife does not have authority over her own body, but the husband. Likewise also the husband does not have authority over his own body, but the wife. **5** Do not deprive one another, unless it is by consent for a season, that you may give yourselves to prayer, and may be together again, that Satan does not tempt you because of your lack of self-control. **6** But this I say by way of concession, not of commandment. **7** Yet I wish that all people were like me. However each one has his own gift from God, one of this kind, and another of that kind. **8** But I say to the unmarried and to widows, it is good for them if they remain even as I am. **9** But if they do not have self-control, let them marry. For it's better to marry than to burn. **10** But to the married I command—not I, but the Lord—that the wife not leave her husband **11** (but if she departs, let her remain unmarried, or else be reconciled to her husband), and that the husband not leave his wife. **12** But to the rest I—not the Lord—say, if any brother has an unbelieving wife, and she is content to live with him, let him not leave her. **13** The woman who has an unbelieving husband, and he is content to live with her, let her not leave her husband. **14** For the unbelieving husband is sanctified in the wife, and the unbelieving wife is sanctified by the brother. Otherwise your children would be unclean, but now they are holy. **15** Yet if the unbeliever departs, let there be separation. The brother or the sister is not under bondage in such cases, but God has called you to peace. **16** For how do you know, wife, whether you will save your husband? Or how do you know, husband, whether you will save your wife? **17** Only, as the Lord has assigned to each one, as God has called each, so let him walk. So I command in all the churches. **18** Was anyone called having been circumcised? Let him not become uncircumcised. Has anyone been called in uncircumcision? Let him not be circumcised. **19** Circumcision is nothing, and uncircumcision is nothing, but the keeping of the commandments of God. **20** Let each person stay in that calling in which he was called. **21** Were you called being a slave? Do not let that bother you, but if you get an opportunity to become free, use it. **22** For he who was called in the Lord being a slave is the Lord's free person. Likewise he who was called being free is Christ's slave. **23** You were bought with a price. Do not become slaves of people. **24** Brothers, let each one, in whatever condition he was called, stay in that condition with God. **25** Now concerning virgins, I have no commandment from the Lord, but I give my judgment as one who has obtained mercy from the Lord to be trustworthy. **26** I think that it is good therefore, because of the distress that is on us, that it is good for a person to remain as he is. **27** Are you bound to a wife? Do not seek to be freed. Are you free from a wife? Do not seek a wife. **28** But if you marry, you have not sinned. If a virgin marries, she has not sinned. Yet such will have oppression in the flesh, and I want to spare you. **29** But I say this, brothers: the time is short, that from now on, those who have wives should be as though they had none; **30** and those who weep, as though they did not weep; and those who rejoice, as though they did not rejoice; and those who buy, as though they did not possess; **31** and those who use the world, as not using it to the fullest. For the form of this world is passing away. **32** But I desire to have you to be free from cares. He who is unmarried is concerned for the things of the Lord, how he may please the Lord; **33** but he who is married is concerned about the things of the world, how he may please his wife, **34** and is divided. And the woman that is unmarried, or a virgin, is concerned about the things of the Lord, so that she may be holy both in body and in spirit. But the one that is married is concerned about the things of the world, how she may please her husband. **35** This I say for your own profit; not that I may ensnare you, but for that which is appropriate, and that you may attend to the Lord without distraction. **36** But if anyone thinks that he is behaving inappropriately toward his virgin, if she is past the flower of her age, and if need so requires, let him do what he desires. He does not sin. Let them marry. **37** But he who stands steadfast in his heart, having no necessity, but has power over his own heart, to keep his own virgin, does well. **38** So then both he who gives his own virgin in marriage does well, and he who does not give her in marriage does better. **39** A wife is bound to her husband as long as he lives; but if the husband is dead, she is free to be married to whomever she desires, only in

1 Corinthians

the Lord. **40** But she is happier if she stays as she is, in my judgment, and I think that I also have God's Spirit.

8 Now concerning things sacrificed to idols: We know that we all have knowledge. Knowledge puffs up, but love builds up. **2** But if anyone thinks that he knows anything, he does not yet know as he ought to know. **3** But if anyone loves God, the same is known by him. **4** Therefore concerning the eating of things sacrificed to idols, we know that no idol is anything in the world, and that there is no God but one. **5** For though there are things that are called "gods," whether in the heavens or on earth; as there are many "gods" and many "lords;" **6** yet to us there is one God, the Father, from whom are all things, and we for him; and one Lord, Jesus Christ, through whom are all things, and we live through him. **7** However, not all have this knowledge. But some, being so accustomed to idols until now, eat as of a thing sacrificed to an idol, and their conscience, being weak, is defiled. **8** But food will not commend us to God. For neither, if we do not eat, are we the worse; nor, if we eat, are we the better. **9** But be careful that by no means does this liberty of yours become a stumbling block to the weak. **10** For if someone sees you who have knowledge sitting in an idol's temple, won't his conscience, if he is weak, be emboldened to eat things sacrificed to idols? **11** And through your knowledge, he who is weak perishes, the brother for whom the Christ died. **12** Thus, sinning against the brothers, and wounding their conscience when it is weak, you sin against Christ. **13** Therefore if food causes my brother to stumble, I will by no means eat meat for this age (**aiōn g165**), that I do not cause my brother to stumble.

9 Am I not free? Am I not an apostle? Have I not seen Jesus our Lord? Are you not my work in the Lord? **2** If to others I am not an apostle, yet at least I am to you; for you are the seal of my office of apostle in the Lord. **3** My defense to those who examine me is this. **4** Have we no right to eat and to drink? **5** Have we no right to take along a wife who is a believer, even as the rest of the apostles, and the brothers of the Lord, and Cephas? **6** Or have only Barnabas and I no right to not work? **7** What soldier ever serves at his own expense? Who plants a vineyard, and does not eat of its fruit? Or who feeds a flock, and does not drink from the flock's milk? **8** Do I say these things according to human authority? Or does not the Law also say the same thing? **9** For it is written in the Law of Moses, "Do not muzzle an ox while it treads out the grain." Is it for the oxen that God cares, **10** or does he say it assuredly for our sake? Yes, it was written for our sake, because he who plows ought to plow in hope, and he who threshes in the hope of having a share. **11** If we sowed to you spiritual things, is it a great thing if we reap your fleshly things? **12** If others partake of this right over you, do not we yet more? Nevertheless we did not use this right, but we bear all things, that we may cause no hindrance to the Good News of Christ. **13** Do you not know that those who serve around sacred things eat from the things of the temple, and those who wait on the altar have their portion with the altar? **14** Even so the Lord ordained that those who proclaim the Good News should live from the Good News. **15** But I have used none of these things, and I do not write these things that it may be done so in my case; for I would rather die, than that anyone should make my boasting void. **16** For if I proclaim the Good News, I have nothing to boast about; for necessity is laid on me; but woe is to me, if I do not proclaim the Good News. **17** For if I do this of my own will, I have a reward. But if not of my own will, I have a stewardship entrusted to me. **18** What then is my reward? That, when I proclaim the Good News, I may present the Good News without charge, so as not to abuse my authority in the Good News. **19** For though I was free from all, I brought myself under bondage to all, that I might gain the more. **20** To the Jews I became as a Jew, that I might gain Jews; to those who are under the law, as under the law, not being myself under the law, that I might gain those who are under the law; **21** to those who are without law, as without law (not being without law toward God, but under law toward Christ), that I might win those who are without law. **22** To the weak I became as weak, that I might gain the weak. I have become all things to all people, that I may by all means save some. **23** Now I do all things for the sake of the Good News, that I may be a joint partaker of it. **24** Do you not know that those who run in a race all run, but one receives the prize? Run like that, that you may win. **25** Now everyone who competes in the games exercises self-control in all things. Now they do it to receive a corruptible crown, but we an incorruptible. **26** I therefore run like that, as not uncertainly. I fight like that, as not beating the air, **27** but I beat my body and bring it into submission, lest by any means, after I have preached to others, I myself should be rejected.

10 Now I would not have you ignorant, brothers, that our fathers were all under the cloud, and all passed through the sea; **2** and were all baptized into Moses in the cloud and in the sea; **3** and all ate the same spiritual food; **4** and all drank the same spiritual drink. For they drank of a spiritual rock that followed them, and the rock was Christ. **5** However with most of them, God was not well pleased, for they were overthrown in the wilderness. **6** Now these things were our examples, to the intent we should not lust after evil things, as they also lusted. **7** Neither be idolaters, as some of them were. As it is written, "The people sat down to eat and drink, and rose up to play." **8** Neither let us commit sexual immorality, as some of them committed, and in one day twenty-three thousand fell. **9** Neither let us test the Christ, as some of them tested, and perished by the serpents. **10** Neither grumble, as some of them also grumbled, and perished by the destroyer. **11** Now all these things happened to them by way of example, and they were written for our admonition, on whom the ends of the ages (**aiōn g165**) have come. **12** Therefore let him who thinks he stands be careful that he does not fall. **13** No temptation has taken you except what is common to humanity. God is faithful, who will not allow you to be tempted above what you are able, but will with the temptation also make the way of escape, that you may be able to endure it. **14** Therefore, my beloved, flee from idolatry. **15** I speak as to wise people. Judge what I say. **16** The cup of blessing which we bless, is it not a sharing of the blood of Christ? The bread which we break, is it not a sharing of the body of Christ? **17** Because there is one loaf of bread, we, who are many, are one body; for we all partake of the one loaf of bread. **18** Consider Israel according to the flesh. Do not those who eat the sacrifices participate in the altar? **19** What am I saying then? That a thing sacrificed to idols is anything, or that an idol is anything? **20** But I say that the things which pagans sacrifice, they sacrifice to demons, and not to God, and I do not desire that you would have fellowship with demons. **21** You cannot both drink the cup of the Lord and the cup of demons. You cannot both partake of the table of the Lord, and of the table of demons. **22** Or do we provoke the Lord to jealousy? Are we stronger than he? **23** "All things are lawful," but not all things are profitable. "All things are lawful," but not all things build up. **24** Let no one seek his own, but his neighbor's good. **25** Whatever is sold in the butcher shop, eat, asking no question for the sake of conscience, **26** for "the earth is the Lord's, and its fullness." **27** But if one of those who do not believe invites you to a meal, and you are inclined to go, eat whatever is set before you, asking no questions for the sake of conscience. **28** But if anyone says to you, "This was offered to idols," do not eat it for the sake of the one who told you, and for the sake of conscience. **29** Conscience, I say, not your own, but the other's conscience. For why is my liberty judged by another conscience? **30** If I partake with thankfulness, why am I denounced for that for which I give thanks? **31** Whether therefore you eat, or drink, or whatever you do, do all to the glory of God. **32** Give no occasions for stumbling, either to Jews, or to Greeks, or to the church of God; **33** even as I also please all people in all things, not seeking my own profit, but the profit of the many, that they may be saved.

11 Be imitators of me, even as I also am of Christ. **2** Now I praise you, that you remember me in all things, and hold firm the traditions, even as I delivered them to you. **3** But I would have you know that the head of every man is Christ, and the head of the woman is the man, and the head of Christ is God. **4** Every man praying or prophesying, having his head covered, dishonors his head. **5** But every woman praying or prophesying with her head unveiled dishonors her head. For it is one and the same thing as if she were shaved. **6** For if a woman is not covered, let her also be shorn. But if it is shameful for a woman to be shorn or shaved, let her be covered. **7** For a man indeed ought not to have his head covered, because he is the image and glory of God, but the woman is the glory of the man. **8** For man is not from woman, but woman from man; **9** for neither was man created for the woman, but woman for the man. **10** For this cause the woman ought to have authority on her head, because of the angels. **11** Nevertheless, neither is the woman independent of the man, nor the man independent of the woman, in the Lord. **12** For as woman came from man, so a man also comes through a woman; but all things are from God. **13** Judge for yourselves. Is it appropriate that a woman pray to God unveiled? **14** Doesn't even nature itself teach you that if a man has long hair, it is a dishonor to him? **15** But if a woman has long hair, it is a glory to her, for her hair is given to her for a covering. **16** But if anyone seems to be contentious, we have no such custom, neither do God's churches. **17** But in giving you this command, I do not praise you, that you come together not for the better but for the worse. **18** For first of all, when you come together in the church, I hear that divisions exist among you, and I partly believe it. **19** For there also must be factions among you, that those who are approved may be revealed among you. **20** When therefore you assemble yourselves together, it is not the Lord's supper that you eat. **21** For in your eating each one takes his own supper first. One is hungry, and another is drunk. **22** What, do you not have houses to eat and to drink in? Or do you despise God's church, and put them to shame who do not have? What should I tell you? Should I praise you? In this I do not praise you. **23** For I received from the Lord that which also I delivered to you, that the Lord Jesus on the night in which he was betrayed took bread. **24** When he had given thanks, he broke it, and said, "This is my body, which is for you. Do this in memory of me." **25** In the same way he also took the cup, after the meal, saying, "This cup is the new covenant in my blood. Do this, as often as you drink, in memory of me." **26** For as often as you eat this bread and drink this cup, you proclaim the Lord's death until he comes. **27** Therefore whoever eats this bread or drinks the Lord's cup in a manner unworthy will be guilty of the body and the blood of the Lord. **28** But let a person examine himself, and so let him eat of the bread, and drink of the cup. **29** For he who eats and drinks eats and drinks judgment to himself, if he does not discern the body. **30** For this cause many among you are weak and sickly, and not a few sleep. **31** For if we discerned ourselves, we would not be judged. **32** But when we are judged, we are punished by the Lord, that we may not be condemned with the world. **33** Therefore, my brothers, when you come together to eat, wait one for another. **34** But if anyone is hungry, let him eat at home, lest your coming together be for judgment. The rest I will set in order whenever I come.

12 Now concerning spiritual things, brothers, I do not want you to be ignorant. **2** You know that when you were unbelievers, you were led away to those mute idols, however you might be led. **3** Therefore I make known to you that no one speaking by God's Spirit says, "Jesus is accursed." No one can say, "Jesus is Lord," but by the Holy Spirit. **4** Now there are various kinds of gifts, but the same Spirit. **5** There are various kinds of service, and the same Lord. **6** There are various kinds of workings, but the same God, who works all things in all. **7** But to each one is given the manifestation of the Spirit for the profit of all. **8** For to one is given through the Spirit the word of wisdom, and to another the word of knowledge, according to the same Spirit; **9** to another faith, by the same Spirit; and to another gifts of healings, by the one

1 Corinthians

Spirit; **10** and to another workings of miracles; and to another prophecy; and to another discernings of spirits; to another different kinds of tongues; and to another the interpretation of tongues. **11** But the one and the same Spirit works all of these, distributing to each one separately as he desires. **12** For as the body is one, and has many members, and all the members of the body, being many, are one body; so also is Christ. **13** For in one Spirit we were all baptized into one body, whether Jews or Greeks, whether bond or free; and were all given to drink of one Spirit. **14** For the body is not one member, but many. **15** If the foot would say, "Because I'm not the hand, I'm not part of the body," it is not therefore not part of the body. **16** If the ear would say, "Because I'm not the eye, I'm not part of the body," it's not therefore not part of the body. **17** If the whole body were an eye, where would the hearing be? If the whole were hearing, where would the smelling be? **18** But now God has set the members, each one of them, in the body, just as he desired. **19** If they were all one member, where would the body be? **20** But now they are many members, but one body. **21** The eye cannot tell the hand, "I have no need for you," or again the head to the feet, "I have no need for you." **22** No, much rather, those members of the body which seem to be weaker are necessary. **23** Those parts of the body which we think to be less honorable, on those we bestow more abundant honor; and our unpresentable parts have more abundant propriety; **24** whereas our presentable parts have no such need. But God composed the body together, giving more abundant honor to the inferior part, **25** that there should be no division in the body, but that the members should have the same care for one another. **26** When one member suffers, all the members suffer with it. Or when one member is honored, all the members rejoice with it. **27** Now you are the body of Christ, and members individually. **28** God has set some in the church: first apostles, second prophets, third teachers, then miracle workers, then gifts of healings, helps, governments, and various kinds of tongues. **29** Are all apostles? Are all prophets? Are all teachers? Are all miracle workers? **30** Do all have gifts of healings? Do all speak with tongues? Do all interpret? **31** But earnestly desire the greater gifts. Moreover, I show a most excellent way to you.

13 If I speak with the tongues of humans and of angels, but do not have love, I have become sounding bronze, or a clanging cymbal. **2** If I have the gift of prophecy, and know all mysteries and all knowledge; and if I have all faith, so as to remove mountains, but do not have love, I am nothing. **3** If I dole out all my goods to feed the poor, and if I surrender my body so that I may boast, but do not have love, it profits me nothing. **4** Love is patient and is kind; love does not envy. Love does not brag, is not proud, **5** does not behave itself inappropriately, does not seek its own way, is not irritable, does not keep a record of wrongs; **6** does not rejoice in unrighteousness, but rejoices with the truth; **7** bears all things, believes all things, hopes all things, endures all things. **8** Love never fails. But where there are prophecies, they will be done away with. Where there are tongues, they will cease. Where there is knowledge, it will be done away with. **9** For we know in part, and we prophesy in part; **10** but when that which is complete has come, that which is partial will be done away with. **11** When I was a child, I spoke as a child, I felt as a child, I thought as a child. Now that I have become an adult, I have put away childish things. **12** For now we see in a mirror, dimly, but then face to face. Now I know in part, but then I will know fully, even as I was also fully known. **13** But now faith, hope, and love remain—these three. The greatest of these is love.

14 Follow after love, and earnestly desire spiritual things, and especially that you may prophesy. **2** For the one who speaks in another language speaks not to people, but to God; for no one understands; but in the Spirit he speaks mysteries. **3** But he who prophesies speaks to people for their encouragement, strengthening, and comfort. **4** He who speaks in another language edifies himself, but he who prophesies edifies the church. **5** Now I desire to have you all speak with other languages, but rather that you would prophesy, and he is greater who prophesies than he who speaks with other languages, unless he interprets, that the church may be built up. **6** But now, brothers, if I come to you speaking with other languages, what would I profit you, unless I speak to you either by way of revelation, or of knowledge, or of prophesying, or of teaching? **7** Even things without life, giving a voice, whether pipe or harp, if they did not give a distinction in the sounds, how would it be known what is piped or harped? **8** For if the trumpet gave an uncertain sound, who would prepare himself for war? **9** So also you, unless you uttered by the tongue words easy to understand, how would it be known what is spoken? For you would be speaking into the air. **10** There are, it may be, so many kinds of sounds in the world, and none is without meaning. **11** If then I do not know the meaning of the sound, I would be to him who speaks a foreigner, and he who speaks would be a foreigner to me. **12** So also you, since you are zealous for spiritual things, seek that you may abound to the building up of the church. **13** Therefore let him who speaks in another language pray that he may interpret. **14** For if I pray in another language, my spirit prays, but my understanding is unfruitful. **15** What is it then? I will pray with the spirit, and I will pray with the understanding also. I will sing with the spirit, and I will sing with the understanding also. **16** Otherwise if you bless with the spirit, how will he who fills the place of the unlearned say the "Amen" at your giving of thanks, seeing he does not know what you say? **17** For you truly give thanks well, but the other person is not built up. **18** I thank God I speak in tongues more than you all. **19** However in the church I would rather speak five words with my understanding, that I might instruct others also, than ten thousand words in another language. **20** Brothers, do not be children in thoughts, yet in malice be babies, but in thoughts be mature. **21** In the law it is written, "By people of strange tongues and by the lips of strangers I will speak to this people; but even then they will not listen to me," says the

Lord. **22** Therefore tongues are for a sign, not to those who believe, but to the unbelieving; but prophesying is for a sign, not to the unbelieving, but to those who believe. **23** If therefore the whole church is assembled together and all speak in tongues, and unlearned or unbelieving people come in, won't they say that you are crazy? **24** But if all prophesy, and someone unbelieving or unlearned comes in, he is reproved by all, and he is judged by all. **25** And thus the secrets of his heart are revealed. So he will fall down on his face and worship God, declaring that God is among you indeed. **26** What is it then, brothers? When you come together, each one has a psalm, has a teaching, has a revelation, has another language, has an interpretation. Let all things be done to build each other up. **27** If anyone speaks in another language, let it be two, or at the most three, and in turn; and let one interpret. **28** But if there is no interpreter, let him keep silent in the church, and let him speak to himself, and to God. **29** Let the prophets speak, two or three, and let the others discern. **30** But if a revelation is made to another sitting by, let the first keep silent. **31** For you can all prophesy one by one, that all may learn and all may be encouraged. **32** The spirits of the prophets are subject to the prophets, **33** for God is not a God of confusion, but of peace. As in all the churches of the saints, **34** let the women keep silent in the churches, for it has not been permitted for them to speak; but let them be in subjection, as the Law also says. **35** If they desire to learn anything, let them ask their own husbands at home, for it is shameful for a woman to chatter in the church. **36** What? Was it from you that the word of God went out? Or did it come to you alone? **37** If anyone thinks himself to be a prophet, or spiritual, let him recognize the things which I write to you, that they are the commandment of the Lord. **38** But if someone does not recognize this, he is not recognized. **39** Therefore, brothers, desire earnestly to prophesy, and do not forbid speaking in tongues. **40** Let all things be done decently and in order.

15 Now I declare to you, brothers, the Good News which I preached to you, which also you received, in which you also stand, **2** by which also you are saved, if you hold firmly the word which I preached to you—unless you believed in vain. **3** For I delivered to you first of all that which I also received: that Christ died for our sins according to the Scriptures, **4** that he was buried, that he was raised on the third day according to the Scriptures, **5** and that he appeared to Cephas, then to the twelve. **6** After that he appeared to over five hundred brothers at once, most of whom remain until now, but some have also fallen asleep. **7** After that he appeared to James, then to all the apostles, **8** and last of all, as to the child born at the wrong time, he appeared to me also. **9** For I am the least of the apostles, who is not worthy to be called an apostle, because I persecuted the church of God. **10** But by the grace of God I am what I am. His grace which was bestowed on me was not futile, but I worked more than all of them; yet not I, but the grace of God which was with me. **11** Whether then it is I or they, so we proclaim, and so you believed. **12** Now if Christ is preached, that he has been raised from the dead, how do some among you say that there is no resurrection of the dead? **13** But if there is no resurrection of the dead, neither has Christ been raised. **14** If Christ has not been raised, then our preaching is in vain, and your faith also is in vain. **15** Yes, we are found false witnesses of God, because we testified about God that he raised up Christ, whom he did not raise up, if it is so that the dead are not raised. **16** For if the dead are not raised, neither has Christ been raised. **17** If Christ has not been raised, your faith is vain; you are still in your sins. **18** Then they also who are fallen asleep in Christ have perished. **19** If we have only hoped in Christ in this life, we are of all people most to be pitied. **20** But now Christ has been raised from the dead, the first fruits of those who are asleep. **21** For since death came by man, the resurrection of the dead also came by man. **22** For as in Adam all die, so also in Christ all will be made alive. **23** But each in his own order: Christ the first fruits, then those who are Christ's, at his coming. **24** Then the end comes, when he will deliver up the Kingdom to God, even the Father; when he will have abolished all rule and all authority and power. **25** For he must reign until he has put all his enemies under his feet. **26** The last enemy that will be abolished is death. **27** For, "He put all things under his feet." But when he says "all things" are put under, it is evident that the one who put all things under is the exception. **28** When all things have been subjected to him, then the Son will also himself be subjected to him who subjected all things to him, that God may be all in all. **29** Or else what will they do who are baptized for the dead? If the dead are not raised at all, why then are they baptized for them? **30** Why do we also stand in jeopardy every hour? **31** I affirm, brothers, by the boasting in you which I have in Christ Jesus our Lord, I die daily. **32** If I fought with animals at Ephesus for human purposes, what does it profit me? If the dead are not raised, then "let us eat and drink, for tomorrow we die." **33** Do not be deceived. "Bad company corrupts good morals." **34** Become sober-minded, and do not sin, for some are ignorant about God. I say this to your shame. **35** But someone will say, "How are the dead raised?" and, "With what kind of body do they come?" **36** You foolish one, that which you yourself sow is not made alive unless it dies. **37** That which you sow, you do not sow the body that will be, but a bare grain, maybe of wheat, or of some other kind. **38** But God gives it a body even as it pleased him, and to each seed a body of its own. **39** All flesh is not the same flesh, but there is one flesh of humans, another flesh of animals, another of fish, and another of birds. **40** There are also celestial bodies, and terrestrial bodies; but the glory of the celestial differs from that of the terrestrial. **41** There is one glory of the sun, another glory of the moon, and another glory of the stars; for one star differs from another star in glory. **42** So also is the resurrection of the dead. It is sown in corruption; it is raised in incorruption. **43** It is sown in dishonor; it is raised in glory. It is sown in weakness; it is raised in power. **44** It is sown a natural body; it is raised a spiritual body. There is a natural body and there is also a spiritual body. **45** So also it is written, "The first man, Adam, became a living soul."

The last Adam became a life-giving spirit. **46** However that which is spiritual is not first, but that which is natural, then that which is spiritual. **47** The first man is of the earth, made of dust. The second man is from heaven. **48** As is the one made of dust, such are those who are also made of dust; and as is the heavenly, such are they also that are heavenly. **49** As we have borne the image of those made of dust, we will also bear the image of the heavenly. **50** Now I say this, brothers, that flesh and blood cannot inherit the Kingdom of God; neither does corruption inherit incorruption. **51** Look, I tell you a mystery. We will not all sleep, but we will all be changed, **52** in a moment, in the twinkling of an eye, at the last trumpet. For the trumpet will sound, and the dead will be raised incorruptible, and we will be changed. **53** For this corruptible must put on incorruption, and this mortal must put on immortality. **54** But when this corruptible will have put on incorruption, and this mortal will have put on immortality, then what is written will happen: "Death is swallowed up in victory." **55** "Death, where is your sting? Hades **(Hadēs g86)**, where is your victory?" **56** The sting of death is sin, and the power of sin is the law. **57** But thanks be to God, who gives us the victory through our Lord Jesus Christ. **58** Therefore, my beloved brothers, be steadfast, immovable, always abounding in the Lord's work, because you know that your labor is not in vain in the Lord.

16 Now concerning the collection for the saints, as I commanded the churches of Galatia, you do likewise. **2** On the first day of the week, let each one of you save, as he may prosper, that no collections be made when I come. **3** When I arrive, I will send whoever you approve with letters to carry your gracious gift to Jerusalem. **4** If it is appropriate for me to go also, they will go with me. **5** But I will come to you when I have passed through Macedonia, for I am passing through Macedonia. **6** But with you it may be that I will stay, or even winter, that you may send me on my journey wherever I go. **7** For I do not wish to see you now in passing, but I hope to stay a while with you, if the Lord permits. **8** But I will stay at Ephesus until Pentecost, **9** for a great and effective door has opened to me, and there are many adversaries. **10** Now if Timothy comes, see that he is with you without fear, for he does the work of the Lord, as I also do. **11** Therefore let no one despise him. But set him forward on his journey in peace, that he may come to me; for I expect him with the brothers. **12** Now concerning Apollos, the brother, I strongly urged him to come to you with the brothers; and it was not at all his desire to come now; but he will come when he has an opportunity. **13** Watch. Stand firm in the faith. Be courageous. Be strong. **14** Let all that you do be done in love. **15** Now I appeal to you, brothers (you know the house of Stephanas, that it is the first fruits of Achaia, and that they have set themselves to serve the saints), **16** that you also be in subjection to such, and to everyone who helps in the work and labors. **17** I rejoice at the coming of Stephanas, Fortunatus, and Achaicus; for that which was lacking on your part, they supplied. **18** For they refreshed my spirit and yours. Therefore acknowledge those who are like that. **19** The churches of Asia greet you. Aquila and Priscilla greet you much in the Lord, together with the church that is in their house. **20** All the brothers greet you. Greet one another with a holy kiss. **21** This greeting is by me, Paul, with my own hand. **22** If anyone does not love the Lord, a curse be on him. Our Lord, come. **23** The grace of the Lord Jesus be with you. **24** My love to all of you in Christ Jesus.

2 Corinthians

1 Paul, an apostle of Christ Jesus through the will of God, and Timothy our brother, to the church of God which is at Corinth, with all the saints who are in the whole of Achaia: **2** Grace to you and peace from God our Father and the Lord Jesus Christ. **3** Blessed be the God and Father of our Lord Jesus Christ, the Father of mercies and God of all comfort; **4** who comforts us in all our affliction, that we may be able to comfort those who are in any affliction, through the comfort with which we ourselves are comforted by God. **5** For as the sufferings of Christ abound to us, even so our comfort also abounds through Christ. **6** But if we are afflicted, it is for your comfort and salvation. If we are comforted, it is for your comfort, which produces in you the patient enduring of the same sufferings which we also suffer. **7** Our hope for you is steadfast, knowing that, since you are partakers of the sufferings, so also are you of the comfort. **8** For we do not desire to have you uninformed, brothers, concerning our affliction which happened in Asia, that we were weighed down exceedingly, beyond our power, so much that we despaired even of life. **9** Yes, we ourselves have had the sentence of death within ourselves, that we should not trust in ourselves, but in God who raises the dead, **10** who delivered us out of so great a death, and he will deliver us. On him we have set our hope that he will also deliver us again; **11** you also helping together on our behalf by your petition; that, for the gift bestowed on us by means of many, thanks may be given by many persons on our behalf. **12** For our boasting is this: the testimony of our conscience, that with pure motives and sincerity of God, not in fleshly wisdom but in the grace of God we conducted ourselves in the world, and more abundantly toward you. **13** For we write no other things to you, than what you read or even acknowledge, and I hope you will fully acknowledge; **14** as also you acknowledged us in part, that we are your boasting, even as you also are ours, in the day of our Lord Jesus. **15** In this confidence, I was determined to come first to you, that you might have a second benefit; **16** and by you to pass into Macedonia, and again from Macedonia to come to you, and to be sent forward by you on my journey to Judea. **17** When I therefore was planning this, did I do it lightly? Or the things that I purpose, do I purpose according to the flesh, that with me there should be the "Yes, yes" and the "No, no?" **18** But as God is faithful, our word toward you is not "Yes and no." **19** For the Son of God, Jesus Christ, who was preached among you by us, by me, Silvanus, and Timothy, was not "Yes and no," but in him is "Yes." **20** For however many are the promises of God, in him they are "Yes." Therefore also through him they are "Amen," to the glory of God through us. **21** Now he who establishes us with you in Christ, and anointed us, is God; **22** who also sealed us, and gave us the down payment of the Spirit in our hearts. **23** But I call God as a witness to my soul, that to spare you I did not come again to Corinth. **24** Not that we rule over your faith, but are fellow workers with you for your joy. For you stand firm in faith.

2 For I determined this for myself, that I would not come to you again in sorrow. **2** For if I make you sorry, then who will make me glad but he who is made sorry by me? **3** And I wrote this very thing, so that, when I came, I would not have sorrow from them of whom I ought to rejoice; having confidence in you all, that my joy would be shared by all of you. **4** For out of much affliction and anguish of heart I wrote to you with many tears, not that you should be made sorry, but that you might know the love that I have so abundantly for you. **5** But if any has caused sorrow, he has caused sorrow, not to me, but in part (that I not press too heavily) to you all. **6** Sufficient to such a one is this punishment which was inflicted by the many; **7** so that on the contrary you should rather forgive him and comfort him, lest by any means such a one should be swallowed up with his excessive sorrow. **8** Therefore I urge you to confirm your love toward him. **9** For to this end I also wrote, that I might know the proof of you, whether you are obedient in all things. **10** Now I also forgive whomever you forgive anything. For if indeed I have forgiven anything, I have forgiven that one for your sakes in the presence of Christ, **11** that no advantage may be gained over us by Satan; for we are not ignorant of his schemes. **12** Now when I came to Troas for the Good News of Christ, and when a door was opened to me in the Lord, **13** I had no relief for my spirit, because I did not find Titus, my brother, but taking my leave of them, I went out into Macedonia. **14** Now thanks be to God, who always leads us in triumph in Christ, and reveals through us the sweet aroma of his knowledge in every place. **15** For we are a sweet aroma of Christ to God, in those who are saved, and in those who perish; **16** to the one a stench from death to death; to the other a sweet aroma from life to life. Who is sufficient for these things? **17** For we are not, like so many, peddling the word of God. But as of sincerity, but as of God, in the sight of God, we speak in Christ.

3 Are we beginning again to commend ourselves? We do not need, as do some, letters of commendation to you or from you, do we? **2** You are our letter, written in our hearts, known and read by everyone; **3** being revealed that you are a letter of Christ, served by us, written not with ink, but with the Spirit of the living God; not in tablets of stone, but in tablets that are hearts of flesh. **4** Such confidence we have through Christ toward God; **5** not that we are sufficient of ourselves, to account anything as from ourselves; but our sufficiency is from God; **6** who also made us sufficient as servants of a new covenant; not of the letter, but of the Spirit. For the letter kills, but the Spirit gives life. **7** But if the service of death, written engraved on stones, came with glory, so that the children of Israel could not look steadfastly on the face of Moses for the glory of his face; which was passing away; **8** won't service of the Spirit be with much more glory? **9** For if the service of condemnation has glory, the service of righteousness exceeds much more in glory. **10** For truly that which has been made glorious has not been made glorious in this respect, by reason of the glory that surpasses. 11 For if that which passes away was with glory, much more that which remains is in glory. 12 Having therefore such a hope, we use great boldness of speech, 13 and not as Moses, who put a veil on his face, that the children of Israel would not look steadfastly on the end of that which was passing away. 14 But their minds were hardened, for until this very day at the reading of the old covenant the same veil remains, because in Christ it passes away. 15 But to this day, when Moses is read, a veil lies on their heart. 16 But whenever one turns to the Lord, the veil is taken away. 17 Now the Lord is the Spirit and where the Spirit of the Lord is, there is liberty. 18 But we all, with unveiled face looking as in a mirror the glory of the Lord, are transformed into the same image from glory to glory, even as from the Lord, the Spirit.

4 Therefore seeing we have this ministry, even as we obtained mercy, we do not faint. 2 But we have renounced the hidden things of shame, not walking in craftiness, nor handling the word of God deceitfully; but by the manifestation of the truth commending ourselves to every man's conscience in the sight of God. 3 Even if our Good News is veiled, it is veiled to those who are perishing; 4 in whom the god of this age (aiōn g165) has blinded the thoughts of the unbelieving, that the light of the Good News of the glory of Christ, who is the image of God, should not shine on them. 5 For we do not preach ourselves, but Christ Jesus as Lord, and ourselves as your slaves because of Jesus. 6 For it is God, who spoke for light to shine out of darkness, who has shone in our hearts to give the light of the knowledge of the glory of God in the face of Christ. 7 But we have this treasure in clay vessels, that the exceeding greatness of the power may be of God, and not from ourselves. 8 We are pressed on every side, yet not crushed; perplexed, yet not to despair; 9 pursued, yet not forsaken; struck down, yet not destroyed; 10 always carrying in the body the death of Jesus, that the life of Jesus may also be revealed in our body. 11 For we who live are always delivered to death for Jesus' sake, that the life also of Jesus may be revealed in our mortal flesh. 12 So then death works in us, but life in you. 13 But having the same spirit of faith, according to that which is written, "I believed, and therefore I spoke." We also believe, and therefore also we speak; 14 knowing that he who raised the Lord Jesus will raise us also with Jesus, and will present us with you. 15 For all things are for your sakes, that the grace, being multiplied through the many, may cause the thanksgiving to abound to the glory of God. 16 Therefore we do not become discouraged, but even though our outer nature is wearing away, yet our inner nature is being renewed day by day. 17 For our present light affliction works for us more and more exceedingly a consummate (aiōnios g166) weight of glory, 18 while we do not look at the things which are seen, but at the things which are not seen. For the things which are seen are temporal, but the things which are not seen are consummate (aiōnios g166).

5 For we know that if the earthly house of our tent is dissolved, we have a building from God, a house not made with hands, consummate (aiōnios g166), in the heavens. 2 For truly in this we groan, longing to be clothed with our habitation which is from heaven, 3 since, after we have put it on, we will not be found naked. 4 For indeed we who are in this tent do groan, being burdened; not that we desire to be unclothed, but that we desire to be clothed, that what is mortal may be swallowed up by life. 5 Now he who made us for this very thing is God, who also gave to us the down payment of the Spirit. 6 Therefore, we are always confident and know that while we are at home in the body, we are absent from the Lord; 7 for we walk by faith, not by sight. 8 We are of good courage, I say, and are willing rather to be absent from the body, and to be at home with the Lord. 9 Therefore also we make it our aim, whether at home or absent, to be well pleasing to him. 10 For we must all appear before the judgment seat of Christ; that each one may receive the things in the body, according to what he has done, whether good or bad. 11 Knowing therefore the fear of the Lord, we persuade people, but we are revealed to God; and I hope that we are revealed also in your consciences. 12 For we are not commending ourselves to you again, but speak as giving you occasion of boasting on our behalf, that you may have something to answer those who boast in appearance, and not in heart. 13 For if we are out of control, it is for God. If we are in a reasonable way, it is for you. 14 For the love of Christ constrains us; because we judge thus, that one died for all, therefore all died. 15 He died for all, that those who live should no longer live to themselves, but to him who for their sakes died and rose again. 16 Therefore we know no one after the flesh from now on. Even though we have known Christ after the flesh, yet now we know him so no more. 17 Therefore if anyone is in Christ, he is a new creation. The old things have passed away. Look, new things have come. 18 But all things are of God, who reconciled us to himself through Jesus Christ, and gave to us the ministry of reconciliation; 19 namely, that God was in Christ reconciling the world to himself, not counting their trespasses against them, and having committed to us the word of reconciliation. 20 We are therefore ambassadors on behalf of Christ, as though God were making his appeal through us. We implore you on behalf of Christ, be reconciled to God. 21 For him who knew no sin he made to be sin on our behalf; so that in him we might become the righteousness of God.

6 Working together, we entreat also that you not receive the grace of God in vain, 2 for he says, "At an acceptable time I listened to you, and in a day of salvation I helped you." Look, now is the "acceptable time." Look, now is the "day of salvation." 3 We give no occasion of stumbling in anything, that our service may not be blamed, 4 but in everything commending ourselves, as servants of God, in great endurance, in afflictions, in hardships, in distresses, 5 in beatings, in imprisonments, in riots, in labors, in watchings, in fastings; 6 in pureness, in knowledge, in patience, in kindness, in the Holy Spirit, in sincere love, **7** in the word of truth, in the power of God; by the armor of righteousness on the right hand and on the left, **8** by glory and dishonor, by evil report and good report; as deceivers, and yet true; **9** as unknown, and yet well known; as dying, and look, we live; as punished, and not killed; **10** as sorrowful, yet always rejoicing; as poor, yet making many rich; as having nothing, and yet possessing all things. **11** Our mouth is open to you, Corinthians. Our heart is enlarged. **12** You are not restricted by us, but you are restricted by your own affections. **13** Now in return, I speak as to my children, you also be open wide. **14** Do not be unequally yoked with unbelievers, for what fellowship have righteousness and iniquity? Or what fellowship has light with darkness? **15** What agreement has Christ with Belial? Or what portion has a believer with an unbeliever? **16** What agreement has a temple of God with idols? For we are a temple of the living God. Even as God said, "I will dwell in them, and walk in them; and I will be their God, and they will be my people." **17** Therefore, "'Go out from their midst, and be separate,' says the Lord, 'and touch no unclean thing,' and I will receive you. **18** "And I will be a Father to you, and you will be my sons and daughters," says the Lord of hosts.

7 Having therefore these promises, beloved, let us cleanse ourselves from all defilement of flesh and spirit, perfecting holiness in the fear of God. **2** Open your hearts to us. We wronged no one. We corrupted no one. We took advantage of no one. **3** I say this not to condemn you, for I have said before, that you are in our hearts to die together and live together. **4** Great is my boldness of speech toward you. Great is my boasting on your behalf. I am filled with comfort. I overflow with joy in all our affliction. **5** For even when we had come into Macedonia, our flesh had no relief, but we were afflicted on every side. Fightings were outside. Fear was inside. **6** Nevertheless, he who comforts the lowly, God, comforted us by the coming of Titus; **7** and not by his coming only, but also by the comfort with which he was comforted in you, while he told us of your longing, your mourning, and your zeal for me; so that I rejoiced still more. **8** For though I made you sorry with my letter, I do not regret it, though I did regret it. For I see that my letter made you sorry, though just for a while. **9** I now rejoice, not that you were made sorry, but that you were made sorry to repentance. For you were made sorry in a godly way, that you might suffer loss by us in nothing. **10** For godly sorrow works repentance to salvation, which brings no regret. But the sorrow of the world works death. **11** For look at this very thing, that you were made sorry in a godly way. What diligence it produced in you, what clearing of yourselves, what indignation, what fear, what longing, what zeal, what vindication. In everything you proved yourselves to be innocent in this matter. **12** So although I wrote to you, I wrote not for his cause that did the wrong, nor for his cause that suffered the wrong, but that your earnest care for us might be revealed in you in the sight of God. **13** Therefore we have been comforted. In our comfort we rejoiced the more exceedingly for the joy of Titus, because his spirit has been refreshed by you all. **14** For if in anything I have boasted to him on your behalf, I was not disappointed. But as we spoke all things to you in truth, so our glorying also which I made before Titus was found to be truth. **15** His affection is more abundantly toward you, while he remembers all of your obedience, how with fear and trembling you received him. **16** I rejoice that in everything I am of good courage concerning you.

8 Moreover, brothers, we make known to you the grace of God which has been given in the churches of Macedonia; **2** how that in much proof of affliction the abundance of their joy and their deep poverty abounded to the riches of their liberality. **3** For according to their power, I testify, yes and beyond their power, they gave of their own accord, **4** begging us with much entreaty to receive this grace and the fellowship in the service to the saints. **5** This was not as we had hoped, but first they gave their own selves to the Lord, and to us through the will of God. **6** So we urged Titus, that as he made a beginning before, so he would also complete in you this grace. **7** But as you abound in everything, in faith, utterance, knowledge, all earnestness, and in the love from us that is in you, see that you also abound in this grace. **8** I speak not by way of commandment, but as proving through the earnestness of others the sincerity also of your love. **9** For you know the grace of our Lord Jesus Christ, that, though he was rich, yet for your sakes he became poor, that you through his poverty might become rich. **10** I give a judgment in this: for this is expedient for you, who were the first to start a year ago, not only to do, but also to be willing. **11** But now complete the doing also, that as there was the readiness to be willing, so there may be the completion also out of your ability. **12** For if the readiness is there, it is acceptable according to what you have, not according to what you do not have. **13** For this is not that others may be eased and you distressed, **14** but for equality. Your abundance at this present time supplies their lack, that their abundance also may become a supply for your lack; that there may be equality. **15** As it is written, "He who gathered much had nothing left over, and he who gathered little had no lack." **16** But thanks be to God, who puts the same earnest care for you into the heart of Titus. **17** For he indeed accepted our exhortation, but being himself very earnest, he went out to you of his own accord. **18** We have sent together with him the brother whose praise in the Good News is known through all the churches. **19** Not only so, but who was also appointed by the churches to travel with us in this grace, which is served by us to the glory of the Lord himself, and to show our readiness. **20** We are avoiding this, that no one should blame us concerning this abundance which is administered by us. **21** Having regard for honorable things, not only in the sight of the Lord, but also in the sight of others. **22** We have sent with them our brother, whom we have many times proved earnest in many things, but now much more earnest, by reason of the great confidence which he has in you. **23** As for Titus, he is my partner and fellow worker for you. As for our brothers, they are messengers of the churches, the glory of Christ.

24 Therefore show the proof of your love to them in front of the churches, and of our boasting on your behalf.

9 It is indeed unnecessary for me to write to you concerning the service to the saints, **2** for I know your readiness, of which I boast on your behalf to them of Macedonia, that Achaia has been prepared for a year past. Your zeal has stirred up very many of them. **3** But I have sent the brothers that our boasting on your behalf may not be in vain in this respect, that, just as I said, you may be prepared, **4** so that I won't by any means, if there come with me any of Macedonia and find you unprepared, we (to say nothing of you) should be disappointed in this confidence. **5** I thought it necessary therefore to entreat the brothers that they would go before to you, and arrange ahead of time the generous gift that you promised before, that the same might be ready as a matter of generosity, and not of greediness. **6** Remember this: he who sows sparingly will also reap sparingly. He who sows bountifully will also reap bountifully. **7** Each person should give according as he has determined in his heart; not grudgingly, or under compulsion; for God loves a cheerful giver. **8** And God is able to make all grace abound to you, that you, always having all sufficiency in everything, may abound to every good work. **9** As it is written, "He has scattered, he has given to the poor. His righteousness remains for the age **(aiōn g165)**." **10** Now he who supplies seed to the sower and bread for food, will supply and multiply your seed for sowing, and increase the fruits of your righteousness; **11** you being enriched in everything to all liberality, which works through us thanksgiving to God. **12** For this service of giving that you perform not only makes up for lack among the saints, but abounds also through many thanksgivings to God; **13** seeing that through the proof given by this service, they glorify God for the obedience of your confession to the Good News of Christ, and for the liberality of your contribution to them and to all; **14** while they themselves also, with petition on your behalf, yearn for you by reason of the exceeding grace of God in you. **15** Thanks be to God for his inexpressible gift.

10 Now I Paul, myself, entreat you by the humility and gentleness of Christ; I who in your presence am lowly among you, but being absent am of good courage toward you. **2** But I implore you that when I am present I may not have to be bold with the confidence with which I intend on showing against some, who consider us to be walking according to the flesh. **3** For though we walk in the flesh, we do not wage war according to the flesh; **4** for the weapons of our warfare are not of the flesh, but mighty in God for the tearing down of strongholds, **5** throwing down imaginations and every high thing that is exalted against the knowledge of God, and bringing every thought into captivity to the obedience of Christ; **6** and being in readiness to avenge all disobedience, when your obedience will be made full. **7** Do you look at things only as they appear in front of your face? If anyone trusts in himself that he is Christ's, let him consider this again with himself, that, even as he is Christ's, so also we are Christ's. **8** For though I should boast somewhat abundantly concerning our authority, (which the Lord gave for building you up, and not for casting you down) I will not be disappointed, **9** that I may not seem as if I desire to terrify you by my letters. **10** For, "His letters," they say, "are weighty and strong, but his bodily presence is weak, and his speech is despised." **11** Let such a person consider this, that what we are in word by letters when we are absent, such are we also in deed when we are present. **12** For we are not bold to number or compare ourselves with some of those who commend themselves. But they themselves, measuring themselves by themselves, and comparing themselves with themselves, are without understanding. **13** But we will not boast beyond proper limits, but within the boundaries with which God appointed to us, which reach even to you. **14** For we do not stretch ourselves too much, as though we did not reach to you. For we came even as far as to you with the Good News of Christ, **15** not boasting excessively in the work done by others, but having hope that as your faith grows, we will be abundantly enlarged by you in our sphere of influence, **16** so as to proclaim the Good News even to the regions beyond you, not to boast in what someone else has already done. **17** But "he who boasts, let him boast in the Lord." **18** For it is not he who commends himself who is approved, but whom the Lord commends.

11 I wish that you would bear with me in a little foolishness, but indeed you do bear with me. **2** For I am jealous over you with a godly jealousy. For I married you to one husband, that I might present you as a pure virgin to Christ. **3** But I am afraid that somehow, as the serpent deceived Eve in his craftiness, so your minds might be corrupted from the sincerity and purity that is in Christ. **4** For if he who comes preaches another Jesus, whom we did not preach, or if you receive a different spirit, which you did not receive, or a different "good news", which you did not accept, you put up with that well enough. **5** For I reckon that I am not at all behind the very best apostles. **6** Even though I am unskilled in speech, I am not unskilled in knowledge. But in every way we have made this known to you in all things. **7** Or did I commit a sin in humbling myself that you might be exalted, because I preached to you God's Good News free of charge? **8** I robbed other churches, taking wages from them that I might serve you. **9** When I was present with you and was in need, I was not a burden on anyone, for the brothers, when they came from Macedonia, supplied the measure of my need. In everything I kept myself from being burdensome to you, and I will continue to do so. **10** As the truth of Christ is in me, no one will stop me from this boasting in the regions of Achaia. **11** Why? Because I do not love you? God knows. **12** But what I do, that I will do, that I may cut off occasion from them that desire an occasion, that in which they boast, they may be found even as we. **13** For such people are false apostles, deceitful workers, masquerading as Christ's apostles. **14** And no wonder, for even Satan masquerades as an angel of light. **15** It is no great thing therefore if his servants also masquerade as servants of righteousness, whose end will be according to their works. **16** I say again, let no one think me foolish. But if so, yet receive me as foolish, that I also may boast a little. **17** That which I speak, I do not speak according to the Lord, but as in foolishness, in this confidence of boasting. **18** Seeing that many boast after the flesh, I will also boast. **19** For you bear with the foolish gladly, being wise. **20** For you put up with it if someone makes slaves of you, if someone exploits you, if someone takes advantage of you, if someone exalts himself, if someone strikes you on the face. **21** I speak by way of disparagement, as though we had been weak. Yet however any is bold (I speak in foolishness), I am bold also. **22** Are they Hebrews? So am I. Are they Israelites? So am I. Are they descendants of Abraham? So am I. **23** Are they servants of Christ? (I speak as one beside himself) I am more so; in labors more abundantly, in prisons more abundantly, in stripes above measure, in deaths often. **24** Five times from the Jews I received forty stripes minus one. **25** Three times I was beaten with rods. Once I was stoned. Three times I suffered shipwreck. I have been a night and a day in the deep. **26** I have been in travels often, perils of rivers, perils of robbers, perils from my countrymen, perils from those who are not Jews, perils in the city, perils in the wilderness, perils in the sea, perils among false brothers; **27** in labor and travail, in watchings often, in hunger and thirst, in fastings often, and in cold and nakedness. **28** Besides those things that are outside, there is that which presses on me daily, anxiety for all the churches. **29** Who is weak, and I am not weak? Who is caused to stumble, and I do not burn with indignation? **30** If I must boast, I will boast of the things that concern my weakness. **31** The God and Father of the Lord Jesus, he who is blessed for the ages **(aiōn g165)**, knows that I do not lie. **32** In Damascus the governor under Aretas the king guarded the city of the Damascenes to arrest me. **33** Through a window I was let down in a basket by the wall, and escaped his hands.

12 It is necessary to boast, though it is not profitable. But I will come to visions and revelations of the Lord. **2** I know a man in Christ, fourteen years ago (whether in the body, I do not know, or whether out of the body, I do not know; God knows), such a one was caught up into the third heaven. **3** I know such a man (whether in the body, or apart from the body, I do not know; God knows), **4** how he was caught up into Paradise, and heard unspeakable words, which it is not lawful for a human to utter. **5** On behalf of such a one I will boast, but on my own behalf I will not boast, except in my weaknesses. **6** For if I would desire to boast, I will not be foolish; for I will speak the truth. But I refrain, so that no one may think more of me than that which he sees in me, or hears from me. **7** And because of the surpassing greatness of the revelations, therefore, to keep me from exalting myself, there was given to me a thorn in the flesh, a messenger of Satan to pound away at me, to keep me from exalting myself. **8** Concerning this thing, I pleaded with the Lord three times that it might depart from me. **9** He has said to me, "My grace is sufficient for you, for power is made perfect in weakness." Most gladly therefore I will rather glory in my weaknesses, that the power of Christ may rest on me. **10** Therefore I take pleasure in weaknesses, in injuries, in necessities, in persecutions, in distresses, for Christ's sake. For when I am weak, then am I strong. **11** I have become foolish. You compelled me, for I ought to have been commended by you, for in nothing was I inferior to the very best apostles, though I am nothing. **12** Truly the signs of an apostle were worked among you in all patience, in signs and wonders and mighty works. **13** For what is there in which you were made inferior to the rest of the churches, unless it is that I myself was not a burden to you? Forgive me this wrong. **14** Look, for the third time I am ready to come to you, and I will not be a burden to you; for I seek not what is yours, but you. For the children ought not to save up for the parents, but the parents for the children. **15** I will most gladly spend and be spent for your souls. If I love you more abundantly, am I loved the less? **16** But be it so, I did not myself burden you. But, being crafty, I caught you with deception. **17** Did I take advantage of you by anyone of them whom I have sent to you? **18** I exhorted Titus, and I sent the brother with him. Did Titus take any advantage of you? Did not we walk in the same spirit? Did not we walk in the same steps? **19** Have you been thinking all this time that we have been defending ourselves before you? In the sight of God we speak in Christ; and all things, beloved, are for your edifying. **20** For I am afraid that by any means, when I come, I might find you not the way I want to, and that I might be found by you as you do not desire; that by any means there would be strife, jealousy, outbursts of anger, factions, slander, whisperings, proud thoughts, riots; **21** that again when I come my God would humble me before you, and I would mourn for many of those who have sinned before now, and not repented of the uncleanness and sexual immorality and lustfulness which they committed.

13 This is the third time I am coming to you. "At the mouth of two or three witnesses will every word be established." **2** I have said beforehand, and I do say beforehand, as when I was present the second time, so now, being absent, to those who have sinned before now, and to all the rest, that, if I come again, I will not spare; **3** seeing that you seek a proof of Christ who speaks in me; who toward you is not weak, but is powerful in you. **4** For indeed he was crucified through weakness, yet he lives through the power of God. For we also are weak in him, but we will live with him through the power of God toward you. **5** Test your own selves, whether you are in the faith. Test your own selves. Or do you not know as to your own selves, that Jesus Christ is in you?—unless indeed you are disqualified. **6** But I hope that you will know that we are not disqualified. **7** Now we pray to God that you do no evil; not that we may appear approved, but that you may do that which is honorable, though we are as reprobate. **8** For we can do nothing against the truth, but for the truth. **9** For we rejoice when we are weak and you are strong. And this we also pray for, even your perfecting. **10** For this cause I write these things while absent, that I may not deal sharply when present, according to the authority which the Lord gave me for building up, and not for tearing down. **11** Finally, brothers, rejoice. Be perfected, be comforted, be of the same mind, live in peace, and the God of love and peace will be with you. **12** Greet one another with a holy kiss. **13** All the saints greet you. **14** The grace of the Lord Jesus Christ, the love of God, and the fellowship of the Holy Spirit, be with you all.

Galatians

1 Paul, an apostle (not from humans, nor through humans, but through Jesus Christ, and God the Father, who raised him from the dead), **2** and all the brothers who are with me, to the churches of Galatia: **3** Grace to you and peace from God our Father, and the Lord Jesus Christ, **4** who gave himself for our sins, that he might deliver us out of this present evil age (aiōn g165), according to the will of our God and Father— **5** to whom be the glory for the ages (aiōn g165) of the ages (aiōn g165). Amen. **6** I am astonished that you are so quickly deserting him who called you by the grace of Christ to a different "good news"; **7** and there is not another "good news." Only there are some who trouble you, and want to pervert the Good News of Christ. **8** But even though we, or an angel from heaven, should proclaim to you a "good news" other than that which we preached to you, let him be cursed. **9** As we have said before, so I now say again: if anyone preaches to you a "good news" other than that which you received, let him be cursed. **10** For am I now seeking the favor of people, or of God? Or am I striving to please people? For if I were still pleasing people, I would not be a servant of Christ. **11** But I make known to you, brothers, concerning the Good News which was preached by me, that it is not of human origin. **12** For neither did I receive it from a human source, nor was I taught it, but it came to me through revelation of Jesus Christ. **13** For you have heard of my former way of life in Judaism, how I severely persecuted the church of God, and tried to destroy it. **14** I advanced in Judaism beyond many of my own age among my countrymen, being more exceedingly zealous for the traditions of my fathers. **15** But when God, who had set me apart from my mother's womb and called me through his grace, was pleased **16** to reveal his Son to me, that I might proclaim him among those who are not Jewish, I did not immediately confer with flesh and blood, **17** nor did I go up to Jerusalem to those who were apostles before me, but I went away into Arabia. Then I returned to Damascus. **18** Then after three years I went up to Jerusalem to see Cephas and get information from him, and stayed with him fifteen days. **19** But of the other apostles I saw no one, except James, the Lord's brother. **20** Now about the things which I write to you, look, before God, I'm not lying. **21** Then I came to the regions of Syria and Cilicia. **22** I was still unknown by face to the churches of Judea which were in Christ, **23** but they only heard: "He who once persecuted us now preaches the faith that he once tried to destroy." **24** And they glorified God because of me.

2 Then after a period of fourteen years I went up again to Jerusalem with Barnabas, taking Titus also with me. **2** I went up by revelation, and I explained to them the Good News which I proclaim among those who are not Jewish, but privately before those who were respected, for fear that I might be running, or had run, in vain. **3** But not even Titus, who was with me, being a Greek, was compelled to be circumcised. **4** This was because of the false brothers secretly brought in, who stole in to spy out our liberty which we have in Christ Jesus, that they might bring us into bondage; **5** to whom we gave no place in the way of subjection, not for an hour, that the truth of the Good News might continue with you. **6** But from those who were reputed to be important (whatever they were, it makes no difference to me; God shows no favoritism between people)—they, I say, who were respected imparted nothing to me, **7** but to the contrary, when they saw that I had been entrusted with the Good News for the uncircumcision, even as Peter with the Good News for the circumcision **8** (for he who appointed Peter to be an apostle of the circumcision appointed me also to the Gentiles); **9** and when they perceived the grace that was given to me, James and Cephas and John, they who were reputed to be pillars, gave to me and Barnabas the right hand of fellowship, that we should go to the Gentiles, and they to the circumcised. **10** They only asked us to remember the poor—which very thing I was also zealous to do. **11** But when Cephas came to Antioch, I resisted him to his face, because he stood condemned. **12** For before some people came from James, he ate with those who were not Jewish. But when they came, he drew back and separated himself, fearing those who were of the circumcision. **13** And the rest of the Jewish believers joined him in his hypocrisy; so that even Barnabas was carried away with their hypocrisy. **14** But when I saw that they did not walk uprightly according to the truth of the Good News, I said to Cephas before them all, "If you, being a Jew, live as the Gentiles do, and not as the Jews do, how can you compel the Gentiles to live as the Jews do? **15** "We, being Jews by birth, and not Gentile sinners, **16** yet knowing that no one is justified by the works of the law but through faith in Jesus Christ, even we believed in Christ Jesus, that we might be justified by faith in Christ, and not by the works of the law, because no flesh will be justified by the works of the law. **17** But if, while we sought to be justified in Christ, we ourselves also were found sinners, is Christ a servant of sin? Certainly not. **18** For if I build up again those things which I destroyed, I prove myself a law-breaker. **19** For I, through the law, died to the law, that I might live to God. **20** I have been crucified with Christ, and it is no longer I that live, but Christ living in me. That life which I now live in the flesh, I live by faith in the Son of God, who loved me, and gave himself up for me. **21** I do not make void the grace of God. For if righteousness is through the law, then Christ died for nothing."

3 Foolish Galatians, who has cunningly deceived you, before whose eyes Jesus Christ was openly set forth as crucified? **2** I just want to learn this from you. Did you receive the Spirit by the works of the law, or by hearing of faith? **3** Are you so foolish? Having begun in the Spirit, are you now completed in the flesh? **4** Did you suffer so many things in vain, if it is indeed in vain? **5** He therefore who supplies the Spirit to you, and works miracles among you, does he do it by the works of the law, or by hearing of faith? **6** Even as Abraham "believed God, and it was credited to him as righteousness." **7** Know therefore that those who are of faith, the same are children of Abraham. **8** The Scripture, foreseeing that God would justify the Gentiles by faith, preached the Good News beforehand to Abraham, saying, "Through you all the nations will be blessed." **9** So then, those who are of faith are blessed with the faithful Abraham. **10** For as many as are of the works of the law are under a curse. For it is written, "Cursed is everyone who does not continue in all things that are written in the book of the law, to do them." **11** Now it is evident that no one is justified by the law before God, for, "The righteous will live by faith." **12** The law is not of faith, but, "The one who does them will live by them." **13** Christ redeemed us from the curse of the law, having become a curse for us. For it is written, "Cursed is everyone who hangs on a tree," **14** that the blessing of Abraham might come on the Gentiles through Christ Jesus; that we might receive the promise of the Spirit through faith. **15** Brothers, I am speaking in human terms. Though it is only a human covenant, once it has been ratified, no one annuls it or adds to it. **16** Now the promises were spoken to Abraham and to his offspring. He does not say, "And to offsprings," as of many, but as of one, "And to your offspring," which is Christ. **17** Now I say this: the law, which came four hundred thirty years later, does not annul a covenant previously ratified by God, so as to cancel the promise. **18** For if the inheritance is of the law, it is no more of promise; but God has granted it to Abraham by promise. **19** What then is the law? It was added because of transgressions, until the offspring should come to whom the promise has been made. It was ordained through angels by the hand of a mediator. **20** Now a mediator is not between one, but God is one. **21** Is the law then against the promises of God? Certainly not. For if there had been a law given which could give life, most certainly righteousness would have been of the law. **22** But the Scriptures imprisoned all things under sin, that the promise by faith in Jesus Christ might be given to those who believe. **23** But before faith came, we were kept in custody under the law, confined for the faith which should afterwards be revealed. **24** So that the law was our tutor to bring us to Christ, that we might be justified by faith. **25** But now that faith has come, we are no longer under a tutor. **26** For you are all children of God, through faith in Christ Jesus. **27** For as many of you as were baptized into Christ have put on Christ. **28** There is neither Jew nor Greek, there is neither slave nor free, there is neither male nor female; for you are all one in Christ Jesus. **29** If you are Christ's, then you are Abraham's offspring and heirs according to promise.

4 But I say that so long as the heir is a child, he is no different from a slave, though he is lord of all; **2** but is under guardians and stewards until the day appointed by the father. **3** So we also, when we were children, were held in bondage under the elemental principles of the world. **4** But when the fullness of the time came, God sent out his Son, born to a woman, born under the law, **5** that he might redeem those who were under the law, that we might receive the adoption of children. **6** And because you are children, God sent out the Spirit of his Son into our hearts, crying, "Abba, Father." **7** So you are no longer a slave, but a son; and if a son, then an heir of God. **8** However at that time, not knowing God, you were slaves to those who by nature are not gods. **9** But now that you have come to know God, or rather to be known by God, why do you turn back again to the weak and miserable elemental principles, to which you desire to be enslaved all over again? **10** You observe days, months, seasons, and years. **11** I am afraid for you, that I might have wasted my labor for you. **12** I beg you, brothers, become as I am, for I also have become as you are. You did me no wrong, **13** but you know that in physical weakness I preached the Good News to you the first time; **14** and though my condition was a trial to you, you did not despise nor reject; but you received me as an angel of God, even as Christ Jesus. **15** Where was the blessing you enjoyed? For I testify to you that, if possible, you would have plucked out your eyes and given them to me. **16** So then, have I become your enemy by telling you the truth? **17** They zealously seek you, but for no good purpose; they desire to alienate you, that you may be zealous for them. **18** But it is always good to be zealous in a good cause, and not only when I am present with you. **19** My little children, of whom I am again in travail until Christ is formed in you— **20** but I could wish to be present with you now, and to change my tone, for I am perplexed about you. **21** Tell me, you that desire to be under the law, do you not listen to the law? **22** For it is written that Abraham had two sons, one by the slave woman, and one by the free woman. **23** However, the son by the slave woman was born according to the flesh, but the son by the free woman was born through promise. **24** These things contain an allegory, for these are two covenants. One is from Mount Sinai, bearing children to slavery, which is Hagar. **25** For this Hagar is Mount Sinai in Arabia, and represents Jerusalem that exists now, for she is in slavery with her children. **26** But the Jerusalem that is above is free, and she is our mother. **27** For it is written, "Rejoice, you barren who do not bear. Break forth and shout, you that do not travail. For more are the children of the desolate than of her who has a husband." **28** Now you, brothers, as Isaac was, are children of promise. **29** But as then, he who was born according to the flesh persecuted him who was born according to the Spirit, so also it is now. **30** However what does the Scripture say? "Cast out the slave woman and her son, for the son of the slave woman will not inherit with the son of the free woman." **31** So then, brothers, we are not children of a handmaid, but of the free woman.

5 Stand firm therefore in the liberty by which Christ has made us free, and do not be entangled again with a yoke of bondage. **2** Listen, I, Paul, tell you that if you receive circumcision, Christ will profit you nothing. **3** Yes, I testify again to every man who receives circumcision, that he is a debtor to do the whole law. **4** You are alienated from Christ, you who desire to be justified by the law. You have fallen away from grace. **5** For we, through the Spirit, by faith wait for the hope of righteousness. **6** For in Christ Jesus neither circumcision amounts to anything, nor uncircumcision, but faith working through love. **7** You were running well. Who interfered with you that you should not obey the truth? **8** This persuasion is not from him who calls you. **9** A little yeast grows through the whole lump. **10** I have confidence toward you in the Lord that you will think no other way. But he who troubles you will bear his judgment, whoever he is. **11** But I, brothers, if I still proclaim circumcision, why am I still persecuted? Then the stumbling block of the cross has been removed. **12** I wish that those who disturb you would cut themselves off. **13** For you, brothers, were called for freedom. Only do not use your freedom for gain to the flesh, but through love be servants to one another. **14** For the whole law is fulfilled in one word, in this: "You are to love your neighbor as yourself." **15** But if you bite and devour one another, be careful that you do not consume one another. **16** But I say, walk by the Spirit, and you will not carry out the desires of the flesh. **17** For the flesh lusts against the Spirit, and the Spirit against the flesh; and these are contrary to one another, that you may not do the things that you desire. **18** But if you are led by the Spirit, you are not under the law. **19** Now the works of the flesh are obvious, which are: sexual immorality, uncleanness, lustfulness, **20** idolatry, sorcery, hatred, strife, jealousies, outbursts of anger, rivalries, divisions, heresies, **21** envyings, murders, drunkenness, orgies, and things like these; of which I forewarn you, even as I also forewarned you, that those who practice such things will not inherit the Kingdom of God. **22** But the fruit of the Spirit is love, joy, peace, patience, kindness, goodness, faithfulness, **23** gentleness, and self-control. Against such things there is no law. **24** Those who belong to Christ have crucified the flesh with its passions and lusts. **25** If we live by the Spirit, let us also walk by the Spirit. **26** Let us not become conceited, provoking one another, and envying one another.

6 Brothers, even if someone is caught in some wrongdoing, you who are spiritual must restore such a one in a spirit of gentleness; looking to yourself so that you also are not tempted. **2** Bear one another's burdens, and so you will fulfill the law of Christ. **3** For if anyone thinks himself to be something when he is nothing, he deceives himself. **4** But let each one test his own work, and then he will take pride in himself and not in his neighbor. **5** For every person will bear his own load. **6** But let him who is taught in the word share all good things with him who teaches. **7** Do not be deceived. God is not mocked, for whatever a person sows, that he will also reap. **8** For he who sows to his own flesh will from the flesh reap corruption. But he who sows to the Spirit will from the Spirit reap consummate (aiōnios g166) life. **9** Let us not be weary in doing good, for we will reap in due season, if we do not give up. **10** So then, as we have opportunity, let us do what is good toward all people, and especially toward those who are of the household of the faith. **11** See with what large letters I write to you with my own hand. **12** As many as desire to make a good showing in the flesh, they compel you to be circumcised; only that they may not be persecuted for the cross of Christ. **13** For even they who receive circumcision do not keep the law themselves, but they desire to have you circumcised, that they may boast in your flesh. **14** But far be it from me to boast, except in the cross of our Lord Jesus Christ, through which the world has been crucified to me, and I to the world. **15** For neither is circumcision anything, nor uncircumcision, but a new creation. **16** As many as walk by this rule, peace and mercy be on them, and on God's Israel. **17** From now on, let no one cause me any trouble, for I bear the marks of Jesus branded on my body. **18** The grace of our Lord Jesus Christ be with your spirit, brothers. Amen.

Ephesians

1 Paul, an apostle of Christ Jesus through the will of God, to the saints (in Ephesus) who are faithful in Christ Jesus: **2** Grace to you and peace from God our Father and the Lord Jesus Christ. **3** Blessed be the God and Father of our Lord Jesus Christ, who has blessed us with every spiritual blessing in the heavenly places in Christ; **4** even as he chose us in him before the foundation of the world, that we would be holy and without blemish before him in love; **5** having predestined us for adoption as children through Jesus Christ to himself, according to the good pleasure of his desire, **6** to the praise of the glory of his grace, which he freely bestowed on us in the Beloved One, **7** in whom we have our redemption through his blood, the forgiveness of our trespasses, according to the riches of his grace, **8** which he made to abound toward us in all wisdom and prudence, **9** making known to us the mystery of his will, according to his good pleasure which he purposed in him **10** to an administration of the fullness of the times, to sum up all things in Christ, the things in the heavens, and the things on the earth, in him; **11** in whom also we were assigned an inheritance, having been foreordained according to the purpose of him who works all things after the counsel of his will; **12** to the end that we should be to the praise of his glory, we who had before hoped in Christ: **13** in whom you also, having heard the word of the truth, the Good News of your salvation, —in whom, having also believed, you were sealed with the Holy Spirit of promise, **14** who is a pledge of our inheritance, to the redemption of God's own possession, to the praise of his glory. **15** For this cause I also, having heard of the faith in the Lord Jesus which is among you, and the love which you have toward all the saints, **16** do not cease to give thanks for you, making mention of you in my prayers, **17** that the God of our Lord Jesus Christ, the Father of glory, may give to you a spirit of wisdom and revelation in the knowledge of him; **18** having the eyes of your heart enlightened, that you may know what is the hope of his calling, and what are the riches of the glory of his inheritance in the saints, **19** and what is the exceeding greatness of his power toward us who believe, according to that working of the strength of his might **20** which he worked in Christ, when he raised him from the dead, and made him to sit at his right hand in the heavenly places, **21 far above all rule and authority and power and dominion and every name that is named, not only in this age (aiōn g165), but also in that which is to come.** **22** He put all things under his feet, and gave him to be head over all things for the church, **23** which is his body, the fullness of him who fills all in all.

2 You were made alive when you were dead in your transgressions and sins, **2 in which you once walked according to the age (aiōn g165) of this world, according to the prince of the power of the air, the spirit who now works in the children of disobedience.** **3** among whom we also all once lived in the lust of our flesh, doing the desires of the flesh and of the mind, and were by nature children of wrath, even as the rest. **4** But God, being rich in mercy, for his great love with which he loved us, **5** even when we were dead through our trespasses, made us alive together with Christ (by grace you have been saved), **6** and raised us up with him, and made us to sit with him in the heavenly places in Christ Jesus, **7 that in the ages (aiōn g165) to come he might show the exceeding riches of his grace in kindness toward us in Christ Jesus;** **8** for by grace you have been saved through faith, and that not of yourselves; it is the gift of God, **9** not of works, that no one would boast. **10** For we are his workmanship, created in Christ Jesus for good works, which God prepared before that we would walk in them. **11** Therefore remember that once you, the Gentiles in the flesh, who are called "uncircumcision" by that which is called "circumcision," (in the flesh, made by hands); **12** that you were at that time separate from Christ, alienated from the commonwealth of Israel, and strangers from the covenants of the promise, having no hope and without God in the world. **13** But now in Christ Jesus you who once were far away have been brought near by the blood of Christ. **14** For he is our peace, who made both one, and broke down the middle wall of partition, **15** having abolished in the flesh the hostility, the law of commandments contained in ordinances, that he might create in himself one new man of the two, making peace; **16** and might reconcile them both in one body to God through the cross, by which he put to death their enmity. **17** He came and preached peace to you who were far off and peace to those who were near. **18** For through him we both have our access in one Spirit to the Father. **19** So then you are no longer strangers and foreigners, but you are fellow citizens with the saints, and of the household of God, **20** being built on the foundation of the apostles and prophets, Christ Jesus himself being the chief cornerstone; **21** in whom the whole building, fitted together, grows into a holy temple in the Lord; **22** in whom you also are built together for a habitation of God in the Spirit.

3 For this cause I, Paul, am the prisoner of Christ Jesus on behalf of you the Gentiles, **2** if it is so that you have heard of the administration of that grace of God which was given me toward you; **3** how that by revelation the mystery was made known to me, as I wrote before in few words, **4** by which, when you read, you can perceive my understanding in the mystery of Christ; **5** which in other generations was not made known to people, as it has now been revealed to his holy apostles and prophets in the Spirit; **6** that the Gentiles are fellow heirs, and fellow members of the body, and fellow partakers of the promise in Christ Jesus through the Good News, **7** of which I was made a servant, according to the gift of that grace of God which was given me according to the working of his power. **8** To me, the very least of all saints, was this grace given, to proclaim to the Gentiles the unsearchable riches of Christ, **9 and to bring to light what is the administration of the mystery which for ages (aiōn g165) has been hidden in God, who created all things;** **10** to the intent that now through the church the manifold wisdom of God might be made known to the rulers and the authorities in the heavenly places, **11**

according to the purpose of the ages (aiōn g165) which he accomplished in Christ Jesus our Lord. **12** in whom we have boldness and access in confidence through our faith in him. **13** Therefore I ask that you not be discouraged because of my sufferings for you, which is your glory. **14** For this cause, I bow my knees before the Father, **15** from whom every family in heaven and on earth is named, **16** that he would grant you, according to the riches of his glory, that you may be strengthened with power through his Spirit in the inner person; **17** that Christ may dwell in your hearts through faith; to the end that you, being rooted and grounded in love, **18** may be strengthened to comprehend with all the saints what is the breadth and length and height and depth, **19** and to know Christ's love which surpasses knowledge, that you may be filled with all the fullness of God. **20** Now to him who is able to do exceedingly abundantly above all that we ask or think, according to the power that works in us, **21** to him be the glory in the church and in Christ Jesus to all generations for the age (aiōn g165) of the ages (aiōn g165). Amen.

4 I therefore, a prisoner in the Lord, urge you to lead a life worthy of the calling to which you have been called, **2** with all humility and gentleness, with patience, bearing with one another in love; **3** being eager to keep the unity of the Spirit in the bond of peace. **4** There is one body, and one Spirit, even as you also were called in one hope of your calling; **5** one Lord, one faith, one baptism, **6** one God and Father of all, who is over all, and through all, and in all. **7** But to each one of us was the grace given according to the measure of the gift of Christ. **8** Therefore he says, "When he ascended on high, he led captivity captive, and gave gifts to people." **9** Now this, "He ascended," what is it but that he also descended into the lower parts of the earth? **10** He who descended is the one who also ascended far above all the heavens, that he might fill all things. **11** He gave some to be apostles; and some, prophets; and some, evangelists; and some, pastors and teachers; **12** for the perfecting of the saints, to the work of serving, to the building up of the body of Christ; **13** until we all attain to the unity of the faith, and of the knowledge of the Son of God, to a mature person, to the measure of the stature of the fullness of Christ; **14** that we may no longer be children, tossed back and forth and carried about with every wind of doctrine, by the trickery of people, by cleverness in deceitful schemes; **15** but speaking truth in love, we may grow up in all things into him, who is the head, Christ; **16** from whom all the body, being fitted and knit together through that which every joint supplies, according to the proper working of each individual part, makes the body increase to the building up of itself in love. **17** This I say therefore, and testify in the Lord, that you no longer walk as the nations also walk, in the futility of their mind, **18** being darkened in their understanding, alienated from the life of God, because of the ignorance that is in them, because of the hardening of their hearts; **19** who having become callous gave themselves up to lust, to work all uncleanness with greediness. **20** But you did not learn Christ that way; **21** if indeed you heard him, and were taught in him, even as truth is in Jesus: **22** that you put away, as concerning your former way of life, the old self, that grows corrupt after the lusts of deceit; **23** and that you be renewed in the spirit of your mind, **24** and put on the new self, who in the likeness of God has been created in righteousness and holiness of truth. **25** Therefore, putting away falsehood, speak truth each one with his neighbor. For we are members of one another. **26** "Be angry, but do not sin." Do not let the sun go down on your anger, **27** neither give place to the devil. **28** Let him who stole steal no more; but rather let him labor, working with his hands the thing that is good, that he may have something to give to him who has need. **29** Let no corrupt speech proceed out of your mouth, but such as is good for building up as the need may be, that it may give grace to those who hear. **30** Do not grieve the Holy Spirit of God, in whom you were sealed for the day of redemption. **31** Let all bitterness, wrath, anger, outcry, and slander, be put away from you, with all malice. **32** And be kind to one another, tenderhearted, forgiving each other, just as God also in Christ forgave you.

5 Be therefore imitators of God, as beloved children. **2** And walk in love, even as Christ also loved us, and gave himself up for us, an offering and a sacrifice to God for a sweet-smelling fragrance. **3** But sexual immorality, and all uncleanness, or covetousness, let it not even be mentioned among you, as becomes saints; **4** nor filthiness, nor foolish talking, nor jesting, which are not appropriate; but rather giving of thanks. **5** Know this for sure, that no sexually immoral or impure or greedy person, that is, an idolater, has any inheritance in the Kingdom of Christ and God. **6** Let no one deceive you with empty words. For because of these things, the wrath of God comes on the children of disobedience. **7** Therefore do not be partakers with them. **8** For you were once darkness, but are now light in the Lord. Walk as children of light, **9** for the fruit of the light is in all goodness and righteousness and truth, **10** proving what is well pleasing to the Lord. **11** Have no fellowship with the unfruitful works of darkness, but rather even reprove them. **12** For the things which are done by them in secret, it is a shame even to speak of. **13** But all things, when they are reproved, are revealed by the light, for everything that reveals is light. **14** Therefore he says, "Awake, you who sleep, and rise from the dead, and Christ will shine on you." **15** Therefore watch carefully how you walk, not as unwise, but as wise; **16** redeeming the time, because the days are evil. **17** Therefore do not be foolish, but understand what the will of the Lord is. **18** Do not get drunk with wine, which is debauchery, but be filled with the Spirit, **19** speaking to one another in psalms, hymns, and spiritual songs, singing and making music in your heart to the Lord; **20** giving thanks always concerning all things in the name of our Lord Jesus Christ to God the Father; **21** subjecting yourselves one to another in the fear of Christ. **22** Wives, be subject to your own husbands, as to the Lord. **23** For the husband is the head of the wife, and Christ also is the head of the church, being himself the savior of the body. **24** But as the church is subject to

Christ, so let the wives also be to their own husbands in everything. **25** Husbands, love your wives, even as Christ also loved the church, and gave himself up for it; **26** that he might sanctify it, having cleansed it by the washing of water with the word, **27** that he might present the church to himself gloriously, not having spot or wrinkle or any such thing; but that it should be holy and without blemish. **28** Even so husbands also ought to love their own wives as their own bodies. He who loves his own wife loves himself. **29** For no one ever hated his own flesh; but nourishes and cherishes it, even as Christ also does the church; **30** because we are members of his body, of his flesh and of his bones. **31** "For this cause a man will leave his father and mother, and will be joined to his wife, and the two will become one flesh." **32** This mystery is great, but I speak concerning Christ and of the church. **33** Nevertheless each of you must also love his own wife even as himself; and let the wife see that she respects her husband.

6 Children, obey your parents in the Lord, for this is right. **2** "Honor your father and mother," which is the first commandment with a promise: **3** "that it may be well with you, and that you may live long in the land." **4** And fathers, do not provoke your children to anger, but nurture them in the discipline and instruction of the Lord. **5** Servants, be obedient to those who according to the flesh are your masters, with fear and trembling, in singleness of your heart, as to Christ; **6** not in the way of service only when eyes are on you, as people-pleasers; but as servants of Christ, doing the will of God from the heart; **7** with good will doing service, as to the Lord, and not to people; **8** knowing that whatever good thing each one does, he will receive the same again from the Lord, whether he is bound or free. **9** You masters, do the same things to them, and give up threatening, knowing that he who is both their Master and yours is in heaven, and there is no partiality with him. **10** Finally, be strong in the Lord, and in the strength of his might. **11** Put on the whole armor of God, that you may be able to stand against the schemes of the devil. **12** For our wrestling is not against flesh and blood, but against the rulers, against the authorities, against the world leaders of this darkness, and against the spiritual forces of evil in the heavenly places. **13** Therefore, put on the whole armor of God, that you may be able to withstand in the evil day, and, having done all, to stand. **14** Stand therefore, having the belt of truth buckled around your waist, and having put on the breastplate of righteousness, **15** and having fitted your feet with the preparation of the Good News of peace; **16** above all, taking up the shield of faith, with which you will be able to quench all the fiery darts of the evil one. **17** And take the helmet of salvation, and the sword of the Spirit, which is the spoken word of God; **18** with all prayer and requests, praying at all times in the Spirit, and being watchful to this end in all perseverance and requests for all the saints: **19** on my behalf, that utterance may be given to me in opening my mouth, to make known with boldness the mystery of the Good News, **20** for which I am an ambassador in chains; that in it I may speak boldly, as I ought to speak. **21** But that you also may know my affairs, how I am doing, Tychicus, the beloved brother and faithful servant in the Lord, will make known to you all things; **22** whom I have sent to you for this very purpose, that you may know our state, and that he may comfort your hearts. **23** Peace be to the brothers, and love with faith, from God the Father and the Lord Jesus Christ. **24** Grace be with all those who love our Lord Jesus Christ with incorruptible love.

Philippians

1 Paul and Timothy, servants of Christ Jesus; To all the saints in Christ Jesus who are at Philippi, with the overseers and deacons: **2** Grace to you and peace from God our Father and the Lord Jesus Christ. **3** I thank my God whenever I remember you, **4** always in every prayer of mine for all of you, making my requests with joy, **5** for your partnership in the Good News from the first day until now; **6** being confident of this very thing, that he who began a good work in you will complete it until the day of Christ Jesus. **7** It is even right for me to think this way about all of you, because I have you in my heart, because, both in my imprisonment and in the defense and confirmation of the Good News, you all are partakers with me of grace. **8** For God is my witness, how I long after all of you in the tender mercies of Christ Jesus. **9** This I pray, that your love may abound yet more and more in knowledge and all discernment; **10** so that you may approve the things that are excellent; that you may be pure and blameless for the Day of Christ; **11** being filled with the fruit of righteousness, which are through Jesus Christ, to the glory and praise of God. **12** Now I desire to have you know, brothers, that the things which happened to me have turned out rather to the progress of the Good News; **13** so that it became evident to the whole praetorian guard, and to all the rest, that my bonds are in Christ; **14** and that most of the brothers in the Lord, being confident through my bonds, are more abundantly bold to speak the word without fear. **15** Some indeed proclaim Christ even out of envy and strife, and some also out of good will. **16** The latter out of love, knowing that I am appointed for the defense of the Good News. **17** The former insincerely proclaim Christ from selfish ambition, thinking that they add affliction to my chains. **18** What does it matter? Only that in every way, whether out of false motives or in truth, Christ is proclaimed. I rejoice in this, yes, and will rejoice. **19** For I know that this will turn out for my deliverance, through your petition and the supply of the Spirit of Jesus Christ, **20** according to my earnest expectation and hope, that I will in no way be disappointed, but with all boldness, as always, now also Christ will be magnified in my body, whether by life, or by death. **21** For to me to live is Christ, and to die is gain. **22** But if I live on in the flesh, this will bring fruit from my work; yet I do not make known what I will choose. **23** But I am in a dilemma between the two, having the desire to depart and be with Christ, which is far better. **24** Yet, to remain in the flesh is more needful for your sake. **25** Having this confidence, I know that I will remain, yes, and remain with you all, for your progress and joy in the faith, **26** that your rejoicing may abound in Christ Jesus in me through my presence with you again. **27** Only let your manner of life be worthy of the Good News of Christ, that, whether I come and see you or am absent, I may hear of your state, that you stand firm in one spirit, with one soul striving for the faith of the Good News; **28** and in nothing frightened by the adversaries, which is for them a proof of destruction, but to you of salvation, and that from God. **29** Because it has been granted to you on behalf of Christ, not only to believe in him, but also to suffer on his behalf, **30** having the same conflict which you saw in me, and now hear is in me.

2 If there is therefore any exhortation in Christ, if any consolation of love, if any fellowship of the Spirit, if any tender mercies and compassion, **2** make my joy full, by being like-minded, having the same love, being of one accord, of one mind; **3** doing nothing through rivalry or through conceit, but in humility, each counting others better than himself; **4** each of you not just looking to his own things, but each of you also to the things of others. **5** Have this in your mind, which was also in Christ Jesus, **6** who, existing in the form of God, did not consider equality with God a thing to be grasped, **7** but emptied himself, taking the form of a servant, being made in the likeness of men. **8** And being found in human form, he humbled himself, becoming obedient to death, yes, the death of the cross. **9** Therefore God also highly exalted him, and gave to him the name which is above every name; **10** that at the name of Jesus every knee should bow, of those in heaven, those on earth, and those under the earth, **11** and that every tongue should confess that Jesus Christ is Lord, to the glory of God the Father. **12** So then, my beloved, even as you have always obeyed, not only in my presence, but now much more in my absence, work out your own salvation with awe and reverence. **13** For it is God who works in you both to will and to work, for his good pleasure. **14** Do all things without murmurings and disputes, **15** that you may become blameless and pure, children of God without blemish in the midst of a crooked and perverse generation, among whom you are seen as lights in the world, **16** holding up the word of life; that I may have something to boast in the day of Christ, that I did not run in vain nor labor in vain. **17** Yes, and if I am poured out on the sacrifice and service of your faith, I rejoice, and rejoice with you all. **18** In the same way, you also rejoice, and rejoice with me. **19** But I hope in the Lord Jesus to send Timothy to you soon, that I also may be cheered up when I know how you are doing. **20** For I have no one else like-minded, who will truly care about you. **21** For they all seek their own, not the things of Jesus Christ. **22** But you know the proof of him, that, as a child serves a father, so he served with me in furtherance of the Good News. **23** Therefore I hope to send him at once, as soon as I see how it will go with me. **24** But I trust in the Lord that I myself also will come shortly. **25** But I counted it necessary to send to you Epaphroditus, my brother, fellow worker, fellow soldier, and your apostle and servant of my need; **26** since he longed for you all, and was very troubled, because you had heard that he was sick. **27** For indeed he was sick, nearly to death, but God had mercy on him; and not on him only, but on me also, that I might not have sorrow on sorrow. **28** I have sent him all the more eagerly, therefore, so that when you see him again you may rejoice, and that I may be less anxious. **29** Receive him therefore in the Lord with all joy, and hold such in honor, **30** because for the work of Christ he came near to death, risking his life to supply that which was lacking in your service toward me.

3 Finally, my brothers, rejoice in the Lord. To write the same things to you is no trouble to me, and is a safeguard for you. **2** Beware of the dogs, beware of the evil workers, beware of the false circumcision. **3** For we are the circumcision, who worship God in the Spirit, and rejoice in Christ Jesus, and have no confidence in the flesh; **4** though I myself might have confidence even in the flesh. If anyone else thinks that he has confidence in the flesh, I yet more: **5** circumcised the eighth day, of the nation of Israel, of the tribe of Benjamin, a Hebrew of Hebrews; concerning the law, a Pharisee; **6** concerning zeal, persecuting the church; concerning the righteousness which is in the law, found blameless. **7** However, what things were gain to me, these have I counted loss for Christ. **8** More than that, I count all things to be a loss compared to the far greater value of knowing Christ Jesus, my Lord, for whom I suffered the loss of all things, and count them nothing but refuse, that I may gain Christ **9** and be found in him, not having a righteousness of my own, that which is of the law, but that which is through faith in Christ, the righteousness which is from God by faith; **10** that I may know him, and the power of his resurrection, and the fellowship of his sufferings, becoming conformed to his death; **11** if by any means I may attain to the resurrection from the dead. **12** Not that I have already obtained, or am already made perfect; but I press on, if it is so that I may take hold of that for which also I was taken hold of by Christ Jesus. **13** Brothers, I do not regard myself as having taken hold of it, but one thing I do. Forgetting the things which are behind, and reaching forward to the things which are ahead, **14** I press on toward the goal for the prize of the high calling of God in Christ Jesus. **15** Let us therefore, as many as are perfect, think this way. If in anything you think otherwise, God will also reveal that to you. **16** Nevertheless, to what we have attained, let us walk by the same rule, being of the same mind. **17** Brothers, be imitators together of me, and note those who walk this way, even as you have us for an example. **18** For many, of whom I have often told you, and now tell you with tears, live as enemies of the cross of Christ, **19** whose end is destruction, whose god is the belly, and whose glory is in their shame, who think about earthly things. **20** For our citizenship is in heaven, from which we also eagerly wait for a Savior, the Lord Jesus Christ; **21** who will transform our lowly body into the likeness of his glorious body, according to the power by which he is able even to subject all things to himself.

4 Therefore, my brothers, whom I love and long for, my joy and crown, so stand firm in the Lord, my beloved. **2** I appeal to Euodia and I appeal to Syntyche to agree in the Lord. **3** Yes, I ask you also, true companion, help these women, for they labored with me in the Good News, with Clement also, and the rest of my fellow workers, whose names are in the Book of Life. **4** Rejoice in the Lord always. Again I will say, Rejoice. **5** Let your gentleness be evident to all people. The Lord is near. **6** Do not be anxious about anything, but in everything, by prayer and petition with thanksgiving, let your requests be made known to God. **7** And the peace of God, which surpasses all understanding, will guard your hearts and your minds in Christ Jesus. **8** Finally, brothers, whatever things are true, whatever things are honorable, whatever things are just, whatever things are pure, whatever things are lovely, whatever things are of good report; if there is any virtue, and if there is any praise, think on these things. **9** And the things you learned and received and heard and saw in me, do these things. And the God of peace will be with you. **10** Now I rejoice in the Lord greatly that at last you have revived your concern for me; in which you were indeed concerned, but you lacked opportunity. **11** I'm not saying this because I am in need, for I have learned to be content in any circumstance. **12** I know what it is to be in need, and I know what it is to have a lot. In any and all circumstances I have learned the secret, whether full or hungry, whether having a lot or being in need. **13** I can do all things through him who strengthens me. **14** Still, you have done well to share my hardship. **15** And you Philippians yourselves know that in the beginning of the Good News, when I departed from Macedonia, no church shared with me in the matter of giving and receiving but you only. **16** For even in Thessalonica you sent me aid twice. **17** Not that I seek the gift, but I seek the fruit that increases to your account. **18** But I have received everything in full, and I have an abundance. I am fully supplied, having received from Epaphroditus the things that came from you, a sweet-smelling fragrance, an acceptable and well-pleasing sacrifice to God. **19** And my God will supply all your needs according to his riches in glory in Christ Jesus. **20** Now to our God and Father be the glory for the ages **(aiōn g165)** of the ages **(aiōn g165)**! Amen. **21** Greet every saint in Christ Jesus. The brothers who are with me greet you. **22** All the saints greet you, especially those who are of Caesar's household. **23** The grace of the Lord Jesus Christ be with your spirit.

Colossians

1 Paul, an apostle of Christ Jesus through the will of God, and Timothy our brother, **2** to the saints and faithful brothers in Christ at Colossae: Grace to you and peace from God our Father. **3** We give thanks to God the Father of our Lord Jesus Christ, praying always for you, **4** having heard of your faith in Christ Jesus, and of the love which you have toward all the saints, **5** because of the hope which is laid up for you in heaven, of which you heard before in the word of truth, the Good News, **6** which has come to you; even as it is in all the world and is bearing fruit and growing, as it does in you also, since the day you heard and knew the grace of God in truth; **7** even as you learned of Epaphras our beloved fellow servant, who is a faithful servant of Christ on our behalf, **8** who also declared to us your love in the Spirit. **9** For this cause, we also, since the day we heard this, do not cease praying and making requests for you, that you may be filled with the knowledge of his will in all spiritual wisdom and understanding, **10** that you may walk worthily of the Lord, to please him in every way, bearing fruit in every good work, and increasing in the knowledge of God; **11** strengthened with all power, according to the might of his glory, for all endurance and perseverance with joy; **12** giving thanks to the Father, who has qualified you to share in the inheritance of the saints in the light; **13** who delivered us out of the power of darkness, and transferred us into the Kingdom of the Son of his love; **14** in whom we have our redemption, the forgiveness of our sins; **15** who is the image of the invisible God, the firstborn over all creation. **16** For by him all things were created, in the heavens and on the earth, things visible and things invisible, whether thrones or dominions or rulers or authorities; all things have been created by him and for him. **17** He is before all things, and in him all things are held together. **18** He is the head of the body, the church, who is the beginning, the firstborn from the dead; that in all things he might have the preeminence. **19** For all the fullness was pleased to dwell in him, **20** and through him to reconcile all things to himself, making peace through the blood of his cross through him, whether things on the earth or things in heaven. **21** You, who once were alienated and were hostile in your minds, doing evil deeds, **22** yet now he has reconciled in the body of his flesh through death, to present you holy and without blemish and blameless before him, **23** if it is so that you continue in the faith, established and firm, and not moved away from the hope of the Good News which you heard, which is being proclaimed in all creation under heaven; of which I, Paul, have become a servant. **24** Now I rejoice in my sufferings for your sake, and I am completing in my flesh what is lacking in the sufferings of Christ for the sake of his body, which is the church; **25** of which I was made a servant, according to the stewardship of God which was given me toward you, to fulfill the word of God, **26** the mystery which has been hidden for the ages (aiōn g165) and for the generations, but now it has been revealed to his saints, **27** to them God was pleased to make known what are the riches of the glory of this mystery among the Gentiles, which is Christ in you, the hope of glory; **28** whom we proclaim, admonishing everyone and teaching everyone all wisdom, that we may present everyone perfect in Christ Jesus; **29** for which I also labor, struggling according to his power, which works in me mightily.

2 For I desire to have you know how greatly I struggle for you, and for those at Laodicea, and for as many as have not seen my face in the flesh; **2** that their hearts may be comforted, they being knit together in love, and gaining all riches of the full assurance of understanding, that they may know the mystery of God, namely, Christ, **3** in whom are all the treasures of wisdom and knowledge hidden. **4** Now I say this so that no one will deceive you with persuasive words. **5** For though I am absent in the flesh, yet am I with you in the spirit, rejoicing and seeing your order, and the steadfastness of your faith in Christ. **6** As therefore you received Christ Jesus, the Lord, walk in him, **7** rooted and built up in him, and established in the faith, even as you were taught, abounding in it with thanksgiving. **8** Be careful not to allow anyone to captivate you through an empty and deceptive philosophy, according to human tradition, according to the elementary principles of the world, and not according to Christ. **9** For in him all the fullness of Deity dwells in bodily form, **10** and in him you are made full, who is the head of all principality and power; **11** in whom you were also circumcised with a circumcision not made with hands, in the putting off of the body of the flesh, in the circumcision of Christ; **12** having been buried with him in baptism, in which you were also raised with him through faith in the working of God, who raised him from the dead. **13** You were dead through your trespasses and the uncircumcision of your flesh. He made you alive together with him, having forgiven us all our trespasses, **14** wiping out the handwriting in ordinances which was against us; and he has taken it out of the way, nailing it to the cross; **15** having disarmed the rulers and authorities, he made a show of them openly, triumphing over them in it. **16** Therefore do not let anyone judge you about food and drink, or with respect to a feast day or a new moon or a Sabbath day, **17** which are a shadow of the things to come; but the body is Christ's. **18** Let no one rob you of your prize by a voluntary humility and worshipping of the angels, dwelling in the things which he has seen, vainly puffed up by his fleshly mind, **19** and not holding firmly to the Head, from whom all the body, being supplied and knit together through the joints and ligaments, grows with God's growth. **20** If you died with Christ from the elementary principles of the world, why, as though living in the world, do you subject yourselves to ordinances, **21** "Do not handle, nor taste, nor touch" **22** (all of which perish with use), according to human commandments and teachings? **23** Which things indeed appear like wisdom in self-imposed worship, and humility, and severity to the body; but are not of any value against the indulgence of the flesh.

3 If then you were raised together with Christ, seek the things that are above, where Christ is, seated on the right hand of God. **2** Set your mind on the things that are above, not on the things that are on the earth. **3** For you died, and your life is hidden with Christ in God. **4** When Christ, your life, is revealed, then you will also be revealed with him in glory. **5** Put to death, therefore, whatever is worldly in you: sexual immorality, impurity, lust, evil desire, and covetousness, which is idolatry. **6** Because of these, the wrath of God is coming on the children of disobedience. **7** You also once walked in those, when you lived in them; **8** but now you also put them all away: anger, wrath, malice, slander, and shameful speaking out of your mouth. **9** Do not lie to one another, seeing that you have put off the old self with its practices, **10** and have put on the new self, who is being renewed in knowledge after the image of his Creator, **11** where there cannot be Greek and Jew, circumcision and uncircumcision, barbarian, Scythian, slave, freeman; but Christ is all, and in all. **12** Put on therefore, as God's chosen ones, holy and beloved, a heart of compassion, kindness, gentleness, humility, and patience; **13** bearing with one another, and forgiving each other, if anyone has a complaint against another; even as the Lord forgave you, so you also do. **14** Above all these things, walk in love, which is the bond of perfection. **15** And let the peace of Christ rule in your hearts, to which also you were called in one body; and be thankful. **16** Let the word of Christ dwell in you richly; in all wisdom teaching and admonishing one another with psalms, hymns, and spiritual songs, singing with grace in your heart to God. **17** Whatever you do, in word or in deed, do all in the name of the Lord Jesus, giving thanks to God the Father, through him. **18** Wives, be in subjection to your husbands, as is fitting in the Lord. **19** Husbands, love your wives, and do not be bitter against them. **20** Children, obey your parents in all things, for this pleases the Lord. **21** Fathers, do not provoke your children, so that they won't be discouraged. **22** Servants, obey in all things those who are your masters according to the flesh, not just when they are looking, as people-pleasers, but in singleness of heart, fearing the Lord. **23** And whatever you do, work heartily, as for the Lord, and not for people, **24** knowing that from the Lord you will receive the reward of the inheritance; for you serve the Lord Christ. **25** But he who does wrong will receive again for the wrong that he has done, and there is no partiality.

4 Masters, give to your servants that which is just and equal, knowing that you also have a Master in heaven. **2** Continue steadfastly in prayer, watching in it with thanksgiving; **3** praying together for us also, that God may open to us a door for the word, to speak the mystery of Christ, for which I am also in bonds; **4** that I may reveal it as I ought to speak. **5** Walk in wisdom toward those who are outside, redeeming the time. **6** Let your speech always be with grace, seasoned with salt, that you may know how you ought to answer each one. **7** All my affairs will be made known to you by Tychicus, the beloved brother, faithful servant, and fellow slave in the Lord. **8** I am sending him to you for this very purpose, that you may know our circumstances and that he may encourage your hearts, **9** together with Onesimus, the faithful and beloved brother, who is one of you. They will make known to you everything that is going on here. **10** Aristarchus, my fellow prisoner greets you, and Mark, the cousin of Barnabas (concerning whom you received commandments, "if he comes to you, receive him"), **11** and Jesus who is called Justus, who are of the circumcision. These are my only fellow workers for the Kingdom of God, and they have been a comfort to me. **12** Epaphras, who is one of you, a servant of Christ, salutes you, always striving for you in his prayers, that you may stand perfect and fully assured in all the will of God. **13** For I testify about him, that he has worked hard for you, and for those in Laodicea, and for those in Hierapolis. **14** Luke, the beloved physician, and Demas greet you. **15** Greet the brothers who are in Laodicea, and to Nympha and the church that is in her house. **16** When this letter has been read among you, cause it to be read also in the church of the Laodiceans; and that you also read the letter from Laodicea. **17** Tell Archippus, "See that you fulfill the ministry that you have been given in the Lord." **18** The salutation of me, Paul, with my own hand: remember my bonds. Grace be with you.

1 Thessalonians

1 Paul, Silvanus, and Timothy, to the church of the Thessalonians in God the Father and the Lord Jesus Christ: Grace to you and peace. **2** We always give thanks to God for all of you, mentioning you in our prayers, **3** remembering without ceasing your work of faith and labor of love and patience of hope in our Lord Jesus Christ, before our God and Father. **4** We know, brothers loved by God, that you are chosen, **5** and that our Good News came to you not in word only, but also in power, and in the Holy Spirit, and with much assurance. You know what kind of persons we showed ourselves to be among you for your sake. **6** You became imitators of us, and of the Lord, having received the word in much affliction, with joy of the Holy Spirit, **7** so that you became an example to all who believe in Macedonia and in Achaia. **8** For from you the word of the Lord has been declared, not only in Macedonia and Achaia, but also in every place your faith toward God has gone out; so that we do not need to say anything. **9** For they themselves report concerning us what kind of a reception we had from you; and how you turned to God from idols, to serve a living and true God, **10** and to wait for his Son from heaven, whom he raised from the dead—Jesus, who delivers us from the wrath to come.

2 For you yourselves know, brothers, our visit to you was not in vain, **2** but having suffered before and been shamefully treated, as you know, at Philippi, we grew bold in our God to tell you the Good News of God in much conflict. **3** For our exhortation is not of error, nor of uncleanness, nor in deception. **4** But even as we have been approved by God to be entrusted with the Good News, so we speak; not as pleasing people, but God, who tests our hearts. **5** For neither were we at any time found using words of flattery, as you know, nor with a pretext for greed (God is witness), **6** nor seeking glory from people (neither from you nor from others), when we might have claimed authority as apostles of Christ. **7** But we were like little children among you, like a nursing mother cherishes her own children. **8** Even so, affectionately longing for you, we were well pleased to impart to you, not the Good News of God only, but also our own souls, because you had become very dear to us. **9** For you remember, brothers, our labor and travail; for working night and day, that we might not burden any of you, we preached to you the Good News of God. **10** You are witnesses with God, how holy, righteously, and blamelessly we behaved ourselves toward you who believe. **11** As you know, as a father with his own children, **12** we exhorted, comforted, and implored every one of you to lead a life worthy of God, who calls you into his own Kingdom and glory. **13** For this cause we also thank God without ceasing, that, when you received from us the word of the message of God, you accepted it not as a human word, but, as it is in truth, the word of God, which also works in you who believe. **14** For you, brothers, became imitators of the churches of God which are in Judea in Christ Jesus; for you also suffered the same things from your own countrymen, even as they did from the Judeans; **15** who killed both the Lord Jesus and the prophets, and drove us out, and did not please God, and are hostile to all people; **16** forbidding us to speak to those who are not Jewish that they may be saved; to fill up their sins always. But wrath has come on them to the uttermost. **17** But we, brothers, being bereaved of you for a short season, in presence, not in heart, tried even harder to see your face with great desire, **18** because we wanted to come to you—indeed, I, Paul, once and again—but Satan hindered us. **19** For what is our hope, or joy, or crown of rejoicing? Is it not even you, before our Lord Jesus at his coming? **20** For you are our glory and our joy.

3 Therefore, when we could not stand it any longer, we thought it good to be left behind at Athens alone, **2** and sent Timothy, our brother and God's fellow worker in the Good News of Christ, to establish you, and to comfort you concerning your faith; **3** that no one be moved by these afflictions. For you know that we are appointed to this task. **4** For truly, when we were with you, we told you beforehand that we are to suffer affliction, even as it happened, and you know. **5** For this cause I also, when I could not stand it any longer, sent that I might know your faith, for fear that by any means the tempter had tempted you, and our labor would have been in vain. **6** But when Timothy came just now to us from you, and brought us glad news of your faith and love, and that you have good memories of us always, longing to see us, even as we also long to see you; **7** for this cause, brothers, we were comforted over you in all our distress and affliction through your faith. **8** For now we live, since you stand firm in the Lord. **9** For what thanksgiving can we render again to God for you, for all the joy with which we rejoice for your sakes before our God; **10** night and day praying exceedingly that we may see your face, and may perfect that which is lacking in your faith? **11** Now may our God and Father himself, and our Lord Jesus, direct our way to you; **12** and the Lord make you to increase and abound in love for one another and for all, even as we also do toward you, **13** to the end he may establish your hearts blameless in holiness before our God and Father, at the coming of our Lord Jesus with all his saints.

4 Finally then, brothers, we ask and urge you in the Lord Jesus, that as you received from us how you ought to live and to please God, even as you are living, that you excel more and more. **2** For you know what instructions we gave you through the Lord Jesus. **3** For this is the will of God: your sanctification, that you abstain from sexual immorality, **4** that each one of you know how to possess himself of his own vessel in sanctification and honor, **5** not in the passion of lust, even as the nations who do not know God; **6** that no one should take advantage of and wrong a brother or sister in this matter; because the Lord is an avenger in all these things, as also we forewarned you and testified. **7** For God called us not for uncleanness, but in sanctification. **8** Therefore he who rejects this does not reject man, but God, who has also given his Holy

Spirit to you. **9** But concerning brotherly love, you have no need that one write to you. For you yourselves are taught by God to love one another, **10** for indeed you do it toward all the brothers who are in all Macedonia. But we exhort you, brothers, that you abound more and more; **11** and that you make it your ambition to lead a quiet life, and to do your own business, and to work with your own hands, even as we instructed you; **12** that you may walk properly toward those who are outside, and may have need of nothing. **13** But we do not want you to be ignorant, brothers, concerning those who have fallen asleep, so that you do not grieve like the rest, who have no hope. **14** For if we believe that Jesus died and rose again, even so God will bring with him those who have fallen asleep in Jesus. **15** For this we tell you by the word of the Lord, that we who are alive, who are left to the coming of the Lord, will in no way precede those who have fallen asleep. **16** For the Lord himself will descend from heaven with a shout, with the voice of the archangel, and with God's trumpet. The dead in Christ will rise first, **17** then we who are alive, who are left, will be caught up together with them in the clouds, to meet the Lord in the air. So we will be with the Lord forever. **18** Therefore comfort one another with these words.

5 But concerning the times and the seasons, brothers, you have no need that anything be written to you. **2** For you yourselves know well that the day of the Lord comes like a thief in the night. **3** Now when they are saying, "Peace and safety," then sudden destruction will come on them, like birth pains on a pregnant woman; and they will in no way escape. **4** But you, brothers, are not in darkness, that the day should overtake you like a thief. **5** You are all children of light, and children of the day. We do not belong to the night, nor to darkness, **6** so then let us not sleep, as the rest do, but let us watch and be sober. **7** For those who sleep, sleep in the night, and those who are drunk are drunk in the night. **8** But let us, since we belong to the day, be sober, putting on the breastplate of faith and love, and, for a helmet, the hope of salvation. **9** For God did not appoint us to wrath, but to the obtaining of salvation through our Lord Jesus Christ, **10** who died for us, that, whether we wake or sleep, we should live together with him. **11** Therefore exhort one another, and build each other up, even as you also do. **12** But we ask you, brothers, to recognize those who labor among you, and are over you in the Lord, and admonish you, **13** and to respect and honor them in love for their work's sake. Be at peace among yourselves. **14** We exhort you, brothers, admonish the disorderly, encourage the fainthearted, support the weak, be patient toward all. **15** See that no one returns evil for evil to anyone, but always seek what is good both for each other and for all. **16** Rejoice always. **17** Pray without ceasing. **18** In everything give thanks, for this is the will of God in Christ Jesus toward you. **19** Do not quench the Spirit. **20** Do not treat prophecies with contempt, **21** but test all things; hold firmly that which is good. **22** Abstain from every form of evil. **23** May the God of peace himself sanctify you completely. May your whole spirit, soul, and body be preserved blameless at the coming of our Lord Jesus Christ. **24** He who calls you is faithful, who will also do it. **25** Brothers, pray for us also. **26** Greet all the brothers with a holy kiss. **27** I solemnly command you by the Lord that this letter be read to all the holy brothers. **28** The grace of our Lord Jesus Christ be with you.

2 Thessalonians

1 Paul, Silvanus, and Timothy, to the church of the Thessalonians in God our Father, and the Lord Jesus Christ: **2** Grace to you and peace from God our Father and the Lord Jesus Christ. **3** We are bound to always give thanks to God for you, brothers, even as it is appropriate, because your faith grows exceedingly, and the love of each and every one of you towards one another abounds; **4** so that we ourselves boast about you in the churches of God for your patience and faith in all your persecutions and in the afflictions which you endure. **5** This is an obvious sign of the righteous judgment of God, to the end that you may be counted worthy of the Kingdom of God, for which you also suffer. **6** Since it is a righteous thing with God to repay affliction to those who afflict you, **7** and to give relief to you who are afflicted with us, when the Lord Jesus is revealed from heaven with his mighty angels in flaming fire, **8** giving vengeance to those who do not know God, and to those who do not obey the Good News of our Lord Jesus, **9** who will pay the penalty: consummate (aiōnios g166) destruction at the face of the Lord and at the glory of his might, **10** when he comes to be glorified in his saints, and to be admired among all those who have believed (because our testimony to you was believed) in that day. **11** To this end we also pray always for you, that our God may count you worthy of your calling, and fulfill every desire of goodness and work of faith, with power; **12** that the name of our Lord Jesus may be glorified in you, and you in him, according to the grace of our God and the Lord Jesus Christ.

2 Now, brothers, concerning the coming of our Lord Jesus Christ, and our gathering together to him, we ask you **2** not to be quickly shaken in your mind, nor yet be troubled, either by spirit, or by word, or by letter as from us, saying that the day of the Lord had come. **3** Let no one deceive you in any way. For it will not be, unless the rebellion comes first, and the man of lawlessness is revealed, the son of destruction, **4** he who opposes and exalts himself against all that is called God or that is worshiped; so that he sits in the temple of God, setting himself up as God. **5** Do you not remember that, when I was still with you, I told you these things? **6** Now you know what is restraining him, to the end that he may be revealed in his own season. **7** For the mystery of lawlessness already works. Only there is one who restrains now, until he is taken out of the way. **8** Then the lawless one will be revealed, whom the Lord will kill with the breath of his mouth, and destroy by the manifestation of his coming; **9** even he whose coming is according to the working of Satan with all power and signs and lying wonders, **10** and with all deception of wickedness for those who are perishing, because they did not receive the love of the truth, that they might be saved. **11** And because of this, God sends them a strong delusion, that they should believe the lie, **12** in order that all might be judged who did not believe the truth, but had pleasure in unrighteousness. **13** But we are bound to always give thanks to God for you, brothers loved by the Lord, because God chose you from the beginning for salvation through sanctification of the Spirit and belief in the truth; **14** to which he called you through our Good News, for the obtaining of the glory of our Lord Jesus Christ. **15** So then, brothers, stand firm, and hold the traditions which you were taught by us, whether by word, or by letter. **16** Now our Lord Jesus Christ himself, and God our Father, who loved us and gave us consummate (aiōnios g166) comfort and good hope through grace, **17** comfort your hearts and establish you in every good work and word.

3 Finally, brothers, pray for us, that the word of the Lord may spread rapidly and be glorified, even as also with you; **2** and that we may be delivered from unreasonable and evil people; for not all have faith. **3** But the Lord is faithful, who will establish you, and guard you from the evil one. **4** We have confidence in the Lord concerning you, that you both do and will do the things we command. **5** May the Lord direct your hearts into the love of God, and into the patience of Christ. **6** Now we command you, brothers, in the name of our Lord Jesus Christ, that you withdraw yourselves from every brother who walks in rebellion, and not after the tradition which they received from us. **7** For you know how you ought to imitate us. For we did not behave ourselves rebelliously among you, **8** neither did we eat bread from anyone's hand without paying for it, but in labor and travail worked night and day, that we might not burden any of you; **9** not because we do not have the right, but to make ourselves an example to you, that you should imitate us. **10** For even when we were with you, we commanded you this: "If anyone will not work, neither let him eat." **11** For we hear of some who walk among you in rebellion, who do not work at all, but are busybodies. **12** Now those who are that way, we command and exhort in the Lord Jesus Christ, that with quietness they work, and eat their own bread. **13** But you, brothers, do not be weary in doing well. **14** If anyone does not obey our word in this letter, note that person, that you have no company with him, to the end that he may be ashamed. **15** Do not count him as an enemy, but admonish him as a brother. **16** Now may the Lord of peace himself give you peace at all times in all ways. The Lord be with you all. **17** The greeting of me, Paul, with my own hand, which is the sign in every letter: this is how I write. **18** The grace of our Lord Jesus Christ be with you all.

1 Timothy

1 Paul, an apostle of Christ Jesus according to the commandment of God our Savior, and Christ Jesus our hope; **2** to Timothy, my true child in faith: Grace, mercy, and peace, from God the Father and Christ Jesus our Lord. **3** As I urged you when I was going into Macedonia, stay at Ephesus that you might command certain people not to teach a different doctrine, **4** neither to pay attention to myths and endless genealogies, which cause speculation, rather than God's stewardship, which is in faith— **5** but the goal of this command is love, out of a pure heart and a good conscience and unfeigned faith; **6** from which things some, having missed the mark, have turned aside to vain talking; **7** desiring to be teachers of the law, though they understand neither what they say, nor about what they strongly affirm. **8** But we know that the law is good, if one uses it lawfully, **9** as knowing this, that law is not made for a righteous person, but for the lawless and insubordinate, for the ungodly and sinners, for the unholy and profane, for those who kill their father or mother, for murderers, **10** for the sexually immoral, for men who have sexual relations with men, for kidnappers, for liars, for perjurers, and for whatever else is contrary to sound teaching; **11** according to the Good News of the glory of the blessed God, which was committed to my trust. **12** And I thank him who enabled me, Christ Jesus our Lord, because he counted me faithful, appointing me to service; **13** although I was before a blasphemer, a persecutor, and insolent. However, I obtained mercy, because I did it ignorantly in unbelief. **14** The grace of our Lord abounded exceedingly with faith and love which is in Christ Jesus. **15** The saying is faithful and worthy of all acceptance, that Christ Jesus came into the world to save sinners; of whom I am chief. **16** However, for this cause I obtained mercy, that in me first, Jesus Christ might display all his patience for an example of those who were going to believe in him for consummate (aiōnios g166) life. **17** Now to the King of the ages (aiōn g165), incorruptible, invisible, only God, be honor and glory for the ages (aiōn g165) of the ages (aiōn g165). Amen. **18** This instruction I commit to you, my child Timothy, according to the prophecies which led the way to you, that by them you may wage the good warfare; **19** holding faith and a good conscience; which some having thrust away made a shipwreck concerning the faith; **20** of whom is Hymenaeus and Alexander; whom I delivered to Satan, that they might be taught not to blaspheme.

2 I exhort therefore, first of all, that petitions, prayers, intercessions, and thanksgivings, be made for all people: **2** for kings and all who are in high places; that we may lead a tranquil and quiet life in all godliness and reverence. **3** For this is good and acceptable in the sight of God our Savior; **4** who desires all people to be saved and come to full knowledge of the truth. **5** For there is one God, and one mediator between God and humanity, a human, Christ Jesus, **6** who gave himself as a ransom for all; the testimony in its own times; **7** to which I was appointed a proclaimer and an apostle (I am telling the truth, I am not lying), a teacher of the Gentiles in faith and truth. **8** I desire therefore that the men in every place pray, lifting up holy hands without anger and doubting. **9** In the same way, that women also adorn themselves in decent clothing, with modesty and propriety; not just with braided hair, gold, pearls, or expensive clothing; **10** but (which becomes women professing godliness) with good works. **11** Let a woman learn in quietness with all subjection. **12** But I do not permit a woman to teach, nor to exercise authority over a man, but to be in quietness. **13** For Adam was first formed, then Eve. **14** Adam was not deceived, but the woman, being deceived, has fallen into disobedience; **15** but she will be delivered through the childbirth, if they continue in faith and love and holiness, with good judgment.

3 This is a faithful saying: If someone aspires to the office of overseer, he desires a good work. **2** The overseer, therefore, must be beyond criticism, the husband of one wife, temperate, sensible, modest, hospitable, good at teaching; **3** not a drunkard, not violent, but gentle, not quarrelsome, not a lover of money; **4** one who rules his own house well, having children in subjection with all reverence; **5** (but if someone does not know how to manage his own house, how will he take care of the church of God?) **6** not a new convert, lest being puffed up he fall into the same condemnation as the devil. **7** Moreover he must have good testimony from those who are outside, to avoid falling into disgrace and the trap of the devil. **8** Deacons, in the same way, must be reverent, not double-tongued, not devoted to a lot of wine, not greedy for money; **9** holding the mystery of the faith in a pure conscience. **10** Let them also first be tested; then let them serve as deacons, if they are blameless. **11** Their wives in the same way must be reverent, not slanderers, temperate, faithful in all things. **12** Let deacons be husbands of one wife, ruling their children and their own houses well. **13** For those who have served well as deacons gain for themselves a good standing, and great boldness in the faith which is in Christ Jesus. **14** These things I write to you, hoping to come to you shortly; **15** but if I wait long, that you may know how people ought to behave themselves in the house of God, which is the church of the living God, the pillar and ground of the truth. **16** Without controversy, the mystery of godliness is great: He was revealed in the flesh, justified by the Spirit, seen by angels, preached among the nations, believed on in the world, and received up in glory.

4 But the Spirit says expressly that in later times some will fall away from the faith, paying attention to seducing spirits and doctrines of demons, **2** through the hypocrisy of liars, branded in their own conscience as with a hot iron; **3** forbidding marriage and commanding to abstain from foods which God created to be received with thanksgiving by those who believe and know the truth. **4** For every creature of God is good, and nothing is to be rejected, if it is received with thanksgiving. **5** For it is sanctified through the word of God and prayer. **6** If you instruct the brothers of these things, you will be a good servant of Christ Jesus, nourished in the words of the faith, and of the good doctrine which you have followed. **7** But refuse profane and old wives' tales. Exercise yourself toward godliness. **8** For bodily exercise has some value, but godliness has value in all things, having the promise of the life which is now, and of that which is to come. **9** This saying is faithful and worthy of all acceptance. **10** For to this end we both labor and strive, because we have set our trust in the living God, who is the Savior of all people, especially of those who believe. **11** Command and teach these things. **12** Let no one despise your youth; but be an example to those who believe, in word, in your way of life, in love, in faith, and in purity. **13** Until I come, pay attention to reading, to exhortation, and to teaching. **14** Do not neglect the gift that is in you, which was given to you by prophecy, with the laying on of the hands of the elders. **15** Be diligent in these things. Give yourself wholly to them, that your progress may be revealed to all. **16** Pay attention to yourself, and to your teaching. Continue in these things, for in doing this you will save both yourself and those who hear you.

5 Do not rebuke an older man, but exhort him as a father; the younger men as brothers; **2** the older women as mothers; the younger as sisters, in all purity. **3** Honor widows who are widows indeed. **4** But if any widow has children or grandchildren, let them learn first to show piety towards their own family, and to repay their parents, for this is acceptable in the sight of God. **5** Now she who is a widow indeed, and desolate, has her hope set on God, and continues in petitions and prayers night and day. **6** But she who gives herself to pleasure is dead while she lives. **7** Also command these things, so that they will be without fault. **8** But if anyone does not provide for his own, and especially his own household, he has denied the faith, and is worse than an unbeliever. **9** Let no one be enrolled as a widow under sixty years old, having been the wife of one man, **10** being approved by good works, if she has brought up children, if she has been hospitable to strangers, if she has washed the saints' feet, if she has relieved the afflicted, and if she has diligently followed every good work. **11** But refuse younger widows, for whenever their passions lead them away from Christ, they desire to marry; **12** having condemnation, because they have rejected their first pledge. **13** Besides, they also learn to be idle, going about from house to house. Not only idle, but also gossips and busybodies, saying things which they ought not. **14** I desire therefore that the younger widows marry, bear children, rule the household, and give no occasion to the adversary for reviling. **15** For already some have turned aside after Satan. **16** If any believing man or believing woman has widows, let them assist them, and do not let the church be burdened; that it might help those widows who are truly in need. **17** Let the elders who rule well be counted worthy of double honor, especially those who labor in the word and in teaching. **18** For the Scripture says, "Do not muzzle the ox when it treads out the grain." And, "The laborer is worthy of his wages." **19** Do not receive an accusation against an elder, except at the word of two or three witnesses. **20** Those who sin, reprove in the sight of all, that the rest also may be in fear. **21** I command you in the sight of God, and Christ Jesus, and the chosen angels, that you observe these things without prejudice, doing nothing by partiality. **22** Do not ordain anyone hastily, nor participate in the sins of others. Keep yourself pure. **23** Be no longer a drinker of water only, but use a little wine for your stomach's sake and your frequent infirmities. **24** The sins of some people are obvious, going before them to judgment, but those of others show up later. **25** In the same way also there are good works that are obvious, and those that are otherwise cannot be hidden.

6 Let as many as are slaves under the yoke count their own masters worthy of all honor, that the name of God and the doctrine not be blasphemed. **2** Those who have believing masters, let them not despise them, because they are brothers, but rather let them serve them, because those who partake of the benefit are believing and beloved. Teach and exhort these things. **3** If anyone teaches a different doctrine, and does not consent to sound words, the words of our Lord Jesus Christ, and to the doctrine which is according to godliness, **4** he is conceited, knowing nothing, but obsessed with arguments, disputes, and word battles, from which come envy, strife, reviling, evil suspicions, **5** constant friction of people of corrupt minds and destitute of the truth, who suppose that godliness is a means of gain. **6** But godliness with contentment is great gain. **7** For we brought nothing into the world, so neither can we carry anything out. **8** But having food and clothing, we will be content with that. **9** But those who are determined to be rich fall into a temptation and a snare and many foolish and harmful lusts, such as plunge people into ruin and destruction. **10** For the love of money is a root of all kinds of evil. Some have been led astray from the faith in their greed, and have pierced themselves through with many sorrows. **11** But you, man of God, flee these things, and follow after righteousness, godliness, faith, love, patience, and gentleness. **12** Fight the good fight of faith. Lay hold of the consummate (aiōnios g166) life to which you were called and did confess the good confession in the sight of many witnesses. **13** I command you before God, who gives life to all things, and before Christ Jesus, who before Pontius Pilate testified the good confession, **14** that you keep the commandment without spot, blameless, until the appearing of our Lord Jesus Christ; **15** which in its own times he will show, who is the blessed and only Ruler, the King of kings, and Lord of lords; **16** who alone has immortality, dwelling in unapproachable light, whom no man has seen, nor can see: to whom be honor and consummate (aiōnios g166) power. Amen. **17** Charge those who are rich in this present age (aiōn g165) that they not be arrogant, nor have their hope set on the uncertainty of riches, but on God, who richly provides us with everything for enjoyment; **18** that they do good, that they be rich in good works, that they be ready to distribute, willing to communicate; **19** laying up in store for themselves a good foundation against the time to come, that they may lay hold of the true life. **20** Timothy, guard that which is committed to you, turning away from the empty chatter and oppositions of the knowledge which is falsely so called; **21** which some professing have erred concerning the faith. Grace be with you.

2 Timothy

1 Paul, an apostle of Christ Jesus through the will of God, according to the promise of the life which is in Christ Jesus, **2** to Timothy, my beloved child: Grace, mercy, and peace, from God the Father and Christ Jesus our Lord. **3** I thank God, whom I serve as my forefathers did, with a pure conscience. How unceasing is my memory of you in my petitions, night and day **4** longing to see you, remembering your tears, that I may be filled with joy; **5** having been reminded of the unfeigned faith that is in you; which lived first in your grandmother Lois, and your mother Eunice, and, I am persuaded, in you also. **6** For this cause, I remind you that you should stir up the gift of God which is in you through the laying on of my hands. **7** For God did not give us a spirit of fear, but of power and love and of a sound mind. **8** Therefore do not be ashamed of the testimony of our Lord, nor of me his prisoner; but endure hardship for the Good News according to the power of God, **9** who saved us and called us with a holy calling, not according to our works, but according to his own purpose and grace, which was given to us in Christ Jesus before the times of the ages (aiōnios g166), **10** but has now been revealed by the appearing of our Savior, Christ Jesus, who abolished death, and brought life and immortality to light through the Good News. **11** For this, I was appointed a preacher, an apostle, and a teacher. **12** For this cause I also suffer these things. Yet I am not ashamed, for I know him whom I have believed, and I am persuaded that he is able to guard that which I have committed to him against that day. **13** Hold the pattern of sound words which you have heard from me, in faith and love which is in Christ Jesus. **14** That good thing which was committed to you, guard through the Holy Spirit who dwells in us. **15** This you know, that all who are in Asia turned away from me; of whom are Phygelus and Hermogenes. **16** May the Lord grant mercy to the house of Onesiphorus, for he often refreshed me, and was not ashamed of my chain, **17** but when he was in Rome, he sought me diligently, and found me **18** (the Lord grant to him to find the Lord's mercy in that day); and in how many things he served at Ephesus, you know very well.

2 You therefore, my child, be strengthened in the grace that is in Christ Jesus. **2** The things which you have heard from me among many witnesses, commit the same to faithful people, who will be able to teach others also. **3** You therefore must share in hardship, as a good soldier of Christ Jesus. **4** No soldier on duty entangles himself in the affairs of life, that he may please him who enrolled him as a soldier. **5** Also, if anyone competes in athletics, he is not crowned unless he has competed by the rules. **6** The farmers who labor must be the first to get a share of the crops. **7** Consider what I say, for the Lord will give you understanding in all things. **8** Remember Jesus Christ, risen from the dead, a descendant of David, according to my Good News, **9** in which I suffer hardship to the point of chains as a criminal. But God's word is not chained. **10** Therefore I endure all things for the chosen ones' sake, that they also may obtain the salvation which is in Christ Jesus with consummate (aiōnios g166) glory. **11** This saying is faithful: "For if we died with him, we will also live with him. **12** If we endure, we will also reign with him. If we deny him, he also will deny us. **13** If we are faithless, he remains faithful, for he cannot deny himself." **14** Remind them of these things, charging them in the presence of God, not to wrangle about words, to no profit, to the subverting of those who hear. **15** Do your best to present yourself approved by God, a worker who does not need to be ashamed, properly handling the word of truth. **16** But shun empty chatter, for they will proceed further in ungodliness, **17** and their word will consume like gangrene, of whom is Hymenaeus and Philetus; **18** who have erred concerning the truth, saying that the resurrection is already past, and overthrowing the faith of some. **19** However God's firm foundation stands, having this seal, "The Lord knows those who are his," and, "Let every one who names the name of the Lord depart from unrighteousness." **20** Now in a large house there are not only vessels of gold and of silver, but also of wood and of clay. Some are for honor, and some for dishonor. **21** If anyone therefore purges himself from these, he will be a vessel for honor, sanctified, and suitable for the master's use, prepared for every good work. **22** Flee from youthful lusts; but pursue righteousness, faith, love, and peace with those who call on the Lord out of a pure heart. **23** But refuse foolish and ignorant questionings, knowing that they generate strife. **24** The Lord's servant must not quarrel, but be gentle towards all, able to teach, patient, **25** in gentleness correcting those who oppose him: perhaps God may give them repentance leading to a full knowledge of the truth, **26** and they may recover themselves out of the devil's snare, having been taken captive by him to his will.

3 But know this, that in the last days, grievous times will come. **2** For people will be lovers of self, lovers of money, boastful, arrogant, blasphemers, disobedient to parents, unthankful, unholy, **3** unloving, unforgiving, slanderers, without self-control, brutal, hateful of good, **4** traitors, headstrong, conceited, lovers of pleasure rather than lovers of God; **5** holding a form of godliness, but denied the power thereof. Turn away from these, also. **6** For among them are those who crawl into households and take captive weak-willed women weighed down with sins, led away by various passions and pleasures, **7** always learning, and never able to come to the knowledge of the truth. **8** Even as Jannes and Jambres opposed Moses, so do these also oppose the truth; people corrupted in mind, disapproved concerning the faith. **9** But they will proceed no further. For their folly will be evident to all, as theirs also was. **10** But you did follow my teaching, conduct, purpose, faith, patience, love, steadfastness, **11** persecutions, and sufferings: those things that happened to me at Antioch, Iconium, and Lystra. I endured those persecutions. Out of them all the Lord delivered me. **12** Yes, and all who desire to live godly in Christ Jesus will suffer persecution. **13** But evil people and impostors will grow worse and worse, deceiving and being deceived. **14** But you remain in the things which you have learned and have been assured of, knowing from whom you have learned them. **15** From infancy, you have known the holy Scriptures which are able to make you wise for salvation through faith, which is in Christ Jesus. **16** All Scripture is God-breathed and profitable for teaching, for reproof, for correction, and for training in righteousness, **17** that the person of God may be complete, thoroughly equipped for every good work.

4 I command you therefore before God and of Christ Jesus, who will judge the living and the dead, and by his appearing and his Kingdom: **2** proclaim the word; be urgent in season and out of season; reprove, rebuke, and exhort, with all patience and teaching. **3** For the time will come when they will not listen to the sound doctrine, but, having itching ears, will heap up for themselves teachers after their own lusts; **4** and will turn away their ears from the truth, and turn aside to myths. **5** But you be sober in all things, endure hardship, do the work of an evangelist, fulfill your ministry. **6** For I am already being offered, and the time of my departure has come. **7** I have fought the good fight. I have finished the course. I have kept the faith. **8** From now on, there is stored up for me the crown of righteousness, which the Lord, the righteous judge, will give to me on that day; and not to me only, but also to all those who have loved his appearing. **9** Be diligent to come to me soon, **10** for Demas left me, having loved this present age **(aiōn g165)**, and went to Thessalonica; Crescens to Galatia; and Titus to Dalmatia. **11** Only Luke is with me. Take Mark, and bring him with you, for he is useful to me for service. **12** But I sent Tychicus to Ephesus. **13** Bring the cloak that I left at Troas with Carpus when you come, and the books, especially the parchments. **14** Alexander, the coppersmith, did much evil to me. The Lord will repay him according to his works, **15** of whom you also must beware; for he greatly opposed our words. **16** At my first defense, no one came to help me, but all left me. May it not be held against them. **17** But the Lord stood by me, and strengthened me, that through me the message might be fully proclaimed, and that all the Gentile people might hear; and I was delivered out of the mouth of the lion. **18** And the Lord will deliver me from every evil work, and will preserve me for his heavenly Kingdom; to whom be the glory for the ages **(aiōn g165)** of the ages **(aiōn g165)**. Amen. **19** Greet Prisca and Aquila, and the house of Onesiphorus. **20** Erastus remained at Corinth, and I left Trophimus at Miletus, ill. **21** Be diligent to come before winter. Eubulus salutes you, as do Pudens, Linus, Claudia, and all the brothers. **22** The Lord be with your spirit. Grace be with you.

Titus

1 Paul, a servant of God, and an apostle of Jesus Christ, according to the faith of God's chosen ones, and the knowledge of the truth which is according to godliness, **2** in hope of the consummate (aiōnios g166) life, which God, who cannnot lie, promised before time began; **3** but in his own time revealed his word in the message with which I was entrusted according to the commandment of God our Savior; **4** to Titus, my true child according to a common faith: Grace and peace from God the Father and Christ Jesus our Savior. **5** I left you in Crete for this reason, that you would set in order the things that were lacking, and appoint elders in every city, as I directed you; **6** if anyone is blameless, the husband of one wife, having children who believe, who are not accused of loose or unruly behavior. **7** For the overseer must be blameless, as God's steward; not self-pleasing, not easily angered, not given to wine, not violent, not greedy for dishonest gain; **8** but given to hospitality, as a lover of good, sober minded, fair, holy, self-controlled; **9** holding to the faithful word which is according to the teaching, that he may be able to exhort in the sound doctrine, and to convict those who contradict him. **10** For there are many rebellious people, empty talkers and deceivers, especially those of the circumcision, **11** whose mouths must be silenced; who are upsetting whole families, teaching things which they should not, for the sake of dishonest gain. **12** One of them, a prophet of their own, said, "Cretans are always liars, evil beasts, and idle gluttons." **13** This testimony is true. For this cause, reprove them sharply, that they may be sound in the faith, **14** not paying attention to Jewish myths and commandments of people who reject the truth. **15** To the pure, all things are pure; but to those who are defiled and unbelieving, nothing is pure; but both their mind and their conscience are defiled. **16** They profess that they know God, but by their works they deny him, being abominable, disobedient, and unfit for any good work.

2 But say the things which fit sound doctrine, **2** that older men should be sober-minded, worthy of respect, self-controlled, sound in faith, in love, and in patience: **3** and that older women likewise be reverent in behavior, not slanderers nor enslaved to much wine, teachers of that which is good; **4** that they may train the young women to love their husbands, to love their children, **5** to be sober minded, chaste, workers at home, kind, being in subjection to their own husbands, that God's word may not be blasphemed. **6** Likewise, exhort the younger men to be sober minded; **7** in all things showing yourself an example of good works. In your teaching show integrity, seriousness, **8** and a sound message that cannot be condemned; that he who opposes you may be ashamed, having no evil thing to say about us. **9** Exhort servants to be in subjection to their own masters, and to be well-pleasing in all things; not contradicting; **10** not stealing, but showing all good fidelity; that they may adorn the doctrine of God, our Savior, in all things. **11** For the grace of God has appeared, bringing salvation to all people, **12** instructing us, that denying ungodliness and worldly lusts, we might live sensibly, righteously, and reverently in this present age (aiōn g165); **13** looking for the blessed hope and appearing of the glory of our great God and Savior, Jesus Christ; **14** who gave himself for us, that he might redeem us from all iniquity, and purify for himself a people for his own possession, zealous for good works. **15** Say these things and exhort and reprove with all authority. Let no one despise you.

3 Remind them to be in subjection to rulers and to authorities, to be obedient, to be ready for every good work, **2** to speak evil of no one, not to be contentious, to be gentle, showing courtesy to all people. **3** For we were also once foolish, disobedient, deceived, serving various lusts and pleasures, living in malice and envy, hateful, and hating one another. **4** But when the kindness and love of God our Savior appeared, **5** not by works of righteousness, which we did ourselves, but according to his mercy, he saved us, through the washing of rebirth and renewing by the Holy Spirit, **6** whom he poured out on us richly, through Jesus Christ our Savior; **7** that being justified by his grace, we might be made heirs according to the hope of the consummate (aiōnios g166) life. **8** This saying is faithful, and concerning these things I desire that you affirm confidently, so that those who have believed God may be careful to maintain good works. These things are good and profitable for people; **9** but shun foolish questionings, genealogies, strife, and disputes about the law; for they are unprofitable and vain. **10** Reject a divisive person after a first and second warning; **11** knowing that such a one is perverted, and sins, being self-condemned. **12** When I send Artemas to you, or Tychicus, be diligent to come to me to Nicopolis, for I have determined to winter there. **13** Send Zenas, the Law scholar, and Apollos on their journey speedily, that nothing may be lacking for them. **14** Let our people also learn to maintain good works for necessary uses, that they may not be unfruitful. **15** All who are with me greet you. Greet those who love us in faith. Grace be with you all.

Philemon

1 Paul, a prisoner of Christ Jesus, and Timothy our brother, to Philemon, our beloved fellow worker, **2** and to Apphia our sister, to Archippus, our fellow soldier, and to the church in your house: **3** Grace to you and peace from God our Father and the Lord Jesus Christ. **4** I thank my God always, making mention of you in my prayers, **5** hearing of your love, and of the faith which you have toward the Lord Jesus, and toward all the saints; **6** that the fellowship of your faith may become effective, in the knowledge of every good thing which is in you in Christ. **7** For I have much joy and comfort in your love, because the hearts of the saints have been refreshed through you, brother. **8** Therefore, though I have all boldness in Christ to command you that which is appropriate, **9** yet on the basis of love I rather appeal, being such a one as Paul, the aged, but also a prisoner of Christ Jesus. **10** I appeal to you for my child, whom I have become the father of in my chains, Onesimus, **11** who once was useless to you, but now is useful to you and to me. **12** I am sending back to you, him who is my very heart, **13** whom I desired to keep with me, that on your behalf he might serve me in my chains for the Good News. **14** But I was willing to do nothing without your consent, that your goodness would not be as of necessity, but of free will. **15** For perhaps he was therefore separated from you briefly, that you would now have him wholly (aiōnios g166), **16** no longer as a slave, but more than a slave, a beloved brother, especially to me, but how much rather to you, both in the flesh and in the Lord. **17** If then you count me a partner, receive him as you would receive me. **18** But if he has wronged you at all, or owes you anything, put that to my account. **19** I, Paul, write this with my own hand: I will repay it (not to mention to you that you owe to me even your own self besides). **20** Yes, brother, let me have joy from you in the Lord. Refresh my heart in Christ. **21** Having confidence in your obedience, I write to you, knowing that you will do even beyond what I say. **22** Also, prepare a guest room for me, for I hope that through your prayers I will be restored to you. **23** Epaphras, my fellow prisoner in Christ Jesus, greets you, **24** as do Mark, Aristarchus, Demas, and Luke, my fellow workers. **25** The grace of the Lord Jesus Christ be with your spirit.

Hebrews

1 God, having in the past spoken to the fathers through the prophets at many times and in various ways, **2** in these last days has spoken to us in a Son, whom he appointed heir of all things, through whom also he made the ages (aiōn g165). **3** He is the radiance of his glory, the very image of his substance, and upholding all things by the word of his power, when he had made purification for sins, sat down on the right hand of the Majesty on high; **4** having become so much better than the angels, as he has inherited a more excellent name than they have. **5** For to which of the angels did he say at any time, "You are my Son. Today I have become your Father"? And again, "I will be his Father, and he will be my Son"? **6** And again, when he brings in the firstborn into the world he says, "Let all the angels of God worship him." **7** Of the angels he says, "Who makes his angels winds, and his servants a flame of fire." **8** But of the Son he says, "Your throne, O God, is for the age (aiōn g165) of the age (aiōn g165) and the scepter of uprightness is the scepter of your Kingdom. **9** You have loved righteousness, and hated iniquity; therefore God, your God, has anointed you with the oil of gladness above your companions." **10** And, "In the beginning, Lord, you established the foundation of the earth. The heavens are the works of your hands. **11** They will perish, but you remain; and they will all wear out like a garment. **12** As a cloak, you will roll them up, and like a garment they will be changed. But you remain the same, and your years will have no end." **13** But which of the angels has he told at any time, "Sit at my right hand, until I make your enemies the footstool of your feet?" **14** Are they not all ministering spirits, sent out to do service for the sake of those who will inherit salvation?

2 Therefore we ought to pay greater attention to the things that were heard, so that we will not drift away. **2** For if the word spoken through angels proved steadfast, and every transgression and disobedience received a just recompense; **3** how will we escape if we neglect so great a salvation—which at the first having been spoken through the Lord, was confirmed to us by those who heard; **4** God also testifying with them, both by signs and wonders, by various works of power, and by gifts of the Holy Spirit, according to his own will? **5** For he did not subject the world to come, of which we speak, to angels. **6** But one has somewhere testified, saying, "What is man, that you think of him? Or the son of man, that you care for him? **7** You made him a little lower than the angels. You crowned him with glory and honor. **8** You have put all things under his feet." For in that he put all things under him, he left nothing that is not under him. But now we do not yet see that all things are under him. **9** But we see him who has been made a little lower than the angels, Jesus, because of the suffering of death crowned with glory and honor, that by the grace of God he should taste of death for everyone. **10** For it became him, for whom are all things, and through whom are all things, in bringing many children to glory, to make the author of their salvation perfect through sufferings. **11** For both he who sanctifies and those who are sanctified are all from one, for which cause he is not ashamed to call them brothers, **12** saying, "I will declare your name to my brothers. In the midst of the assembly I will praise you." **13** And again, "I will put my trust in him." And again, "Look, I and the children whom God has given me." **14** Since then the children have shared in flesh and blood, he also himself in like manner partook of the same, that through death he might bring to nothing him who had the power of death, that is, the devil, **15** and might deliver all of them who through fear of death were all their lifetime subject to bondage. **16** For, truly, he did not come to help the angels, but to help the offspring of Abraham. **17** Therefore he was obligated in all things to be made like his brothers, that he might become a merciful and faithful high priest in things pertaining to God, to make atonement for the sins of the people. **18** For in that he himself has suffered being tempted, he is able to help those who are tempted.

3 Therefore, holy brothers, partakers of a heavenly calling, consider the Apostle and High Priest of our confession, Jesus; **2** who was faithful to him who appointed him, as also was Moses in all his house. **3** For he has been counted worthy of more glory than Moses, just as he who built the house has more honor than the house. **4** For every house is built by someone; but he who built all things is God. **5** Moses indeed was faithful in all his house as a servant, for a testimony of those things which were afterward to be spoken, **6** but Christ is faithful as a Son over his house; whose house we are, if we hold fast our confidence and the boast of our hope. **7** Therefore, even as the Holy Spirit says, "Today if you will hear his voice, **8** do not harden your hearts, as in the provocation, like as in the day of the trial in the wilderness, **9** where your fathers tested me and challenged me, and saw my works for forty years. **10** Therefore I was displeased with this generation, and said, 'They always err in their heart, but they did not know my ways;' **11** as I swore in my wrath, 'They will not enter into my rest.'" **12** Beware, brothers, lest perhaps there be in any one of you an evil heart of unbelief, in falling away from the living God; **13** but exhort one another day by day, so long as it is called "today;" lest any one of you be hardened by the deceitfulness of sin. **14** For we have become partakers of Christ, if we hold fast the beginning of our confidence firm to the end: **15** while it is said, "Today if you will hear his voice, do not harden your hearts, as in the rebellion." **16** For who, when they heard, rebelled? No, did not all those who came out of Egypt by Moses? **17** With whom was he displeased forty years? Was not it with those who sinned, whose bodies fell in the wilderness? **18** To whom did he swear that they would not enter into his rest, but to those who were disobedient? **19** We see that they were not able to enter in because of unbelief.

4 Let us fear therefore, lest perhaps anyone of you should seem to have come short of a promise of entering into his rest. **2** For indeed we have had good news preached to us, even as they also did, but the word they heard did not profit them, because they were not united by faith with those who heard. **3** For we who have believed do enter into that rest, even as he has said, "As I swore in my wrath, they will not enter into my rest;" although the works were finished from the foundation of the world. **4** For he has said this somewhere about the seventh day, "And God rested on the seventh day from all his works;" **5** and in this place again, "They will not enter into my rest." **6** Since therefore it remains for some to enter it, and they to whom the good news was before preached failed to enter in because of disobedience, **7** he again appoints a certain day, "Today," saying through David so long a time afterward (just as has been said), "Today if you will hear his voice, do not harden your hearts." **8** For if Joshua had given them rest, he would not have spoken afterward of another day. **9** There remains therefore a Sabbath rest for the people of God. **10** For he who has entered into his rest has himself also rested from his works, as God did from his. **11** Let us therefore give diligence to enter into that rest, lest anyone fall after the same example of disobedience. **12** For the word of God is living, and active, and sharper than any two-edged sword, and piercing even to the dividing of soul and spirit, of both joints and marrow, and is able to discern the thoughts and intentions of the heart. **13** There is no creature that is hidden from his sight, but all things are naked and laid open before the eyes of him with whom we have to do. **14** Having then a great high priest, who has passed through the heavens, Jesus, the Son of God, let us hold tightly to our confession. **15** For we do not have a high priest who cannot be touched with the feeling of our infirmities, but one who has been in all points tempted like we are, yet without sin. **16** Let us therefore draw near with boldness to the throne of grace, that we may receive mercy, and may find grace for help in time of need.

5 For every high priest, being taken from among people, is appointed for people in things pertaining to God, that he may offer both gifts and sacrifices for sins. **2** The high priest can deal gently with those who are ignorant and going astray, because he himself is also surrounded with weakness. **3** Because of this, he must offer sacrifices for sins for the people, as well as for himself. **4** Nobody takes this honor on himself, but he is called by God, just like Aaron was. **5** So also Christ did not glorify himself to be made a high priest, but it was he who said to him, "You are my Son. Today I have become your Father." **6** As he says also in another place, "You are a priest for the age **(aiōn g165)**, after the order of Melchizedek." **7** In the days of his flesh, he offered up prayers and petitions with loud cries and tears to him who was able to save him from death, and he was heard because of his reverence. **8** Although he was a Son, he learned obedience by the things which he suffered. **9** Having been made perfect, he became to all of those who obey him the author of consummate **(aiōnios g166)** salvation, **10** named by God a high priest after the order of Melchizedek. **11** About him we have many words to say, and hard to interpret, seeing you have become dull of hearing. **12** For when by reason of the time you ought to be teachers, you again need to have someone teach you the rudiments of the first principles of the oracles of God. You have come to need milk, not solid food. **13** For everyone who lives on milk is not experienced in the word of righteousness, for he is a baby. **14** But solid food is for those who are full grown, who by reason of use have their senses exercised to discern good and evil.

6 Therefore leaving the doctrine of the first principles of Christ, let us press on to perfection—not laying again a foundation of repentance from dead works, of faith toward God, **2** of the teaching of baptisms, of laying on of hands, of resurrection of the dead, and of consummate judgment **(aiōnios g166)**. **3** And this we will do if God permits. **4** For concerning those who were once enlightened and tasted of the heavenly gift, and were made partakers of the Holy Spirit, **5** and tasted the good word of God and the powers of the age **(aiōn g165)** to come, **6** and then fell away, it is impossible to renew them again to repentance; seeing they crucify the Son of God for themselves again, and put him to open shame. **7** For the land which has drunk the rain that comes often on it, and brings forth a crop suitable for them for whose sake it is also tilled, receives blessing from God; **8** but if it bears thorns and thistles, it is rejected and near being cursed, whose end is to be burned. **9** But, beloved, we are persuaded of better things for you, and things that accompany salvation, even though we speak like this. **10** For God is not unrighteous, so as to forget your work and the love which you showed toward his name, in that you served the saints, and still do serve them. **11** We desire that each one of you may show the same diligence to the fullness of hope even to the end, **12** that you won't be sluggish, but imitators of those who through faith and patience inherited the promises. **13** For when God made a promise to Abraham, since he could swear by none greater, he swore by himself, **14** saying, "I will indeed bless you, and I will greatly multiply you." **15** Thus, having patiently endured, he obtained the promise. **16** For people swear oaths by something greater, and in every dispute of theirs the oath is final for confirmation. **17** In this way God, being determined to show more abundantly to the heirs of the promise the immutability of his counsel, interposed with an oath; **18** that by two immutable things, in which it is impossible for God to lie, we may have a strong encouragement, who have fled for refuge to take hold of the hope set before us. **19** This hope we have as an anchor of the soul, a hope both sure and steadfast and entering into that which is within the curtain; **20** where as a forerunner Jesus entered for us, having become a high priest for the age **(aiōn g165)** after the order of Melchizedek.

7 For this Melchizedek, king of Salem, priest of God Most High, who met Abraham returning from the slaughter of the kings and blessed him, **2** to whom also Abraham divided "a tenth part of everything" (being first, by interpretation, king of righteousness, and then also king of Salem, which is king of peace; **3** without father, without mother, without genealogy, having neither beginning of days nor end of life, but made like the Son of God), remains a priest continually. **4** Now consider how great this man was, to whom even Abraham, the patriarch, gave a tenth out of the most valuable plunder. 5 They indeed of the sons of Levi who receive the priest's office have a commandment to take tithes of the people according to the Law, that is, of their brothers, though these have come out of the body of Abraham, 6 but he whose genealogy is not counted from them has accepted tithes from Abraham, and has blessed him who has the promises. 7 But without any dispute the lesser is blessed by the greater. 8 Here people who die receive tithes, but there one receives tithes of whom it is testified that he lives. 9 We can say that through Abraham even Levi, who receives tithes, has paid tithes, 10 for he was yet in the body of his father when Melchizedek met him. 11 Now if there was perfection through the Levitical priesthood (for under it the people have received the law), what further need was there for another priest to arise after the order of Melchizedek, and not be called after the order of Aaron? 12 For the priesthood being changed, there is of necessity a change made also in the law. 13 For he of whom these things are said belongs to another tribe, from which no one has officiated at the altar. 14 For it is evident that our Lord has sprung out of Judah, about which tribe Moses spoke nothing concerning priests. 15 This is yet more abundantly evident, if after the likeness of Melchizedek there arises another priest, 16 who has been made, not after the law of a fleshly commandment, but after the power of an endless life: 17 for it is testified, "You are a priest for the age (aiōn g165), according to the order of Melchizedek." 18 For there is an annulling of a foregoing commandment because of its weakness and uselessness 19 (for the law made nothing perfect), and a bringing in of a better hope, through which we draw near to God. 20 Inasmuch as he was not made priest without the taking of an oath, 21 (for they indeed have been made priests without an oath), but he with an oath by him that says of him, "The Lord swore and will not change his mind, 'You are a priest for the age (aiōn g165), according to the order of Melchizedek.'" 22 Accordingly Jesus has become the guarantor of a better covenant. 23 Many, indeed, have been made priests, because they are hindered from continuing by death. 24 But he, because he lives for the age (aiōn g165), has his priesthood unchangeable. 25 Therefore he is also able to save completely those who draw near to God through him, seeing that he lives forever to make intercession for them. 26 For such a high priest was indeed fitting for us: holy, guiltless, undefiled, separated from sinners, and made higher than the heavens; 27 who does not need, like those high priests, to offer up sacrifices daily, first for his own sins, and then for those of the people. For he did this once for all, when he offered up himself. 28 For the law appoints men as high priests who have weakness, but the word of the oath which came after the law appoints a Son for the age (aiōn g165) who has been perfected.

8 Now in the things which we are saying, the main point is this. We have such a high priest, who sat down on the right hand of the throne of the Majesty in the heavens, 2 a servant of the sanctuary, and of the true tabernacle, which the Lord set up, and not man. 3 For every high priest is appointed to offer both gifts and sacrifices. Therefore it is necessary that this high priest also have something to offer. 4 Now if he were on earth, he would not be a priest at all, seeing there are priests who offer the gifts according to the Law; 5 who serve a copy and shadow of the heavenly things, even as Moses was warned when he was about to make the tabernacle, for he said, "See that you make everything according to the pattern that was shown to you on the mountain." 6 But now he has obtained a more excellent ministry, by so much as he is also the mediator of a better covenant, which on better promises has been given as Law. 7 For if that first covenant had been faultless, then no place would have been sought for a second. 8 For finding fault with them, he said, "Look, the days are coming," says the Lord, "when I will make a new covenant with the house of Israel and with the house of Judah; 9 not according to the covenant that I made with their fathers, in the day that I took them by the hand to lead them out of the land of Egypt; for they did not continue in my covenant, and I disregarded them," says the Lord. 10 "For this is the covenant that I will make with the house of Israel. After those days," says the Lord; "I will put my laws into their mind, I will also write them on their heart. I will be their God, and they will be my people. 11 They will not teach each one his fellow citizen, and each one his brother, saying, 'Know the Lord,' for all will know me, from the least of them to the greatest of them. 12 For I will be merciful to their unrighteousness. I will remember their sins no more." 13 In that he says, "new," he has made the first old. But that which is becoming old and grows aged is near to vanishing away.

9 Now indeed even the first covenant had ordinances of divine service, and an earthly sanctuary. 2 For a tabernacle was prepared. In the first part were the lampstand, the table, and the show bread; which is called the Holy Place. 3 After the second curtain was the tabernacle which is called the Holy of Holies, 4 having a golden censer, and the ark of the covenant overlaid on all sides with gold, in which was a gold jar containing the manna, Aaron's rod that budded, and the tablets of the covenant; 5 and above it cherubim of glory overshadowing the mercy seat, of which things we cannot speak now in detail. 6 Now these things having been thus prepared, the priests go in continually into the first tabernacle, accomplishing the services, 7 but into the second the high priest alone, once in the year, not without blood, which he offers for himself, and for the errors of the people. 8 The Holy Spirit is indicating this, that the way into the Holy Place was not yet revealed while the first tabernacle was still standing; 9 which is a symbol of the present age, where gifts and sacrifices are offered that are incapable, concerning the conscience, of making the worshipper perfect; 10 but deal only with foods and drinks and various washings; they are regulations for the flesh imposed until the time of setting things right. 11 But Christ having come as a high priest of the good things that have come, through the greater and more perfect tabernacle, not made with hands, that is to say, not of this creation, **12** nor yet through the blood of goats and calves, but through his own blood, entered in once for all into the Holy Place, having obtained consummate **(aiōnios g166)** redemption. **13** For if the blood of goats and bulls, and the ashes of a heifer sprinkling those who have been defiled, sanctify to the cleanness of the flesh: **14** how much more will the blood of Christ, who through the consummate **(aiōnios g166)** Spirit offered himself unblemished to God, cleanse your conscience from dead works to serve the living God? **15** For this reason he is the mediator of a New Covenant, since a death has occurred for the redemption of the transgressions that were under the first covenant, that those who have been called may receive the promise of the consummate **(aiōnios g166)** inheritance. **16** For where a last will and testament is, there must of necessity be the death of him who made it. **17** For a will is in force where there has been death, for it is never in force while he who made it lives. **18** Therefore even the first covenant has not been dedicated without blood. **19** For when every commandment had been spoken by Moses to all the people according to the Law, he took the blood of the calves and the goats, with water and scarlet wool and hyssop, and sprinkled both the scroll itself and all the people, **20** saying, "This is the blood of the covenant which God has commanded you." **21** Moreover he sprinkled the tabernacle and all the vessels of the ministry in like manner with the blood. **22** According to the Law, nearly everything is cleansed with blood, and apart from shedding of blood there is no forgiveness. **23** It was necessary therefore that the copies of the things in the heavens should be cleansed with these; but the heavenly things themselves with better sacrifices than these. **24** For Christ hasn't entered into holy places made with hands, which are representations of the true, but into heaven itself, now to appear in the presence of God for us; **25** nor yet that he should offer himself often, as the high priest enters into the holy place year by year with blood not his own, **26** or else he must have suffered often since the foundation of the world. But now once at the completion of the ages **(aiōn g165)**, he has been revealed for the annulment of sin by the sacrifice of himself. **27** Inasmuch as it is appointed for people to die once, and after this, judgment, **28** so Christ also, having been offered once to bear the sins of many, will appear a second time, without sin, to those who are eagerly waiting for him for salvation.

10 For the Law, having a shadow of the good to come, not the very image of the things, can never with the same sacrifices year by year, which they offer continually, make perfect those who draw near. **2** Or else would not they have ceased to be offered, because the worshippers, having been once cleansed, would have had no more consciousness of sins? **3** But in those sacrifices there is yearly reminder of sins. **4** For it is impossible that the blood of bulls and goats should take away sins. **5** Therefore when he comes into the world, he says, "Sacrifice and offering you did not desire, but a body you prepared for me. **6** Whole burnt offerings and sin-offerings you took no pleasure in. **7** Then I said, 'Look, I have come. It is written about me in the scroll of a book; to do your will, God.'" **8** Previously saying, "Sacrifices and offerings and whole burnt offerings and sin-offerings you did not desire, nor took pleasure in" (which are offered according to the Law), **9** then he said, "Look, I have come to do your will." He takes away the first, that he may establish the second, **10** by which will we have been sanctified through the offering of the body of Jesus Christ once for all. **11** Every priest indeed stands day by day serving and often offering the same sacrifices, which can never take away sins, **12** but this one, when he had offered one sacrifice for sins forever, sat down on the right hand of God; **13** from that time waiting until his enemies are made the footstool of his feet. **14** For by one offering he has perfected forever those who are being sanctified. **15** The Holy Spirit also testifies to us, for after saying, **16** "This is the covenant that I will make with them: 'After those days,' says the Lord, 'I will put my laws on their hearts, I will also write them on their minds.'" **17** "And I will remember their sins and their iniquities no more." **18** Now where forgiveness of these is, there is no more offering for sin. **19** Having therefore, brothers, boldness to enter into the holy place by the blood of Jesus, **20** by the way which he dedicated for us, a new and living way, through the curtain, that is to say, his flesh; **21** and having a great priest over the house of God, **22** let us draw near with a true heart in fullness of faith, having our hearts sprinkled from an evil conscience, and having our body washed with pure water, **23** let us hold fast the confession of our hope without wavering; for he who promised is faithful. **24** Let us consider how to motivate one another to love and good works, **25** not forsaking our own assembling together, as the custom of some is, but exhorting one another; and so much the more, as you see the Day approaching. **26** For if we sin willfully after we have received the knowledge of the truth, there remains no more a sacrifice for sins, **27** but a certain fearful expectation of judgment, and a fierceness of fire which will devour the adversaries. **28** Anyone who disregards the Law of Moses dies without compassion on the word of two or three witnesses. **29** How much worse punishment, do you think, will he be judged worthy of, who has trodden under foot the Son of God, and has counted the blood of the covenant with which he was sanctified an unholy thing, and has insulted the Spirit of grace? **30** For we know him who said, "Vengeance belongs to me; I will repay." Again, "The Lord will judge his people." **31** It is a fearful thing to fall into the hands of the living God. **32** But remember the former days, in which, after you were enlightened, you endured a great struggle with sufferings; **33** partly, being exposed to insults and abuse in public, and sometimes you came to share with others who were treated in the same way. **34** For you both had compassion on them that were in chains, and joyfully accepted the plundering of your possessions, since you knew that you yourselves had a better possession and an enduring one. **35** Therefore do not throw away your boldness, which has a great reward. **36** For you need patient endurance so that, having done the will of God, you may receive the promise. **37** "For in just a little while, he who is coming will come and will not delay. **38** But the righteous will live by faith, and if he holds back, my soul has no pleasure in him." **39** But we are not of those who shrink back to destruction, but of those who have faith to the saving of the soul.

11 Now faith is being confident of what we hope for, convinced about things we do not see. **2** For by this, the people of old were attested. **3** By faith, we understand that the ages (aiōn g165) have been aligned by the word of God, so that what is seen has not been made out of things which are visible. **4** By faith, Abel offered to God a better sacrifice than Cain, through which he was attested as righteous, God testifying with respect to his gifts; and though he died he still speaks through it. **5** By faith, Enoch was taken away, so that he would not see death, "and he was not found, because God took him away." For before he was taken he was attested as having pleased God. **6** Now without faith it is impossible to be well pleasing to him, for he who comes to God must believe that he exists, and that he is a rewarder of those who seek him. **7** By faith, Noah, being warned about things not yet seen, in reverence prepared a box-shaped vessel for the salvation of his household, through which he condemned the world, and became heir of the righteousness which is according to faith. **8** By faith, Abraham, when he was called, obeyed to go out to a place which he was to receive for an inheritance. He went out, not knowing where he was going. **9** By faith, he sojourned in a land of promise, as a foreigner, living in tents with Isaac and Jacob, the heirs with him of the same promise. **10** For he looked for the city which has foundations, whose architect and builder is God. **11** By faith, even barren Sarah herself received power to conceive when she was past age, and gave birth, since she considered him faithful who had promised. **12** Therefore as many as the stars of the sky in multitude, and as innumerable as the sand which is by the sea shore, were fathered by one man, and him as good as dead. **13** These all died in faith, not having received the promises, but having seen them and embraced them from afar, and having acknowledged that they were strangers and temporary residents on the earth. **14** For those who say such things make it clear that they are seeking a country of their own. **15** If indeed they had been thinking of that country from which they went out, they would have had enough time to return. **16** Instead, they were longing for a better country, that is, a heavenly one. Therefore God is not ashamed of them, to be called their God, for he has prepared a city for them. **17** By faith, Abraham, being tested, offered up Isaac; and he who had gladly received the promises was offering up his one and only son; **18** even he to whom it was said, "In Isaac will your descendants be called;" **19** concluding that God is able to raise up even from the dead. Figuratively speaking, he also did receive him back from the dead. **20** By faith, Isaac blessed Jacob and Esau, even concerning things to come. **21** By faith, Jacob, when he was dying, blessed each of the sons of Joseph, and bowed over the top of his staff. **22** By faith, Joseph, when his end was near, made mention of the departure of the children of Israel; and gave instructions concerning his bones. **23** By faith, Moses, when he was born, was hidden for three months by his parents, because they saw that he was a beautiful child, and they were not afraid of the king's commandment. **24** By faith, Moses, when he had grown up, refused to be called the son of Pharaoh's daughter, **25** choosing rather to share ill treatment with God's people, than to enjoy the pleasures of sin for a time; **26** considering the abuse suffered for the Christ greater riches than the treasures of Egypt; for he looked to the reward. **27** By faith, he left Egypt, not fearing the wrath of the king; for he endured, as seeing him who is invisible. **28** By faith, he kept the Passover, and the sprinkling of the blood, that the destroyer of the firstborn should not touch them. **29** By faith, they passed through the Red Sea as on dry land. When the Egyptians tried to do so, they were swallowed up. **30** By faith, the walls of Jericho fell down, after they had been encircled for seven days. **31** By faith, Rahab the prostitute did not perish with those who were disobedient, having received the spies in peace. **32** And what more should I say? For the time would fail me if I told of Gideon, Barak, Samson, Jephthah, David, Samuel, and the prophets; **33** who, through faith subdued kingdoms, worked out righteousness, obtained promises, stopped the mouths of lions, **34** quenched the power of fire, escaped the edge of the sword, from weakness were made strong, grew mighty in war, and caused foreign armies to flee. **35** Women received their dead by resurrection. And others were tortured, not accepting the payment for release, that they might obtain a better resurrection. **36** Others were tried by mocking and scourging, yes, moreover by bonds and imprisonment. **37** They were stoned, they were sawed apart, they were put to the test, they were killed with the sword. They went around in sheepskins and in goatskins, being destitute, afflicted, mistreated **38** (of whom the world was not worthy), wandering in deserts, mountains, caves, and the holes of the earth. **39** These all, having had testimony given to them through their faith, did not receive the promise, **40** God having provided some better thing concerning us, so that apart from us they should not be made perfect.

12 Therefore let us also, seeing we are surrounded by so great a cloud of witnesses, lay aside every weight and the sin which so easily entangles us, and let us run with patience the race that is set before us, **2** looking to Jesus, the founder and completer of the faith, who for the joy that was set before him endured the cross, disregarding its shame, and has sat down at the right hand of the throne of God. **3** For consider him who has endured such hostility from sinners against himself, so that you may not become tired and give up. **4** You have not yet resisted to the point of shedding blood in your struggle against sin; **5** and you have forgotten the exhortation which reasons with you as with children, "My son, do not take lightly the discipline of the Lord, nor lose heart when you are corrected by him. **6** For whom the Lord loves he disciplines, and punishes every son he accepts." **7** If you are enduring discipline, God is dealing with you as children. For what child is there whom his father does not discipline? **8** But if you are without discipline, of which all have been made partakers, then you are illegitimate, and not children. **9** Furthermore, we had earthly fathers who disciplined us, and we paid them respect. Should we not much rather be subject to the Father of spirits, and live? **10** For they indeed, for a few days, disciplined us as seemed good to them; but he for our profit, that we may be partakers of his holiness. **11** All discipline seems for the moment painful, not joyful; yet afterward it yields the peaceful fruit of righteousness to those who have been exercised thereby. **12** Therefore, lift up the hands that hang down and the feeble knees, **13** and make straight paths for your feet, so that which is lame may not be dislocated, but rather be healed. **14** Pursue peace with everyone, and the sanctification without which no one will see the Lord, **15** looking carefully lest there be anyone who falls short of the grace of God; that no root of bitterness springing up cause trouble, and by it many become defiled; **16** that there be no sexually immoral or profane person like Esau, who sold his own birthright for one meal. **17** For you know that even when he afterward desired to inherit the blessing, he was rejected, for he found no place for a change of mind though he sought it diligently with tears. **18** For you have not come to something that might be touched, and that burned with fire, and darkness, gloom, and storm, **19** the sound of a trumpet, and the voice of words; which those who heard it begged that not one more word should be spoken to them, **20** for they could not stand that which was commanded, "If even an animal touches the mountain, it must be stoned;" **21** and so fearful was the appearance, that Moses said, "I am terrified and trembling." **22** But you have come to Mount Zion, and to the city of the living God, the heavenly Jerusalem, and to innumerable multitudes of angels, **23** to the assembly of the firstborn who are enrolled in heaven, to God the Judge of all, to the spirits of righteous people made perfect, **24** to Jesus, the mediator of a new covenant, and to the blood of sprinkling that speaks better than that of Abel. **25** See that you do not refuse him who speaks. For if they did not escape when they refused him who warned on the earth, how much more will we not escape who turn away from him who warns from heaven, **26** whose voice shook the earth then, but now he has promised, saying, "Yet once more I will shake not only the earth, but also the heavens." **27** This phrase, "Yet once more," signifies the removing of those things that are shaken, as of things that have been made, that those things which are not shaken may remain. **28** So since we are receiving a Kingdom that cannot be shaken, let us give thanks, through which we may offer service pleasing to God, with reverence and awe, **29** for our God is a consuming fire.

13 Let brotherly love continue. **2** Do not forget to show hospitality to strangers, for in doing so, some have entertained angels without knowing it. **3** Remember those who are in bonds, as bound with them; and those who are ill-treated, since you are also in the body. **4** Let marriage be held in honor among all, and let the bed be undefiled: for God will judge the sexually immoral and adulterers. **5** Be free from the love of money, content with such things as you have, for he has said, "I will never leave you or forsake you." **6** So we can confidently say, "The Lord is my helper; I will not fear. What can humans do to me?" **7** Remember your leaders, who spoke to you the word of God, and considering the results of their conduct, imitate their faith. **8** Jesus Christ is the same yesterday, today, and for the ages (aiōn g165). **9** Do not be carried away by all kinds of strange teachings, for it is good that the heart be established by grace, not by food, through which those who were so occupied were not benefited. **10** We have an altar from which those who serve the holy tabernacle have no right to eat. **11** For the bodies of those animals, whose blood is brought into the holy place by the high priest as an offering for sin, are burned outside of the camp. **12** Therefore Jesus also, that he might sanctify the people through his own blood, suffered outside of the gate. **13** Let us therefore go out to him outside of the camp, bearing the abuse he bore. **14** For we do not have here an enduring city, but we seek that which is to come. **15** Through him, then, let us offer up a sacrifice of praise to God continually, that is, the fruit of lips that confess his name. **16** But do not forget to be doing good and sharing, for with such sacrifices God is well pleased. **17** Obey your leaders and submit to them, for they watch on behalf of your souls, as those who will give account, that they may do this with joy, and not with groaning, for that would be unprofitable for you. **18** Pray for us, for we are persuaded that we have a good conscience, desiring to live honorably in all things. **19** I strongly urge you to do this, that I may be restored to you sooner. **20** Now may the God of peace, who brought again from the dead the great Shepherd of the sheep with the blood of the consummate (aiōnios g166) covenant, our Lord Jesus, **21** align you in every good thing so as to do his will, doing in us that which is wellpleasing before him, through Jesus Christ, to whom be the glory for the ages (aiōn g165) of the ages (aiōn g165). Amen. **22** But I exhort you, brothers, endure the word of exhortation, for I have written to you in few words. **23** Know that our brother Timothy has been freed, with whom, if he comes shortly, I will see you. **24** Greet all of your leaders and all the saints. Those from Italy send you greetings. **25** Grace be with you all.

James

1 James, a servant of God and of the Lord Jesus Christ, to the twelve tribes which are in the Diaspora: Greetings. **2** Count it all joy, my brothers, when you encounter various trials, **3** knowing that the testing of your faith produces endurance. **4** Let endurance have its perfect work, that you may be perfect and complete, lacking in nothing. **5** But if any of you lacks wisdom, let him ask of God, who gives to all generously and without finding fault; and it will be given to him. **6** But let him ask in faith, without any doubting, for the one who doubts is like a wave of the sea, driven and tossed by the wind. **7** For let that person not think that he will receive anything from the Lord. **8** He is a double-minded person, unstable in all his ways. **9** But let the brother in humble circumstances glory in his high position; **10** and the rich, in that he is made humble, because like the flower in the grass, he will pass away. **11** For the sun arises with the scorching wind, and withers the grass, and the flower in it falls, and the beauty of its appearance perishes. So also will the rich person fade away in his pursuits. **12** Blessed is the one who perseveres under trial, for when he has been approved, he will receive the crown of life, which he promised to those who love him. **13** Let no one say when he is tempted, "I am tempted by God," for God cannot be tempted by evil, and he himself tempts no one. **14** But each one is tempted, when he is drawn away by his own lust, and enticed. **15** Then the lust, when it has conceived, bears sin; and the sin, when it is full grown, brings forth death. **16** Do not be deceived, my beloved brothers. **17** All generous giving and every perfect gift is from above, coming down from the Father of lights, with whom can be no variation, nor turning shadow. **18** Of his own will he brought us forth by the word of truth, that we should be a kind of first fruits of his creatures. **19** This you know, my beloved brothers. But let every person be swift to hear, slow to speak, and slow to anger; **20** for human anger does not produce the righteousness of God. **21** Therefore, putting away all filthiness and overflowing of wickedness, receive with humility the implanted word, which is able to save your souls. **22** But be doers of the word, and not only hearers, deluding your own selves. **23** For if anyone is a hearer of the word and not a doer, he is like someone looking at his natural face in a mirror; **24** for he sees himself, and goes away, and immediately forgets what kind of person he was. **25** But he who looks into the perfect Law of freedom, and continues, not being a hearer who forgets, but a doer of the work, this person will be blessed in what he does. **26** If anyone thinks himself to be religious while he does not bridle his tongue, but deceives his heart, this man's religion is worthless. **27** Pure religion and undefiled before our God and Father is this: to visit the fatherless and widows in their affliction, and to keep oneself unstained by the world.

2 My brothers, do not hold the faith of our Lord Jesus Christ of glory with partiality. **2** For if someone with a gold ring, in fine clothing, comes into your synagogue, and a poor person in filthy clothing also comes in; **3** and you pay special attention to the one who wears the fine clothing, and say, "Sit here in a good place;" but you tell the poor person, "Stand there," or "Sit by my footstool." **4** Have you not discriminated among yourselves, and become judges with evil thoughts? **5** Listen, my beloved brothers. Did not God choose those who are poor in this world to be rich in faith, and heirs of the Kingdom which he promised to those who love him? **6** But you have dishonored the poor person. Do not the rich oppress you, and personally drag you before the courts? **7** Do not they blaspheme the honorable name by which you are called? **8** However, if you fulfill the royal law, according to the Scripture, "You are to love your neighbor as yourself," you do well. **9** But if you show partiality, you commit sin, being convicted by the law as transgressors. **10** For whoever keeps the whole law, and yet stumbles in one point, he has become guilty of all. **11** For he who said, "Do not commit adultery," also said, "Do not commit murder." Now if you do not commit adultery, but murder, you have become a transgressor of the law. **12** So speak, and so do, as those who are to be judged by a law of freedom. **13** For judgment is without mercy to him who has shown no mercy. Mercy triumphs over judgment. **14** What good is it, my brothers, if someone says he has faith, but has no works? Can faith save him? **15** And if a brother or sister is poorly clothed and may be lacking in daily food, **16** and one of you tells them, "Go in peace, be warmed and filled;" and yet you did not give them the things the body needs, what good is it? **17** Even so faith, if it has no works, is dead in itself. **18** But someone will say, "You have faith, and I have works." Show me your faith without works, and I by my works will show you my faith. **19** You believe that God is one. You do well. The demons also believe, and shudder. **20** But do you want to know, foolish person, that faith apart from works is useless? **21** Wasn't Abraham our father justified by works, in that he offered up Isaac his son on the altar? **22** You see that faith worked with his works, and by works faith was perfected; **23** and the Scripture was fulfilled which says, "And Abraham believed God, and it was credited to him as righteousness;" and he was called the friend of God. **24** You see that a person is justified by works and not by faith alone. **25** In like manner was not Rahab the prostitute also justified by works, in that she received the messengers, and sent them out another way? **26** For as the body apart from the spirit is dead, even so faith apart from works is dead.

3 Let not many of you be teachers, my brothers, knowing that we will receive heavier judgment. **2** For in many things we all stumble. If anyone does not stumble in word, this one is a perfect person, able to bridle the whole body also. **3** Now if we put bits into the horses' mouths so that they may obey us, we guide their whole body. **4** And look at the ships also, though they are so big and are driven by fierce winds, are yet guided by a very small rudder, wherever the pilot desires. **5** So the tongue is also a little member, and boasts great things. See how a small fire can spread to a large forest. **6** And the tongue is a fire. The world of iniquity set among our members is the tongue, which defiles the whole body, and sets on fire the course of nature, and is set on fire by Gehenna (Geenna g1067). **7** For all kinds of animals, and birds, of reptiles and sea creatures, are being tamed and have been tamed by humankind. **8** But nobody can tame the tongue. It is a restless evil, full of deadly poison. **9** With it we bless our Lord and Father, and with it we curse people, who are made in the image of God. **10** Out of the same mouth comes forth blessing and cursing. My brothers, these things ought not to be so. **11** Does a spring send out from the same opening fresh and bitter water? **12** Can a fig tree, my brothers, yield olives, or a vine figs? Nor is salt water able to produce sweet. **13** Who is wise and understanding among you? Let him show by his good conduct that his deeds are done in gentleness of wisdom. **14** But if you have bitter jealousy and selfish ambition in your heart, do not boast and do not lie against the truth. **15** This wisdom is not that which comes down from above, but is earthly, sensual, and demonic. **16** For where jealousy and selfish ambition are, there is confusion and every evil deed. **17** But the wisdom that is from above is first pure, then peaceful, gentle, reasonable, full of mercy and good fruits, without partiality, without hypocrisy. **18** Now the fruit of righteousness is sown in peace by those who make peace.

4 Where do conflicts and quarrels among you come from? Do they not come from your passions that war in your members? **2** You lust, and do not have. You kill, covet, and cannot obtain. You fight and make war. You do not have, because you do not ask. **3** You ask, and do not receive, because you ask with wrong motives, so that you may spend it for your pleasures. **4** You adulterers and adulteresses, do you not know that friendship with the world is hostility toward God? Therefore whoever wants to be a friend of the world makes himself an enemy of God. **5** Or do you think that the Scripture says in vain, "The Spirit which he made to dwell in us yearns jealously"? **6** But he gives more grace. Therefore it says, God resists the proud, but gives grace to the humble. **7** Be subject therefore to God. But resist the devil, and he will flee from you. **8** Draw near to God, and he will draw near to you. Cleanse your hands, you sinners; and purify your hearts, you double-minded. **9** Lament, mourn, and weep. Let your laughter be turned to mourning, and your joy to gloom. **10** Humble yourselves in the sight of the Lord, and he will exalt you. **11** Do not speak against one another, brothers. He who speaks against a brother or judges his brother, speaks against the law and judges the law. But if you judge the law, you are not a doer of the law, but a judge. **12** Only one is the lawgiver and judge, who is able to save and to destroy. But who are you to judge your neighbor? **13** Come now, you who say, "Today or tomorrow let us go into this city, and spend a year there, trade, and make a profit." **14** Whereas you do not know what tomorrow will be like. What is your life? For you are a vapor that appears for a little time and then vanishes away. **15** For you ought to say, "If the Lord wills, we will both live, and do this or that."

16 But now you glory in your boasting. All such boasting is evil. **17** To him therefore who knows to do good, and does not do it, to him it is sin.

5 Come now, you rich, weep and cry aloud for your miseries that are coming on you. **2** Your riches are corrupted and your garments are moth-eaten. **3** Your gold and your silver are corroded, and their corrosion will be for a testimony against you, and will eat your flesh like fire. You have laid up your treasure in the last days. **4** Look, the wages of the laborers who mowed your fields, which you have kept back by fraud, cry out, and the cries of those who reaped have entered into the ears of the Lord of hosts. **5** You have lived delicately on the earth, and taken your pleasure. You have nourished your hearts in a day of slaughter. **6** You have condemned, you have murdered the righteous one. He does not resist you. **7** Be patient therefore, brothers, until the coming of the Lord. Look, the farmer waits for the precious fruit of the earth, being patient over it, until it receives the early and late rain. **8** You also be patient. Establish your hearts, for the coming of the Lord is near. **9** Do not grumble, brothers, against one another, so that you won't be judged. Look, the judge stands at the door. **10** Take, brothers, for an example of suffering and of patience, the prophets who spoke in the name of the Lord. **11** Look, we call them blessed who endured. You have heard of the patience of Job, and have seen the Lord in the outcome, and how the Lord is full of compassion and mercy. **12** But above all things, my brothers, do not swear, neither by heaven, nor by the earth, nor by any other oath; but let your "yes" be "yes," and your "no," "no;" so that you do not fall under judgment. **13** Is anyone among you suffering? He should pray. Is anyone cheerful? He should sing praises. **14** Is anyone among you sick? He should call for the elders of the church, and they should pray over him, anointing him with oil in the name of the Lord. **15** And the prayer of faith will save the one who is sick, and the Lord will raise him up. If he has committed sins, he will be forgiven. **16** Therefore confess your sins to one another, and pray for one another, that you may be healed. The prayer of the righteous person is powerfully effective. **17** Elijah was a human being with a nature like ours, and he prayed earnestly that it might not rain, and it did not rain on the land for three years and six months. **18** He prayed again, and the sky gave rain, and the earth brought forth its fruit. **19** My brothers, if any among you wanders from the truth, and someone turns him back, **20** let him know that he who turns a sinner from the error of his way will save his soul from death, and will cover a multitude of sins.

1 Peter

1 Peter, an apostle of Jesus Christ, to the chosen ones who are living as foreigners in the Diaspora in Pontus, Galatia, Cappadocia, Asia, and Bithynia, **2** according to the foreknowledge of God the Father, in sanctification of the Spirit, that you may obey Jesus Christ and be sprinkled with his blood: Grace to you and peace be multiplied. **3** Blessed be the God and Father of our Lord Jesus Christ, who according to his great mercy caused us to be born again to a living hope through the resurrection of Jesus Christ from the dead, **4** to an incorruptible and undefiled inheritance that does not fade away, reserved in Heaven for you, **5** who by the power of God are guarded through faith for a salvation ready to be revealed in the last time. **6** Wherein you greatly rejoice, though now for a little while, if necessary, you have been grieved by various trials, **7** that the genuineness of your faith, which is more precious than gold that perishes even though it is tested by fire, may be found to result in praise, glory, and honor at the revelation of Jesus Christ— **8** whom not having seen you love; in whom, though now you do not see him, yet believing, you rejoice greatly with joy inexpressible and full of glory— **9** receiving the result of your faith, the salvation of your souls. **10** Concerning this salvation, the prophets sought and searched diligently, who prophesied of the grace that would come to you, **11** searching for who or what kind of time the Spirit of Christ, which was in them, pointed to, when he predicted the sufferings of Christ, and the glories that would follow them. **12** To them it was revealed, that not to themselves, but to you, they ministered these things, which now have been announced to you through those who preached the Good News to you by the Holy Spirit sent out from heaven; which things angels desire to look into. **13** Therefore, prepare your minds for action, be sober and set your hope fully on the grace that will be brought to you at the revelation of Jesus Christ. **14** As obedient children, do not be conformed to the desires as in your ignorance, **15** but just as he who called you is holy, you yourselves also be holy in all of your behavior; **16** because it is written, "Be holy, for I am holy." **17** If you call on him as Father, who without respect of persons judges according to each man's work, pass the time of your living as foreigners here in reverent fear: **18** knowing that you were redeemed, not with corruptible things, with silver or gold, from the useless way of life handed down from your fathers, **19** but with precious blood, as of an unblemished and spotless lamb, namely Christ; **20** who was foreknown indeed before the foundation of the world, but was revealed in these last times for your sake, **21** who through him are believers in God, who raised him from the dead, and gave him glory; so that your faith and hope might be in God. **22** Seeing you have purified your souls in your obedience to the truth in sincere brotherly affection, love one another from a pure heart fervently: **23** having been born again, not of corruptible seed, but of incorruptible, through the living and remaining word of God. **24** For, "All flesh is like grass, and all its glory like the flower in the grass. The grass withers, and its flower falls; **25** but the Lord's word endures for the age **(aiōn g165)**." This is the word of Good News which was preached to you.

2 Putting away therefore all wickedness, and all deceit, and hypocrisy, and envy, and all slander, **2** as newborn babies, long for the pure milk of the word, that you may grow thereby to salvation, **3** if indeed you have tasted that the Lord is good: **4** coming to him, a living stone, though rejected by people but chosen by God, precious. **5** You also, as living stones, are built up as a spiritual house, to be a holy priesthood, to offer up spiritual sacrifices, acceptable to God through Jesus Christ. **6** Because it is contained in Scripture, "Look, I am laying in Zion a stone, a chosen precious cornerstone, and whoever believes in him will not be put to shame." **7** For you who believe therefore is the honor, but for those who do not believe, "The stone which the builders rejected, has become the chief cornerstone," **8** and, "a stone to stumble over, and a rock to trip over." For they stumble at the word, being disobedient, to which also they were appointed. **9** But you are a chosen race, a royal priesthood, a holy nation, a people for his own possession, that you may proclaim the excellence of him who called you out of darkness into his marvelous light: **10** who once were not a people, but now are God's people, who had not obtained mercy, but now have obtained mercy. **11** Beloved, I urge you as foreigners and temporary residents, to abstain from fleshly lusts, which war against the soul; **12** having good behavior among the nations, so in that of which they speak against you as evildoers, they may by your good works, which they see, glorify God in the day of visitation. **13** Subject yourselves to every human institution for the Lord's sake: whether to the king, as supreme; **14** or to governors, as sent by him for vengeance on evildoers and for praise to those who do well. **15** For this is the will of God, that by well-doing you should put to silence the ignorance of foolish people: **16** as free, and not using your freedom as a cover-up for evil, but as slaves of God. **17** Honor all people. Love the brotherhood. Fear God. Honor the king. **18** Servants, be in subjection to your masters with all fear; not only to the good and gentle, but also to the wicked. **19** For it is commendable if someone endures pain, suffering unjustly, because of conscience toward God. **20** For what glory is it if, when you sin, you patiently endure beating? But if, when you do well, you patiently endure suffering, this is commendable with God. **21** For to this you were called, because Christ also suffered for you, leaving you an example, that you should follow his steps, **22** who "committed no sin, nor was deceit found in his mouth." **23** Who, when he was cursed, did not curse back. When he suffered, did not threaten, but committed himself to him who judges righteously; **24** who his own self bore our sins in his body on the tree, that we, having died to sins, might live to righteousness; by whose wounds you were healed. **25** For you were going astray like sheep; but now have returned to the Shepherd and Overseer of your souls.

3 In like manner, wives, be in subjection to your own husbands; so that, even if any do not obey the word, they may be won by the behavior of their wives without a word; **2** seeing your pure behavior in fear. **3** Let your beauty be not just the outward adorning of braiding the hair, and of wearing jewels of gold, or of putting on fine clothing; **4** but in the hidden person of the heart, in the incorruptible adornment of a gentle and quiet spirit, which is in the sight of God very precious. **5** For this is how the holy women before, who hoped in God also adorned themselves, being in subjection to their own husbands: **6** as Sarah obeyed Abraham, calling him lord, whose children you now are, if you do well, and are not put in fear by any terror. **7** You husbands, in like manner, live with your wives according to knowledge, giving honor to the woman, as to the weaker vessel, as being also joint heirs of the grace of life; that your prayers may not be hindered. **8** Finally, be all like-minded, compassionate, loving as brothers, tenderhearted, humble, **9** not rendering evil for evil, or reviling for reviling; but instead blessing; because to this were you called, that you may inherit a blessing. **10** For, "He who would love life, and see good days, let him keep his tongue from evil, and his lips from speaking deceit. **11** Let him turn away from evil, and do good. Let him seek peace, and pursue it. **12** For the eyes of the Lord are on the righteous, and his ears open to their prayer; but the face of the Lord is against those who do evil." **13** Now who is he who will harm you, if you become zealous of that which is good? **14** But even if you should suffer for righteousness' sake, you are blessed. "And do not fear what they fear, nor be troubled." **15** But sanctify in your hearts Christ as Lord; and always be ready to give an answer to everyone who asks you a reason concerning the hope that is in you, yet with humility and fear: **16** having a good conscience; so that when they speak evil against you, they may be put to shame who slander your good manner of life in Christ. **17** For it is better, if it is God's will, that you suffer for doing well than for doing evil. **18** Because Christ also suffered for sins once, the righteous for the unrighteous, that he might bring you to God; being put to death in the flesh, but made alive in the spirit; **19** in which he also went and made a proclamation to the spirits in prison, **20** who before were disobedient, when God waited patiently in the days of Noah, while the box-shaped vessel was being built. In it, few, that is, eight souls, were saved by means of water. **21** This is a symbol of baptism, which now saves you—not the removal of dirt from the body, but an appeal to God for a good conscience, through the resurrection of Jesus Christ, **22** who is at the right hand of God, having gone into heaven, angels and authorities and powers being made subject to him.

4 Forasmuch then as Christ suffered in the flesh, arm yourselves also with the same mind; for he who has suffered in the flesh has ceased from sin; **2** that you no longer should live the rest of your time in the flesh for human desires, but for the will of God. **3** For enough time in the past has been spent doing the will of the unbelievers, and having walked in lewdness, lusts, drunkenness, orgies, carousings, and abominable idolatries. **4** They think it is strange that you do not run with them into the same flood of debauchery, blaspheming: **5** who will give account to him who is ready to judge the living and the dead. **6** For this reason also the Good News was preached to those who are now dead, that they might be judged according to man in the flesh, but might live according to God in the Spirit. **7** But the end of all things is near. Therefore be serious and disciplined in your prayers. **8** Above all things be earnest in your love among yourselves, for love covers a multitude of sins. **9** Be hospitable to one another without grumbling. **10** As each has received a gift, employ it in serving one another, as good managers of the grace of God in its various forms. **11** If anyone speaks, let it be as it were the very words of God. If anyone serves, let it be as of the strength which God supplies, that in all things God may be glorified through Jesus Christ, to whom belong the glory and the dominion for the ages **(aiōn g165)** of the ages **(aiōn g165)**. Amen. **12** Beloved, do not be astonished at the fiery trial which has come upon you, to test you, as though a strange thing happened to you. **13** But because you are partakers of Christ's sufferings, rejoice; that at the revelation of his glory you also may rejoice with exceeding joy. **14** If you are insulted for the name of Christ, you are blessed; because the Spirit of glory and of God rests on you. On their part he is blasphemed, but on your part he is glorified. **15** For let none of you suffer as a murderer, or a thief, or an evil doer, or a meddler. **16** But if as a Christian, let him not be ashamed, but let him glorify God in this name. **17** For the time has come for judgment to begin with the household of God; and if it begins first with us, what will happen to those who do not obey the Good News of God? **18** And "If the righteous is delivered with difficulty, where will the ungodly and the sinner appear?" **19** Therefore let them also who suffer according to the will of God in doing good entrust their souls to him, as to a faithful Creator.

5 Therefore, I exhort the elders among you, as a fellow elder, and a witness of the sufferings of Christ, and who will also share in the glory that will be revealed. **2** Shepherd the flock of God which is among you, exercising the oversight, not under compulsion, but voluntarily, as God wants; not for dishonest gain, but willingly; **3** neither as lording it over those entrusted to you, but making yourselves examples to the flock. **4** When the chief Shepherd is revealed, you will receive the crown of glory that does not fade away. **5** Likewise, you younger ones, be subject to the elder. Yes, all of you clothe yourselves with humility, towards one another; for God resists the proud, but gives grace to the humble. **6** Humble yourselves therefore under the mighty hand of God, that he may exalt you in due time; **7** casting all your worries on him, because he cares for you. **8** Be sober and self-controlled. Be watchful. Your adversary the devil, walks around like a roaring lion, seeking whom he may devour. **9** Withstand him steadfast in your faith, knowing that your brothers who are in the world are undergoing the same sufferings. **10** Now the the God of all grace, who called you to his consummate **(aiōnios g166)** glory by Christ Jesus, after you have suffered a little while, will himself align, confirm, strengthen, and establish you. 11 To him be the power for the ages (aiōn g165) of the ages (aiōn g165). Amen. 12 Through Silvanus, our faithful brother, as I consider him, I have written to you briefly, exhorting, and testifying that this is the true grace of God. Stand firm in it. 13 She who is in Babylon, chosen together with you, greets you; and so does Mark, my son. 14 Greet one another with a kiss of love. Peace be to you all who are in Christ.

2 Peter

1 Simeon Peter, a servant and apostle of Jesus Christ, to those who have obtained a like precious faith with us in the righteousness of our God and Savior, Jesus Christ: **2** Grace to you and peace be multiplied in the knowledge of God and of Jesus our Lord, **3** seeing that his divine power has granted to us all things that pertain to life and godliness, through the knowledge of him who called us by his own glory and virtue; **4** by which he has granted to us his precious and exceedingly great promises; that through these you may become partakers of the divine nature, having escaped from the corruption that is in the world by lust. **5** Yes, and for this very cause adding on your part all diligence, in your faith supply moral excellence; and in moral excellence, knowledge; **6** and in knowledge, self-control; and in self-control patience; and in patience godliness; **7** and in godliness brotherly affection; and in brotherly affection, love. **8** For if these things are yours and abound, they make you to be not idle nor unfruitful to the knowledge of our Lord Jesus Christ. **9** For he who lacks these things is blind, seeing only what is near, having forgotten the cleansing from his old sins. **10** Therefore, brothers, be more diligent to make your calling and election sure. For if you do these things, you will never stumble. **11** For thus you will be richly supplied with the entrance into the consummate **(aiōnios g166)** Kingdom of our Lord and Savior, Jesus Christ. **12** Therefore I will be ready always to remind you of these things, though you know them, and are established in the present truth. **13** I think it right, as long as I am in this tent, to stir you up by reminding you; **14** knowing that the putting off of my tent comes swiftly, even as our Lord Jesus Christ made clear to me. **15** Yes, I will make every effort that you may always be able to remember these things even after my departure. **16** For we did not follow cunningly devised tales, when we made known to you the power and coming of our Lord Jesus Christ, but we were eyewitnesses of his majesty. **17** For he received from God the Father honor and glory, when the voice came to him from the Majestic Glory, "This is my beloved Son, in whom I am well pleased." **18** We heard this voice come out of heaven when we were with him on the holy mountain. **19** We have the more sure word of prophecy; and you do well that you heed it, as to a lamp shining in a dark place, until the day dawns, and the morning star arises in your hearts: **20** knowing this first, that no prophecy of Scripture is of private interpretation. **21** For no prophecy ever came by human will, but people spoke from God, being moved by the Holy Spirit.

2 But false prophets also arose among the people, as false teachers will also be among you, who will secretly bring in destructive heresies, denying even the Master who bought them, bringing on themselves swift destruction. **2** Many will follow their immoral ways, and as a result, the way of the truth will be maligned. **3** In covetousness they will exploit you with deceptive words: whose sentence now from of old does not linger, and their destruction is not asleep. **4** For if God did not spare angels when they sinned, but cast them down to Tartarus **(Tartaroō g5020)**, and committed them to pits of darkness, being kept for judgment; **5** and did not spare the ancient world, but preserved Noah with seven others, a proclaimer of righteousness, when he brought a flood on the world of the ungodly; **6** and turning the cities of Sodom and Gomorrah into ashes, condemned them to destruction, having made them an example of what is going to happen to the ungodly; **7** and delivered righteous Lot, who was very distressed by the lustful life of the wicked **8** (for that righteous man dwelling among them, was tormented in his righteous soul from day to day with seeing and hearing lawless deeds): **9** the Lord knows how to deliver the godly out of temptation and to keep the unrighteous under punishment for the day of judgment; **10** but chiefly those who walk after the flesh in the lust of defilement, and despise authority. Daring, self-willed, they are not afraid to blaspheme the glories; **11** whereas angels, though greater in might and power, do not bring a railing judgment against them before the Lord. **12** But these, as unreasoning creatures, born natural animals to be taken and destroyed, speaking evil in matters about which they are ignorant, will in their destroying surely be destroyed, **13** suffering the penalty as the wages of evil; people who count it pleasure to revel in the daytime, spots and blemishes, reveling in their deceit while they feast with you; **14** having eyes full of adultery, and insatiable for sin, enticing unstable people, having a heart trained in greed. Children under a curse. **15** Forsaking the right way they went astray, having followed the way of Balaam the son of Beor, who loved the wages of unrighteousness. **16** But he was rebuked for his own transgression; a donkey that could not talk spoke with a human voice and stopped the irrationality of the prophet. **17** These are wells without water, clouds driven by a storm; for whom the blackness of darkness has been reserved. **18** For, uttering great swelling words of emptiness, they entice in the lusts of the flesh, by licentiousness, those who actually escape from those who live in error; **19** promising them liberty, while they themselves are slaves of corruption; for a person is brought into bondage by whoever overcomes him. **20** For if, after they have escaped the defilement of the world through the knowledge of the Lord and Savior Jesus Christ, they are again entangled in it and overcome, the last state has become worse for them than the first. **21** For it would be better for them not to have known the way of righteousness, than, after knowing it, to turn back from the holy commandment delivered to them. **22** It has happened to them according to the true proverb, "The dog turns to his own vomit again," and "the sow that has washed to wallowing in the mire."

3 This is now, beloved, the second letter that I have written to you; and in both of them I stir up your sincere mind by reminding you; **2** that you should remember the words which were spoken before by the holy prophets, and the commandment of the Lord and Savior through your apostles: **3** knowing this first, that in the last days scoffers will come, mocking and walking after their own lusts, **4**

and saying, "Where is the promise of his coming? For, from the day that the fathers fell asleep, all things continue as they were from the beginning of the creation." **5** For this they willfully forget, that there were heavens from of old, and an earth formed out of water and amid water, by the word of God; **6** by which means the world that then was, being deluged with water, was destroyed. **7** But the heavens that now are, and the earth, by the same word have been stored up for fire, being reserved against the day of judgment and destruction of ungodly people. **8** But do not forget this one thing, beloved, that one day is with the Lord as a thousand years, and a thousand years as one day. **9** The Lord is not slow concerning his promise, as some count slowness; but is patient toward you, not wishing that any should perish, but that all should come to repentance. **10** But the day of the Lord will come as a thief; in which the heavens will pass away with a great noise, and the elements will be dissolved with fervent heat, and the earth and the works on it will not be found. **11** Therefore since all these things will be destroyed like this, what kind of people ought you to be in holy living and godliness, **12** looking for and earnestly desiring the coming of the day of God, which will cause the burning heavens to be dissolved, and the elements will melt with fervent heat? **13** But, according to his promise, we look for new heavens and a new earth, in which righteousness dwells. **14** Therefore, beloved, seeing that you look for these things, be diligent to be found in peace, without blemish and blameless in his sight. **15** Regard the patience of our Lord as salvation; even as our beloved brother Paul also, according to the wisdom given to him, wrote to you; **16** as also in all of his letters, speaking in them of these things. In those, there are some things that are hard to understand, which the ignorant and unsettled twist, as they also do to the other Scriptures, to their own destruction. **17** You therefore, beloved, knowing these things beforehand, beware, lest being carried away with the error of the wicked, you fall from your own steadfastness. **18** But grow in the grace and knowledge of our Lord and Savior Jesus Christ. To him be the glory both now and in the day of that age **(aiōn g165)**. Amen.

1 John

1 That which was from the beginning, that which we have heard, that which we have seen with our eyes, that which we saw, and our hands touched, concerning the Word of life **2** (and the life was revealed, and we have seen, and testify, and declare to you the consummmate (aiōnios g166) life, which was with the Father, and was revealed to us); **3** that which we have seen and heard we declare to you also, that you also may have fellowship with us. Yes, and our fellowship is with the Father, and with his Son, Jesus Christ. **4** And we write these things, that our joy may be fulfilled. **5** This is the message which we have heard from him and announce to you, that God is light, and in him is no darkness at all. **6** If we say that we have fellowship with him and walk in the darkness, we lie, and do not tell the truth. **7** But if we walk in the light, as he is in the light, we have fellowship with one another, and the blood of Jesus, his Son, cleanses us from all sin. **8** If we say that we have no sin, we deceive ourselves, and the truth is not in us. **9** If we confess our sins, he is faithful and righteous to forgive us the sins, and to cleanse us from all unrighteousness. **10** If we say that we have not sinned, we make him a liar, and his word is not in us.

2 My little children, I write these things to you so that you may not sin. If anyone sins, we have an advocate with the Father, Jesus Christ, the righteous. **2** And he is the atoning sacrifice for our sins, and not for ours only, but also for the whole world. **3** This is how we know that we know him: if we keep his commandments. **4** One who says, "I know him," and does not keep his commandments, is a liar, and the truth is not in him. **5** But whoever keeps his word, God's love has truly been perfected in him. This is how we know that we are in him: **6** he who says he remains in him ought himself also to walk just like he walked. **7** Beloved, I write no new commandment to you, but an old commandment which you had from the beginning. The old commandment is the word which you heard. **8** Again, I write a new commandment to you, which is true in him and in you; because the darkness is passing away, and the true light already shines. **9** He who says he is in the light and hates his brother, is in the darkness even until now. **10** He who loves his brother remains in the light, and there is no occasion for stumbling in him. **11** But he who hates his brother is in the darkness, and walks in the darkness, and does not know where he is going, because the darkness has blinded his eyes. **12** I write to you, little children, because your sins are forgiven you for his name's sake. **13** I am writing to you, fathers, because you know him who is from the beginning. I write to you, young people, because you have overcome the evil one. I write to you, little children, because you know the Father. **14** I have written to you, fathers, because you know him who is from the beginning. I have written to you, young people, because you are strong, and the word of God remains in you, and you have overcome the evil one. **15** Do not love the world, neither the things that are in the world. If anyone loves the world, the Father's love is not in him. **16** For all that is in the world, the lust of the flesh, the lust of the eyes, and the pride of life, is not the Father's, but is the world's. **17** The world is passing away with its lusts, but he who does God's will remains for the age (aiōn g165). **18** Little children, these are the end times, and as you heard that the antichrist is coming, even now many antichrists have arisen. By this we know that it is the final hour. **19** They went out from us, but they did not belong to us; for if they had belonged to us, they would have continued with us. But they left, that they might be revealed that none of them belong to us. **20** You have an anointing from the Holy One, and you all have knowledge. **21** I have not written to you because you do not know the truth, but because you know it, and because no lie is of the truth. **22** Who is the liar but he who denies that Jesus is the Christ? This is the antichrist, he who denies the Father and the Son. **23** Whoever denies the Son, the same does not have the Father. He who confesses the Son has the Father also. **24** As for you, let that remain in you which you heard from the beginning. If that which you heard from the beginning remains in you, you also will remain in the Son, and in the Father. **25** This is the promise which he promised us, the consummate (aiōnios g166) life. **26** These things I have written to you concerning those who would lead you astray. **27** As for you, the anointing which you received from him remains in you, and you do not need for anyone to teach you. But as his anointing teaches you concerning all things, and is true, and is no lie, and even as it taught you, you remain in him. **28** Now, little children, remain in him, that when he appears, we may have boldness, and not be ashamed before him at his coming. **29** If you know that he is righteous, you know that everyone also who practices righteousness is born of him.

3 See what kind of love the Father has bestowed on us, that we should be called children of God; and we are. For this reason the world does not know us, because it did not know him. **2** Beloved, now we are children of God, and it is not yet revealed what we will be. We know that, when he is revealed, we will be like him; for we will see him just as he is. **3** Everyone who has this hope set on him purifies himself, even as he is pure. **4** Everyone who sins also commits lawlessness. Sin is lawlessness. **5** You know that he was revealed to take away sins, and in him is no sin. **6** Whoever remains in him does not sin. Whoever sins hasn't seen him, neither knows him. **7** Children, let no one lead you astray. He who does righteousness is righteous, even as he is righteous. **8** He who sins is of the devil, for the devil has been sinning from the beginning. To this end the Son of God was revealed, to destroy the works of the devil. **9** Whoever is born of God does not commit sin, because his seed remains in him; and he cannot sin, because he is born of God. **10** In this the children of God are revealed, and the children of the devil. Whoever does not do righteousness is not of God, neither is he who does not love his brother. **11** For this is the message which you heard from the beginning, that we should love one another; **12** unlike Cain, who was of the evil one, and killed his brother. Why did he kill him? Because his works were evil, and his brother's righteous. **13** Therefore do not be surprised, brothers, if the world hates you. **14** We know that we have passed out of death into life, because we love the brothers. He who does not love remains in death. **15** Whoever hates his brother is a murderer, and you know that no murderer has consummate **(aiōnios g166)** life remaining in him. **16** By this we know love, because he laid down his life for us. And we ought to lay down our lives for the brothers. **17** But whoever has the world's goods, and sees his brother in need, and closes his heart of compassion against him, how does the love of God remain in him? **18** Little children, let us not love in word only, neither with the tongue only, but in deed and truth. **19** And by this we will know that we are of the truth, and persuade our heart before him, **20** because if our heart condemns us, God is greater than our heart, and knows all things. **21** Beloved, if our hearts do not condemn us, we have confidence before God; **22** and whatever we ask, we receive from him, because we keep his commandments and do the things that are pleasing in his sight. **23** This is his commandment, that we should believe in the name of his Son, Jesus Christ, and love one another, even as he commanded us. **24** He who keeps his commandments remains in him, and he in him. By this we know that he remains in us, by the Spirit which he gave us.

4 Beloved, do not believe every spirit, but test the spirits, whether they are of God, because many false prophets have gone out into the world. **2** By this you know the Spirit of God: every spirit who confesses that Jesus Christ has come in the flesh is of God, **3** and every spirit who does not confess Jesus is not of God; and this is that of the antichrist, of whom you have heard that it comes. Now it is in the world already. **4** You are of God, little children, and have overcome them; because greater is he who is in you than he who is in the world. **5** They are of the world. Therefore they speak of the world, and the world hears them. **6** We are of God. He who knows God listens to us. He who is not of God does not listen to us. By this we know the spirit of truth, and the spirit of error. **7** Beloved, let us love one another, for love is of God; and everyone who loves is born of God, and knows God. **8** He who does not love does not know God, for God is love. **9** By this God's love was revealed in us, that God has sent his one and only Son into the world that we might live through him. **10** In this is love, not that we have loved God, but that he loved us, and sent his Son as the atoning sacrifice for our sins. **11** Beloved, if God loved us in this way, we also ought to love one another. **12** No one has seen God at any time. If we love one another, God remains in us, and his love has been perfected in us. **13** By this we know that we remain in him and he in us, because he has given us of his Spirit. **14** We have seen and testify that the Father has sent the Son as the Savior of the world. **15** Whoever confesses that Jesus is the Son of God, God remains in him, and he in God. **16** We know and have believed the love which God has for us. God is love, and he who remains in love remains in God, and God remains in him.

17 In this love has been made perfect among us, that we may have boldness in the day of judgment, because as he is, even so are we in this world. **18** There is no fear in love; but perfect love casts out fear, because fear has punishment. He who fears is not made perfect in love. **19** We love, because he first loved us. **20** If anyone says, "I love God," and hates his brother, he is a liar; for he who does not love his brother whom he has seen, cannot love God whom he has not seen. **21** This commandment we have from him, that he who loves God should also love his brother.

5 Whoever believes that Jesus is the Christ is born of God. Whoever loves the Father also loves the child who is born of him. **2** By this we know that we love the children of God, when we love God and do his commandments. **3** For this is the love of God, that we keep his commandments. His commandments are not grievous. **4** For whatever is born of God overcomes the world. This is the victory that has overcome the world: our faith. **5** Who is he who overcomes the world, but he who believes that Jesus is the Son of God? **6** This is he who came by water and blood, Jesus Christ; not with the water only, but with the water and the blood. It is the Spirit who testifies, because the Spirit is the truth. **7** For there are three who testify: **8** the Spirit, the water, and the blood; and the three agree as one. **9** If we accept human testimony, the witness of God is greater; for this is God's testimony that he has testified concerning his Son. **10** He who believes in the Son of God has the testimony in himself. He who does not believe God has made him a liar, because he has not believed in the testimony that God has given concerning his Son. **11** The testimony is this, that God gave to us consummate **(aiōnios g166)** life, and this life is in his Son. **12** He who has the Son has the life. He who does not have God's Son does not have the life. **13** These things I have written to you who believe in the name of the Son of God, that you may know that you have consummate **(aiōnios g166)** life. **14** This is the boldness which we have toward him, that, if we ask anything according to his will, he listens to us. **15** And if we know that he listens to us, whatever we ask, we know that we have the petitions which we have asked of him. **16** If anyone sees his brother sinning a sin not leading to death, he should ask, and he will give him life for those who sin not leading to death. There is a sin leading to death. I do not say that he should make a request concerning this. **17** All unrighteousness is sin, and there is a sin not leading to death. **18** We know that whoever is born of God does not sin, but he who was born of God protects him, and the evil one does not touch him. **19** We know that we are of God, and the whole world lies in the power of the evil one. **20** We know that the Son of God has come, and has given us an understanding, that we know the true one, and we are in the true one, in his Son, Jesus Christ. This is the true God and consummate **(aiōnios g166)** life. **21** Little children, keep yourselves from idols.

1 John

2 John

1 The elder, to the chosen lady and her children, whom I love in truth; and not I only, but also all those who know the truth; **2** for the truth's sake, which remains in us, and it will be with us for the age **(aiōn g165)**: **3** Grace, mercy, and peace will be with us, from God the Father, and from Jesus Christ, the Son of the Father, in truth and love. **4** I rejoice greatly that I have found some of your children walking in truth, even as we have been commanded by the Father. **5** And now I ask you, dear lady, not as though I wrote to you a new commandment, but that which we had from the beginning, that we love one another. **6** This is love, that we should walk according to his commandments. This is the commandment, even as you heard from the beginning, that you should walk in it. **7** For many deceivers have gone out into the world, those who do not confess that Jesus Christ came in the flesh. This is the deceiver and the antichrist. **8** Watch yourselves, that you do not lose the things which we have accomplished, but that you receive a full reward. **9** Whoever goes on and does not remain in the teaching of Christ, does not have God. He who remains in the teaching, the same has both the Father and the Son. **10** If anyone comes to you, and does not bring this teaching, do not receive him into your house, and do not welcome him, **11** for he who welcomes him participates in his evil works. **12** Having many things to write to you, I do not want to do so with paper and ink, but I hope to come to you, and to speak face to face, that our joy may be made full. **13** The children of your chosen sister greet you.

3 John

1 The elder to Gaius the beloved, whom I love in truth. **2** Beloved, I pray that you may prosper in all things and be in good health, even as your soul prospers. **3** For I rejoiced greatly, when brothers came and testified about your truth, even as you walk in truth. **4** I have no greater joy than this, to hear about my children walking in truth. **5** Beloved, you do a faithful work in whatever you accomplish for those who are brothers and strangers. **6** They have testified about your love before the church. You will do well to send them forward on their journey in a manner worthy of God, **7** because for the sake of the Name they went out, taking nothing from the non-believers. **8** We therefore ought to receive such, that we may be fellow workers for the truth. **9** I wrote something to the church, but Diotrephes, who loves to be first among them, does not accept what we say. **10** Therefore, if I come, I will call attention to his deeds which he does, unjustly accusing us with wicked words. Not content with this, neither does he himself receive the brothers, and those who would, he forbids and throws out of the church. **11** Beloved, do not imitate that which is evil, but that which is good. He who does good is of God. He who does evil hasn't seen God. **12** Demetrius has the testimony of all, and of the truth itself; yes, we also testify, and you know that our testimony is true. **13** I had many things to write to you, but I am unwilling to write to you with ink and pen; **14** but I hope to see you soon, and we will speak face to face. Peace be to you. The friends greet you. Greet the friends by name.

Jude

1 Jude, a servant of Jesus Christ, and brother of James, to those who are called, loved by God the Father, and kept for Jesus Christ: **2** Mercy to you and peace and love be multiplied. **3** Beloved, while I was very eager to write to you about our common salvation, I was constrained to write to you exhorting you to contend earnestly for the faith which was once for all delivered to the saints. **4** For there are certain people who crept in secretly, even those who were long ago written about for this condemnation: ungodly people, turning the grace of our God into sensuality, and denying our only Master and Lord, Jesus Christ. **5** Now I want to remind you, though you already know all these things, that the Lord, having saved a people out of the land of Egypt, afterward destroyed those who did not believe. **6** Angels who did not keep their first domain, but deserted their own dwelling place, he has kept in everlasting (aïdios g126) bonds under darkness for the judgment of the great day. **7** Even as Sodom and Gomorrah and the cities around them, having in the same way as these given themselves over to sexual immorality and gone after unusual desires, are shown as an example, suffering the punishment of consummate (aiōnios g166) fire. **8** Yet in like manner these also in their dreaming defile the flesh, despise authority, and blaspheme the glories. **9** But Michael, the archangel, when contending with the devil and arguing about the body of Moses, dared not bring against him an abusive condemnation, but said, "May the Lord rebuke you." **10** But these speak evil of whatever things they do not know. What they understand naturally, like the creatures without reason, they are destroyed in these things. **11** Woe to them. For they went in the way of Cain, and ran riotously in the error of Balaam for profit, and perished in Korah's rebellion. **12** These are hidden rocky reefs in your love feasts when they feast with you, shepherds who without fear feed themselves; clouds without water, carried along by winds; autumn leaves without fruit, twice dead, plucked up by the roots; **13** wild waves of the sea, foaming out their own shame; wandering stars, for whom the blackness of darkness has been reserved for an age (aiōn g165). **14** About these also Enoch, the seventh from Adam, prophesied, saying, "Look, the Lord comes with ten thousands of his holy ones, **15** to execute judgment on all, and to convict every person of all their works of ungodliness which they have done in an ungodly way, and of all the hard things which ungodly sinners have spoken against him." **16** These are murmurers and complainers, walking after their lusts (and their mouth speaks proud things), showing respect of persons to gain advantage. **17** But you, beloved, remember the words which have been spoken before by the apostles of our Lord Jesus Christ. **18** They said to you that "In the end time there will be mockers, walking after their own ungodly lusts." **19** These are they who cause divisions, and are sensual, not having the Spirit. **20** But you, beloved, keep building yourselves up in your most holy faith, praying in the Holy Spirit. **21** Keep yourselves in the love of God, awaiting the mercy of our Lord Jesus Christ to consummate (aiōnios g166) life. **22** And some pity who are wavering, **23** and some save, snatching them out of the fire, and on some have mercy with fear; hating even the clothing stained by the flesh. **24** Now to him who is able to keep you from stumbling, and to present you faultless before the presence of his glory in great joy, **25** to the only God our Savior, through Jesus Christ our Lord, be glory, greatness, power, and authority before every age (aiōn g165), and now, and for all the ages (aiōn g165). Amen.

Revelation

1 This is the Revelation of Jesus Christ, which God gave him to show to his servants the things which must happen soon, which he sent and made known by his angel to his servant, John, **2** who testified to God's word, and of the testimony of Jesus Christ, about everything that he saw. **3** Blessed is he who reads and those who hear the words of the prophecy, and keep the things that are written in it, for the time is near. **4** John, to the seven churches that are in Asia: Grace to you and peace, from him who is and who was and who is to come; and from the seven Spirits who are before his throne; **5** and from Jesus Christ, the faithful witness, the firstborn of the dead, and the ruler of the kings of the earth. To him who loves us, and freed us from our sins by his blood; **6** and he made us to be a Kingdom, priests to his God and Father—to him be the glory and the dominion for the ages **(aiōn g165)** of the ages **(aiōn g165)**. Amen. **7** Look, he is coming with the clouds, and every eye will see him, including those who pierced him. And all the tribes of the earth will mourn over him. Even so, Amen. **8** "I am the Alpha and the Omega," says the Lord God, "who is and who was and who is to come, the Almighty." **9** I John, your brother and fellow-partner with you in persecution, Kingdom, and patient endurance in Jesus, was on the island that is called Patmos because of the word of God and the testimony of Jesus. **10** I was in the Spirit on the Lord's day, and I heard behind me a loud voice, like a trumpet **11** saying, "What you see, write on a scroll and send to the seven churches: to Ephesus, Smyrna, Pergamum, Thyatira, Sardis, Philadelphia, and to Laodicea." **12** I turned to see the voice that spoke with me. Having turned, I saw seven golden lampstands. **13** And among the lampstands was one like a son of man, clothed with a robe reaching down to his feet, and with a golden sash around his chest. **14** His head and his hair were white as white wool, like snow. His eyes were like a flame of fire. **15** His feet were like burnished bronze, as if it had been refined in a furnace. His voice was like the voice of many waters. **16** He had seven stars in his right hand. Out of his mouth proceeded a sharp two-edged sword. His face was like the sun shining at its brightest. **17** When I saw him, I fell at his feet like a dead man. He laid his right hand on me, saying, "Do not be afraid. I am the first and the last, **18** and the Living one. I was dead, but look, I am alive for the ages **(aiōn g165)** of the ages **(aiōn g165)**, and I have the keys of Death and of Hades **(Hadēs g86)**. **19** Write therefore the things which you have seen, and the things which are, and the things which will happen hereafter; **20** the mystery of the seven stars which you saw in my right hand, and the seven golden lampstands. The seven stars are the angels of the seven churches. The seven lampstands are seven churches.

2 "To the angel of the church in Ephesus write: "He who holds the seven stars in his right hand, he who walks among the seven golden lampstands says these things: **2** "I know your works, and your toil and perseverance, and that you cannot tolerate those who are evil, and have tested those who call themselves apostles, and they are not, and found them false. **3** You have perseverance and have endured for my name's sake, and have not grown weary. **4** But I have this against you, that you left your first love. **5** Remember therefore from where you have fallen, and repent and do the first works; or else I am coming to you, and will move your lampstand out of its place, unless you repent. **6** But this you have, that you hate the works of the Nicolaitans, which I also hate. **7** He who has an ear, let him hear what the Spirit says to the churches. To him who overcomes I will give to eat of the tree of life, which is in the Paradise of God. **8** "To the angel of the church in Smyrna write: "The first and the last, who was dead, and has come to life says these things: **9** "I know your tribulation and your poverty (but you are rich), and the blasphemy of those who say they are Jews, and they are not, but are a synagogue of Satan. **10** Do not be afraid of the things which you are about to suffer. Look, the devil is about to throw some of you into prison, that you may be tested; and you will have oppression for ten days. Be faithful until death, and I will give you the crown of life. **11** He who has an ear, let him hear what the Spirit says to the churches. He who overcomes won't be harmed by the second death. **12** "To the angel of the church in Pergamum write: "He who has the sharp two-edged sword says these things: **13** "I know where you dwell, where Satan's throne is. You hold firmly to my name, and did not deny my faith even in the days of Antipas, my witness, my faithful one, who was killed among you, where Satan dwells. **14** But I have a few things against you, because you have there some who hold the teaching of Balaam, who taught Balak to throw a stumbling block before the children of Israel, to eat things sacrificed to idols, and to commit sexual immorality. **15** So you also have some who hold to the teaching of the Nicolaitans likewise. **16** Repent therefore, or else I am coming to you quickly, and I will make war against them with the sword of my mouth. **17** He who has an ear, let him hear what the Spirit says to the churches. To him who overcomes, to him I will give of the hidden manna, and I will give him a white stone, and on the stone a new name written, which no one knows but he who receives it. **18** "To the angel of the church in Thyatira write: "The Son of God, who has his eyes like a flame of fire, and his feet are like burnished bronze, says these things: **19** "I know your works, your love, faith, service, patient endurance, and that your last works are more than the first. **20** But I have this against you, that you tolerate the woman, Jezebel, who calls herself a prophetess. She teaches and seduces my servants to commit sexual immorality, and to eat things sacrificed to idols. **21** I gave her time to repent, but she refuses to repent of her sexual immorality. **22** Look, I will throw her into a sickbed, and those who commit adultery with her into great oppression, unless they repent of her works. **23** I will kill her children with Death, and all the churches will know that I am he who searches the minds and hearts. I will give to each one of you according to your deeds. **24** But to you I say, to the rest who are in Thyatira, as many as do not have this teaching, who do not know what some call 'the deep things of Satan,' to you I say, I am not putting any other burden on you. **25** Nevertheless, hold that which you have firmly until I come. **26** He who overcomes, and he who keeps my works to the end, to him I will give authority over the nations. **27** He will rule them with an iron scepter, shattering them like clay pots; as I also have received of my Father: **28** and I will give him the morning star. **29** He who has an ear, let him hear what the Spirit says to the churches.

3 "And to the angel of the church in Sardis write: "He who has the seven Spirits of God, and the seven stars says these things: "I know your works, that you have a reputation of being alive, but you are dead. **2** Wake up, and keep the things that remain, which were about to die, for I have found no works of yours perfected before my God. **3** Remember therefore how you have received and heard. Keep it, and repent. If therefore you do not wake up, I will come as a thief, and you won't know what hour I will come to you. **4** Nevertheless you have a few names in Sardis that did not defile their garments. They will walk with me in white, for they are worthy. **5** He who overcomes will be arrayed in white garments, and I will in no way blot his name out of the Book of Life, and I will confess his name before my Father, and before his angels. **6** He who has an ear, let him hear what the Spirit says to the churches. **7** "To the angel of the church in Philadelphia write: "These are the words of the Holy One, the True One, he who has the key of David, he who opens and no one can shut, and who shuts and no one opens: **8** "I know your works. Look, I have set before you an open door, which no one can shut. For you have a little power, and have kept my word, and did not deny my name. **9** Look, I give of the synagogue of Satan, of those who say they are Jews, and they are not, but lie; look, I will make them to come and worship before your feet, and to know that I have loved you. **10** Because you kept my command to endure, I also will keep you from the hour of testing, which is to come on the whole world, to test those who dwell on the earth. **11** I am coming quickly. Hold firmly that which you have, so that no one takes your crown. **12** He who overcomes, I will make him a pillar in the temple of my God, and he will go out from there no more. I will write on him the name of my God, and the name of the city of my God, the new Jerusalem, which comes down out of heaven from my God, and my own new name. **13** He who has an ear, let him hear what the Spirit says to the churches. **14** "To the angel of the church in Laodicea write: "The Amen, the Faithful and True Witness, the Head of God's creation, says these things: **15** "I know your works, that you are neither cold nor hot. I wish you were cold or hot. **16** So, because you are lukewarm, and neither hot nor cold, I will vomit you out of my mouth. **17** Because you say, 'I am rich, and have gotten riches, and have need of nothing;' and do not know that you are wretched, miserable, poor, blind, and naked; **18** I counsel you to buy from me gold refined by fire, that you may become rich; and white garments, that you may clothe yourself, and that the shame of your nakedness may not be revealed; and eye salve to put on your eyes, that you may see. **19** As many as I love, I rebuke and discipline. Be zealous therefore, and repent. **20** Look, I stand at the door and knock. If anyone hears my voice and opens the door, I will come in to him, and will dine with him, and he with me. **21** He who overcomes, I will give to him to sit down with me on my throne, as I also overcame, and sat down with my Father on his throne. **22** He who has an ear, let him hear what the Spirit says to the churches."

4 After these things I looked and saw a door opened in heaven, and the first voice that I heard, like a trumpet speaking with me, was one saying, "Come up here, and I will show you the things which must happen after this." **2** Immediately I was in the Spirit; and look, there was a throne set in heaven, and one sitting on the throne. **3** And the one who sat there looked like a jasper stone and a sardius. There was a rainbow around the throne, like an emerald to look at. **4** Around the throne were twenty-four thrones. On the thrones were twenty-four elders sitting, dressed in white garments, with crowns of gold on their heads. **5** And from the throne came flashes of lightning and sounds and peals of thunder. And there were seven torches of fire burning before the throne, which are the seven Spirits of God. **6** Before the throne was something like a sea of glass, similar to crystal. In the midst of the throne, and around the throne were four living creatures full of eyes before and behind. **7** The first living creature was like a lion, and the second living creature like a calf, and the third living creature had a face like a man, and the fourth living creature was like a flying eagle. **8** The four living creatures, each one of them having six wings, are full of eyes around and within. They have no rest day and night, saying, "Holy, holy, holy is the Lord God Almighty, who was and who is and who is to come." **9** When the living creatures give glory, honor, and thanks to him who sits on the throne, to him who lives for the ages (aiōn g165) of the ages (aiōn g165), **10** the twenty-four elders fall down before him who sits on the throne, and worship him who lives for the ages (aiōn g165) of the ages (aiōn g165), and throw their crowns before the throne, saying, **11** "Worthy are you, our Lord and God, to receive the glory, the honor, and the power, for you created all things, and because of your desire they existed, and were created."

5 I saw, in the right hand of him who sat on the throne, a scroll written inside and on the back, sealed shut with seven seals. **2** I saw a mighty angel proclaiming with a loud voice, "Who is worthy to open the scroll, and to break its seals?" **3** No one in heaven above, or on the earth, or under the earth, was able to open the scroll, or to look in it. **4** And I wept much, because no one was found worthy to open the scroll, or to look in it. **5** One of the elders said to me, "Do not weep. Look, the Lion who is of the tribe of Judah, the Root of David, has overcome so that he can open the scroll and loose its seven seals." **6** I saw in the midst of the throne and of the four living creatures, and in the midst of the elders, a Lamb standing, as though it had been slain, having seven horns, and seven eyes, which are the seven Spirits of God, sent out into all the earth.

7 Then he came, and he took it out of the right hand of him who sat on the throne. 8 Now when he had taken the scroll, the four living creatures and the twenty-four elders fell down before the Lamb, each one having a harp, and golden bowls full of incense, which are the prayers of the saints. 9 They sang a new song, saying, "You are worthy to take the scroll, and to open its seals: for you were killed, and redeemed for God with your blood those from every tribe, language, people, and nation, 10 and made them a kingdom and priests to our God, and they will reign on earth." 11 I saw, and I heard the voice of many angels around the throne, the living creatures, and the elders; and the number of them was ten thousands of ten thousands, and thousands of thousands; 12 saying with a loud voice, "Worthy is the Lamb who has been killed to receive the power, wealth, wisdom, strength, honor, glory, and blessing." 13 I heard every created thing which is in heaven, on the earth, under the earth, on the sea, and everything in them, saying, "To him who sits on the throne, and to the Lamb be the blessing, the honor, the glory, and the dominion, for the ages (aiōn g165) of the ages (aiōn g165)! Amen!" 14 The four living creatures said, "Amen!" Then the elders fell down and worshiped.

6 I saw when the Lamb opened one of the seven seals, and I heard one of the four living creatures saying, as with a voice of thunder, "Come." 2 And I looked, and suddenly there was a white horse, and he who sat on it had a bow. A crown was given to him, and he came forth conquering, and to conquer. 3 When he opened the second seal, I heard the second living creature saying, "Come." 4 Another came forth, a fiery red horse. To him who sat on it was given power to take peace from the earth, and that they should kill one another. There was given to him a great sword. 5 When he opened the third seal, I heard the third living creature saying, "Come." And I saw, and suddenly there was a black horse and he who sat on it had a balance in his hand. 6 I heard something like a voice in the midst of the four living creatures saying, "A choenix of wheat for a denarius, and three choenixes of barley for a denarius. Do not damage the oil and the wine." 7 When he opened the fourth seal, I heard the fourth living creature saying, "Come." 8 And I saw, and behold, a pale horse, and the name of he who sat on it was Death. Hades (Hadēs g86) followed with him. Authority over one fourth of the earth, to kill with the sword, with famine, with death, and by the wild animals of the earth was given to him. 9 When he opened the fifth seal, I saw underneath the altar the souls of people who had been killed for the Word of God, and for the testimony which they had. 10 They called out with a loud voice, saying, "How long, Master, the holy and true, until you judge and avenge our blood on those who dwell on the earth?" 11 A long white robe was given to each of them. They were told that they should rest yet for a little longer, until their fellow servants and their brothers, who would also be killed even as they were, should complete their course. 12 I saw when he opened the sixth seal, and there was a great earthquake. The sun became black as sackcloth made of hair, and the whole moon became as blood. 13 The stars of the sky fell to the earth, like a fig tree dropping its unripe figs when it is shaken by a great wind. 14 The sky was removed like a scroll when it is rolled up. Every mountain and island were moved out of their places. 15 The kings of the earth, the princes, the commanding officers, the rich, the strong, and every slave and free person, hid themselves in the caves and in the rocks of the mountains. 16 They told the mountains and the rocks, "Fall on us, and hide us from the face of him who sits on the throne, and from the wrath of the Lamb, 17 for the great day of their wrath has come; and who is able to stand?"

7 And after this, I saw four angels standing on the four quarters of the earth, holding the four winds of the earth, so that no wind would blow on the earth, or on the sea, or on any tree. 2 I saw another angel ascend from the sunrise, having the seal of the living God. He called out with a loud voice to the four angels to whom it was given to harm the earth and the sea, 3 saying, "Do not harm the earth, neither the sea, nor the trees, until we have sealed the servants of our God on their foreheads." 4 I heard the number of those who were sealed, one hundred forty-four thousand, sealed out of every tribe of the children of Israel: 5 of the tribe of Judah were sealed twelve thousand, of the tribe of Reuben twelve thousand, of the tribe of Gad twelve thousand, 6 of the tribe of Asher twelve thousand, of the tribe of Naphtali twelve thousand, of the tribe of Manasseh twelve thousand, 7 of the tribe of Simeon twelve thousand, of the tribe of Levi twelve thousand, of the tribe of Issachar twelve thousand, 8 of the tribe of Zebulun twelve thousand, of the tribe of Joseph twelve thousand, of the tribe of Benjamin were sealed twelve thousand. 9 After these things I looked, and suddenly there was a great multitude, which no one could number, out of every nation and of all tribes, peoples, and languages, standing before the throne and before the Lamb, dressed in white robes, with palm branches in their hands. 10 They shouted with a loud voice, saying, "Salvation be to our God, who sits on the throne, and to the Lamb." 11 All the angels were standing around the throne, the elders, and the four living creatures; and they fell on their faces before the throne, and worshiped God, 12 saying, "Amen! Blessing, glory, wisdom, thanksgiving, honor, power, and might, be to our God for the ages (aiōn g165) of the ages (aiōn g165)! Amen." 13 One of the elders answered, saying to me, "These who are arrayed in white robes, who are they, and from where did they come?" 14 So I said to him, "My lord, you know." He said to me, "These are the ones who came out of the great tribulation. They washed their robes, and made them white in the Lamb's blood. 15 Therefore they are before the throne of God, they serve him day and night in his temple. He who sits on the throne will spread his tabernacle over them. 16 They will hunger no more, neither thirst any more; neither will the sun beat on them, nor any heat; 17 for the Lamb who is in the midst of the throne shepherds them, and leads them to springs of waters of life. And God will wipe away every tear from their eyes."

8 When he opened the seventh seal, there was silence in heaven for about half an hour. **2** I saw the seven angels who stand before God, and seven trumpets were given to them. **3** Another angel came and stood over the altar, having a golden censer. Much incense was given to him to offer up, with the prayers of all the saints, on the golden altar which was before the throne. **4** The smoke of the incense, with the prayers of the saints, went up before God out of the angel's hand. **5** The angel took the censer, and he filled it with the fire of the altar, and threw it on the earth. There followed thunders, sounds, lightnings, and an earthquake. **6** The seven angels who had the seven trumpets prepared themselves to sound. **7** And the first angel sounded, and there followed hail and fire, mixed with blood, and they were thrown to the earth. One third of the earth was burnt up, and one third of the trees were burnt up, and all green grass was burnt up. **8** The second angel sounded, and something like a great mountain burning with fire was thrown into the sea. One third of the sea became blood, **9** and one third of the living creatures which were in the sea died. One third of the ships were destroyed. **10** The third angel sounded, and a great star fell from the sky, burning like a torch, and it fell on one third of the rivers, and on the springs of the waters. **11** The name of the star is called "Wormwood." One third of the waters became wormwood. Many people died from the waters, because they were made bitter. **12** The fourth angel sounded, and one third of the sun was struck, and one third of the moon, and one third of the stars; so that one third of them would be darkened, and the day would not shine for one third of it, and the night in the same way. **13** I saw, and I heard an eagle, flying in mid heaven, saying with a loud voice, "Woe. Woe. Woe for those who dwell on the earth, because of the other voices of the trumpets of the three angels, who are yet to sound."

9 The fifth angel sounded, and I saw a star from the sky which had fallen to the earth. The key to the pit of the Abyss **(Abyssos g12)** was given to him. **2** He opened the shaft of the Abyss **(Abyssos g12)**, and smoke went up out of the shaft, like the smoke from a burning furnace. The sun and the air were darkened because of the smoke from the shaft. **3** Then out of the smoke came forth locusts on the earth, and power was given to them, as the scorpions of the earth have power. **4** They were told that they should not hurt the grass of the earth, neither any green thing, neither any tree, but only those people who do not have God's seal on their foreheads. **5** They were given power not to kill them, but to torment them for five months. Their torment was like the torment of a scorpion, when it strikes a person. **6** In those days people will seek death, and will in no way find it. They will desire to die, and death will flee from them. **7** The shapes of the locusts were like horses prepared for war. On their heads were something like golden crowns, and their faces were like people's faces. **8** They had hair like women's hair, and their teeth were like those of lions. **9** They had breastplates, like breastplates of iron. The sound of their wings was like the sound of chariots, or of many horses rushing to war. **10** They have tails like those of scorpions, and stings. In their tails is their power to harm people for five months. **11** They have over them as king the angel of the Abyss **(Abyssos g12)**. His name in Hebrew is "Abaddon", and in Greek, he has the name "Apollyon". **12** The first woe is past. Look, there are still two woes coming after this. **13** The sixth angel sounded. I heard a voice from the four horns of the golden altar which is before God, **14** saying to the sixth angel who had one trumpet, "Free the four angels who are bound at the great river Euphrates." **15** The four angels were freed who had been prepared for this hour and day and month and year, so that they might kill one third of humanity. **16** The number of the armies of the horsemen was two hundred million. I heard the number of them. **17** Thus I saw the horses in the vision, and those who sat on them, having breastplates of fiery red, hyacinth blue, and sulfur yellow; and the heads of lions. Out of their mouths proceed fire, smoke, and sulfur. **18** By these three plagues were one third of humanity killed: from the fire, the smoke, and the sulfur, which proceeded out of their mouths. **19** For the power of the horses is in their mouths, and in their tails. For their tails are like serpents, and have heads, and with them they harm. **20** The rest of humanity, who were not killed with these plagues, did not repent of the works of their hands, that they would not worship demons, and the idols of gold, and of silver, and of bronze, and of stone, and of wood; which can neither see, nor hear, nor walk. **21** They did not repent of their murders, nor of their sorceries, nor of their sexual immorality, nor of their thefts.

10 I saw another mighty angel coming down out of the sky, clothed with a cloud. A rainbow was on his head. His face was like the sun, and his legs like pillars of fire. **2** He had in his hand a little open scroll. He set his right foot on the sea, and his left on the land. **3** He shouted with a loud voice, as a lion roars. When he shouted, the seven thunders uttered their voices. **4** When the seven thunders sounded, I was about to write; but I heard a voice from the sky saying, "Seal up the things which the seven thunders said, and do not write them." **5** The angel whom I saw standing on the sea and on the land lifted up his right hand to the sky, **6** and swore by him who lives for the ages **(aiōn g165)** of the ages **(aiōn g165)**, who created heaven and the things that are in it, the earth and the things that are in it, and the sea and the things that are in it, that there will no longer be delay, **7** but in the days of the voice of the seventh angel, when he is about to sound, then the mystery of God is finished, as he declared to his servants, the prophets. **8** The voice which I heard from heaven, again speaking with me, said, "Go, take the scroll which is open in the hand of the angel who stands on the sea and on the land." **9** I went to the angel, telling him to give me the little scroll. He said to me, "Take it, and eat it up. It will make your stomach bitter, but in your mouth it will be as sweet as honey." **10** I took the little scroll out of the angel's hand, and ate it up. It was as sweet as honey in my mouth. When I had eaten it, my stomach was made bitter. **11** They told me, "You must prophesy again about many peoples, nations, languages, and kings."

11 A reed like a rod was given to me. Someone said, "Rise and measure God's temple, and the altar, and those who worship in it. **2** Leave out the court which is outside of the temple, and do not measure it, for it has been given to the nations. They will tread the holy city under foot for forty-two months. **3** I will give power to my two witnesses, and they will prophesy one thousand two hundred sixty days, clothed in sackcloth." **4** These are the two olive trees and the two lampstands, standing before the Lord of the earth. **5** If anyone desires to harm them, fire proceeds out of their mouth and devours their enemies. If anyone desires to harm them, he must be killed in this way. **6** These have the power to shut up the sky, that it may not rain during the days of their prophecy. They have power over the waters, to turn them into blood, and to strike the earth with every plague, as often as they desire. **7** When they have finished their testimony, the beast that comes up out of the Abyss **(Abyssos g12)** will make war with them, and overcome them, and kill them. **8** Their dead bodies will be in the street of the great city, which spiritually is called Sodom and Egypt, where also their Lord was crucified. **9** From among the peoples, tribes, languages, and nations people will look at their dead bodies for three and a half days, and will not allow their dead bodies to be placed in a tomb. **10** Those who dwell on the earth rejoice over them, and they will be glad. They will give gifts to one another, because these two prophets tormented those who dwell on the earth. **11** After the three and a half days, the breath of life from God entered into them, and they stood on their feet. Great fear fell on those who saw them. **12** I heard a loud voice from heaven saying to them, "Come up here." They went up into heaven in the cloud, and their enemies saw them. **13** In that hour there was a great earthquake, and a tenth of the city fell. Seven thousand people were killed in the earthquake, and the rest were terrified, and gave glory to the God of heaven. **14** The second woe is past. Look, the third woe comes quickly. **15** The seventh angel sounded, and great voices in heaven followed, saying, "The kingdom of the world has become the Kingdom of our Lord, and of his Christ. He will reign for the ages **(aiōn g165)** of the ages **(aiōn g165)**!" **16** The twenty-four elders, who sit on their thrones before God's throne, fell on their faces and worshiped God, **17** saying: "We give you thanks, Lord God Almighty, the one who is and who was; because you have taken your great power, and reigned. **18** The nations were angry, and your wrath came, as did the time for the dead to be judged, and to give your servants the prophets, their reward, as well as to the saints, and those who fear your name, to the small and the great; and to destroy those who destroy the earth." **19** God's temple that is in heaven was opened, and the ark of his covenant was seen in his temple. Lightnings, sounds, thunders, an earthquake, and great hail followed.

12 A great sign was seen in heaven: a woman clothed with the sun, and the moon under her feet, and on her head a crown of twelve stars. **2** She was with child. She screamed out in pain, laboring to give birth. **3** Another sign was seen in heaven. Look, a great fiery red serpent, having seven heads and ten horns, and on his heads seven crowns. **4** His tail drew one third of the stars of the sky, and threw them to the earth. The serpent stood before the woman who was about to give birth, so that when she gave birth he might devour her child. **5** She gave birth to a son, a male child, who is to rule all the nations with an iron scepter. Her child was caught up to God, and to his throne. **6** The woman fled into the wilderness, where she has a place prepared by God, that there they may nourish her one thousand two hundred sixty days. **7** There was war in the sky. Michael and his angels made war on the serpent. The serpent and his angels made war. **8** They did not prevail, neither was a place found for them any more in heaven. **9** The great serpent was thrown down, the ancient serpent, he who is called the devil and Satan, the deceiver of the whole world. He was thrown down to the earth, and his angels were thrown down with him. **10** I heard a loud voice in heaven, saying, "Now is come the salvation, the power, and the Kingdom of our God, and the authority of his Christ; for the accuser of our brothers has been thrown down, who accuses them before our God day and night. **11** They overcame him by the blood of the Lamb, and by the word of their testimony. They did not love their life, even to death. **12** Therefore rejoice, heavens, and you who dwell in them. Woe to the land and the sea, because the devil has gone down to you, having great wrath, knowing that he has but a short time." **13** When the serpent saw that he was thrown down to the earth, he persecuted the woman who gave birth to the male child. **14** Two wings of the great eagle were given to the woman, that she might fly into the wilderness to her place, so that she might be nourished for a time, and times, and half a time, from the face of the serpent. **15** The serpent spewed water out of his mouth after the woman like a river, that he might cause her to be carried away by the stream. **16** The earth helped the woman, and the earth opened its mouth and swallowed up the river which the serpent spewed out of his mouth. **17** The serpent grew angry with the woman, and went away to make war with the rest of her offspring, who keep God's commandments and hold to the testimony of Jesus.

13 And he stood on the sand of the sea. And I saw a beast coming up out of the sea, having ten horns and seven heads. On his horns were ten crowns, and on his heads, blasphemous names. **2** The beast which I saw was like a leopard, and his feet were like those of a bear, and his mouth like the mouth of a lion. The serpent gave him his power, his throne, and great authority. **3** One of his heads looked like it had been wounded fatally. His fatal wound was healed, and the whole earth was amazed and followed the beast. **4** They worshiped the serpent, because he gave his authority to the beast, and they worshiped the beast, saying, "Who is like the beast? Who is able to make war with him?" **5** A mouth was given to him speaking proud words and blasphemies. There was given to him authority to act for forty-two months. **6** He opened his mouth for blasphemies against God, to blaspheme his name, and his dwelling, those who dwell in heaven. **7** It was given to him to make war with the saints, and to overcome them. Authority over every tribe, people, language, and nation was given to him. **8** All who dwell on the earth will worship him, everyone whose name has not been written from the foundation of the world in the Book of Life of the Lamb who has been killed. **9** If anyone has an ear, let him hear. **10** If anyone is to go into captivity, he will go into captivity. If anyone is to be killed with the sword, he must be killed with the sword. Here is the endurance and the faith of the saints. **11** I saw another beast coming up out of the earth. He had two horns like a lamb, and he spoke like a serpent. **12** He exercises all the authority of the first beast in his presence. He makes the earth and those who dwell in it to worship the first beast, whose fatal wound was healed. **13** He performs great signs, even making fire come down out of heaven to the earth in the sight of people. **14** He deceives those who dwell on the earth because of the signs he was granted to do in front of the beast; saying to those who dwell on the earth, that they should make an image to the beast who had been wounded by the sword and yet lived. **15** It was given to him to give breath to it, to the image of the beast, that the image of the beast could both speak and cause those who would not worship the image of the beast to be killed. **16** He causes all, the small and the great, the rich and the poor, and the free and the slave, to be given a mark on their right hand, or on their forehead; **17** and that no one could be able to buy or to sell, unless he has that mark, the name of the beast or the number of his name. **18** Here is wisdom. He who has understanding, let him calculate the number of the beast, for it is the number of a man. His number is six hundred sixty-six.

14 And I looked, and suddenly on Mount Zion stood the Lamb, and with him one hundred forty-four thousand, having his name, and the name of his Father, written on their foreheads. **2** I heard a sound from heaven, like the sound of many waters, and like the sound of a great thunder. The sound which I heard was like that of harpists playing on their harps. **3** They sing a new song before the throne, and before the four living creatures and the elders. No one could learn the song except the one hundred forty-four thousand, those who had been redeemed out of the earth. **4** These are those who were not defiled with women, for they are virgins. These are those who follow the Lamb wherever he goes. These were redeemed from among humanity, the first fruits to God and to the Lamb. **5** In their mouth was found no lie; they are blameless. **6** I saw an angel flying in mid heaven, having the consummate **(aiōnios g166)** Good News to proclaim to those who dwell on the earth, and to every nation, tribe, language, and people. **7** He said with a loud voice, "Fear God, and give him glory; for the hour of his judgment has come. Worship him who made the heaven, the earth, the sea, and the springs of waters." **8** Another, a second angel, followed, saying, "Babylon the great has fallen, which has made all the nations to drink of the wine of the wrath of her sexual immorality." **9** Another angel, a third, followed them, saying with a great voice, "If anyone worships the beast and his image, and receives a mark on his forehead, or on his hand, **10** he also will drink of the wine of the wrath of God, which is prepared unmixed in the cup of his anger. He will be tormented with fire and sulfur in the presence of the holy angels, and in the presence of the Lamb. **11** The smoke of their torment goes up for ages **(aiōn g165)** of ages **(aiōn g165)**. They have no rest day and night, those who worship the beast and his image, and whoever receives the mark of his name. **12** Here is the patience of the saints, those who keep the commandments of God, and the faith of Jesus." **13** I heard the voice from heaven saying, "Write, 'Blessed are the dead who die in the Lord from now on.'" "Yes," says the Spirit, "that they may rest from their labors; for their works follow with them." **14** And I looked, and suddenly there was a white cloud; and on the cloud one sitting like a son of man, having on his head a golden crown, and in his hand a sharp sickle. **15** Another angel came out from the temple, crying with a loud voice to him who sat on the cloud, "Send forth your sickle, and reap; for the hour to reap has come; for the harvest of the earth is ripe." **16** He who sat on the cloud thrust his sickle on the earth, and the earth was reaped. **17** Another angel came out from the temple which is in heaven. He also had a sharp sickle. **18** Another angel came out from the altar, he who has power over fire, and he called with a loud voice to him who had the sharp sickle, saying, "Send forth your sharp sickle, and gather the clusters of the vine of the earth, for its grapes are fully ripe." **19** The angel thrust his sickle into the earth, and gathered the vintage of the earth, and threw it into the great winepress of the wrath of God. **20** The winepress was trodden outside of the city, and blood came out from the winepress, even to the bridles of the horses, as far as one hundred eighty four miles.

15 I saw another great and marvelous sign in the sky: seven angels having the seven last plagues, for in them God's wrath is finished. **2** I saw something like a sea of glass mixed with fire, and those who overcame the beast, his image, and the number of his name, standing on the sea of glass, having harps of God. **3** They sang the song of Moses, the servant of God, and the song of the Lamb, saying, "Great and marvelous are your works, Lord God Almighty. Righteous and true are your ways, O King eternal. **4** Who would not fear you, Lord, and glorify your name? For you only are holy. For all the nations will come and worship before you. For your righteous acts have been revealed." **5** After these things I looked, and the temple of the tabernacle of the testimony in heaven was opened. **6** The seven angels came out of the temple who had the seven plagues, clothed with pure, bright linen, and wearing golden sashes around their chests. **7** One of the four living creatures gave to the seven angels seven golden bowls full of the wrath of God, who lives for the ages **(aiōn g165)** of the ages **(aiōn g165)**. **8** The temple was filled with smoke from the glory of God, and from his power. No one was able to enter into the temple, until the seven plagues of the seven angels would be finished.

16 I heard a loud voice out of the temple, saying to the seven angels, "Go and pour out the seven bowls of the wrath of God on the earth." **2** The first went, and poured out his bowl into the earth, and it became a harmful and evil sore on the people who had the mark of the beast, and who worshiped his image. **3** The second one poured out his bowl into the sea, and it became blood as of a corpse. And every living thing in the sea died. **4** The third poured out his bowl into the rivers and springs of water, and they became blood. **5** I heard the angel of the waters saying, "You are righteous, who is and who was, the Holy One, because you have judged these things. **6** For they poured out the blood of the saints and the prophets, and you have given them blood to drink. They deserve this." **7** I heard the altar saying, "Yes, Lord God Almighty, true and righteous are your judgments." **8** The fourth poured out his bowl on the sun, and it was given to him to scorch people with fire. **9** People were scorched with great heat, and they blasphemed the name of God who has the power over these plagues. They did not repent and give him glory. **10** The fifth poured out his bowl on the throne of the beast, and his kingdom was darkened. They gnawed their tongues because of the pain, **11** and they blasphemed the God of heaven because of their pains and their sores. They did not repent of their works. **12** The sixth poured out his bowl on the great river, the Euphrates. Its water was dried up, that the way might be made ready for the kings that come from the sunrise. **13** I saw coming out of the mouth of the serpent, and out of the mouth of the beast, and out of the mouth of the false prophet, three unclean spirits, something like frogs; **14** for they are spirits of demons, performing signs; which go forth to the kings of the whole inhabited earth, to gather them together for the war of the great day of God, the Almighty. **15** "Look, I am coming like a thief. Blessed is he who watches, and keeps his clothes, so that he does not walk naked, and they see his shame." **16** He gathered them together into the place which is called in Hebrew, Har Megiddo. **17** The seventh poured out his bowl into the air. A loud voice came forth out of the temple, from the throne, saying, "It is done." **18** There were lightnings, voices, and peals of thunder; and there was a great earthquake, such as was not since man was on the earth, so great an earthquake, so mighty. **19** The great city was divided into three parts, and the cities of the nations fell. Babylon the great was remembered in the sight of God, to give to her the cup of the wine of the fierceness of his wrath. **20** Every island fled away, and the mountains were not found. **21** Great hailstones, about one hundred pounds each, came down out of the sky on people. People blasphemed God because of the plague of the hail, for this plague is exceedingly severe.

17 One of the seven angels who had the seven bowls came and spoke with me, saying, "Come here. I will show you the judgment of the great prostitute who sits on many waters, **2** with whom the kings of the earth committed sexual immorality, and those who dwell in the earth were made drunk with the wine of her sexual immorality." **3** He carried me away in the Spirit into a wilderness. I saw a woman sitting on a scarlet-colored animal, full of blasphemous names, having seven heads and ten horns. **4** The woman was dressed in purple and scarlet, and decked with gold and precious stones and pearls, having in her hand a golden cup full of abominations and the impurities of her sexual immorality. **5** And on her forehead a name was written, "MYSTERY, BABYLON THE GREAT, THE MOTHER OF THE PROSTITUTES AND OF THE ABOMINATIONS OF THE EARTH." **6** I saw the woman drunk with the blood of the saints, and with the blood of the martyrs of Jesus. When I saw her, I wondered with great amazement. **7** The angel said to me, "Why do you wonder? I will tell you the mystery of the woman, and of the beast that carries her, which has the seven heads and the ten horns. **8** The beast that you saw was, and is not; and is about to come up out of the Abyss **(Abyssos g12)** and to go to destruction. Those who dwell on the earth and whose names have not been written in the Book of Life from the foundation of the world will marvel when they see that the beast was, and is not, and is present. **9** Here is the mind that has wisdom. The seven heads are seven mountains, on which the woman sits. **10** They are seven kings. Five have fallen, the one is, the other has not yet come. When he comes, he must continue a little while. **11** The beast that was, and is not, is himself also an eighth, and is of the seven; and he goes to destruction. **12** The ten horns that you saw are ten kings who have received no kingdom as yet, but they receive authority as kings, with the beast, for one hour. **13** These have one mind, and they give their power and authority to the beast. **14** These will war against the Lamb, and the Lamb will overcome them, for he is Lord of lords, and King of kings. They also will overcome who are with him, called and chosen and faithful." **15** He said to me, "The waters which you saw, where the prostitute sits, are peoples, multitudes, nations, and languages. **16** The ten horns which you saw, and the beast, these will hate the prostitute, and will make her desolate and naked, and will eat her flesh, and will burn her utterly with fire. **17** For God has put in their hearts to do what he has in mind, and to be of one mind, and to give their kingdom to the beast, until the words of God should be accomplished. **18** The woman whom you saw is the great city, which reigns over the kings of the earth."

18 After these things, I saw another angel coming down out of the sky, having great authority. The earth was illuminated with his glory. **2** He shouted with a mighty voice, saying, "Fallen, fallen is Babylon the great, and she has become a habitation of demons, a prison of every unclean spirit, and a prison of every unclean bird, and a prison of every unclean and detestable beast. **3** For all the nations have drunk of the wine of the wrath of her sexual immorality, the kings of the earth committed sexual immorality with her, and the merchants of the earth grew rich from the abundance of her luxury." **4** I heard another voice from heaven, saying, "Come out of her, my people, that you have no participation in her sins, and that you do not receive of her plagues, **5** for her sins have reached to the sky, and God has remembered her iniquities. **6** Return to her just as she returned, and repay her double as she did, and according to her works. In the cup which she mixed, mix to her double. **7** However much she glorified herself, and grew wanton, so much give her of torment and mourning. For she says in her heart, 'I sit a queen, and am no widow, and will in no way see mourning.' **8** Therefore in one day her plagues will come: death, mourning, and famine; and she will be utterly burned with fire; for the Lord God who has judged her is strong. **9** The kings of the earth, who committed sexual immorality and lived wantonly with her, will weep and wail over her, when they look at the smoke of her burning, **10** standing far away for the fear of her torment, saying, 'Woe, woe, the great city, Babylon, the strong city. For your judgment has come in one hour.' **11** The merchants of the earth weep and mourn over her, for no one buys their merchandise any more; **12** merchandise of gold, silver, precious stones, pearls, fine linen, purple, silk, scarlet, all expensive wood, every vessel of ivory, every vessel made of most precious wood, and of bronze, and iron, and marble; **13** and cinnamon, spice, incense, perfume, frankincense, wine, olive oil, fine flour, wheat, cattle, sheep, horses, chariots, slaves and human lives. **14** The fruits which your soul lusted after have been lost to you, and all things that were luxury and splendor have perished from you, and you will never ever find them again. **15** The merchants of these things, who were made rich by her, will stand far away for the fear of her torment, weeping and mourning; **16** saying, 'Woe, woe, the great city, she who was dressed in fine linen, purple, and scarlet, and decked with gold and precious stones and pearls. **17** For in an hour such great riches are made desolate.' Every shipmaster, and everyone who sails anywhere, and mariners, and as many as gain their living by sea, stood far away, **18** and exclaimed as they looked at the smoke of her burning, saying, 'What is like the great city?' **19** They cast dust on their heads, and shouting, weeping and mourning, saying, 'Woe, woe, the great city, in which all who had their ships in the sea were made rich by reason of her great wealth.' For in one hour is she made desolate. **20** "Rejoice over her, O heaven, you saints, apostles, and prophets; for God has judged your judgment on her." **21** A mighty angel took up a stone like a great millstone and cast it into the sea, saying, "Thus with violence will Babylon, the great city, be thrown down, and will be found no more at all. **22** The voice of harpists, minstrels, flute players, and trumpeters will be heard no more at all in you. No craftsman, of whatever craft, will be found any more at all in you. The sound of a mill will be heard no more at all in you. **23** The light of a lamp will shine no more at all in you. The voice of the bridegroom and of the bride will be heard no more at all in you; your merchants were the princes of the earth; for with your sorcery all the nations were deceived. **24** In her was found the blood of prophets and of saints, and of all who have been slain on the earth."

19 After these things I heard something like a loud voice of a great multitude in heaven, saying, "Hallelujah. Salvation, glory, and power belong to our God: **2** for true and righteous are his judgments. For he has judged the great prostitute, who corrupted the earth with her sexual immorality, and he has avenged the blood of his servants at her hand." **3** A second said, "Hallelujah! Her smoke goes up for the ages **(aiōn g165)** of the ages **(aiōn g165)**." **4** The twenty-four elders and the four living creatures fell down and worshiped God who sits on the throne, saying, "Amen. Hallelujah." **5** A voice came forth from the throne, saying, "Give praise to our God, all you his servants, you who fear him, the small and the great." **6** I heard something like the voice of a great multitude, and like the voice of many waters, and like the voice of mighty thunders, saying, "Hallelujah. For the Lord our God of hosts reigns. **7** Let us rejoice and be exceedingly glad, and let us give the glory to him. For the marriage of the Lamb has come, and his wife has made herself ready." **8** It was given to her that she would array herself in bright, pure, fine linen: for the fine linen is the righteous acts of the saints. **9** He said to me, "Write, 'Blessed are those who are invited to the marriage supper of the Lamb.'" He said to me, "These are true words of God." **10** I fell down before his feet to worship him. He said to me, "Look. Do not do it. I am a fellow servant with you and with your brothers who hold the testimony of Jesus. Worship God, for the testimony of Jesus is the Spirit of Prophecy." **11** I saw the heaven opened, and suddenly there was a white horse, and he who sat on it is called Faithful and True. In righteousness he judges and makes war. **12** His eyes are a flame of fire, and on his head are many crowns. He had a name written which no one knows but he himself. **13** He is clothed in a garment dipped in blood. His name is called "The Word of God." **14** The armies which are in heaven followed him on white horses, clothed in white, pure, fine linen. **15** Out of his mouth proceeds a sharp sword, that with it he should strike the nations. He will rule them with an iron scepter. He treads the winepress of the fierceness of the wrath of God, the Almighty. **16** He has on his garment and on his thigh a name written, "King of kings, and Lord of lords." **17** I saw an angel standing in the sun. He shouted with a loud voice, saying to all the birds that fly in the sky, "Come. Be gathered together to the great supper of God, **18** that you may eat the flesh of kings, the flesh of captains, the flesh of mighty people, and the flesh of horses and of those who sit on them, and the flesh of all people., both free and slave, and small and great." **19** I saw the beast, and the kings of the earth, and their armies, gathered together to make war against him who sat on the horse, and against his army. **20** The beast was taken, and with him the false prophet who worked the signs in his sight, with which he deceived those who had received the mark of the beast and those who worshiped his image. These two were thrown alive into the Lake of Fire **(Limnē Pyr g3041 g4442)** that burns with sulfur. **21** The rest were killed with the sword of him who sat on the horse, the sword which came forth out of his mouth. All the birds were filled with their flesh.

20 I saw an angel coming down out of heaven, having the key of the Abyss **(Abyssos g12)** and a great chain in his hand. **2** He seized the serpent, the ancient snake, which is the devil and Satan, and bound him for a thousand years, **3** and cast him into the Abyss **(Abyssos g12)**, and shut and sealed it over him, that he should no longer deceive the nations, until the thousand years were finished. After this, he must be freed for a short time. **4** I saw thrones, and they sat on them, and judgment was given to them. I saw the souls of those who had been beheaded for the testimony of Jesus, and for the word of God, and such as did not worship the beast nor his image, and did not receive the mark on their forehead and on their hand. They lived, and reigned with Christ for a thousand years. **5** The rest of the dead did not live until the thousand years were finished. This is the first resurrection. **6** Blessed and holy is he who has part in the first resurrection. Over these, the second death has no power, but they will be priests of God and of Christ, and will reign with him one thousand years. **7** And after the thousand years, Satan will be released from his prison, **8** and he will come out to deceive the nations which are in the four quarters of the earth, Gog and Magog, to gather them together to the war; the number of whom is as the sand of the sea. **9** They went up over the breadth of the earth, and surrounded the camp of the saints, and the beloved city, and fire came down out of heaven and devoured them. **10** The devil who deceived them was thrown into the Lake of Fire **(Limnē Pyr g3041 g4442)** and sulfur, where the beast and the false prophet are also. They will be tormented day and night for the ages **(aiōn g165)** of the ages **(aiōn g165)**. **11** I saw a great white throne, and him who sat on it, from whose face the earth and the heaven fled away. There was found no place for them. **12** I saw the dead, the great and the small, standing before the throne, and they opened books. Another book was opened, which is the Book of Life. The dead were judged out of the things which were written in the books, according to their works. **13** The sea gave up the dead who were in it. Death and Hades **(Hadēs g86)** gave up the dead who were in them. They were judged, each one according to his works. **14** Death and Hades **(Hadēs g86)** were thrown into the Lake of Fire. This is the second death, the Lake of Fire **(Limnē Pyr g3041 g4442)**. **15** If anyone was not found written in the Book of Life, he was cast into the Lake of Fire **(Limnē Pyr g3041 g4442)**.

21 I saw a new heaven and a new earth: for the first heaven and the first earth have passed away, and the sea is no more. **2** I saw the holy city, New Jerusalem, coming down out of heaven from God, made ready like a bride adorned for her husband. **3** I heard a loud voice from the throne saying, "Look, the tabernacle of God is with humans, and he will dwell with them, and they will be his people, and God himself will be with them and be their God. **4** And he will wipe away every tear from their eyes, and death will be no more, nor will there be mourning, nor crying, nor pain anymore, for the first things have passed away." **5** He who sits on the throne said, "Look, I am making all things new." He said, "Write, for these words are faithful and true." **6** He said to me, "It is done. I am the Alpha and the Omega, the Beginning and the End. I will give freely to him who is thirsty from the spring of the water of life. **7** He who overcomes, I will give him these things. I will be his God, and he will be my son. **8** But for the cowardly, unbelieving, fouled, murderers, sexually immoral, sorcerers, idolaters, and all liars, their part is in the Lake that burns with fire **(Limnē Pyr g3041 g4442)** and sulfur, which is the second death." **9** One of the seven angels who had the seven bowls, full of the seven last plagues came, and he spoke with me, saying, "Come here. I will show you the bride, the wife of the Lamb." **10** He carried me away in the Spirit to a great and high mountain, and showed me the holy city, Jerusalem, coming down out of heaven from God, **11** having the glory of God. Her light was like a most precious stone, as if it was a jasper stone, clear as crystal; **12** having a great and high wall; having twelve gates, and at the gates twelve angels; and names written on them, which are the names of the twelve tribes of the children of Israel. **13** On the east were three gates; and on the north three gates; and on the south three gates; and on the west three gates. **14** The wall of the city had twelve foundations, and on them twelve names of the twelve apostles of the Lamb. **15** He who spoke with me had for a measure, a golden reed, to measure the city, its gates, and its wall. **16** The city lies foursquare, and its length is as great as its breadth. He measured the city with the reed, one thousand three hundred eighty miles. Its length, breadth, and height are equal. **17** Its wall is one hundred forty-four cubits, by human measurement, that is, of an angel. **18** The construction of its wall was jasper. The city was pure gold, like pure glass. **19** The foundations of the city's wall were adorned with all kinds of precious stones. The first foundation was jasper; the second, sapphire; the third, chalcedony; the fourth, emerald; the fifth, sardonyx; the sixth, sardius; the seventh, chrysolite; the eighth, beryl; the ninth, topaz; the tenth, chrysoprasus; the eleventh, jacinth; and the twelfth, amethyst. **21** The twelve gates were twelve pearls. Each one of the gates was made of one pearl. The street of the city was pure gold, like transparent glass. **22** I saw no temple in it, for the Lord God Almighty and the Lamb are its temple. **23** The city has no need for the sun, neither of the moon, to shine, for the very glory of God illuminated it, and its lamp is the Lamb. **24** The nations will walk in its light. The kings of the earth bring their splendor into it. **25** Its gates will in no way be shut by day (for there will be no night there), **26** and they will bring the glory and the honor of the nations into it. **27** There will in no way enter into it anything profane, or one who causes an abomination or a lie, but only those who are written in the Lamb's Book of Life.

22 He showed me a river of water of life, clear as crystal, proceeding out of the throne of God and of the Lamb, **2** in the middle of its street. On this side of the river and on that was the tree of life, bearing twelve kinds of fruits, yielding its fruit every month. The leaves of the tree were for the healing of the nations. **3** There will be no curse any more. The throne of God and of the Lamb will be in it, and his servants serve him. **4** They will see his face, and his name will be on their foreheads. **5** There will no longer be night, and they will not need the light of a lamp nor the light of the sun; for the Lord God will shine light on them. They will reign for the ages **(aiōn g165)** of the ages **(aiōn g165)**. **6** He said to me, "These words are faithful and true. The Lord God of the spirits of the prophets sent his angel to show to his servants the things which must happen soon." **7** "Look, I am coming quickly. Blessed is he who keeps the words of the prophecy of this book." **8** Now I, John, am the one who heard and saw these things. When I heard and saw, I fell down to worship before the feet of the angel who had shown me these things. **9** He said to me, "See you do not do it. I am a fellow servant with you and with your brothers, the prophets, and with those who keep the words of this book. Worship God." **10** He said to me, "Do not seal up the words of the prophecy of this book, for the time is near. **11** He who acts unjustly, let him act unjustly still. He who is filthy, let him be filthy still. He who is righteous, let him do righteousness still. He who is holy, let him be holy still." **12** "Look, I am coming quickly. My reward is with me, to repay to each person according to his work. **13** I am the Alpha and the Omega, the First and the Last, the Beginning and the End. **14** Blessed are they who wash their robes, that they may have the right to the tree of life, and may enter in by the gates into the city. **15** Outside are the dogs, the sorcerers, the sexually immoral, the murderers, the idolaters, and everyone who loves and practices falsehood. **16** I, Jesus, have sent my angel to testify these things to you for the churches. I am the root and the offspring of David; the bright morning star." **17** The Spirit and the bride say, "Come." He who hears, let him say, "Come." He who is thirsty, let him come. He who desires, let him take the water of life freely. **18** I testify to everyone who hears the words of the prophecy of this book, if anyone adds to them, God will add to him the plagues which are written in this book. **19** If anyone takes away from the words of the book of this prophecy, God will take away his part from the tree of life, and out of the holy city, which are written in this book. **20** He who testifies these things says, "Yes, I come quickly." Amen. Come, Lord Jesus. **21** The grace of the Lord Jesus be with all.

The New Jerusalem

I saw the holy city, New Jerusalem, coming down out of heaven from God, made ready like a bride adorned for her husband. I heard a loud voice from the throne saying, 'Look, the tabernacle of God is with humans, and he will dwell with them, and they will be his people, and God himself will be with them and be their God.

Revelation 21:2-3

Reader's Guide
AionianBible.org/Readers-Guide

The Aionian Bible republishes public domain and Creative Common Bible texts that are 100% free to copy and print. The original translation is unaltered and notes are added to help your study. The notes show the location of ten special Greek and Hebrew Aionian Glossary words to help us better understand God's love for individuals and for all mankind, and the nature of afterlife destinies.

Who has the authority to interpret the Bible and examine the underlying Hebrew and Greek words? That is a good question! We read in 1 John 2:27, *"As for you, the anointing which you received from him remains in you, and you do not need for anyone to teach you. But as his anointing teaches you concerning all things, and is true, and is no lie, and even as it taught you, you remain in him."* Every Christian is qualified to interpret the Bible! Now that does not mean we will all agree. Each of us is still growing in our understanding of the truth. However, it does mean that there is no infallible human or tradition to answer all our questions. Instead the Holy Spirit helps each of us to know the truth and grow closer to God and each other.

The Bible is a library with 66 books in the Protestant Canon. The best way to learn God's word is to read entire books. Read the book of Genesis. Read the book of John. Read the entire Bible library. Topical studies and cross-referencing can be good. However, the safest way to understand context and meaning is to read whole Bible books. Chapter and verse numbers were added for convenience in the 16th century, but unfortunately they can cause the Bible to seem like an encyclopedia. The Aionian Bible is formatted with simple verse numbering, minimal notes, and no cross-referencing in order to encourage the reading of Bible books.

Bible reading must also begin with prayer. Any Christian is qualified to interpret the Bible with God's help. However, this freedom is also a responsibility because without the Holy Spirit we cannot interpret accurately. We read in 1 Corinthians 2:13-14, *"And we speak of these things, not with words taught by human wisdom, but with those taught by the Spirit, comparing spiritual things with spiritual things. Now the natural person does not receive the things of the Spirit of God, for they are foolishness to him, and he cannot understand them, because they are spiritually discerned."* So we cannot understand in our natural self, but we can with God's help through prayer.

The Holy Spirit is the best writer and he uses literary devices such as introductions, conclusions, paragraphs, and metaphors. He also writes various genres including historical narrative, prose, and poetry. So Bible study must spiritually discern and understand literature. Pray, read, observe, interpret, and apply. Finally, *"Do your best to present yourself approved by God, a worker who does not need to be ashamed, properly handling the word of truth."* 2 Timothy 2:15. *"God has granted to us his precious and exceedingly great promises; that through these you may become partakers of the divine nature, having escaped from the corruption that is in the world by lust. Yes, and for this very cause adding on your part all diligence, in your faith supply moral excellence; and in moral excellence, knowledge; and in knowledge, self-control; and in self-control patience; and in patience godliness; and in godliness brotherly affection; and in brotherly affection, love. For if these things are yours and abound, they make you to be not idle nor unfruitful to the knowledge of our Lord Jesus Christ,"* 2 Peter 1:4-8.

Glossary
AionianBible.org/Glossary

The Aionian Bible un-translates and instead transliterates ten special words to help us better understand the extent of God's love for individuals and all mankind, and the nature of afterlife destinies. The original translation is unaltered and a note is added to 63 Old Testament and 200 New Testament verses. Compare the meanings below to the Strong's Concordance and Glossary definitions.

Abyssos
Language: Koine Greek
Speech: proper noun, place
Usage: 9 times in 3 books, 6 chapters, and 9 verses
Strongs: g12
Meaning:
　　Temporary prison for special fallen angels such as Apollyon, the Beast, and Satan.

aïdios
Language: Koine Greek
Speech: adjective
Usage: 2 times in Romans 1:20 and Jude 6
Strongs: g126
Meaning:
　　Lasting, enduring forever, eternal.

aiōn
Language: Koine Greek
Speech: noun
Usage: 127 times in 22 books, 75 chapters, and 102 verses
Strongs: g165
Meaning:
　　A lifetime or time period with a beginning and end, an era, an age, the completion of which is beyond human perception, but known only to God the creator of the aiōns, Hebrews 1:2. Never meaning simple endless or infinite chronological time in Koine Greek usage. Read Dr. Heleen Keizer and Ramelli and Konstan for proofs.

aiōnios
Language: Koine Greek
Speech: adjective
Usage: 71 times in 19 books, 44 chapters, and 69 verses
Strongs: g166
Meaning:
　　From start to finish, pertaining to the age, lifetime, entirety, complete, or even consummate. Never meaning simple endless or infinite chronological time in Koine Greek usage. Read Dr. Heleen Keizer and Ramelli and Konstan for proofs.

Geenna
Language: Koine Greek
Speech: proper noun, place
Usage: 12 times in 4 books, 7 chapters, and 12 verses
Strongs: g1067
Meaning:
   Valley of Hinnom, Jerusalem's trash dump, a place of ruin, destruction, and judgment in this life, or the next, though not eternal to Jesus' audience.

Hadēs
Language: Koine Greek
Speech: proper noun, place
Usage: 11 times in 5 books, 9 chapters, and 11 verses
Strongs: g86
Meaning:
   Synonomous with Sheol, though in New Testament usage Hades is the temporal place of punishment for deceased unbelieving mankind, distinct from Paradise for deceased believers.

Limnē Pyr
Language: Koine Greek
Speech: proper noun, place
Usage: Phrase 5 times in the New Testament
Strongs: g3041 g4442
Meaning:
   Lake of Fire, final punishment for those not named in the Book of Life, prepared for the Devil and his angels, Matthew 25:41.

Sheol
Language: Hebrew
Speech: proper noun, place
Usage: 65 times in 17 books, 50 chapters, and 63 verses
Strongs: h7585
Meaning:
   The grave or temporal afterlife world of both the righteous and unrighteous, believing and unbelieving, until the general resurrection.

Tartaroō
Language: Koine Greek
Speech: proper noun, place
Usage: 1 time in 2 Peter 2:4
Strongs: g5020
Meaning:
   Temporary prison for particular fallen angels awaiting final judgment.

Glossary +
AionianBible.org/Bibles/English---Aionian-Bible/Noted

Glossary references are below. Strong's Hebrew and Greek number notes are added to 63 Old Testament and 200 New Testament verses. Questioned verse translations do not contain Aionian Glossary words and may wrongly imply *eternal* or *Hell*. * The note placement is skipped or adjusted for verses with non-standard numbering.

Abyssos
Luke 8:31
Romans 10:7
Revelation 9:1
Revelation 9:2
Revelation 9:11
Revelation 11:7
Revelation 17:8
Revelation 20:1
Revelation 20:3

aïdios
Romans 1:20
Jude 1:6

aiōn
Matthew 12:32
Matthew 13:22
Matthew 13:39
Matthew 13:40
Matthew 13:49
Matthew 21:19
Matthew 24:3
Matthew 28:20
Mark 3:29
Mark 4:19
Mark 10:30
Mark 11:14
Luke 1:33
Luke 1:55
Luke 1:70
Luke 16:8
Luke 18:30
Luke 20:34
Luke 20:35
John 4:14
John 6:51
John 6:58
John 8:35
John 8:51
John 8:52
John 9:32
John 10:28
John 11:26
John 12:34
John 13:8
John 14:16

Acts 3:21
Acts 15:18
Romans 1:25
Romans 9:5
Romans 11:36
Romans 12:2
Romans 16:27
1 Corinthians 1:20
1 Corinthians 2:6
1 Corinthians 2:7
1 Corinthians 2:8
1 Corinthians 3:18
1 Corinthians 8:13
1 Corinthians 10:11
2 Corinthians 4:4
2 Corinthians 9:9
2 Corinthians 11:31
Galatians 1:4
Galatians 1:5
Ephesians 1:21
Ephesians 2:2
Ephesians 2:7
Ephesians 3:9
Ephesians 3:11
Ephesians 3:21
Ephesians 6:12*
Philippians 4:20
Colossians 1:26
1 Timothy 1:17
1 Timothy 6:17
2 Timothy 4:10
2 Timothy 4:18
Titus 2:12
Hebrews 1:2
Hebrews 1:8
Hebrews 5:6
Hebrews 6:5
Hebrews 6:20
Hebrews 7:17
Hebrews 7:21
Hebrews 7:24
Hebrews 7:28
Hebrews 9:26
Hebrews 11:3
Hebrews 13:8
Hebrews 13:21
1 Peter 1:23*

1 Peter 1:25
1 Peter 4:11
1 Peter 5:11
2 Peter 3:18
1 John 2:17
2 John 1:2
Jude 1:13
Jude 1:25
Revelation 1:6
Revelation 1:18
Revelation 4:9
Revelation 4:10
Revelation 5:13
Revelation 7:12
Revelation 10:6
Revelation 11:15
Revelation 14:11
Revelation 15:7
Revelation 19:3
Revelation 20:10
Revelation 22:5

aiōnios
Matthew 18:8
Matthew 19:16
Matthew 19:29
Matthew 25:41
Matthew 25:46
Mark 3:29
Mark 10:17
Mark 10:30
Luke 10:25
Luke 16:9
Luke 18:18
Luke 18:30
John 3:15
John 3:16
John 3:36
John 4:14
John 4:36
John 5:24
John 5:39
John 6:27
John 6:40
John 6:47
John 6:54
John 6:68

John 10:28
John 12:25
John 12:50
John 17:2
John 17:3
Acts 13:46
Acts 13:48
Romans 2:7
Romans 5:21
Romans 6:22
Romans 6:23
Romans 16:25
Romans 16:26
2 Corinthians 4:17
2 Corinthians 4:18
2 Corinthians 5:1
Galatians 6:8
2 Thessalonians 1:9
2 Thessalonians 2:16
1 Timothy 1:16
1 Timothy 6:12
1 Timothy 6:16
1 Timothy 6:19*
2 Timothy 1:9
2 Timothy 2:10
Titus 1:2
Titus 3:7
Philemon 1:15
Hebrews 5:9
Hebrews 6:2
Hebrews 9:12
Hebrews 9:14
Hebrews 9:15
Hebrews 13:20
1 Peter 5:10
2 Peter 1:11
1 John 1:2
1 John 2:25
1 John 3:15
1 John 5:11
1 John 5:13
1 John 5:20
Jude 1:7
Jude 1:21
Revelation 14:6

Geenna

Matthew 5:22
Matthew 5:29
Matthew 5:30
Matthew 10:28
Matthew 18:9
Matthew 23:15
Matthew 23:33
Mark 9:43
Mark 9:45
Mark 9:47

Luke 12:5
James 3:6

Hadēs

Matthew 11:23
Matthew 16:18
Luke 10:15
Luke 16:23
Acts 2:27
Acts 2:31
1 Corinthians 15:55
Revelation 1:18
Revelation 6:8
Revelation 20:13
Revelation 20:14

Limnē Pyr

Revelation 19:20
Revelation 20:10
Revelation 20:14
Revelation 20:15
Revelation 21:8

Sheol

Genesis 37:35
Genesis 42:38
Genesis 44:29
Genesis 44:31
Numbers 16:30
Numbers 16:33
Deuteronomy 32:22
1 Samuel 2:6
2 Samuel 22:6
1 Kings 2:6
1 Kings 2:9
Job 7:9
Job 11:8
Job 14:13
Job 17:13
Job 17:16
Job 21:13
Job 24:19
Job 26:6
Psalms 6:5
Psalms 9:17
Psalms 16:10
Psalms 18:5
Psalms 30:3
Psalms 31:17
Psalms 49:14
Psalms 49:15
Psalms 55:15
Psalms 86:13
Psalms 88:3
Psalms 89:48
Psalms 116:3
Psalms 139:8

Psalms 141:7
Proverbs 1:12
Proverbs 5:5
Proverbs 7:27
Proverbs 9:18
Proverbs 15:11
Proverbs 15:24
Proverbs 23:14
Proverbs 27:20
Proverbs 30:16
Ecclesiastes 9:10
Song of Solomon 8:6
Isaiah 5:14
Isaiah 14:9
Isaiah 14:11
Isaiah 14:15
Isaiah 28:15
Isaiah 28:18
Isaiah 38:10
Isaiah 38:18
Isaiah 57:9
Ezekiel 31:15
Ezekiel 31:16
Ezekiel 31:17
Ezekiel 32:21
Ezekiel 32:27
Hosea 13:14
Amos 9:2
Jonah 2:2
Habakkuk 2:5

Tartaroō

2 Peter 2:4

Questioned

None yet noted

Abraham's Journey

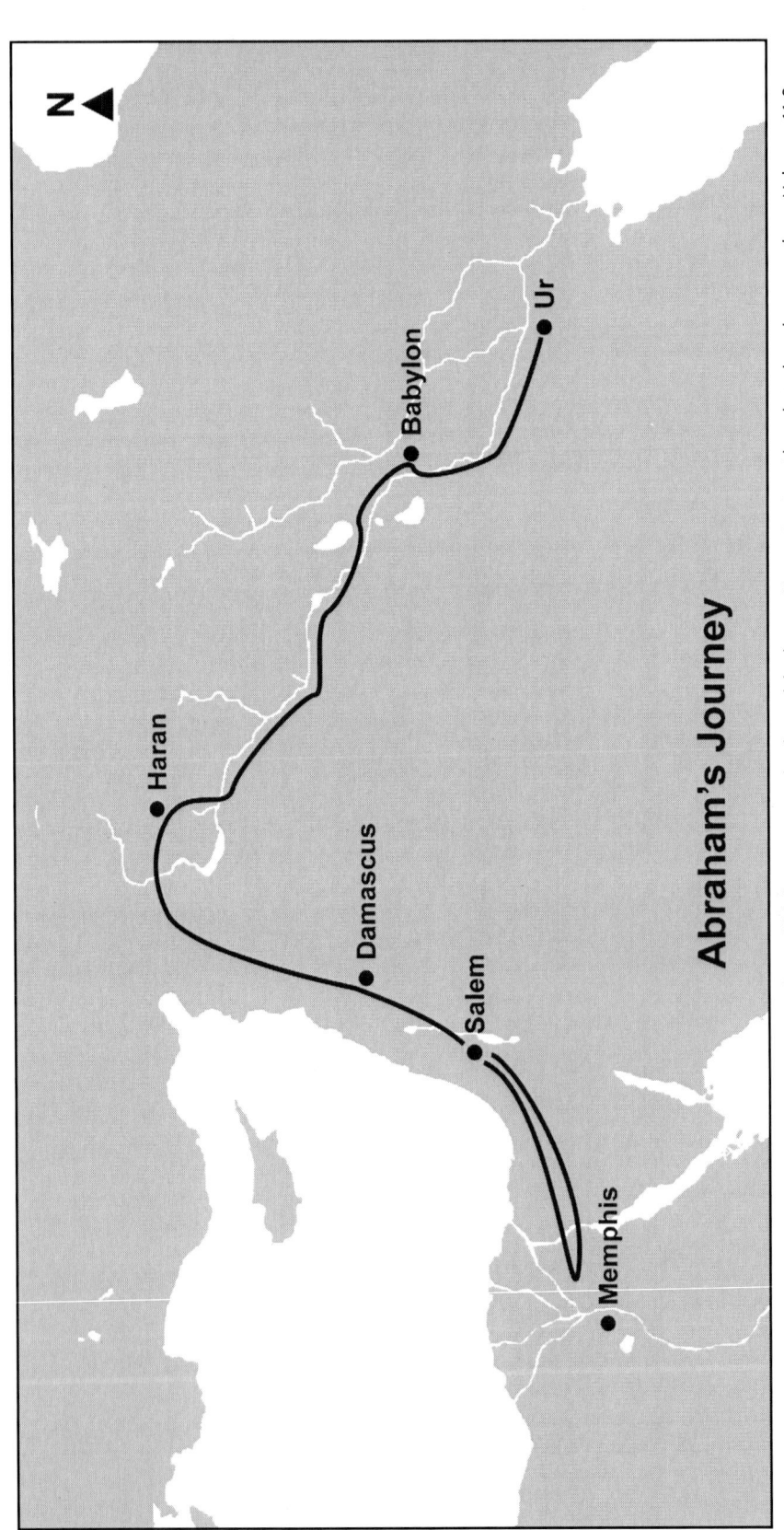

By faith, Abraham, when he was called, obeyed to go out to a place which he was to receive for an inheritance. He went out, not knowing where he was going. - Hebrews 11:8

Israel's Exodus

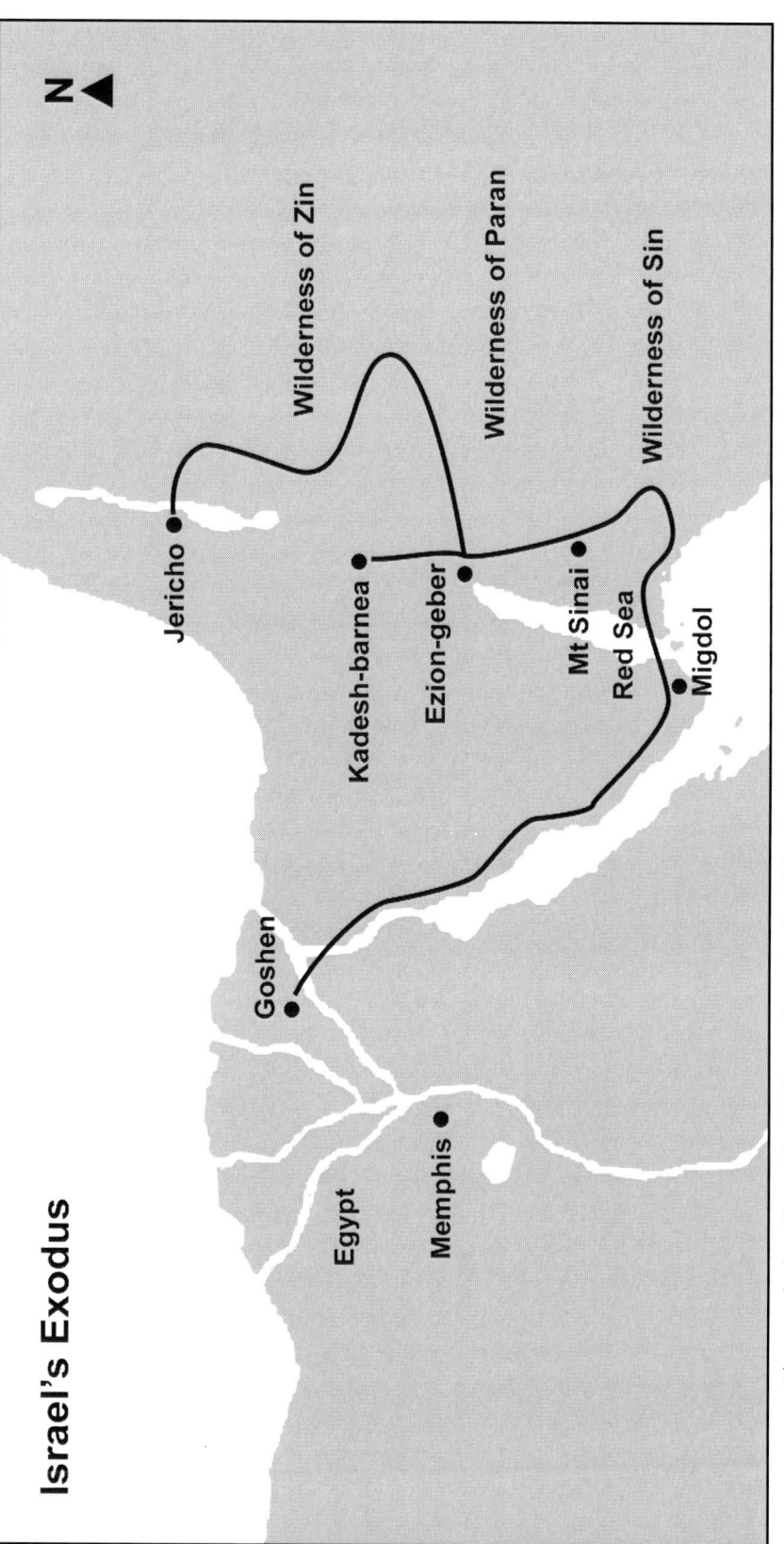

It happened, when Pharaoh had let the people go, that God did not lead them by the way of the land of the Philistines, although that was near; for God said, 'Lest perhaps the people change their minds when they see war, and they return to Egypt;' - Exodus 13:17

Jesus' Journeys

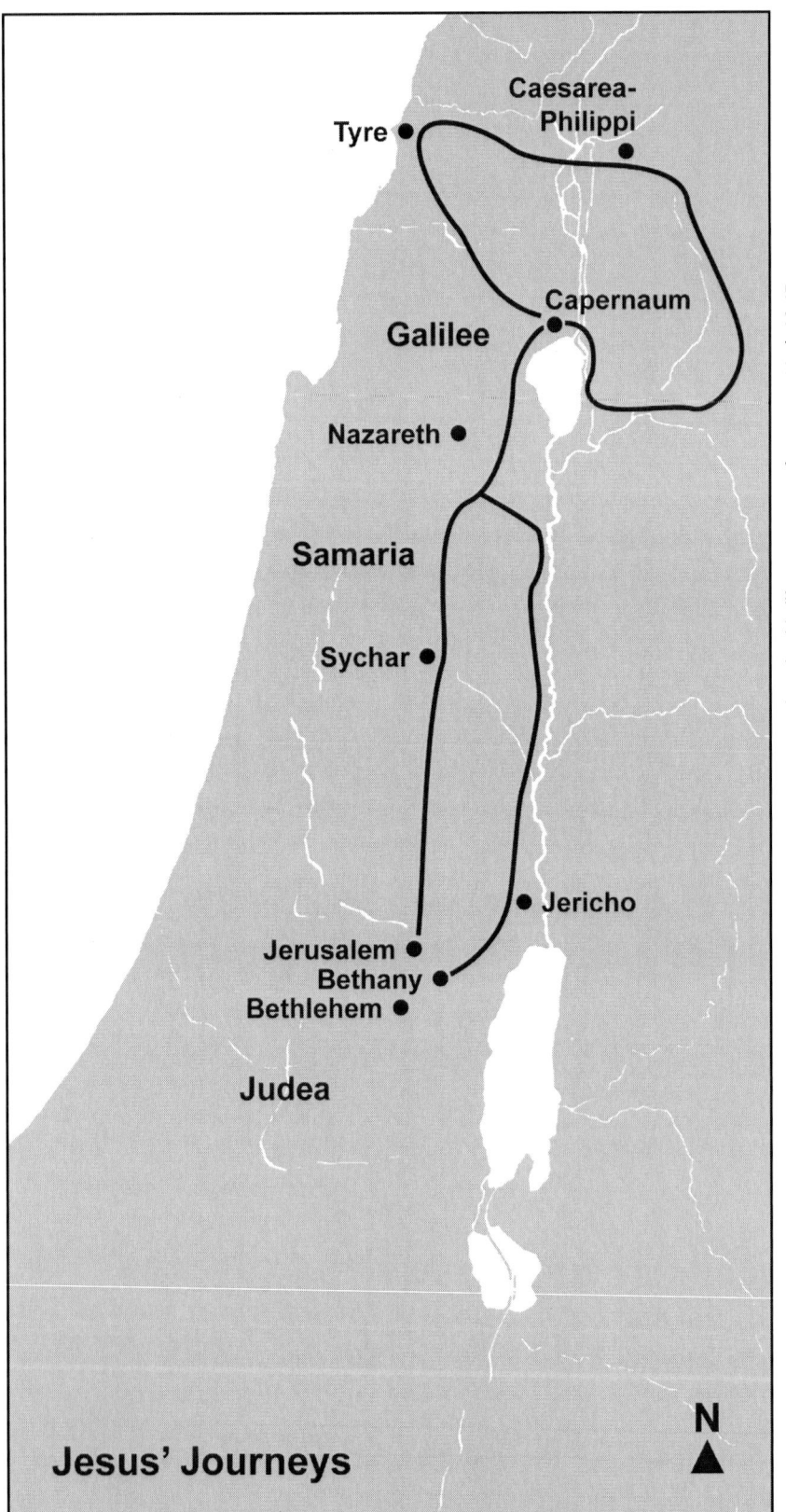

For the Son of Man also did not come to be served, but to serve, and to give his life as a ransom for many. - Mark 10:45

Paul's Missionary Journeys

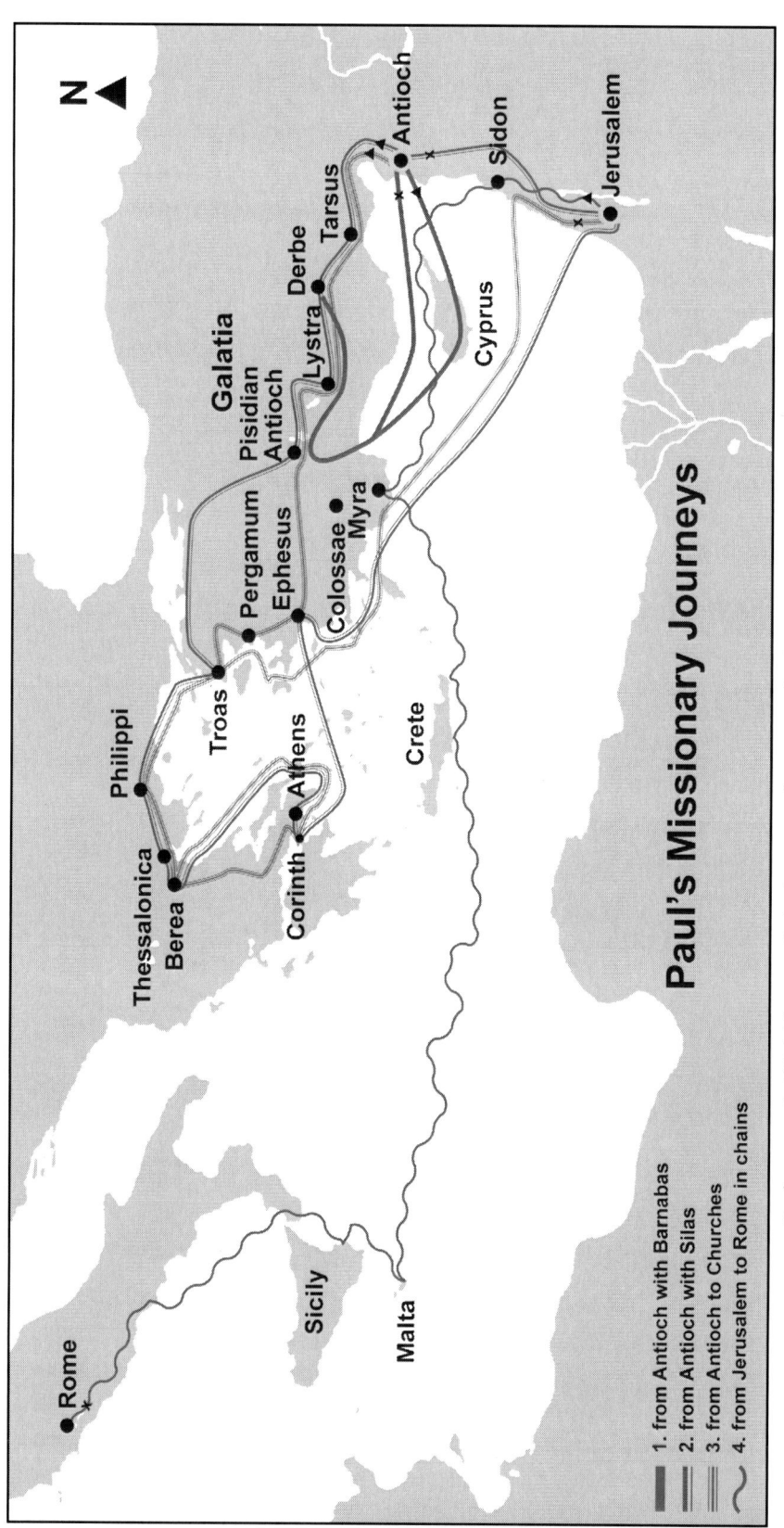

1. from Antioch with Barnabas
2. from Antioch with Silas
3. from Antioch to Churches
4. from Jerusalem to Rome in chains

Paul, a servant of Christ Jesus, called to be an apostle, set apart for the Good News of God. - Romans 1:1

Creation 4004 B.C.

Adam and Eve created	4004
Tubal-cain forges metal	3300
Enoch walks with God	3017
Methuselah dies at age 969	2349
God floods the Earth	2349
Tower of Babel thwarted	2247
Abraham sojourns to Canaan	1922
Jacob moves to Egypt	1706
Moses leads Exodus from Egypt	1491
Gideon judges Israel	1245
Ruth embraces the God of Israel	1168
David installed as King	1055
King Solomon builds the Temple	1018
Elijah defeats Baal's prophets	896
Jonah preaches to Nineveh	800
Assyrians conquer Israelites	721
King Josiah reforms Judah	630
Babylonians capture Judah	605
Persians conquer Babylonians	539
Cyrus frees Jews, rebuilds Temple	537
Nehemiah rebuilds the wall	454
Malachi prophecies the Messiah	416
Greeks conquer Persians	331
Seleucids conquer Greeks	312
Hebrew Bible translated to Greek	250
Maccabees defeat Seleucids	165
Romans subject Judea	63
Herod the Great rules Judea	37

(The Annals of the World, James Uusher)

Jesus Christ born 4 B.C.

New Heavens and Earth

	Christ returns for his people
1956	Jim Elliot martyrd in Ecuador
1830	John Williams reaches Polynesia
1731	Zinzendorf leads Moravian mission
1614	Japanese kill 40,000 Christians
1572	Jesuits reach Mexico
1517	Martin Luther leads Reformation
1455	Gutenberg prints first Bible
1323	Franciscans reach Sumatra
1276	Ramon Llull trains missionaries
1100	Crusades tarnish the church
1054	The Great Schism
997	Adalbert marytyrd in Prussia
864	Bulgarian Prince Boris converts
716	Boniface reaches Germany
635	Alopen reaches China
569	Longinus reaches Alodia / Sudan
432	Saint Patrick reaches Ireland
397	Carthage ratifies Bible Canon
341	Ulfilas reaches Goth / Romania
325	Niceae proclaims God is Trinity
250	Denis reaches Paris, France
197	Tertullian writes Christian literature
70	Titus destroys the Jewish Temple
61	Paul imprisoned in Rome, Italy
52	Thomas reaches Malabar, India
39	Peter reaches Gentile Cornelius
33	Holy Spirit empowers the Church

(Wikipedia, Timeline of Christian missions)

Resurrected 33 A.D.

What are we?	Genesis 1:26 - 2:3
How are we sinful?	Romans 5:12-19

Where are we?

			Innocence	
			Eternity Past	Creation 4004 B.C.

Who are we?

God	Father	John 10:30 God's perfect fellowship	Genesis 1:31 God's perfect fellowship with Adam in The Garden of Eden	
	Son	:::	:::	
	Holy Spirit	:::	:::	
Mankind	Living	Genesis 1:1 No Creation No people	:::	
	Deceased believing	:::	:::	
	Deceased unbelieving	:::	:::	
Angels	Holy	:::	Genesis 1:31 No Fall No unholy Angels	
	Imprisoned	:::	:::	
	Fugitive	:::	:::	
	First Beast	:::	:::	
	False Prophet	:::	:::	
	Satan	:::	:::	

Why are we?	Romans 11:25-36, Ephesian 2:7

Mankind is created in God's image, male and female He created us

Sin entered the world through Adam and then death through sin

When are we? ▼

Fallen				Glory
Fall to sin No Law	Moses' Law 1500 B.C.	Christ 33 A.D.	Church Age Kingdom Age	New Heavens and Earth
1 Timothy 6:16 Living in unapproachable light				Acts 3:21 Philippians 2:11 Revelation 20:3 God's perfectly restored fellowship with all Mankind praising Christ as Lord in the Holy City
John 8:58 Pre-incarnate		John 1:14 Incarnate	Luke 23:43 Paradise	
Psalm 139:7 Everywhere		John 14:17 Living in believers		
Ephesians 2:1-5 Serving the Savior or Satan on Earth				
Luke 16:22 Blessed in Paradise				
Luke 16:23, Revelation 20:5,13 Punished in Hades until the final judgment				
Hebrews 1:14 Serving mankind at God's command				
2 Peter 2:4, Jude 6 Imprisoned in Tartarus				Matthew 25:41 Revelation 20:10 Lake of Fire prepared for the Devil and his Angels
1 Peter 5:8, Revelation 12:10 Rebelling against Christ Accusing mankind				Revelation 20:13 Thalaasa
^			Revelation 19:20 Lake of Fire	
^			Revelation 20:2 Abyss	

For God has bound all over to disobedience in order to show mercy to all

World Nations

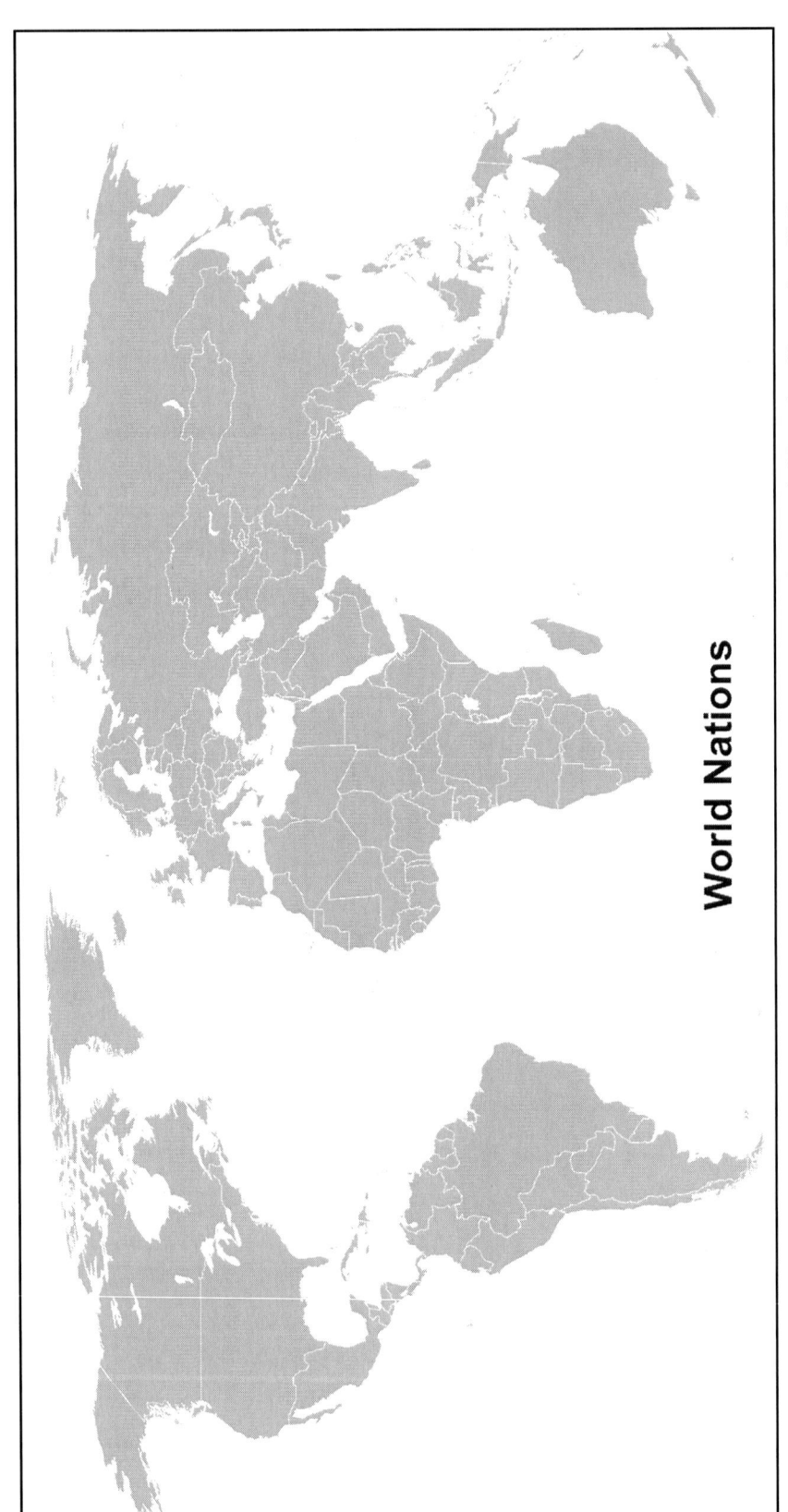

Therefore go, and make disciples of all nations, baptizing them in the name of the Father and of the Son and of the Holy Spirit. - Matthew 28:19